# Lecture Notes in Computer Scien

T0238318

*Commenced Publication in 1973*
Founding and Former Series Editors:
Gerhard Goos, Juris Hartmanis, and Jan van Leeuwen

## Editorial Board

George Almási   Călin Caşcaval
Peng Wu (Eds.)

# Languages and Compilers for Parallel Computing

19th International Workshop, LCPC 2006
New Orleans, LA, USA, November 2-4, 2006
Revised Papers

 Springer

Volume Editors

George Almási
Călin Cascaval
Peng Wu

IBM Research Division
Thomas J. Watson Research Center
Yorktown Heights, New York 10598
E-mail: {gheorghe, cascaval, pengwu}@us.ibm.com

Library of Congress Control Number: 2007926757

CR Subject Classification (1998): D.3, D.1.3, F.1.2, B.2.1, C.2.4, C.2, E.1, D.4

LNCS Sublibrary: SL 1 – Theoretical Computer Science and General Issues

| ISSN | 0302-9743 |
| ISBN-10 | 3-540-72520-2 Springer Berlin Heidelberg New York |
| ISBN-13 | 978-3-540-72520-6 Springer Berlin Heidelberg New York |

Springer is a part of Springer Science+Business Media

springer.com

© Springer-Verlag Berlin Heidelberg 2007
Printed in Germany

Typesetting: Camera-ready by author, data conversion by Scientific Publishing Services, Chennai, India
Printed on acid-free paper     SPIN: 12063598     06/3180     5 4 3 2 1 0

# Preface

The 19th Workshop on Languages and Compilers for Parallel Computing was held in November 2006 in New Orleans, Louisiana USA. More than 40 researchers from around the world gathered together to present their latest results and to exchange ideas on topics ranging from parallel programming models, code generation, compilation techniques, parallel data structure and parallel execution models, to register allocation and memory management in parallel environments.

Out of the 49 paper submissions, the Program Committee, with the help of external reviewers, selected 24 papers for presentation at the workshop. Each paper had at least three reviews and was extensively discussed in the committee meeting. The papers were presented in 30-minute sessions at the workshop. One of the selected papers, while still included in the proceedings, was not presented because of an unfortunate visa problem that prevented the authors from attending the workshop.

We were fortunate to have two outstanding keynote addresses at LCPC 2006, both from UC Berkeley. Kathy Yelick presented "Compilation Techniques for Partitioned Global Address Space Languages." In this keynote she discussed the issues in developing programming models for large-scale parallel machines and clusters, and how PGAS languages compare to languages emerging from the DARPA HPCS program. She also presented compiler analysis and optimization techniques developed in the context of UPC and Titanium source-to-source compilers for parallel program and communication optimizations.

David Patterson's keynote focused on the "Berkeley View: A New Framework and a New Platform for Parallel Research." He summarized trends in architecture design and application development and he discussed how these will affect the process of developing system software for parallel machines, including compilers and libraries. He also presented the Research Accelerator for Multiple Processors (RAMP), an effort to develop a flexible, scalable and economical FPGA-based platform for parallel architecture and programming systems research. Summaries and slides of the keynotes and the program are available from the workshop Web site http://www.lcpcworkshop.org.

The success of the LCPC 2006 workshop would not have been possible without help from many people. We would like to thank the Program Committee members for their time and effort in reviewing papers. We wish to thank Gerald Baumgartner, J. Ramanujam, and P. Sadayappan for being wonderful hosts. The LCPC Steering Committee, especially David Padua, provided continuous support and encouragement. And finally, we would like to thank all the authors who submitted papers to LCPC 2006.

March 2007

Gheorghe Almási
Călin Caşcaval
Peng Wu

# Organization

## Steering Committee

Utpal Banerjee                 Intel Corporation
David Gelernter             Yale University
Alex Nicolau                University of California, Irvine
David Padua                University of Illinois, Urbana-Champaign

## Organizing Committee

Program Co-chairs        Gheorghe Almási, IBM Research
                         Călin Caşcaval, IBM Research
                         Peng Wu, IBM Research
Local Co-chairs           Gerald Baumgartner, Louisiana State University
                         J. Ramanujam, Louisiana State University
                         P. Sadayappan, Ohio State University

## Program Committee

Vikram Adve                University of Illinois at Urbana-Champaign
Gheorghe Almási         IBM Research
Eduard Ayguad           Universitat de Politècnica de Catalunya
Gerald Baumgartner     Louisiana State University
Călin Caşcaval           IBM Research
Rudolf Eigenmann       Purdue University
Maria-Jesus Garzaran    University of Illinois at Urbana-Champaign
Zhiyuan Li                 Purdue University
Sam Midkiff                Purdue University
Paul Petersen             Intel Corp.
J. Ramanujam            Louisiana State University
P. Sadayappan           Ohio State University
Peng Wu                    IBM Research

# Table of Contents

## Keynote II

## Session 4: Compilation Techniques

## Session 5: Data Structures

## Session 6: Register Allocation

## Session 7: Memory Management

# Compilation Techniques for Partitioned Global Address Space Languages

Kathy Yelick

EECS Department, UC Berkeley
Computational Research Division, Lawrence Berkeley National Lab

**Abstract.** Partitioned global address space (PGAS) languages have emerged as a viable alternative to message passing programming models for large-scale parallel machines and clusters. They also offer an alternative to shared memory programming models (such as threads and OpenMP) and the possibility of a single programming model that will work well across a wide range of shared and distributed memory platforms. Although the major source of parallelism in these languages is managed by the application programmer, rather than being automatically discovered by a compiler, there are many opportunities for program analysis to detect programming errors and for performance optimizations from the compiler and runtime system. The three most mature PGAS languages (UPC, CAF and Titanium) offer a statically partitioned global address space with a static SPMD control model, while languages emerging from the DARPA HPCS program are more dynamic.

In this talk I will describe some of the analysis and optimizations techniques used in the Berkeley UPC and Titanium compilers, both of which source-to-source translators based on a common runtime system. Both compilers are publicly released and run on most serial, parallel, and cluster platforms. Building on the strong typing of the underlying Java language, the Titanium compiler includes several forms of type-based analyses for both error detection and to enable code transformations. The Berkeley UPC compiler extends the Open64 analysis framework on which it is built to handle the language features of UPC. Both compilers perform communication optimizations to overlap, aggregate, and schedule communication, as well as pointer localization, and other optimizations on parallelism constructs in the language. The HPCS languages can use some of the implementation techniques of the older PGAS languages, but offer new opportunities for expressiveness and suggest new open questions related to compiler and runtime support, especially as machines scale towards a petaflop.

G. Almási, C. Caşcaval, and P. Wu (Eds.): LCPC 2006, LNCS 4382, p. 1, 2007.

# Can Transactions Enhance Parallel Programs?*

Troy A. Johnson, Sang-Ik Lee, Seung-Jai Min, and Rudolf Eigenmann

School of Electrical and Computer Engineering
Purdue University, West Lafayette, IN 47907
{troyj, sangik, smin, eigenman}@purdue.edu

**Abstract.** Transactional programming constructs have been proposed as key elements of advanced parallel programming models. Currently, it is not well understood to what extent such constructs enable efficient parallel program implementations and ease parallel programming beyond what is possible with existing techniques. To help answer these questions, we investigate the technology underlying transactions and compare it to existing parallelization techniques. We also consider the most important parallelizing transformation techniques and look for opportunities to further improve them through transactional constructs or – vice versa – to improve transactions with these transformations. Finally, we evaluate the use of transactions in the SPEC OMP benchmarks.

## 1 Transaction-Supported Parallel Programming Models

Although a large number of parallel programming models have been proposed over the last three decades, there are reasons to continue the search for better models. Evidently, the ideal model has not yet been discovered; creating programs for parallel machines is still difficult, error-prone, and costly. Today, the importance of this issue is increasing because all computer chips likely will include parallel processors within a short period of time. In fact, some consider finding better parallel programming models one of today's most important research topics. Models are especially needed for non-numerical applications, which typically are more difficult to parallelize.

### 1.1 Can Transactions Provide New Solutions?

Recently, programming models that include transactional constructs have received significant attention [1,4,12,15]. At a high level, transactions are optimistically executed atomic blocks. The effect of an atomic block on the program state happens *at once*; optimistic execution means that multiple threads can execute the block in parallel, as long as some mechanism ensures atomicity. To this end, both hardware and software solutions have been proposed. An interesting observation is that these contributions make few references to technology in languages and compilers for parallel computing. These omissions are puzzling because the

---

* This work is supported in part by the National Science Foundation under Grants No. 0103582-EIA, and 0429535-CCF.

G. Almási, C. Caşcaval, and P. Wu (Eds.): LCPC 2006, LNCS 4382, pp. 2–16, 2007.

two topics pursue the same ultimate goal: making parallel programming easier and more efficient. While the programming models are arguably different, both areas need advanced compiler, run-time, and hardware optimization techniques. Hence, one expects that the underlying techniques supporting these models are closely related. In this paper, we investigate these relationships. We examine how much the concept of transactions can improve parallel program design and implementation beyond existing technology and to what extent transactions are just an interesting new way of looking at the same problem. We also review the ability of existing technology to optimize the implementation of transactions.

## 1.2    The Promise of Programming with Transactions

How can transactional constructs improve parallel programs? A transaction, in its basic meaning, is simply a set of instructions and memory operations. In many situations (e.g., in databases and parallel programming) it is important that the transactions are performed in such a way that their effects become visible simultaneously, or *atomically*. For example, in a bank, it is important that an amount of money gets deducted from one account and put into the other atomically, so that the total balance remains invariant at all times. Similarly, when incrementing a counter by two parallel threads, it is important that reading, modifying, and writing the counter be done atomically.

The concept of atomicity is not new per se. Constructs such as semaphores [5], locks [22], and critical sections [11] have been known for a long time. Nevertheless, language constructs that express atomicity typically allow only single memory updates (e.g., the OpenMP [21] `atomic` directive). Blocks of atomic memory operations are expressed through critical sections, which prevent concurrent execution of the block. This implementation is conservative or "pessimistic." The new promise of transactions is to eliminate some of the disadvantages that come with state-of-the-art constructs, namely reducing overhead through "optimistic execution" (if threads end up not accessing the same data inside a critical section, they should execute concurrently) and managing locks (avoiding deadlock and bookkeeping of multiple locks). These overheads naturally occur, as programs are written conservatively. For example, a banking software engineer may protect all account operations with one critical section, even though it could be known, in some cases, that the operations happen to different classes of accounts. The engineer may optimize the accounting software by creating separate locks for the two account classes; however, this increases the amount of bookkeeping information and requires more effort to avoid deadlocks.

The new idea behind transactions is that the programmer can rely on an efficient execution mechanism that executes in parallel *whenever possible*. Thus, the programmer uses the same "critical section" everywhere by simply writing *atomic*. At run time, two account operations or loop-counter updates can occur simultaneously. If different accounts are accessed or different counters are updated, then the program continues normally; if the same account or same counter is updated, then the transaction's implementation properly orders the operations. It is the transaction implementation's responsibility to provide efficient mechanisms for detecting when concurrency is possible and for serializing the operations when necessary.

Two questions arise: (i) Are transactions an adequate user model, and (ii) can transactions be implemented efficiently? Although the idea of an atomic language construct is not new [20], only time and experience can answer whether programmers find transactions useful. Today, only few real programs have been written with transactional constructs. An important challenge is that much parallel programming experience exists in the area of numerical programs; however, transactions aim at all classes of programs. The second question is the focus of this paper. Our thesis is that the technology underlying efficient transactions is very similar to the one that exists today for program parallelization – parallelizing compiler techniques [3,9], implementation techniques of parallel language constructs [18], and hardware techniques for speculative parallelization [8,10]. The ultimate question for the language and compiler community is whether or not we have missed something that we can now learn from the ideas behind transactional constructs. If so, we may be able to incorporate that new knowledge into our compilers, run-time systems, and supporting hardware.

## 2   Comparing the Technology Underlying Transactions and Program Parallelization

### 2.1   Technology Underlying Transactions

Within transactions, threads that do not conflict should execute in parallel unhindered. Conflict detection is therefore at the heart of implementation technology for transactions. Conflict detection can be performed statically or dynamically.

Static conflict detection relies on the compiler's ability to tell that threads access disjoint data. Provably non-conflicting threads can execute safely in parallel without the guard of a transaction; the compiler can remove the transaction altogether. The compiler also may remove conflict-free code out of the transaction, hence narrowing the guarded section. This optimization capability is important because it allows the programmer to insert transactions at a relatively coarse level and rely on the compiler's ability to narrow them to the smallest possible width. Furthermore, if a compiler can identify instructions that always conflict, it may guard these sections directly with a classical critical section. Applying common data dependence tests for conflict resolution is not straightforward, as conflicts among *all* transactions must be considered. For *strong atomicity* [4] this analysis is even necessary between transactions and all other program sections. Note that common data-dependence tests attempt to prove independence, not dependence; i.e., failure to prove independence does not imply dependence.

Compile-time solutions are highly efficient because they avoid run-time overhead. Nevertheless, their applicability is confined to the range of compile-time analyzable programs. Often, these are programs that manipulate large, regular data sets – typically found in numerical applications. Compile-time conflict resolution is difficult in programs that use pointers to manipulate dynamic data structures, which is the case for a large number of non-numerical programs.

For threads that are not provably conflict-free, the compiler still can assist by narrowing the set of addresses that may conflict. At run time, this conflict set must be monitored. The monitoring can happen either through compiler-inserted code (e.g., code that logs every reference) or through interpreters (e.g., virtual machines). At the end of the transaction, the logs are inspected for possible conflicts; in the event of a conflict, the transaction is rolled back and re-executed. Rollback must undo all modifications and can be accomplished by redirecting all write references to a temporary buffer during the transaction. The buffer is discarded upon a rollback; a successful transaction commits the buffer to the real address space. Again, interpreters may perform this redirection of addresses and the final commit operation on-the-fly. Evidently, there is significant overhead associated with software implementations of transactions, giving rise to optimization techniques [1,12].

Fully dynamic implementations of transactions perform conflict detection, rollback and commit in hardware. During the execution of a transaction, data references are redirected to a temporary buffer and monitored for conflicts with other threads' buffers. Detected conflicts cause a rollback, whereby the buffer is emptied and threads are restarted. At the end of a successful, conflict-free transaction, the thread's buffer is committed. Conflict detection in hardware is substantially faster than software solutions, but still adds extra cycles to every data reference. The cost of a rollback is primarily in the wasted work attempting the transaction. Commit operations may be expensive, if they immediately copy the buffered data (for speculative parallelization, hardware schemes have been proposed to commit in a non-blocking style, without immediate copy [24]). An important source of overhead stems from the size of the buffer. While small hardware buffers enable fast conflict detection, they may severely limit the size of a transaction that can be executed. If the buffer fills up during a transaction, parallel execution stalls.

## 2.2   Technology Underlying Program Parallelization

A serial program region can be executed in parallel if it can be divided into multiple threads that access disjoint data elements. Implementing this concept requires techniques analogous to the ones in Section 2.1. There are compile-time, compiler-assisted run-time, and hardware solutions.

*Compile-time parallelization.* Data-dependence analysis is at the heart of compile-time, automatic parallelization. Provably independent program sections can be executed as fully parallel threads. The analysis is the same as what is needed for conflict detection of transactions. Data-dependence tests have proven most successful in regular, numerical applications; data dependence analysis in the presence of pointers [13] is still a largely unsolved problem. Where successful, automatic parallelization is highly efficient, as it produces fully-parallel sections, avoiding run-time overheads.

*Run-time data-dependence tests.* These tests [23] have been introduced to defer the detection of parallelism from compile time to run time, where the actual data values and memory locations are known. Run-time data-dependence tests select the arrays to be monitored and insert monitoring code at compile time. At run time, memory references are recorded; if a conflict is detected, the parallel section is rolled back, usually followed by a serial execution. Run-time data dependence tests are efficient when the address space to be monitored is small. As this is not often the case, these methods are difficult to apply in general.

Hardware parallelization mechanisms are also known as speculative architectures [7,16]. They execute potentially independent threads in parallel, while tracking conflicts. Upon a conflict the thread is rolled back. During the speculative execution, memory references are redirected to a speculation buffer [8], which is committed to the actual memory upon successful speculation (no conflicts detected) or cleared (upon rollback). Hardware speculation mechanisms have essentially the same overheads as mentioned above for hardware transactions: data dependence tracking adds a cost to each memory reference, rollbacks represent significant overheads, and speculation buffer overflow is a known problem.

## 2.3 Comparison

*Compile-time solutions.* Transactions and automatic program parallelization models need implementation technologies that are very similar. Compile-time solutions hinge on the compiler's ability to detect memory conflicts – or data dependences. It can be expected that, for both models, this solution succeeds in regular, numerical programs, whereas pointer-based, non-numerical code patterns pose significant challenges. In terms of efficiency, neither transactions nor automatic parallelization seem to offer advantages over the other model. For both models, static, compile-time solutions – where applicable – are most efficient, as they are void of run-time overheads. They also exhibit the same weaknesses in irregular and pointer-based programs.

*Run-time solutions.* Compiler-assisted run-time solutions underlie both software-based transaction schemes and run-time parallelization techniques. Both schemes rely on the compiler's ability to narrow the range of data that needs to be inspected at run time. Many techniques have been proposed to perform the inspection; the big challenge is to reduce run-time overhead. Sophisticated bit-manipulating inspection code has been used in run-time data-dependence tests [23]. Other techniques detect if re-invocations of the same code regions happen under the same data context, in which case the serial or parallel outcome is already known and reinspection becomes unnecessary [17]. These techniques are compiler-based. Interpreters and virtual machines are most flexible in performing inspection and conflict analysis; however, their performance has yet to be proven.

Hardware-assisted schemes must provide the same basic mechanisms for transactions and speculative parallelization: data-dependence tracking, temporary buffering, rollback, and commit. The associated overheads are essentially the same. Adaptive synchronization techniques have been proposed for speculative synchronization [19], as effective means to eliminate repeated rollback. The same mechanisms would be effective for transactions. A subtle difference stems from the order of thread execution. The effect of a speculatively parallelized program must be the same as in its serial execution. This requirement is most easily implemented by committing the threads in the order that they would execute in the serial program version. By contrast, as transactions are entered from within a parallel program, correctness demands no such order. This might allow for a more efficient implementation, as we will discuss further in Section 3.

*Differences stemming from the user models.* While the underlying technology is very similar, interesting differences lie in the user models. Transactions are embedded inside a program that is already parallel.By contrast, automatic parallelization and speculative parallelization start from a sequential program; the compiler has the additional task of partitioning the program into potentially parallel threads. Parallelizing compilers commonly perform this task at the level of loops, considering each loop iteration as a potential parallel thread. Partitioning techniques for speculative parallelization have been developed that split programs so as to maximize parallelism and minimize overheads [14,26]. Another difference resulting from the user model is that, by explicitly parallelizing a program and inserting transactional regions, the programmer focuses the compiler and run-time system's attention on specific code sections, whereas automatic or implicit parallelization must analyze the entire program. The tradeoffs between automatic and manual parallelization are well-known. Automatic parallelization has been most successful in regular, numerical programs, and similarly for speculative parallelization. As transactional models aim at a broad class of programs, explicit parallelization may be a necessity. Evidently, there is an important tradeoff: large transactions are user-friendly, but lose the important advantage of focusing the compiler's attention on small regions. The extreme case of a whole-program transaction likely requires compiler optimizations similar to those for automatically parallelizing whole programs. It is also worth noting that the most advanced optimization techniques require whole-program analysis, even if their goal is to improve a small code section. For example, interprocedural pointer analysis [27] may gather information from other subroutines that helps improve a small transaction. Hence, once we develop highly-optimized techniques, implementing the different user models becomes increasingly similar.

## 3   Improving Parallelization Techniques Through Transactions and Vice Versa

Three parallelization techniques have proven most important [6]: data privatization, parallelization of reduction operations, and substitution of induction variables. This section discusses opportunities for improving these techniques through the use of transactions and vice versa.

## 3.1   Data Privatization

Privatization [25] is the most widely applicable parallelization technique. It recognizes data values that are only used temporarily within a parallel thread and thus are guaranteed not to be involved in true data dependences across threads. In data dependence terms, the technique removes anti-dependences, which occur because two or more threads use the same storage cell to hold different values. The privatization technique creates a separate storage cell for each thread (through renaming or `private` language constructs), thus eliminating the storage-related dependence. Figure 1 shows a program pattern that is amenable to privatization. Such patterns do not exhibit read, modify, and write sequences typical of transactions. Transaction concepts cannot be used to improve or replace privatization.

```
                                   #pragma OMP parallel private(t)
for (i=1;i<n;i++){                  for (i=1;i<n;i++){
   t = <...>;                          t = <...>;
   . . .             ==>               . . .
   <...> = t;                          <...> = t;
}                                   }
```

**Fig. 1.** Simple form of a program pattern that is amenable to privatization and its parallel form, expressed in the OpenMP directive language: To perform this transformation, the compiler or programmer must recognize that t is *defined* before it is *used* in every loop iteration. No true dependence exists across loop iterations. A more complex form of privatizable data would have t as an array; the compiler would have to analyze the subscripts of the references defining and using t.

By contrast, privatization is important for optimizing transaction implementations. Variables that can be recognized as private can be removed from the conflict set. They do not need to be monitored for conflicts and their accesses never necessitate a rollback; however, private data still needs to be redirected to the temporary storage during the execution of the transaction. If the data is not used after the transaction (i.e, not live-out of the transactional region), it also does not need to be committed. Notice that live-out private data leads to a race condition (by program semantics), as the value of the transaction that happens to complete last will prevail.

The lack of a program order again differentiates the implementation of a transaction from parallelizing a sequential region in subtle ways. (i) In a parallelized program, the compiler and run-time system must ensure that the value of the *youngest* thread prevails. (ii) In speculative parallelization, private data – even if it is not recognized as such – never necessitates a rollback. Only a write reference following a premature read reference is a conflict (thus, anti-dependence violations are not a problem). The presence of a (sequential) program order clearly defines what is premature. Anti-dependences are implicitly enforced through the speculative buffering mechanism and the commit actions, which happen in program order. For transaction implementations, the absence of a program order dictates that all read and write references to the same address cause rollbacks. Privatization is essential to eliminate such overheads.

## 3.2   Reduction Parallelization

Figure 2 shows a reduction program pattern and two forms of parallel transformations. While Transformation 1 looks more elegant, the absence of efficient implementations of the `atomic` construct (often a software implementation of a critical section) make Transformation 2 the preferred option. In the latter form, the atomic section is entered once per processor versus $n$ times in Transformation 1. The size of the reduction, $n$, generally must be large for the transformation to be beneficial.

```
                                                      21 #pragma OMP parallel private(lsum)
                                                      22 {  lsum=0;
                        11 #pragma OMP parallel for    23    #pragma OMP for
01 for (i=1,i<n,i++){   12   for (i=1,i<n,i++){        24      for (i=1,i<n,i++){
02    sum += <...>      13 #pragma OMP atomic          25        lsum += <...>;
03                      14    sum += <...>             26      }
04 }                    15 }                           27    #pragma OMP atomic
                                                      28    sum += lsum;
                                                      29 }

    Original            Transformation 1              Transformation 2
```

**Fig. 2.** Reduction pattern and parallel form expressed in OpenMP: notice that according to OpenMP semantics, statements 22 and 28 are executed once per processor, whereas the processors share the iterations of loops 12 and 24

Consider a transactional implementation of the atomic construct: in Transformation 1, the transaction will never proceed in parallel, as there is always a conflict on `sum`. There will be only some parallelism, if the processors happen to enter the transaction at different times, due to load imbalance. The same holds when using a critical section. Furthermore, the overheads of transactions (conflict tracking and rollbacks) make a plain critical section the much preferred choice.

If the expression `<...>` involves a substantial computation (e.g., a function call), its concurrent execution may be beneficial. To exploit this parallelism, the programmer or compiler moves the expression out of the transaction into the fully-parallel part of the code. Transformation 2 achieves exactly this effect. Hence, this transformation also yields an optimized form of a reduction implemented by a transaction.

For array (or irregular) reductions, the situation is different. The variable `sum` in Figure 2 would have a subscript, such as `sum[expr]`, where `expr` is a loop-variant expression. In this case, different loop iterations modify different elements of `sum`, hence a transactional implementation of the atomic construct in Transformation 1 can exploit some parallelism. The sparser the reduction (i.e., `expr` is different in more iterations), the more parallelism is exploited. Transformation 2 (not shown for array reductions, but similar to Figure 2) will incur substantial overhead, as the variable lsum, which is now also an array, may be large, making the additional statements 22 and 28 expensive. Hence, Transformation 1 with transactions would be preferred for sparse array reductions, whereas the classical transformation with a plain critical section is preferred for dense array reductions. Deciding this tradeoff is difficult, as the degree of sparsity is not likely to be known at compile time.

### 3.3   Induction Variable Substitution

Induction variable substitution removes data dependences at the cost of increasing the strength of the computation. In Figure 3, the original loop has cross-iteration data dependences. These dependences are removed in the transformed version, but the expression $5 + i * 2$ now involves a multiplication instead of just an addition. To obtain parallelism without increasing strength, one might consider guarding the original induction statement with a transaction, capturing the resulting value in a private variable, as in Transformation 2. This code version exploits parallelism among the statements <... ind ...>, which may be beneficial if this computation is large compared to the induction statement. Nevertheless, the same parallelism also would be exploited with an implementation of atomic through a plain critical section. In fact, this version would be more efficient; whenever two threads enter the transaction, there is a conflict, making a critical section the best implementation.

```
ind = 5;                  #pragma OMP parallel      ind0 = 5;
for (i=1,i<n,i++) {         for (i=1,i<n,i++) {      #pragma OMP parallel private (ind)
  ind += 2;                  ind = 5+i*2;              for (i=1,i<n,i++) {
  <... ind ...>              <... ind ...>           #pragma OMP atomic
}                         }                             {ind0 += 2; ind=ind0;}
                                                        <... ind ...>
                                                      }

     Original              Transformation 1          Transformation 2
```

**Fig. 3.** Induction Variable Substitution: Transformation 1 is the common parallelizing transformation. Transformation 2 is possible, if the loop variable $i$ is not used in the loop body. Notice that the atomic block requires two memory cells to be updated, which is not currently supported by OpenMP.

## 4   Evaluating Transactions for the SPEC OMP Benchmarks

SPEC OMP2001 [2] is a benchmark suite used for the performance evaluation and comparison of Shared-Memory Multiprocessor(SMP) systems and consists of three C applications and nine FORTRAN applications, including *gafort*, a non-numerical application. Each of the applications in SPEC OMP2001 is either automatically or manually parallelized using OpenMP directives. There are three types of critical sections in SPEC OMP2001, which have been implemented

```
!$OMP PARALLEL PRIVATE(rand, i, tmp1, tmp2)
!$OMP DO
  DO j=1,npopsiz-1
    CALL ran3(rand)
    iother=j+1+DINT(DBLE(npopsiz-j)*rand)
    IF (j < iother) THEN
        CALL omp_set_lock(lck(j))
        CALL omp_set_lock(lck(iother))
    ELSE
        CALL omp_set_lock(lck(iother))
        CALL omp_set_lock(lck(j))
    END IF
    tmp1 = iparent(iother)
    iparent(iother) = iparent(j)
    iparent(j) = tmp1
    tmp2=fitness(iother)
    fitness(iother)=fitness(j)
    fitness(j)=tmp2
    IF (j < iother) THEN
        CALL omp_unset_lock(lck(iother))
        CALL omp_unset_lock(lck(j))
    ELSE
        CALL omp_unset_lock(lck(j))
        CALL omp_unset_lock(lck(iother))
    END IF
  END DO
!$OMP END PARALLEL DO

  (a) TYPE I - "gafort.f90" from gafort
```

```
!$OMP CRITICAL
    IF (SCALE .LT. LSCALE) THEN
        SSQ = ((SCALE/LSCALE)**2)*SSQ+LSSQ
        SCALE = LSCALE
    ELSE
        SSQ = SSQ+((LSCALE/SCALE)**2)*LSSQ
    END IF
!$OMP END CRITICAL

  (b) TYPE II - "dznrm2.f" from wupwise


    EXNER = 0.0
!$OMP PARALLEL PRIVATE(J,K,T_EXNER)
    T_EXNER = 0.0
!$OMP DO
    DO J=1, NY
        DO K=2, NZ
            ..
            T_EXNER = T_EXNER + P(I,J,...)
            ..
        ENDDO
    ENDDO
!$OMP END DO
!$OMP ATOMIC
    EXNER = EXNER + T_EXNER
!$OMP END PARALLEL

  (c) TYPE III - "apsi.f" from apsi
```

**Fig. 4.** Critical section types

using lock-based synchronization. Figure 4 illustrates examples for each type of critical section. Type I is the critical section guarded by the omp_set_lock() and omp_unset_lock() OpenMP API runtime library routines and type II is the critical section specified by the *OMP CRITICAL* and *OMP END CRITICAL* directives. Both type I and type II exist in source form in SPEC OMP2001, whereas type III is the critical section generated by the underlying OpenMP implementation when converting *OMP reduction* into an efficient form as depicted in Figure 2. While these critical sections can be converted into transactions with little effort, the runtime overheads may offset the benefit of the transaction. In order to estimate these overheads, we measured the probability $p$ that a transaction would conflict and thus roll back. To this end, we count the number of runtime conflicts that happened in the current critical section implementation. We performed our experiments on a four-processor 480MHz SPARC machine using the *ref* dataset of the benchmarks.

Type I critical sections are found six times in *ammp* and once in *gafort*. In *ammp*, Type I critical sections access the same shared data structure type through pointers, which are dynamically changing at runtime. From the program code, one cannot determine whether or not conflicts will arise. In *gafort*, as shown in Figure 4 (a), a critical section guards the swap of an array element with a randomly chosen element; due to the random choice, conflicts cannot be determined statically. To determine the conflict probability, we created a wrapper function of the *omp_set_lock()* and *omp_unset_lock()* library routines,

**Table 1.** Conflict analysis of critical sections in SPEC OMP2001. "Conflict prob." expresses the likelihood that a transactional execution will not commit successfully and, instead, roll back and re-execute. "Compile-time dep." indicates whether or not the conflict is certain at compile time.

| Id | Benchmark | Source file | TYPE | Conflict prob. | Compile-time dep. |
|----|-----------|-------------|------|----------------|-------------------|
| 1  | ammp      | rectmm.c    | I    | 0%             | N                 |
| 2  |           |             | I    | 0%             | N                 |
| 3  |           |             | I    | 0%             | N                 |
| 4  |           | nonbon.c    | I    | 0%             | N                 |
| 5  |           |             | I    | 0%             | N                 |
| 6  |           |             | I    | 0%             | N                 |
| 7  | gafort    | gafort.f90  | I    | 0.02%          | N                 |
| 8  |           |             | III  | 23.4%          | Y                 |
| 9  | apsi      | apsi.f      | III  | 33.0%          | Y                 |
| 10 | fma3d     | platq.f90   | II   | 8.1%           | N                 |
| 11 | wupwise   | dznrm2.f    | II   | 33.7%          | Y                 |
| 12 |           | zdotc.f     | III  | 22.9%          | Y                 |
| 13 |           |             | III  | 21.8%          | Y                 |
| 14 | swim      | swim.f      | III  | 25.0%          | Y                 |
| 15 | mgrid     | mgrid.f     | III  | 27.7%          | Y                 |
| 16 | applu     | l2norm.f    | III  | 31.2%          | Y                 |

respectively. When there is a thread $T$ trying to enter a critical section, the wrapper function of $omp\_set\_lock()$ function is called and it checks if there are other threads executing within a critical section, accessing the same shared memory location as the thread $T$ is going to access. From our experiment, we found that there are no conflicts in all six critical sections in *ammp*. The critical section in *gafort* has a very small number of conflicts, less than 1% of the total number of invocations of the critical section. Nevertheless, the critical section requires a very large array of locks, the `lck` array in Figure 4 (a), for correct execution.

Type II critical sections are found in *wupwise* and *fma3d*. The conflict probability of the critical section from *wupwise*, shown in Figure 4 (b), is only 33.7%, even though the critical section contains a statically known dependence on the shared variable *SSQ*. Due to load imbalance, the parallel threads enter the critical section at different times. The *fma3d* code has a large critical section that contains a small loop. Although it cannot be proven at compile-time, there is a dependency to the shared array, *MATERIAL(\*)*, in the critical section. Despite this dependency, the critical section in *fma3d* exhibits a low conflict probability of 8.1% that we also attribute to load imbalance.

We transformed all *OMP reduction* clauses found in SPEC OMP2001 into the *Transformation 2* form of Figure 2 so that the transformed code consists of a parallel loop and a critical section pair. These Type III critical sections contain reduction statements, where a reduction variable is a source of conflicts from a transaction point of view. The conflict probability of Type III critical sections

**Table 2.** When to use Transactions versus Critical Sections: Case 1 is fully parallel. In Case 4, a compiler can detect a dependence. Cases 2 and 3 are the grey area where the compiler can prove neither. The numbers in the Code Examples column refer to Table 1.

| Cases | Provably Independent | Provably Dependent | Predicted Conflict | Actual Conflict | Use Trans.? | Use C.S.? | Code Examples |
|-------|---------------------|--------------------|--------------------|-----------------|-------------|-----------|---------------|
| 1 | T | F | 0% | 0% | No | No | * |
| 2 | F | F | | 0-1% | Yes | No | 1-7 |
| 3 | F | F | | 8.1% | No | Yes | 10 |
| 4 | F | T | 100% | 21.8-33.7% | No | Yes | 8-9, 11-16 |

varies between 21.8% and 33% depending on the applications. Again, load imbalance frequently prevents the threads from entering the section simultaneously.

One of the key assumptions of transactional memory is that most transactions commit successfully. Table 1 shows that, for Type I critical sections, the probability of successful commit is almost 100%, which coincides with the cases where compile-time analysis cannot prove the absence of conflicts. Hence, these critical sections are good candidates for transactions. In most Type II and Type III cases, the existence of dependences is provable at compile time, except in *fma3d*. When there is a dependency in the critical section, the probability of conflict ranges from 8.1% to 33.7%.

Table 2 summarizes our findings. The four cases differ by the available compile-time knowledge. Case 1 is statically known to be non-conflicting. The compiler can remove all synchronization. Case 4 has a compile-time provable dependence. Critical sections are always the preferred choice. Recall that, due to load imbalance, runtime conflicts happen only 21.8-33.7% of the time. Case 2 has statically unknown dependences. Transactions are beneficial and conflict with a small likelihood of 0-1%. Case 3 has a dependence, but it is not detectable with state-of-the-art compiler technology. A transactional implementation would conflict 8.1% of the time; again, load imbalance prevents many conflicts. In actuality, given the dependence, a critical section implementation would be better.

The above guidelines for when to use a transaction versus a critical section are very loose; the actual tradeoff depends on the efficiency of the transaction and critical section implementations. The tradeoff that must be made is:

$$time[CriticalSection] > time[Transaction]$$

When the inequality is true, a transaction should be used. At a greater level of detail, the inequality becomes:

$$N * time[work] > time[TSetup] + time[work] + MeanReexec * time[work]$$
$$+ time[TCommit]$$

On the left side of the inequality above, $N$ is the number of threads and *work* represents the code within the critical section. The critical section serializes the *work*, so the total execution time is $N * time[work]$. On the right side of the inequality above, $TSetup$ is any setup work that needs to be done to initiate the transaction, *work* represents the code within the transaction, $MeanReexec$ is the average number of times the transaction will be re-executed, and $TCommit$ is any work that needs to be done to complete the successful transaction. Ideally, there are no conflicts during the transaction and, assuming perfect overlap, the execution time for the work is $time[work]$. For each re-execution, there is an additional $time[work]$.

Because the *time* function yields values that are either implementation or application-specific, the inequality cannot be made much more detailed, but we can estimate the $MeanReexec$ given the conflict probability $p$. Due to fewer threads re-executing as some manage to successfully commit, $p$ in fact may not be constant, but we approximate it as the probability of a conflict during the transaction's first attempt. Thus, the chance of no conflict is $1 - p$, the chance of one conflict followed by no conflict is $p(1 - p)$, and so forth such that the chance of $k$ conflicts is approximated as $p^k(1 - p)$. $MeanReexec$ is found using the weighted infinite sum $\sum_{k=0}^{\infty} kp^k(1 - p) = \frac{p}{1-p}$. Therefore, the inequality becomes:

$$N * time[work] > time[TSetup] + time[work] + \frac{p}{1-p} * time[work]$$
$$+ time[TCommit]$$

Observe that for $p = 0$, the inequality compares an ideal execution of a transaction (i.e., no re-executions) to a critical section. For that case, unless $time[work]$ is very brief or the transaction's implementation is inefficient, it is best to use a transaction. For some greater value of $p$, it becomes better to use a critical section. Solving for $p$ and then simplifying, we obtain the break-even point:

$$p < \frac{(N - 1) * time[work] - time[TSetup] - time[TCommit]}{N * time[work] - time[TSetup] - time[TCommit]}$$

When this inequality is true, it is more efficient to use a transaction. The inequality has several interesting properties. The limit of the fraction is 1 as $N \to \infty$, so for a very large number of processors, it nearly always will be better to use a transaction. As transactional overhead becomes very small ($time[TSetup] \to 0$ and $time[TCommit] \to 0$), or as the amount of work becomes very large ($time[work] \to \infty$), the fraction becomes $\frac{N-1}{N}$. For example, for $N = 4$, $p < 0.75$ implies that a transaction should be used. Programs can be optimized using this inequality by obtaining $time[work]$ and $p$ from a profile run of the application. The $time[TSetup]$ and $time[TCommit]$ values can be obtained a single time (i.e., they are application-independent) by profiling an empty transaction.

## 5  Conclusions

We have compared the technology underlying transactions and program parallelization. We find that, while the two user models differ, the underlying implementation technology is essentially the same. Advanced optimizations are necessary for both models. We reviewed the most important optimization techniques for parallel programs and found that these techniques are essential for optimizing transaction implementations as well.

We have analyzed the SPEC OMP benchmarks for the applicability of transactions. While many locks and critical sections could be replaced by transactions, this replacement is beneficial in only a few cases – where data dependences are statically unknown. In provably-independent code sections, synchronization can be eliminated; in provably-dependent code, critical sections are preferred over transactions. We have also found many cases with a definite conflict, but a low runtime conflict probability, suggesting that transactions may be beneficial. In actuality, it is load imbalance that prevents the section from simultaneous access; critical sections are the preferred choice.

Our evaluation has focused on the SPEC OMP benchmarks, which contain numerical applications, in all but one code. Compiler optimizations for parallel programs are most mature in this application area. Non-numerical programs are known to pose substantial challenges for compiler optimizations. As implementation technology for transactions is very similar, we expect this challenge to hold. Studies similar to the one presented in this paper are needed for this large and growing area of parallel programs.

# References

1. A.-R. Adl-Tabatabai et al. Compiler and Runtime Support for Efficient Software Transactional Memory. In *Proceedings of the Conference on Programming Language Design and Implementation*, pages 26–37, June 2006.
2. V. Aslot et al. SPEComp: A New Benchmark Suite for Measuring Parallel Computer Performance. In *Proc. of the Workshop on OpenMP Applications and Tools (WOMPAT2001), Lecture Notes in Computer Science, 2104*, pages 1–10, July 2001.
3. W. Blume et al. Parallel Programming with Polaris. *IEEE Computer*, pages 78–82, December 1996.
4. B. D. Carlstrom et al. The ATOMOS Transactional Programming Language. In *Proceedings of the Conference on Programming Language Design and Implementation*, pages 1–13, June 2006.
5. E. W. Dijkstra. Co-operating Sequential Processes. In F. Genuys, editor, *Programming Languages*, pages 43–112, 1968.
6. R. Eigenmann, J. Hoeflinger, and D. Padua. On the Automatic Parallelization of the Perfect Benchmarks. *IEEE Transactions of Parallel and Distributed Systems*, 9(1):5–23, Jan. 1998.
7. M. Franklin. *The Multiscalar Architecture*. PhD thesis, University of Wisconsin-Madison, November 1993.
8. S. Gopal et al. Speculative Versioning Cache. In *4th IEEE Symposium on HPCA*, pages 195–205, February 1998.
9. M. W. Hall et al. Maximizing Multiprocessor Performance with the SUIF Compiler. *IEEE Computer*, pages 84–89, December 1996.
10. L. Hammond, M. Willey, and K. Olukotun. Data Speculation Support for a Chip Multiprocessor. In *Proc. of the 8th International Conference on ASPLOS*, 1998.

11. P. B. Hansen. *Operating System Principles*. Prentice Hall, 1973.
12. T. Harris et al. Optimizing Memory Transactions. In *Proceedings of the Conference on Programming Language Design and Implementation*, pages 14–25, June 2006.
13. J. Hummel, L. J. Hendren, and A. Nicolau. A general data dependence test for dynamic, pointer-based data structures. In *PLDI '94: Proceedings of the ACM SIGPLAN 1994 conference on Programming language design and implementation*, pages 218–229, New York, NY, USA, 1994. ACM Press.
14. T. A. Johnson, R. Eigenmann, and T. N. Vijaykumar. Min-Cut Program Decomposition for Thread-Level Speculation. In *Proceedings of the Conference on Programming Language Design and Implementation*, pages 59–70, June 2004.
15. S. Kumar et al. Hybrid Transactional Memory. In *Proceedings of the Symposium on Principles and Practices of Parallel Programming*, pages 209–220, 2006.
16. Lance Hammond and Basem A. Nayfeh and Kunle Olukotun. A Single-Chip Multiprocessor. *IEEE Computer*, 30(9):79–85, 1997.
17. S.-J. Min and R. Eigenmann. Combined Compile-time and Runtime-driven Proactive Data Movement in Software DSM Systems. In *Proc. of Seventh Workshop on Languages, Compilers, and Run-Time Systems for Scalable Computers (LCR2004)*, pages 1–6, 2004.
18. S.-J. Min, S. W. Kim, M. Voss, S.-I. Lee, and R. Eigenmann. Portable Compilers for OpenMP. In *OpenMP Shared-Memory Parallel Programming*, Lecture Notes in Computer Science #2104, pages 11–19, Springer Verlag, July 2001.
19. A. Moshovos et al. Dynamic Speculation and Synchronization of Data Dependences. In *Proceedings of the 24th ISCA*, pages 181–193, June 1997.
20. OpenMP Architecture Review Board. OpenMP Fortran Application Program Interface, October 1997.
21. OpenMP Architecture Review Board. OpenMP Application Program Interface. http://www.openmp.org/, May 2005.
22. G. L. Peterson. Myths about the Mutual Exclusion Problem. *Information Processing Letters*, 12(3):115–116, June 1981.
23. L. Rauchwerger and D. Padua. The LRPD test: Speculative run-time parallelization of loops with privatization and reduction parallelization. In *The ACM SIGPLAN '95 Conference on Programming Language Design and Implementation (PLDI'95)*, pages 218–232, June 1995.
24. G. S. Sohi, S. E. Breach, and T. N. Vijaykumar. Multiscalar processors. In *The 22th International Symposium on Computer Architecture (ISCA-22)*, pages 414–425, June 1995.
25. P. Tu and D. Padua. Automatic Array Privatization. In U. Banerjee, D. Gelernter, A. Nicolau, and D. Padua, editors, *Proc. Sixth Workshop on Languages and Compilers for Parallel Computing, Portland, OR. Lecture Notes in Computer Science.*, volume 768, pages 500–521, August 12-14, 1993.
26. T. N. Vijaykumar and G. S. Sohi. Task Selection for a Multiscalar Processor. In *Proc. of the 31st International Symposium on Microarchitecture*, December 1998.
27. J. Whaley and M. S. Lam. Cloning-based context-sensitive pointer alias analysis using binary decision diagrams. In *PLDI '04: Proceedings of the ACM SIGPLAN 2004 conference on Programming language design and implementation*, pages 131–144, New York, NY, USA, 2004. ACM Press.

# Design and Use of htalib – A Library for Hierarchically Tiled Arrays*

Ganesh Bikshandi[1], Jia Guo[1], Christoph von Praun[2], Gabriel Tanase[3],
Basilio B. Fraguela[4], María J. Garzarán[1], David Padua[1],
and Lawrence Rauchwerger[3]

[1] University of Illinois, Urbana-Champaign, IL
[2] IBM T. J. Watson Research Center, Yorktown Heights, NY
[3] Texas A&M University, College Station, TX
[4] Universidade da Coruña, Spain

**Abstract.** Hierarchically Tiled Arrays (HTAs) are data structures that facilitate locality and parallelism of array intensive computations with block-recursive nature. The model underlying HTAs provides programmers with a global view of distributed data as well as a single-threaded view of the execution. In this paper we present htalib, a C++ implementation of HTAs. This library provides several novel constructs: (i) *A map-reduce operator framework* that facilitates the implementation of distributed operations with HTAs. (ii) *Overlapped tiling* in support of tiling in stencil codes. (iii) *Data layering*, facilitating the use of HTAs in adaptive mesh refinement applications. We describe the interface and design of htalib and our experience with the new programming constructs.

## 1 Introduction

### 1.1 Hierarchically Tiled Arrays

A Hierarchically Tiled Array (HTA) [7,4] is a recursive array data type where elements are either HTAs or scalars (at the bottom of the recursion). HTAs adopt tiling as a first class construct for array-based computations and empower programmers to control data distribution and the granularity of computation explicitly through the specification of tiling [2,8,9,16,18]. An HTA has the conventional array functionality: scalar access, pointwise operators, and assignment. The functionality of HTAs goes a significant step beyond mere arrays: HTAs provide a rich set of generic, block-recursive operations that execute with high efficiency in sequential or parallel manner. When programming with HTAs, a

* This work was supported by the National Science Foundation under the NGS program (Grant No. 0103610) and under the CSR-AES program (Grant No. 0509432). Basilio Fraguela was partially supported by the Ministry of Education and Science of Spain, FEDER funds of the European Union (Project TIN2004-07797-C02-02), and by the Galician Government (Project PGIDIT03-TIC10502PR). This work was also supported by the Defense Advanced Research Projects Agency (Contract NBCH30390004).

G. Almási, C. Caşcaval, and P. Wu (Eds.): LCPC 2006, LNCS 4382, pp. 17–32, 2007.
© Springer-Verlag Berlin Heidelberg 2007

programmer seeks to harness the built-in operators or develop new operators by extending the generic framework and HTA-specific functionality.

HTAs are not only a library construct but also a programming model: HTAs provide a global shared memory abstraction, and support (encourage) the programmer to structure algorithms in a block-recursive manner, yet following sequential program logic. This programming style can be efficiently mapped onto todays parallel and distributed computer architectures and memory hierarchies using standard compiler and communication systems. Unlike approaches that are entirely controlled by the compiler [2] or integrated into a specific programming language [9], HTAs offer an attractive programming model and performance while preserving the convenience of standard tools, and libraries (library-based approach).

In earlier work, we introduced the concepts of programming with HTAs [4] and an early prototype based on MATLAB [7]. This paper describes htalib, a portable C++ library and framework for HTAs, and three application-driven extensions to the original HTA proposal [4] that facilitate the use of HTAs in certain application domains and broaden the potential application scope. We report on our experience with HTAs on an IBM BlueGene/L system.

### 1.2   Contributions

We present the design and implementation of an operator framework for HTAs following the principles of *map-reduce* [12] that we illustrate with examples from the NAS kernel programs.

*Overlapped tiling*, a mechanism for implicit allocation and consistency of shadow regions and ghost cells. It provides flexible indexing scheme for HTA tiles and facilitates access to neighbor elements of adjacent tiles, a common access pattern in stencil computations. Overlapped tiling also provides a clean syntax.

*Data layering*, an extension of htalib where a hierarchy of scalar arrays (not just a single array) can be controlled and accessed through one HTA. Data layering makes HTAs a highly expressive and compact data structure for multigrid and AMR (Adaptive Mesh Refinement) [6,17] applications.

## 2   Design and Use of htalib

### 2.1   Overview

The core data structures of the htalib API fall into four categories:

**Logical index space.** Classes used to define index space and tiling of an HTA are `Tuple<N>`, an N-dimensional index value; `Triplet`, a 1-dimensional range with optional stride (`(low:high:step)`); and `Region<N>`, an N-dimensional rectangular index space spanned by N triplets. Arithmetic, shift, and iterator

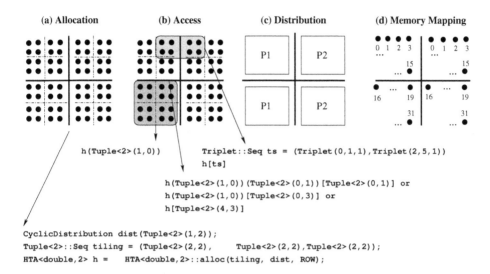

**Fig. 1.** HTA allocation, access, distribution and memory mapping

functionality are implemented and compatible with the STL library. Instances of Tuple<N> and Triplet are values, i.e., once defined, their value cannot change.

**HTA.** Class HTA<T,N> defines an HTA with scalar elements of type T and N dimensions. The data type implements scalar access (operator[]), tile access (operator()) and built-in array operations, e.g., transpose, permute, dpermute, reduce that are described in earlier publications [7]. An HTA is part of a hierarchical structure of recursively composed HTAs. The *root* of the hierarchy is designated as level 0, with its tiles at level 1, etc..

**Machine mapping.** The machine mapping of an HTA specifies (i) where the HTA is allocated in a distributed system and (ii) the memory layout of the scalar data array underlying the HTA. The former aspect is captured by instances of class Distribution that specifies the *home location* of the scalar data for each of the tiles of an HTA. The latter aspect is represented by instances of class MemoryMapping that specify the layout (row-major across tiles, row-major per tile etc.), size and stride of the flat array data underlying the HTA.

The machine mapping is accessed internally by the htalib, for example, to orchestrate implicit communication. The machine mapping is also available through the API of the library to facilitate direct access and communication of array data in case the programmer intends to bypass the access mechanisms provided by HTAs.

**Operator framework.** htalib provides a powerful operator framework following the design of the STL operator classes. This framework consists of routines that evaluate specific operators on HTAs and base classes that serve as a foundation for user-defined operators. A detailed discussion of the operator framework is given in Section 3.

```
HTA<double,1> A, B;
double S = 0.125;
while (!converged) {
  // boundary exchange                    htalib::async();
  B(1:n)[0] = B(0:n-1)[d];                B(1:n)[0] = B(0:n-1)[d];
  B(0:n-1)[d+1] = B(1:n)[1];              B(0:n-1)[d+1] = B(1:n)[1];
  // stencil computation                  htalib::sync();
  A()[1:d] = S * (B()[2:d+1] + B()[0:d-1]);
  ...
}
```

(a)                                          (b)

**Fig. 2.** HTA examples (a) HTA code for 1D Jacobi with one level of tiling. (b) Relaxing sequential evaluation order to facilitate overlap of communication and computation.

## 2.2   Example

In Figure 1, the distribution of the HTA occurs at the root of the tiling hierarchy in a cyclic manner over 2 processors along the second dimension (columns). At each processor, the scalar array corresponding to the tiles is allocated in row-major layout (spawning sub-tiles). The memory mapping in Figure 1 illustrates the logical index of the scalar variables in each processor.

To simplify the presentation in subsequent examples, the C++ code is slightly modified: Instead of the instances `Tuple<DIM>(x,y,...)` and `Triplet(low,high,step)`, we use a comma separated list of integers of the form `(x,y,...)` to represent coordinate points, and the `low:high:step` triplet notation. Regions are constructed from sequences of triplets as in Figure 1. Template arguments are elided when their value is apparent from the context.

Figure 2(a) illustrates a Jacobi computation with HTAs. A and B are HTAs with one level of tiling; there are n tiles at the root of the tiling hierarchy (level 0), each tile holding d+2 variables (level 1). Variables at index 0 and d+1 in each tile are ghost cells. The boundary exchange first updates the ghost cells at index 0, then at index d+1. The iteration across tiles is implicit in all assignments. In the stencil computation, the region is not specified at tile access and thus all tiles at level 0 are considered in the operation. The example illustrates that scalars and arrays can be combined as operator arguments; htalib follows Fortran90 [3] conventions for conformability and automatically promotes scalars to arrays in expressions.

## 2.3   Programming Model

The programming model supported by htalib has the following key properties:

**Global view.** Remote and local data are accessed though the same syntax and address space. In the Jacobi computation in Figure 2(a), the tiles of the HTA could be distributed, yet scalars and tiles are seamlessly accessed within one global logical index space.

**Implicit communication.** Data is communicated when necessary as part of the evaluation of one of the following constructs: array assignment, certain array transformations, and when materializing temporary arrays during the evaluation of complex array expressions (spilling).

**Serial program logic.** Statements and expressions that involve arrays are evaluated according to serial semantics, in particular array assignment follows Fortran90 conventions [3]. Parallelism is achieved when data-parallel array operators are evaluated in a block-recursive manner following the tile distribution.

**Automated memory management.** The implementation maintains reference counts for HTAs and associated structures, facilitating automatic de-allocation. Tuples, triplets and sequences thereof have a very light-weight implementations and are, by convention, allocated on the stack or inlined in objects.

## 2.4   Implementation

This section briefly describes four key implementation aspects of htalib:

**Owner computes.** At allocation time, the top-level tiling of an HTA determines the data distribution, i.e., each tile is assigned a *home* location where the master copy of the scalar data is allocated. The computation of an array expression is distributed among the owners of tiles that receive the result of the expression. Arguments data is communicated when necessary.

**SPMD computation and communication.** The execution and communication mechanisms inside htalib follows the SPMD principle. The communication of tiles or part of tiles is based on two-sided message passing (MPI).

**Dynamic optimizations.** htalib implements *lazy evaluation* to reduce or avoid the overhead due to temporary arrays. At an array assignment, the evaluation of the rhs is delayed until the target of the assignment is determined. If lhs and rhs have no data dependence, the assignment is directly evaluated into the lhs.

**Relaxation of serial evaluation semantics.** htalib provides a mechanism to temporarily relax the serial evaluation ordering and overlap of communication with computation. The example in Figure 2(b) shows the boundary exchange in the Jacobi example in Figure 2(a). As there is no data dependence among the assignments, both statements can proceed concurrently. This is achieved through the runtime calls to asyc and sync. Similarly, the runtime system permits to selectively disable strict evaluation order for array assignment and resort to split-phase semantics [11].

## 3   Operator Framework

### 3.1   Primitive Operators

htalib defines several primitive operators over the scalar and array domain. To provide an uniform interface, all these operators are wrapped in STL like functor

```
struct plus {                        struct ft {
    double operator() (const double a,     void operator() (Array* x) {
                const double b) {          //...
        return a+b;                        mkl.dftForward(x);
    } }                                    //...
                                       } }
```

**Fig. 3.** Primitive Operators

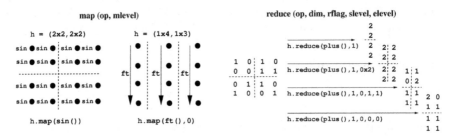

**Fig. 4.** HTA map operator          **Fig. 5.** HTA reduce operator

objects that define method `operator()` with appropriate arguments. Primitive operators are applied to HTAs directly or through *high-order* operators (Section 3.2).

htalib includes primitive operators for standard arithmetic, logical, relational, vector and matrix operations. For example, in the Figure 3, `plus` is the addition operation defined on scalars, while `ft` is *Fourier Transform* defined on an array.

## 3.2   Higher-Order Operators

htalib provides the following higher-order operators: `map`, `reduce`, `scan`. Higher-order operators are parametrized with primitive operators and define the strategy and result format resulting form the application of primitive operators to the tiles or scalar values in an HTA.

**Map.** map applies a function $f$ to each one of the elements of the input HTA at a given level. The syntax of `map` is shown in Figure 4, along with examples. In the figure, h = (n × m ,..., x × y) indicates the region of each level of the HTA h from leaf to root. map takes as input a primitive operator *op*, and a level *mlevel*. The *mlevel* specifies the level of the HTA at which *op* will be invoked. The default value of *mlevel* is *LEAF_LEVEL*. Invocation of `map` on HTA h, results in the mapping function being applied to the top level of h. If its elements are tiles themselves, then the function is invoked recursively on each of their elements until *level = LEAF_LEVEL* or *level = mlevel*. The op is invoked over the elements at that level.

The method *op* is required to be a *PURE* function. The result of `map` is an HTA with identical index space and tiling. Though not shown in the figure, `map` can also take one or more HTAs as its argument, along with *op*. The argument HTAs should be conformable with the receiver of the method. map forms the basis for several point-wise HTA operations. For example, scalar addition of two HTAs, h1 and h2, is implemented using map as follows: r = h1.map(plus(), h2);

The order of iteration in the map does not affect the result of the computation. During its application, there is no communication between the sibling elements (i.e. elements at the same level) of an HTA. Thus, map is a useful abstraction for *do-all* parallelism. A map invocation on a distributed HTA is an equivalent of a *do-all* parallel loop.

**Reduce.** An operation which is applied to all components of a vector to produce a scalar is called a *reduction*. For example, $reduce(+, x)$ is *sum* and $reduce(\times, x)$ is *product* of a vector x. The reduction operation can be generalized for n-dimensions, resulting in an (n-1)-dimensional space.

The reduction operation is extended to HTAs in the form of the reduce operator. Like map, reduce is also a recursive operation. The dimension of the elements at each level will be reduced by one. However, it is possible to control the starting and ending level of the reduction operation. The HTA reductions are parameterized by the following arguments:

- *op*: This is any associative operation from the primitive operator set.
- *dim*: This is the dimension of reduction.
- *rflag*: This is a bit vector, whose $i^{th}$ bit, if set to true, will imply replication of the result along dim, for level $i$. The resulting HTA will have the same number of dimensions as the input HTA, at the level $i$. This is the equivalent of an *all-to-all* reduction. Default value is set to 0 for all dimensions.
- *slevel*: This is the starting level of the reduction. Default value is *LEAF_LEVEL*.
- *elevel*: This is the ending level of the reduction. Default value is *ROOT_LEVEL*. For example, if *elevel* = *LEAF_LEVEL* and the HTA has one-level of tiling, then the reduction is applied over each leaf tiles of the HTA. Also, *elevel* ≤ *slevel*.

For example, if the HTA has a single level of tiling and *slevel* = *elevel* = 1, then the scalar elements of the leaf tiles are reduced along *dim*. If *slevel* = *elevel* = 0, the tiles of the top level HTA are reduced along *dim*. These two cases occur in the IS program of NAS benchmark suite, and an example is shown in the third and fourth row in Figure 5.

**Scan.** scan computes the reductions of all prefixes of a vector. For example, if the vector $v = (1, 2, 3, 4, 5)$, then $scan(+, v) = (1, 3, 6, 10, 14)$. htalib provides a similar scan operation for HTAs. The syntax is very similar to that of reduce. However, unlike map and reduce, scan is an ordered computation; the result is dependent on the order of iteration over the elements. scan represents *do-across* parallelism. Owing to space restrictions, scan is not explained in detail.

**MapReduce.** Certain computations require composition of map and reduce. mapReduce is a higher-order operator that combines the two steps in an efficient manner. mapReduce takes as input instances of a map-reduce operator.

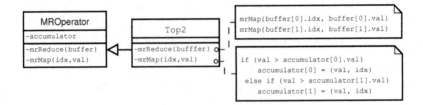

**Fig. 6.** MROperator and Top2

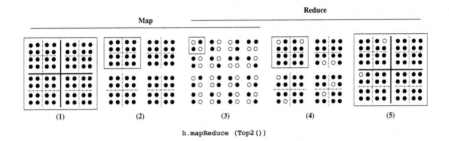

h.mapReduce (Top2())

**Fig. 7.** mapReduce operation

The implementation of this map-reduce operator is based on class MROperator with two key abstract methods, mrMap and mrReduce, and a generic variable accumulator that holds at first intermediate data and finally the results of the operator evaluation.

To implement an application specific map-reduce operator, programmers must extend MROperator and provide implementations for mrMap and mrReduce. Figure 6 shows the MRoperator and a subclass, Top2, which finds the top 2 values and their indices from a numerical matrix. A programmer only implements the core sequential logic: the code for accumulating the results in the accumulator in mrMap, and the code for combining two accumulators in mrReduce. The invocation of mrMap with arguments, and the parallel reduction strategy and data exchange are the responsibility of htalib.

Figure 7 illustrates the semantics of mapReduce invoked with an instance of Top2. In the figure, the mapReduce is applied to an HTA with two levels of tiling. A solid rectangle is used to show the scope of mapReduce at each stage. mapReduce is evaluated recursively across the tile hierarchy down to a specified level, i.e. method mapReduce is recursively invoked on each tile (step 1-2). When the bottom or the recursion is reached, the method mrMap is applied to each scalar of the tiles at this level (step 3). This is followed by calls to mrReduce as the operator evaluation ascends in the tile hierarchy (steps 3-5). In the figure, the top 2 elements chosen at each level are shown with white dots.

mapReduce offers better abstraction and performance benefits over applying map and reduce separately. Since the reductions involve an associative operation, potentially large intermediate buffers can be replaced by much smaller accumulators. This saves both memory usage and network bandwidth. Furthermore, several `maps` or `reduces` can be combined in to a single operation, eliminating several unwanted buffers.

# 4   Overlapped Tiling

Many scientific codes contain operations on several neighboring points within an array. A typical example is iterative PDE solvers based on finite difference techniques, also known as *stencil* codes. Jacobi is a simple example of an iterative PDE solver, which is similar to the stencil computation in NAS MG benchmark. These codes benefit from tiling, and thus from HTAs, both because it improves their locality [15] and because it can be used to distribute their data in order to parallelize them. However, the processing of the data located in the borders of the tiles requires accesses to neighboring data located in other tiles. The usual approach to deal with this problem in parallel codes is to resort to shadow regions or ghost cells that the programmer is responsible for keeping updated. Such situation is shown in Figure 2(a) for a 1D Jacobi code. There are two statements to update shadow regions of HTA B before the stencil computation. In htalib, we have opted for a cleaner approach: overlapped tiling. It consists in specifying at construction time that the contents of each tile of the HTA overlap with a given number of elements of each neighbor tile. The HTA becomes responsible for creating shadow regions of storage if they are needed, and updating them as necessary.

## 4.1   Syntax

**Creation.** When a tile T is defined, we say that the region it comprises is owned by T. The size of this owned region for each tile is given by the tiling parameter, the first parameter in HTA constructor in Figure 8(a). The regions that can be accessed across tile boundaries are defined as *shadow* regions. In particular, outside the region owned by T, are the extended regions that T can access. We call them *shadow-out* regions. Inside T, there are regions that other tiles are allowed to access. We call those *shadow-in* regions. For example, in Figure 8(b), we show the shadow-in and shadow-out regions for the first tile of A defined in Figure 8(a). The sizes of the shadow-in and shadow-out regions are given by a parameter of type `Overlap`. First, we show how to construct an object of type `Overlap`. The general form is,

```
Overlap<DIM> ol = Overlap<DIM>( T<DIM> negativeDir, T<DIM> positiveDir, boundaryMode mode);
```

The `negativeDir` specifies the amount of the overlap for each tile in the *negative direction* (decreasing index value) in each dimension. The `positiveDir` specifies the amount of the overlap for each tile in the *positive direction* (increasing index values). The `mode` parameter specifies the nature of the boundary regions in the original array with three options: `zero`, `preset`, `periodic`. The `zero` mode means shadow regions filled with all zeros will be allocated to the

```
Tuple<1>::seq tiling=(Tuple<1>(4), Tuple<1>(3));

Overlap<1> ol(Tuple<1>(1), Tuple<1>(1), zero);

A=HTA<double,1>::alloc(tiling, array, ROW, ol);
```

(a)

```
HTA<double, 1> A, B;
while (!converged){
    A()[All] = S* ( B()[All-1]+ B()[All+1]);
    ... ...
}
```

(c)

Shadow−out   Owned   Shadow−out

Shadow−in

0                        (b)                        0

**Fig. 8.** Example of overlapped tiling. (a) The constructor for an HTA with tiles overlap to both directions and shadow regions in the boundary are inserted.(b) The pictorial view. (c) HTA code for 1D Jacobi with overlapped tiling.

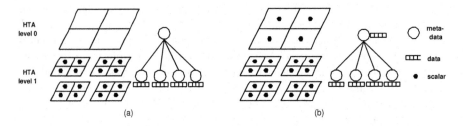

HTA level 0

HTA level 1

(a)                                    (b)

○ meta-data

▭ data

● scalar

**Fig. 9.** (a) HTA with no data layering. (b) Multi layered HTA stores data at different levels of the hierarchy.

boundary of the array by htalib. The **preset** mode means the shadow regions for the array elements in the boundary have been allocated and preset by the programmer. The **periodic** mode means the shadow regions for the array elements satisfy the periodic boundary conditions. In the 1D array case, for instance, the last element of the array treats the first element as its neighbor. The **Overlap** object is used as the last parameter in the HTA constructor to create the HTA with overlapped tiling.

Figure 8(a) shows an example code that creates an $1 \times 3$ HTA **A** with 4 elements per tile. Each tile in the HTA overlaps one element in both directions. Around the boundaries of the array, the shadow regions are allocated by htalib with zeros. The pictorial view is shown in Figure 8(b). As a result of the **zero** mode overlap, the two shadow-out regions for the third tile are the last element of the second tile and the last zero element added to **A**'s boundary by htalib.

**Indexing.** The overlapped tiling provides flexible indexing to HTAs so that each tile can index the neighboring elements in adjacent tiles.

The indexing for the owned region of each tile remains the same as if no overlapped tiling had been applied. The index range for the owned data starts from 0 to the maximum size of the tile in each dimension. The indexing for the shadow regions extends the owner's range in both positive and negative directions in each dimension. For example, let us consider a one dimensional tile T of size 4, with overlapped tiling in both direction with the length 2. Then, the region owned by T can be indexed as T[0:3]. The left shadow region can be indexed as T[-2:-1] and the right shadow region can be indexed as T[4:5]. We define the symbolic shape All to index all elements in the region owned by T. The expression T[All+1] indexes a region which shifts T to the right by 1. It can also be thought as adding value 1 to each index in T[All].

Figure 8(c) shows the same code as Figure 2(a), but uses overlapped tiling. Compared with the original code, it helps simplify the program with only one statement in computation. Furthermore, the simpler indexing scheme makes the code more readable.

### 4.2   Shadow Region Consistency

When there is a write to the shadow region, every tile that has access to this region should be consistent with this change. The shadow region consistency problem is handled by htalib. Consistency is trivial for some data layouts such as row or column major. However, for some special data layouts such as distributed HTAs, proper updates should be performed by htalib in order to keep all copies of the overlapped region consistent.

We use the update-on-write policy to keep the shadow region consistent. Since every element only belongs to one owned region, we only allow that owner tile to perform the write to its data. Once the owner tile modifies the data, it updates the set of tiles whose shadow-out regions contain the data.

## 5   Data Layering

So far the hierarchical nature of HTAs serves to achieve data distribution and access locality. We now investigate HTAs for applications where the hierarchy reflects a property of the application domain. The key extension we propose for HTAs is to associate scalar data with different layers of an HTA (not just with the lowest layer in the hierarchy) to facilitate applications requiring mesh refinement.

When HTAs are used for locality or to control data distribution, data is stored only in the leaf tiles, while tiles above the leaves store only meta data about their children in the tiling hierarchy (see Figure 9(a)). We extend HTAs to provide support for refinement, by allowing any level in the hierarchy to store both data and tiling information about refined levels (see Figure 9(b)). For example, the NAS benchmark MG [1] defines a set of grids that are successive refinements of an original grid, as it can be seen in Figure 10(a), where levels 0, 1 and 2 are shown. Every cell in a grid is expanded by a factor of two along all dimensions, at the next level. The set of grids defined by MG can be naturally represented as a hierarchy of tiled arrays.

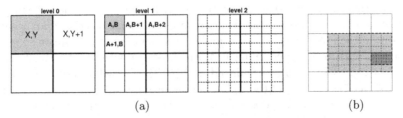

**Fig. 10.** Mesh Refinement (a) MG (b) Adaptive Mesh Refinement

## 5.1 HTA Support for Mesh Refinement in MG

Figure 11(a) shows code for a subset of functions in the NAS MG benchmark, based on HTAs without layering support. In this code, the user has to explicitly allocate space for the HTAs corresponding to different levels of refinement. Function setup(), in Figure 11(a), allocates the HTAs and stores them in an array. The position in the array corresponds to different refinement levels. The users will also have to explicitly store information on how data at a certain level relates to data in the refined and coarse grids. This information is used to communicate data between different levels. In Figure 11(a), function interp(), data from the coarse grid z is used to initialize data in the refined one u. The (A,B) and (X,Y) tuples specify how data elements between two levels correspond and this information has to be provided by the user. The explicit specification of the coordinate mapping is error prone and a tedious task for a programmer. We extend the HTA library to handle the refinement, and to automatically provide these mappings.

For the NAS MG benchmark, allocating the grids for the refined levels is relatively simple. Every cell is refined uniformly, in all directions by a constant factor. In a general adaptive mesh refinement problem there are extra complications that have to be addressed: When the refinement is not uniform, as shown in Figure 10(b), the user will have to allocate explicit space for all refined sections and to store, separated from the grid data structure, more complex information on how grids at different levels are correlated. Both aspects can be naturally expressed with our extensions to HTA, such that to simplify the programmer's effort in maintaining refinement information.

## 5.2 The Extensions for Multiple Levels of Data

Layered HTAs extend the interface of HTA with a set of primitives that facilitate computation requiring refinement as follows:

**void refine(level lev, region, refinement_factor):** at level lev, refine the specified region (see Section 2.1), using the specified refinement_factor. The refinement factor is a tuple specifying the refinement in each dimension. In Figure 10(a), e.g., level 1 is a refinement of the original grid, created through refine(0, All, Tuple(2,2)).

**<region_coarse, region_fine> = project (level):** computes how elements from two adjacent levels correspond to each other. region_coarse and

```
#define Grid HTA                          #define Grid HTA
void setup(...) {                         void setup(...) {
 for i = 0..num_levels {                   allocate H, HTA level 0;
   compute tiling level i                  for i = 1..num_levels {
   array[i] = allocate HTA level i          H.refine(level_i, refinement_factor)
 }                                          }
}                                         }

void interp (Grid z, Grid u ) {          void interp(Grid u, level lev) {
  //get info about tiles                    Weight w;
  Weight w;                                 Region r_coarse(X,Y), r_fine(A,B);
  int iSize = ..                            <r_coarse, r_fine> = u.project(lev);
  int jSize = ..                            //project level lev of u down; return mapping
  int kSize = ..                            u.get_level(lev+1)(r_fine) += w *
  Triplet X(0, iSize-2);                                 u.level(lev)(r_coarse);
  Triplet Y(0, jSize-2);                    r_fine.X += 1;
  Triplet A(0, 2 * (iSize-2), 2);           u.get_level(lev+1)(r_fine) += w *
  Triplet B(0, 2 * (jSize-2), 2);                        u.level(lev)(r_coarse);
                                            ...
  u()((A,B)) += w * z()((X,Y));           }
  u()((A+1,B)) += w * z()((X,Y));
  ...
}

              (a)                                           (b)
```

**Fig. 11.** MG `setup()` and `interp()` functions adapted for 2D Grids: (a) without refinement support and (b) with refinement support

region_fine are initialized by this method. Both regions will have the same size (iteration space) and they encapsulate the mapping information that is used to perform operations between elements on two adjacent levels. Figure 10(a), illustrates an HTA with two levels of refinement; the call <region_coarse, region_fine> = HTA.project (0), initializes the two regions such that element (X,Y) from region_coarse will be associated with element (A,B) from region_fine, (X,Y+1) with (A,B+2), and similarly for all elements at the coarse level. The corresponding regions initialized with project() are used to perform assignments and different operations between elements of HTAs at adjacent levels. To exemplify the use of the project() method, we show in Figure 11(b), function interp() from the NAS MG kernel. The function has the same functionality as the interp() method in Figure 11(a), the mapping corresponding to the refinement are however not computed explicitly, but provided by the layered HTA.

**HTA get_level(level lev):** To simplify the design, layered HTAs can't be used in expressions with regular HTAs. Layered HTAs provide get_level(), a cast type of method that returns an HTA representing the tiling and data at a specific level. This mechanism allows to apply regular HTA operations to a specific layer of a multi layered HTA.

The extensions described in this section, provide an interface that facilitates the development of applications requiring mesh refinement. The hierarchy of refinement levels existent in the application is naturally mapped onto the hierarchy of an HTA. We are currently exploring an adaptive mesh refinement application[17] to analyze the impact of the proposed HTA extensions on productivity and performance.

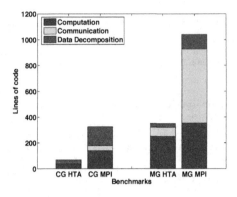

| Number of | Benchmark | | | |
|---|---|---|---|---|
| Processors | CG A | CG B | MG A | MG B |
| 1 | 68.63 | 2631.39 | - | - |
| 2 | 35.27 | 1335.76 | - | - |
| 4 | 17.94 | 671.96 | - | - |
| 8 | 12.49 | 451.84 | 9.57 | 38.03 |
| 16 | 6.47 | 227.78 | 5.06 | 20.37 |
| 32 | 6.94 | 186.08 | 2.84 | 11.7 |
| 64 | 4.19 | 93.02 | 1.91 | 8.27 |

**Fig. 12.** Linecount of key sections of HTA and MPI programs

**Fig. 13.** Execution times of the NAS HTA codes on BlueGene/L

## 6   Experimental Results

HTA programs benefit from a high level notation, much more expressive than that of other approaches to implement parallel programs. Thus it is expected that they will boost programmer's productivity. Figure 12 measures this property by comparing the number of lines of code used by the htalib implementation of the CG and MG NAS benchmarks with that of their corresponding MPI counterparts. As we can see, the HTA codes have substantially fewer lines of code in each one the three categories in which we have classified them.

Figure 13 shows the execution times for CG and MG for classes A and B for different numbers of processors on the BlueGene/L. Some experiments could not be run due to the limited amount of main memory available in a single compute node. We observe good scalability and our current efforts are focused on identifying and optimizing the primitives that will further improve this to match the speedup numbers achieved by the FORTRAN + MPI versions. In terms of absolute performance, the FORTRAN + MPI versions of the benchmarks included in Figure 13 run on average 2.2 times faster than the htalib version.

## 7   Related Work

The programming for distributed memory systems has traditionally followed a SPMD, message-passing model. Programmers specify the path of execution for each processor, and messages are exchanged either using standard libraries like MPI [14] or higher level constructs provided by languages like Co-Array Fortran (CAF) [16] and UPC [8]. This paradigm produces very efficient programs at the cost of high development and maintenance costs, as the programmer has to distribute and communicate data, synchronize processes and choose execution paths for each processor manually.

There are three principal approaches to implement global view programming models for distributed memory systems: (i) extensions of existing languages with directives such as HPF [2], (ii) novel languages like ZPL [9], and (iii) libraries like htalib or STAPL [5]. We find the latter strategy most attractive as it facilitates the reuse of existing codes. Moreover, the library-based approach allows the gradual migration of sequential codes to a parallel form without relying on complex compiler technology that is not always effective in optimizing the overheads associated with the global view model.

What differentiates the HTA from other approaches is (a) its unique treatment of the tile as a first-class object that is explicitly addressed and manipulated and (b) its emphasis in the recursive subdivision of the tiles in order to adapt the data storage and computation structure of the codes to the underlying machine. This latter characteristic is shared with Sequoia [13], although its principal construct is procedural (the *task*), while our approach is data centric. Also, Sequoia tasks are not associated to particular processors; instead they can run in any node in which their working set fits. HTAs provide on the contrary a clear model of data and task placement and communications. Finally, Matrix+$^+$ [10] also allows the construction of hierarchical matrices and implements recursive operations on them, but it lacks the flexible notation of the HTAs to access and manipulate the tiles. Rather, it is focused on computations involving the whole resulting matrices.

## 8    Concluding Remarks

In this paper we describe three extensions to HTAs that facilitate their use in a wide variety of application contexts. Our extensions factor out functionality that is commonly encountered in array-based codes. Using the *operator framework*, programmers can specify powerful, block-recursive array operations in a sequential logic, while the skeleton of reduction and iteration is provided by htalib. *Overlapped tiling* relieves the programmer from explicitly allocating and maintaining ghost cells in stencil computations. Support for *multi-layering* helps users express refinement and computations that involve arrays at adjacent layers of the hierarchy. Our experience with a portable C++ library shows that the new HTA features permit to implement the NAS kernels in a structured and concise manner without compromising scalability or performance on a BlueGene/L system.

**Acknowledgment.** We thank George Almási, Nancy Amato, and Calin Cascaval for their advice and comments on our work.

## References

1. NAS Parallel Benchmarks. Website. http://www.nas.nasa.gov/Software/NPB/.
2. High Performance Fortran Forum. *HPF Specification Version 2.0*, January 1997.
3. J. C. Adams, W. S. Brainerd, J. T. Martin, B. T. Smith, and J. L. Wagener. *Fortran 90 Handbook*. McGraw-Hill, 1992.
4. G. Almási, L. D. Rose, B. B. Fraguela, J. Moreira, and D. Padua. Programming for Locality and Parallelism with Hierarchically Tiled Arrays. In *Proc. of LCPC*, pages 162–176, Oct 2003.

5. P. An, A. Jula, S. Rus, S. Saunders, T. Smith, G. Tanase, N. Thomas, N. Amato, and L. Rauchwerger. STAPL: An Adaptive, Generic Parallel Programming Library for C++. In *Proc. of LCPC*, pages 193–208, August 2001.

6. M. J. Berger and P. Colella. Local adaptive mesh refinement for shock hydrodynamics. *Journal of Computational Physics*, 82(1):64–84, 1989.

7. G. Bikshandi, J. Guo, D. Hoeflinger, G. Almasi, B. B. Fraguela, M. J. Garzarán, D. Padua, and C. von Praun. Programming for parallelism and locality with hierarchically tiled arrays. In *Proc. of the ACM SIGPLAN Symposium on Principles and Practice of Parallel Programming (PPoPP'06)*, pages 48–57, 2006.

8. W. Carlson, J. Draper, D. Culler, K. Yelick, E. Brooks, and K. Warren. Introduction to UPC and Language Specification. Technical Report CCS-TR-99-157, IDA Center for Computing Sciences, 1999.

9. B. L. Chamberlain, S. Choi, E. Lewis, C. Lin, S. Snyder, and W. Weathersby. The Case for High Level Parallel Programming in ZPL. *IEEE Computational Science and Engineering*, 5(3):76–86, July–September 1998.

10. T. Collins and J. C. Browne. Matrix++: An object-oriented environment for parallel high-performance matrix computations. In *Proc. of the 28th Annual Hawaii Intl. Conf. on System Sciences (HICSS)*, page 202, 1995.

11. D. E. Culler, A. Dusseau, S. C. Goldstein, A. Krishnamurthy, S. Lumetta, T. von Eicken, and K. Yelick. Parallel programming in split-c. In *Conference on Supercomputing (SC)*, pages 262–273, 1993.

12. J. Dean and S. Ghemawat. Mapreduce: Simplified data processing on large clusters. In *Symposium on Operating System Design and Implementation (OSDI)*, 2004.

13. K. Fatahalian, T. J. Knight, M. Houston, M. Erez, D. R. Horn, L. Leem, J. Y. Park, M. Ren, A. Aiken, W. J. Dally, and P. Hanrahan. Sequoia: Programming the memory hierarchy. In *To appear in Proc. of Supercomputing 2006*, Nov 2006.

14. W. Gropp, E. Lusk, and A. Skjellum. *Using MPI (2nd ed.): Portable Parallel Programming with the Message-Passing Interface"*. MIT Press, 1999.

15. H. Han, G. Rivera, and C. Tseng. Software support for improving locality in scientific codes. In *Proc. of the Eighth International Workshop on Compilers for Parallel Computers (CPC'2000)*, Aussois, France, Jan 2000.

16. R. W. Numrich and J. Reid. Co-array Fortran for Parallel Programming. *SIGPLAN Fortran Forum*, 17(2):1–31, 1998.

17. T. Wen and P. Colella. Adaptive mesh refinement in Titanium. *IPDPS*, 2005.

18. M. E. Wolf and M. S. Lam. A data locality optimizing algorithm. In *PLDI*, pages 30–44, 1991.

# SP@CE - An SP-Based Programming Model for Consumer Electronics Streaming Applications*

Ana Lucia Varbanescu[1], Maik Nijhuis[2], Arturo González- Escribano[3],
Henk Sips[1], Herbert Bos[2], and Henri Bal[2]

[1] Department of Computer Science, Delft University of Technology, The Netherlands
[2] Department of Computer Science, Vrije Universiteit, Amsterdam, The Netherlands
[3] Departamento Informatica, Universidad de Valladolid, Spain

**Abstract.** Efficient programming of multimedia streaming applications for Consumer Electronics (CE) devices is not trivial. As a solution for this problem, we present SP@CE, a novel programming model designed to balance the specific requirements of CE streaming applications with the simplicity and efficiency of the Series-Parallel Contention (SPC) programming model. To enable the use of SP@CE, we have designed a framework that guides the programmer to design, evaluate, optimize and execute the application on the target CE platform. To evaluate the entire system, we have used SP@CE to implement a set of real-life streaming applications and we present the results obtained by running them on the Wasabi/SpaceCAKE architecture from Philips, a multi-processor system-on-chip (MPSoC) CE platform. The experiments show that SP@CE enables rapid application development, induces low overhead, offers high code reuse potential, and takes advantage of the inherent application parallelism.

**Keywords:** streaming applications, consumer electronics, programming models, SP@CE, component-based framework, MPSoC.

## 1 Introduction

Only a few years ago, the field of consumer electronics (CE) was limited to television, home hi-fi, and home appliances. Nowadays, it has expanded to include many other modern electronics fields, ranging from mobile phones to car navigation systems, from house security devices to interactive information displays. These systems spend most of their resources on processing complex multimedia, including video and sound playing, real-time animations, real-time information retrieval and presentation. The applications have to process data streams (i.e., continuous and virtually infinite flows of data), and they have to be able to run concurrently, to react to user-generated events and to reconfigure themselves on-demand.

To meet the programming challenges of these applications, we present SP@CE, a novel SPC-based programming model for streaming applications for multiprocessor CE devices. Besides the features inherited from SPC, like ease of programming, explicit parallelism, and predictability, SP@CE offers solutions for

---

* This work is supported by the Dutch government's STW/PROGRESS project DES.6397.

G. Almási, C. Caşcaval, and P. Wu (Eds.): LCPC 2006, LNCS 4382, pp. 33–48, 2007.

dealing with streaming and user-interaction, both essential to CE applications. The *SP@CE framework* is a natural extension of the programming model, providing the user a productive tool for application design, performance evaluation, optimization and execution.

The paper is structured as follows: Section 2 presents the specifics of streaming applications and Section 3 discusses requirements identified as essential for consumer electronics applications. Section 4 details the SP@CE programming model, while Section 5 presents our experiments and their results. Section 6 discusses some related work, while Section 7 presents our conclusions and the future work directions.

## 2   Streaming Applications

A *streaming application* is a data-intensive application that has to read, process, and output streams of data [1,2]. *Data streams*, are continuous, virtually infinite flows of data, with a given *data rate*. The elements of a data-stream are of the same type, and they exhibit low reusability: an element is useful/used for a limited (usually short) period of time and then discarded. The *active window* of a data stream contains the elements required for the current processing. The application processes data via its *components* (*filters*), which are, ideally, independent entities, implemented such that they allow concurrent execution, which facilitates the use of task-parallelism.

With respect to its *data flow*, the application is executed as an implicit infinite loop, and we assume it to be synchronous. Each *application iteration* takes the time needed for the active window of the application input stream to be processed and written to the output stream. Depending on the filters organization and/or parallelization, the application may process data at higher or lower rates. The *control flow* of the application allows (1) taking different execution paths based on conditionals, and (2) reshaping the component graph. The interaction between the data flow and the control flow of the application must be specified and formalized.

While an up-to-date "Streaming Programming" paradigm is not yet entirely agreed upon - see the various definitions in [3,4,1], the consumer electronics industry demands dedicated, more productive and more efficient tools for such applications. The SP@CE framework is a possible answer to these demands.

## 3   Consumer Electronics Platforms

An essential requirement for consumer electronics software is to be *reactive*, i.e., to be able to respond and manage user interaction. Thus, besides streaming, CE applications must feature event awareness and handling, dynamic reconfigurability and performance predictability. This section provides insights on these three specific aspects. To exemplify the concepts, we use a TV-like picture-in-picture (PiP) environment, where the user can dynamically control the number of pictures on display (show/remove a picture), as well as their positioning (move the picture on the screen).

**Dynamic application reconfigurability** is the ability of the system to modify the graph of a running application without completely stopping and restarting it. For example, if the user decides to add a new picture in the PiP environment, the new image should not affect the displaying of the previously visible pictures. At the implementation level, dynamic reconfigurability translates into the ability of the application to reconfigure itself transparently to the user. Typically, such a reconfiguration implies application graph restructuring by nodes and/or edges addition or removal. Furthermore, reconfigurability requires a dynamic resource scheduler, able to map the new application graph on the existing resources on-the-fly.

**Event awareness and handling** refer to the ability of an application to detect user requests and respond accordingly. In the PiP environment, if the user pushes a button to add an extra picture, an external event for the application is generated. This event can interrupt the current processing at a suitable moment (event awareness) and the application reconfigures according to the generated event (event handling). At the implementation level, event awareness requires the application control flow to be able to receive and adapt to external commands, while event handling imposes the application to determine and execute the appropriate action in a timely manner (i.e., not necessarily instantly, but within the limits of user non-observability).

**Performance predictability** is a characteristic of the application that allows for performance evaluation without complete simulation or execution. In the case of CE applications, performance prediction is used to evaluate if the soft real-time deadlines, typically imposed by user satisfaction, are met. Guided by the performance predictions, the user may take the appropriate decisions for optimizing the parallelization or resource allocation strategies. In other words, performance prediction enables a broad design space exploration for application parallelization and mapping. In the PiP example, assume 3 active pictures and 4 processors available. There are two possible solutions for resource mapping: (1) decode each frame on one processor, and let the fourth processor make the assembly and display, or (2) make each processor compute one quarter of each active picture and display its part. The performance prediction mechanism has to decide, for each of these implementations, if they meet the deadline imposed by the required frame rate.

## 4   SP@CE

This section describes the design of the novel programming model SP@CE, and it briefly presents the early prototype implementation of its subsequent framework.

### 4.1   The SPC Programming Model

SPC is a programming model that imposes specific restrictions on the dependency graph of an application in order to achieve analyzable performance. SPC

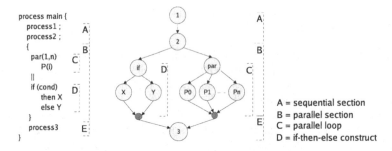

**Fig. 1.** An SP code snippet and its corresponding graph

expresses parallel computations in terms of processes and resources. The "SP" prefix stands for *series-parallel* and it suggests that the application must be expressed in terms of an SP structured computation, which constraints the condition synchronization patterns to only SP graphs[1] [5].The suffix "C" in SPC stands for *contention* and it refers to the use of resource contention to express mutual exclusion and, as a consequence, to describe scheduling constraints [6].

Despite these apparent expressivity limitations, it has been proved that SPC can capture the essential parallelism of an application. The loss in performance when remodeling a non-SP application to its best SP equivalent is typically bounded to few percents [7].

From the user point of view, SPC can be seen as a coordination paradigm that specifies the synchronization model of the application. Programming in SPC loosely refers to (1) expressing data computation as processes, (2) applying compositions between these processes, and (3) expressing mutual exclusion between processes in terms of resource contention (when required). Processes are usually expressed in a familiar sequential language, like C. Composition operators between processes allow sequential composition and loops, parallel composition and loops, with `fork/join` semantics, and conditionals. Figure 1 presents an example that illustrates the usage of these operators.

While the processes are implemented to exploit the unbounded parallelism of the problem, resources are introduced as limitations of the actual parallelism of the system. The mutual exclusion provided by SPC is based on resource contention: two processes are in contention if they require the same resource to execute. For example: `process(i) -> channelA` specifies that all `process(i)`'s must use the resource `channelA` mutually exclusive. To solve the contention, processes are dynamically scheduled with a user-specified scheduling policy (like FCFS, for example). Please note that resources are universal in SPC: they can be either logical (critical sections in the program) or physical (processing units), to allow for a generic approach. And although resources in SPC are only meant as synchronization providers, they can be further used to facilitate the application mapping on real hardware resources.

We have chosen SPC as the basis of our SP@CE model because of three main characteristics: ease of programming, unbounded parallelism, and analyzability.

---

[1] Another common name for *SP programming* is *nested-parallel programming*.

We argue that SP is a natural way of reasoning about parallel applications [8], while resource contention for synchronization avoids the typical hard-to-detect synchronization errors. Furthermore, it allows for data and task parallelism combinations. In its SP form, an application exploits the unbounded parallelism of the problem, without being constrained by any resource mappings transition from its abstract resources to the real hardware resources. Finally, performance prediction is based on estimating the application critical path augmented with the contention serialization penalties.

## 4.2   The Novel SP@CE Programming Model

The SP@CE model coherently extends the SPC model with the addition of data streams, event awareness and reconfigurability capabilities. The main features that make SP@CE suitable and efficient for programming streaming multimedia applications for CE platforms are:

- Construct the application graph in an SP form, which provides (among others) performance predictability
- Model data streaming by providing data streams as a predefined data type
- Facilitate component-based design to simplify code reuse and to rise the level of abstraction
- Combine data and control flow in a coherent model
- Use a synchronous execution model, which allows synchronization points to be used for reconfiguration
- Allow dynamic reconfigurability of the application graph, by designing standard component interfaces that allow runtime plug-and-play capabilities
- Provide event awareness and handling

*Building the data flow.* To define the data flow of an application, the user has to specify the components of the application (i.e., the nodes of the graph) and their interconnections (i.e., the streams that make the graph edges). To completely specify a component, one has to define (1) its data ports (type and direction), (2) its event ports, and (3) its functionality (typically using a "classical" programming language, like C). Data dependencies between the components are specified by connecting compatible data ports, while even awareness is specified by connecting the components even ports (input only) with the centralized event manager.

*Building the control flow.* We divide the application control flow into three subcategories: (1) *internal* control flow, i.e., inside the components, (2) *border* control flow, i.e., conditionals inside a process that affect its streaming behavior, and (3) *external* control flow, i.e., application events, either self- or user-generated.

Internal control flow is naturally managed by the components implementation language (in our case, C), as it is part of the processing. Because border control flow may influence the streaming behavior of the application, an additional constraint has to be imposed here: to preserve the fixed data rate for the streams (i.e., the number of consumed items should be the same in every iteration), the programmer should define a "null-action" for each stream whose data rate may be affected by a border conditional. Finally, because external control has to be

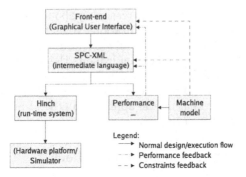

**Fig. 2.** The SP@CE framework components and their interaction

processed at the level of the entire application, SP@CE uses a global *event manager* to gather events and propagate them to the application components. The event manager is implemented as a finite state machine (FSM) which has the possible events as inputs, and the generated events as outputs. The user's task is to decide the logic of the FSM, and to correctly connect its outputs (i.e., the generated commands) to the event ports of the components. The FSM is evaluated at the end of each application iteration, allowing event handling in a timely manner, and with very little interruptions in the data flow.

*Reconfiguration.* Reconfiguration in SP@CE is supported by declaring reconfigurable subgraphs. These subgraphs contain optional parts that can be enabled or disabled as needed. Reconfiguration can only occur at special synchronization points, when the whole subgraph is idle, e.g., at the start or at the end of the subgraph iteration. By restricting reconfiguration to subgraphs, other parts of the application can continue execution without being interrupted.

Reconfiguration typically implies addition and/or removal or components and streams. As an application is initialized with *all* the classes of required components (although only *some* of these are actually instantiated for the initial structure of the application), adding a component requires a simple instantiation of the required component class and the stream interconnections. Similarly, removing a component means removing its instance from the enabled graph.

### 4.3   The SP@CE Framework

To provide the user with all the means for implementing applications in SP@CE, we have designed the SP@CE framework, presented in Figure 2. Top-down, the layers are: the front-end layer, i.e., the user interface, the intermediate representation layer, and the dual-path execution layer, instrumented by PAM-SoC [9] for performance prediction and Hinch[10] for application execution on the target platform.

**Front end.** The front end is the main user interface with SP@CE, allowing users to draw the application graph, interconnecting functional components with the corresponding data streams. To simplify the task of constructing the application

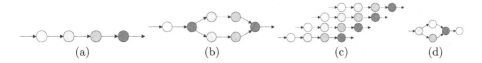

**Fig. 3.** Predefined compositions in SP@CE (similarly shaded bubbles execute the same code): (a) sequential, (b) parallel, (c) pipeline, (d) branch

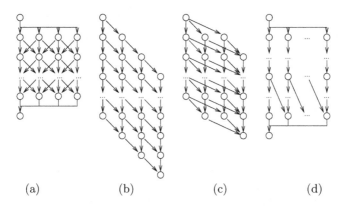

(a)            (b)            (c)            (d)

**Fig. 4.** Supported non-SP compositions in SP@CE: (a)neighbor synchronization, (b)macropipeline, (c)fork-join/broadcast-reduction and (d)paired synchronization

graph, the graphical user interface provides a few predefined SP-compliant constructs (see Figure 3): *sequential* and *sequential loop*, *parallel* and *parallel loop*, (with barrier semantics), *pipeline* and *branch*.

To further extend he capabilities of the framework, we plan to support several well-known non-SP data-parallel computation structures, like neighbor synchronization, macropipeline, fork-join/broadcast-reduction and paired synchronization, presented in Figure 4. These structures can be automatically transformed into their SP equivalents with little overhead [6]. The transformation can be performed during the conversion from the graphical interface to the intermediate representation, but the effort of supporting these complex structures requires further analysis into their real usage (if any) in streaming applications.

**SPC-XML.** A first precompilation step converts this graphical representation into an SPC representation, for which we have chosen an existing language, namely SPC-XML [11]. The generated SPC-XML specification represents the high level structure of the application, i.e., an XML form of the drawn application graph, fully SPC compliant. The components code and interface details are simply propagated in SPC-XML. Thus, the final SPC-XML representation of an application specifies both functionality and coordination. It contains enough information to generate, by direct transformations, both the application code and the application model needed for the performance prediction module.

**Hinch.** The application execution is supported by Hinch [10], a runtime system that takes care of load balancing the application over the available computation nodes, provides streaming communication primitives to the components, and supports dynamic reconfiguration.

Hinch components have to be a one-to-one representation of the SP@CE components. To preserve this identity, several implementation decisions have been made:

- All components adhere to a single interface, which provides an abstraction of the *component* to Hinch. In this way, connecting and executing are addressed similarly for all component instances.
- Components can be recursively grouped, allowing hierarchical compositions
- Component reuse is enabled by allowing multiple instances of a component to be active
- Components can be parametrized to accommodate different stream sizes, or, if given functions as parameters, to act as skeletons for sets of functions.

In Hinch, the application is built by grouping components recursively. The application model is a dataflow process network [12], in which the components are the actors. The application is run by executing *iterations* of the dataflow graph. In each iteration, each actor is fired one or several times, depending on the application data rates. One firing corresponds to running one iteration of the component. For example, in a video processing application, one iteration of a component may consist of processing one image frame from the video stream.

A graph iteration begins by scheduling the initial component(s). The other components are scheduled as soon as their predecessors in the dataflow graph have finished. Given that SP@CE supports iteration pipelining, multiple iterations can be active concurrently, which requires components to be aware of this and provide the necessary locking of their internal data structures to avoid race conditions. Although Hinch has no restriction on the shape of the dataflow graph, the graph will generally be SP-compliant, as it is generated from the high-level SP representation of the application.

**PAM-SoC.** PAM-SoC is based on the PAMELA methodology[13], a static performance prediction methodology for general purpose parallel platforms (GPPPs). The PAMELA toolchain facilitates symbolic cost modeling. It features a modeling language, a compiler, and a performance analysis technique that enables PAMELA models to be compiled into symbolic performance models. The prediction trades accuracy for the lowest possible solution complexity. In this symbolic cost modeling, SP-compliant parallel programs are mapped into explicit, algebraic performance expressions in terms of program parameters (e.g., problem size), and machine parameters (e.g., number of processors). Instead of being simulated, the model is automatically *compiled* into a *symbolic cost model*, that can be further compiled into a *time-domain cost model* and, finally, evaluated into a *time estimate*.

In order to address the specifics of embedded multi-core hardware platforms, we have developed PAM-SoC, a toolchain that includes, beside PAMELA, new techniques for machine modeling and dedicated tools for gathering memory behavior statistics [9]. To predict the performance of an application, PAM-SoC couples the application model with the target machine model, computing an average execution time of the application on the target architecture. Both models are written in the PAMELA modeling language, a process-oriented language designed to capture concurrency and timing behavior of parallel systems [14].

The role of PAM-SoC in the SP@CE framework is to predict the performance of the application in a form that can be used as feedback for the application design. PAM-SoC is able to (1) estimate the average execution time of a given application and (2) identify the potential resources that generate bottlenecks. Given these information, the user should be able to tune the application design and/or implementation to alleviate the bottlenecks and bring the execution time within the required limits.

## 5   Experiments

In this section, we present our initial results with the SP@CE prototype. We focus mainly on the expressiveness issues, discussing the way streaming consumer electronics applications can be programmed. We first describe the experimental setup, followed by the applications used in the experiments and the results. In this paper, we focus on evaluating (1) the overhead of the SP@CE framework by comparing functionally equivalent applications, developed with and without the SP@CE framework, and (2) the performance of the SP@CE applications when running in parallel. More specific details about the runtime system implementation and behaviour in terms of performance, reconfigurability lantecy and reconfiguration overhead are presented in [10].

### 5.1   Experimental Setup

All experiments are performed using the SpaceCake architecture[15], provided by Philips. This architecture has multiple identical processing tiles that communicate using distributed memory. Each tile is a shared memory multiprocessor on chip, called Wasabi. Wasabi contains a general purpose processor core, multiple TriMedia DSP cores, and specialized hardware to speedup specific operations. Per tile, each core has its own L1 cache, while the L2 cache is shared between all cores.

Since SpaceCake hardware is not available, all experiments are run using Wasabi's cycle accurate simulator, provided by Philips, which simulates a single tile with multiple TriMedia cores.

In all the experiments, we measure and compare the relative performance of the main computational part of the applications. To avoid distorting the results with the overhead introduced by the simulation I/O mechanisms, the input file(s) are fully read at initialization, and the final output results are discarded. The SP@CE component architecture simplifies the transition from these testing prototypes to real applications, as these "dummy" input and output components may be easily replaced with functional ones.

### 5.2   Applications

**Motion JPEG.** The first application we evaluated is a Motion-JPEG decoder (MJPEG). It takes a file with 50 concatenated 1280x720 jpeg coded images as input and decodes these into planar Y, U and V buffers. As shown in Figure 6, this application consists of three main components:

1. MJPEG input. This is a simple component that splits the mjpeg file into separate jpeg files. It supplies the next component with a jpeg file in each application iteration.

2. JPEG bit stream decoder. This component decodes the jpeg file into Discrete Cosine Transformed (DCT) blocks for each color component in the image. This includes: jpeg header decoding, Huffman decompression, and inverse-zigzag coding.

   The component can either run in a pipeline fashion, decoding multiple jpeg images concurrently, or it can run in a sliced mode, decoding one jpeg image split up into slices (i.e., adjacent sets of lines). In the sliced mode, the data processing in the bit stream decoder is fully sequential (slice after slice), but the model allows the next component to start running as soon as the first image slice is available. In the non-sliced mode, the next component can be run when all DCT blocks are decoded, but the following image is already in the pipeline. The estimates given by PAM-SoC, confirmed by real measurements, have indicated that the non-sliced mode performs better. Thus, guided by the SP@CE integrated tools, we have taken the appropriate design decisions and used the non-sliced version.

3. JPEG DCT decoder. This component generates pixel data from the input DCT blocks by performing an inverse discrete cosine transform (IDCT) followed by shift and bound operations. There is one DCT decoder for each color component in the image. Since there is no data dependency between the DCT blocks, data parallelism can be exploited by decoding multiple image slices simultaneously.

**Picture-in-Picture.** The second application we have evaluated is Picture-in-Picture (PiP). The application combines 96 images from multiple uncompressed 720x576 image streams into a single image stream by scaling down image streams and blending these into the main (background) image stream. We have four versions of the PiP application (PiP-0 to PiP-3), with 0, 1, 2, and 3 pictures-in-picture, respectively.

The components and data streams in the PiP application are shown in Figure 5(a). The downscale and blend components are run using data-parallelism. The full arrows in the figure correspond to luminance (Y) and packed chrominance (UV) streams. As the original graph is non-SP, we have converted it to its SP form by introducing a new synchronization point before the blender components. The resulting application graph is shown in Figure 5(b)[2].

This procedure shows how a non-SP graph is redesigned as SP. Although the SP version presents more dependences and the two blend components may have to wait for both luminance and chrominance streams downscaling, the inherent load-balance of the downscaling process alleviates performance penalties. Other forms of SP-graphs could be selected for applications with similar structure but different load-balance conditions. The SP@CE prediction tool shows which gives the best performance.

---

[2] For clarity, the graphs only show the dependencies between the components, and not all individual streams. Each dependency corresponds to a luminance stream (Y), chrominance stream (UV), or both (YUV).

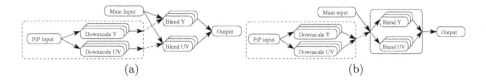

**Fig. 5.** Picture-in-Picture application graph: (a)Non-SP, (b)SP-compliant

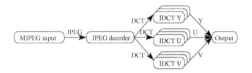

**Fig. 6.** Motion JPEG, SP@CE implementation

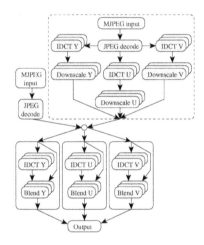

**Fig. 7.** Combined Motion JPEG/Picture-In-Picture application

**Motion JPEG + Picture-in-Picture.** We have also created an application (JPiP) by adjusting PiP to use components from MJPEG as input components, instead of the standard input components. The application combines 16 images from multiple jpeg-compressed 1280x720 image streams into a single 1280x720 image stream. Similarly to PiP, we have four versions JPiP (JPiP-0 to JPiP-3), with 0, 1, 2, and 3 pictures-in-picture, respectively.

The structure of JPiP, with one picture-in-picture, is shown in Figure 7. Being a combination of PiP and MJPEG, JPiP has three downscaling components for each picture-in-picture and three blenders, instead of two. To reduce synchronization overhead, the data-parallel components from both applications are grouped together.

The JPiP application is also a good example of the usability of SP@CE. Without SP@CE, it would have taken quite some effort to build a JPiP equivalent, as all communication and scheduling have to be programmed manually. Further more, code re-use would have been hindered: even though equivalents of MJPEG and PiP are available, various parts of these applications have to be adjusted to fit the new communication and scheduling patterns. With SP@CE, the only thing that had to be done was initializing and connecting existing components. Code reuse is practically optimal, as the components themselves needed no modifications at all.

## 5.3 Sequential Overhead

To estimate the SP@CE model overhead, we have compared the execution time of the SP@CE versions of PiP and MJPEG against their reference implementations. These reference implementations are sequential. Figure 8 shows the execution times of the non-SP@CE implementations, compared to a sequential and a parallel SP@CE version. SP@CE adds a small overhead (within 10%), due to its component-based structure. However, exactly due to its parameterized component-based structure, it allows for the same application to be executed in parallel. Given the much better execution time of the parallel version, we consider the sequential overhead not significant.

The overhead in the (sequential) SP@CE PiP applications is due to the fact that the blender is a separate component, while it is integrated in the downscaler in the non-SP@CE version. Profiling information shows that down scaling the image takes an almost equal amount of cycles for both versions. The difference lies in the amount of data copies, which is larger with a separate blender. However, we expect redundant buffering introduced by the SP structured form of component composition to be easily detected and eliminated by an optimization stage.

The non-SP@CE version of MJPEG decodes the DCT blocks as soon as they are decoded from the bit stream. It is 14% faster than the sequential SP@CE version. Profiling information shows that half the difference is due to communication overhead of the DCT buffers. Buffering DCT data causes data cache misses, both at the writing side (bit stream decoder) and the reading side (DCT decoder). The other half of the difference is added by the SP@CE model, due to some inefficiencies in data management and some code redundancies, mostly derived from generalization and support for parallelism. Better optimization in the SP@CE-generated code may alleviate them. The runtime system (Hinch) does not add significant overhead.

## 5.4 Parallel Performance

Figure 9 shows the speedup of the SP@CE applications when run on multiple TriMedia nodes. Because reference parallel implementations of the used benchmarks are not (publicly) available, we compare the parallel performance against the sequential SP@CE versions. PiP-0 does not exhibit much speedup because it is a trivial application that merely copies its input to its output. It is limited by memory bandwidth, not by processing power. The efficiency of PiP-1 decreases beyond seven nodes because there is no more parallelism to exploit. PiP-2 and PiP-3 do not suffer from this problem and show efficiencies of above 98% at nine nodes. The speedup for MJPEG does not increase much when it is run at more

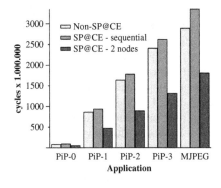

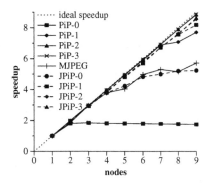

**Fig. 8.** SP@CE overhead                    **Fig. 9.** SP@CE speedup

than four nodes. Beyond this point, the added compute power is hardly used because there is only little additional parallelism to exploit.

The performance of JPiP-0 resembles that of MJPEG since these applications are highly identical: the main differences are the blender components, which are only present in JPiP. Like in PiP-0, the blend components in JPiP-0 do nothing but copying their single input to their output. Profiling information shows that less than two percent of all computation in JPiP-0 is spent in the blend components. In JPiP-1, JPiP-2, and JPiP-3 there is an abundance of parallelism to exploit. These applications therefore achieve good speedup figures, e.g., JPiP-3 has an efficiency of 96 % at 9 nodes.

To summarize, the results of the experiments presented in this section provide evidence that the SP@CE model is a suitable option for implementing predictable parallel streaming applications. Furthermore, while the model and its framework do not induce high overheads, they provide good performance in terms of applications speed-ups.

## 6   Related Work

We relate our work with different types of solutions - languages, design frameworks, and models - for programming streaming applications. For a reference survey on the origins and developments of streaming programming languages, we relate the reader to [1]. The survey presents reference languages like Lucid, LUSTRE, ESTEREL, and many others, until the mid-90's. Our data-flow approach on streaming, together with the representation of streams by their temporal instances largely follows the Lucid approach [16]. The model of synchronizing the application by iteration is similar to the approach of synchronous languages presented by [17] for LUSTRE and [18] for ESTEREL. However, none of these languages take into consideration issues like parallelization or reconfiguration, while events are only marginally discussed.

The most influential "modern" streaming language is StreamIt [19], which also expresses an application as a hierarchical graph of filters connected by streams. To insure correct composition of the filters, only a small number of composition operators are permitted. Components functionality is developed in C and/or Java, allowing code reusability and making the language reasonably user-friendly. However, StreamIt solutions for dealing with reconfiguration and events are cumbersome and limited compared to our approach. Finally, while StreamIt is elegantly exploiting task parallelism, data parallelism is only partially supported. Compared to the lower-level model of languages like Brook [3] or Stream-C/Kernel-C [20], our component-based model raises the level of abstraction, being easier to use for both design and implementation.

Nizza is a framework proposed in [21] as a methodology for developing multimedia streaming applications. Similar to our framework, Nizza uses a data-flow model, and it proposes a complete design-to-implementation flow, but it lacks a generic concept of events and reconfiguration is not entirely dynamic (it requires a restart of the framework). Also, as Nizza targets desktop applications, no performance feedback loop is included.

TStreams [4] is an abstract, dedicated model for parallel streaming applications, based on the same explicit parallelism approach as SP@CE. It remains to be seen if the model implementation is able to preserve these features. The Space-Time Memory abstraction (STM) [22] is a model with a different look on streams: an application is a collection of streams that need processing, so threads can attach them, process, and detach from them as required. The system is dynamic, natively reconfigurable and time-synchronous, being able to exploit both task and data parallelism. Again, the major drawback is in the model implementation that preserves these properties and remains programmer-friendly. Although SP@CE's model is simpler, it allows for a user-friendly implementation that offers a good compromise between the abstraction level and usability.

Kahn Process Networks (KPN) [23] are a popular streaming model for the embedded systems industry, because they are determinate and compositional. However, KPNs have no global state, and they are not reactive to external events. Models like Context Aware Process Networks model (CAPN) [24] and Reactive Process Networks (RPN) [25] alleviate this problems by extending KPN with global state and event awareness, but they sacrifice its determinate property. As a result, they are not predictable. These models do not tackle dynamic reconfiguration and do not include data parallelism facilities, which are both strong points of SP@CE.

Data-flow models are extensively used for expressing streaming applications [12,26]. SP@CE follows a similar graph-of-tasks approach as these models, and it is similar, in its synchronous approach, with the Synchronous Data-Flow [27,28] model. Still, most data-flow models implementations do not tackle dynamic reconfiguration (with an exception in the Parameterized Data Flow model [29]) and do not include data parallelism features. Furthermore, note that an important advantage of SP@CE over generic data-flow models is predictability and analyzability.

# 7   Conclusions and Future Work

We have presented SP@CE, a new programming model for streaming applications for MPSoC Consumer Electronics platforms. One of the main contributions of this work is the analysis of the specific requirements for streaming applications running on consumer electronics platforms. We believe that we have identified and listed *all* the properties that *must* be provided by a dedicated programming model aiming to increase programming correctness, efficiency and productivity. A further step was the SP@CE programming model itself, as an extension of the SPC model that embeds all the aforementioned properties

To prove the usability of SP@CE, we have designed a three-layer framework that assists the programmer in the design-to-execution flow of a streaming application. The SP@CE framework includes an user-friendly front-end, an XML-based intermediate representation, a runtime system and a performance feedback loop. A prototype of this framework has been used to experiment with several real streaming applications on a given multiprocessor CE platform. We have presented the results of these experiments, which prove that SP@CE's component-based approach provides good performance numbers, low overhead and nearly optimal code reuse.

For future work, on short term, our main target is to further validate the results by implementing more applications and more CE platforms. Further, we aim to make several enhancements of the framework prototype, including a complete graphical implementation of the front-end, more aggressive optimization engines for both SPC-XML and Hinch, and fully static performance prediction with PAM-SoC.

# References

1. Stephens, R.: A survey of stream processing. Acta Informatica **34** (1997) 491–541
2. Thies, W., Gordon, M.I., Karczmarek, M., Lin, J., Maze, D., Rabbah, R.M., Amarasinghe, S.: Language and compiler design for streaming applications. In: IPDPS'04 - Workshop 10. Volume 11. (2004)
3. Buck, I., Foley, T., Horn, D., Sugerman, J., Fatahalian, K., Houston, M., Hanrahan, P.: Brook for GPUs: Stream computing on graphics hardware. In: SIGGRAPH 2004, (ACM Press)
4. Knobe, K., Offner, C.D.: Compiling to TStreams, a new model of parallel computation. Technical report (2005)
5. Valdes, J., Tarjan, R.E., Lawler, E.L.: The recognition of series parallel digraphs. In: STOC '79, New York, NY, USA, ACM Press (1979) 1–12
6. González-Escribano, A.: Synchronization Architecture in Parallel Programming Models. PhD thesis, Dpto. Informatica, University of Valladolid (2003)
7. van Gemund, A.: The importance of synchronization structure in parallel program optimization. In: ICS '97: Proc. 11th international conference on Supercomputing, New York, NY, USA, ACM Press (1997) 164–171
8. Skillicorn, D.B., Talia, D.: Models and languages for parallel computation. ACM Comput. Surv. **30** (1998) 123–169
9. Varbanescu, A.L., van Gemund, A., Sips, H.: PAM-SoC: A toolchain for predicting MPSoC performance. In: Euro-Par'06. (2006) 111–123
10. Nijhuis, M., Bos, H., Bal, H.: Supporting reconfigurable parallel multimedia applications. In: Euro-Par'06. (2006) 765–776
11. González-Escribano, A., van Gemund, A., Cardeñoso-Payo, V.: SPC-XML: A structured representation for nested-parallel programming languages. Volume 3648., Springer-Verlag (2005) 782–792

12. Lee, E.A., Parks, T.M.: Dataflow process networks. In: Proc. of the IEEE. (1995) 773–799
13. van Gemund, A.: Performance Modeling of Parallel Systems. PhD thesis, Delft University of Technology (1996)
14. van Gemund, A.: Symbolic performance modeling of parallel systems. IEEE TPDS (2003)
15. Stravers, P., Hoogerbrugge, J.: Single chip multiprocessing for consumer electronics. In Bhattacharyya, ed.: Domain-Specific Processors. Marcel Dekker (2003)
16. Ashcroft, E., Wadge, W.: Lucid, the Dataflow Programming Language. Academic Press (1985)
17. Halbwachs, N., Caspi, P., Raymond, P., Pilaud, D.: The synchronous data-flow programming language LUSTRE. Proc. IEEE **79** (1991) 1305–1320
18. Berry, G., Gonthier, G.: The ESTEREL synchronous programming language: Design, semantics, implementation. Science of Computer Programming **19** (1992) 87–152
19. Thies, W., Karczmarek, M., Amarasinghe, S.: StreamIt: A language for streaming applications. In: Computational Complexity. (2002) 179–196
20. Kapasi, U., Dally, W.J., Rixner, S., Owens, J.D., Khailany, B.: The Imagine stream processor. In: ICCD'02, IEEE (2002) 282–288
21. Tanguay, D., Gelb, D., Baker, H.H.: Nizza: A framework for developing real-time streaming multimedia applications. Technical report (2004)
22. Rehg, J., Ramachandran, U., Jr., R.H., Joerg, C., Kontothanassis, L., Nikhil, R., Kang, S.: Space-Time Memory: a parallel programming abstraction for dynamic vision applications. Technical report (1997)
23. Kahn, G.: The semantics of a simple language for parallel programming. In: IFIP Congress '74, New York, NY, North-Holland (1974) 471–475
24. van Dijk, H.W., Sips, H., Deprettere, E.F.: Context-aware process networks, Los Alamitos, CA, USA, IEEE Computer Society (2003) 6–16
25. Geilen, M., Basten, T.: Reactive process networks. In: EMSOFT'04. (2004) 137–146
26. Ko, D.I., Bhattacharyya, S.S.: Modeling of block-based DSP systems. Volume 40., Kluwer Academic Publishers (2005) 289–299
27. Lee, E., Messerschmitt, D.: Synchronous Data Flow. IEEE Trans. Comp. **36** (1987) 24–35
28. Stuijk, S., Basten, T.: Analyzing concurrency in streaming applications. Technical report (2005)
29. Bhattacharya, B., Bhattacharyya, S.S.: Parameterized dataflow modeling for DSP systems. IEEE Trans. on Signal Processing **49** (2001) 2408–2421

# Data Pipeline Optimization for Shared Memory Multiple-SIMD Architecture[*]

Weihua Zhang[1,2], Tao Bao[1], Binyu Zang[1], and Chuanqi Zhu[1]

[1] Parallel Processing Institute, Fudan University, Shanghai, China
[2] Key Laboratory of Computer System and Architecture, Institute of Computing Technology, Chinese Academy of Sciences
{zhangweihua,052053006,byzang,cqzhu}@fudan.edu.cn

**Abstract.** The rapid growth of multimedia applications has been putting high pressure on the processing capability of modern processors, which leads to more and more modern multimedia processors employing parallel single instruction multiple data (SIMD) units to achieve high performance. In embedded system on chips (SOCs), shared memory multiple-SIMD architecture becomes popular because of its less power consumption and smaller chip size. In order to match the properties of some multimedia applications, there are interconnections among multiple SIMD units. In this paper, we present a novel program transformation technique to exploit parallel and pipelined computing power of modern shared-memory multiple-SIMD architecture. This optimizing technique can greatly reduce the conflict of shared data bus and improve the performance of applications with inherent data pipeline characteristics. Experimental results show that our method provides impressive speedup. For a shared memory multiple-SIMD architecture with 8 SIMD units, this method obtains more than 3.6X speedup for the multimedia programs.

## 1 Introduction

In recent years, multimedia and game applications have experienced rapid growth at an explosive rate both in quantity and complexity. Currently, since these applications typically demand $10^{10}$ to $10^{11}$ operations to be executed per second [1], higher processing capability is expected. Generally speaking, there are two kinds of solutions to the issue - hardware solutions and software solutions. Hardware solutions such as application specific integrated circuits (ASICs) have the advantages of higher performance with lower power consumption; However, their flexibility and adaptability to new applications are very limited. As a result, it is much popular to handle the problem with software solutions which enhance the processing capability of general-purpose processor with multimedia extensions. In the past several years, the key idea in those extensions was to exploit

---

[*] This research was supported by Specialized Research Fund for the Doctoral Program of Chinese Higher Education under Grant No. 20050246020 and supported by the Key Laboratory of Computer System and Architecture, Institute of Computing Technology, Chinese Academy of Sciences.

G. Almási, C. Caşcaval, and P. Wu (Eds.): LCPC 2006, LNCS 4382, pp. 49–63, 2007.
© Springer-Verlag Berlin Heidelberg 2007

subword parallelism in a SIMD (Single Instruction Multiple Data) fashion, such as Intel's SSE, MIPS's MDMX, TI (Texas Instruments)'s TMS320C64xx series etc.

However, with various multimedia applications becoming more complicated, using only single SIMD unit as a multimedia accelerator can not satisfy the performance requirements of these applications. Although it can improve computing capability by increasing processing elements (PEs) in one SIMD unit, this approach is unacceptable from both hardware and software perspective. Therefore, multiple-SIMD architecture instead of single SIMD unit is becoming a dominant multimedia accelerator in modern multimedia processors. At present, there are two types of multiple-SIMD architectures: one is *shared memory multiple-SIMD architecture* (SM-SIMD)[3,4,5,6,7,8,9] , where multiple SIMD units share a common memory (cache) on chip. The other is *distributed memory multiple-SIMD architecture* (DM-SIMD)[10], on which each SIMD unit has its local memory.

Since SM-SIMD architecture can get smaller die size and less power consumption, SM-SIMD architecture is widely used in embedded SOCs [3,4,5,6,7,8,9]. Although the details of these SOCs are not completely the same, there are some common characteristics among them in order to fit mobile computing circumstance.

1. There is a shared memory (cache) on chip for better locality, and multiple SIMD units access shared memory through a shared data bus. Shared data bus can replicate one vector to all SIMD units at the same time.
2. There are limited registers in each SIMD unit.
3. Multiple SIMD units are controlled by a general purpose processor core. Most of SM-SIMD architectures use very long instruction word (VLIW) to exploit the parallelism among multiple SIMD units since such an approach offers the potential advantage of simpler hardware design compared with the superscalar approach while still exhibiting good performance through extensive compiler optimization.
4. There are interconnections among SIMD units to make one SIMD unit get data from the registers of its connected SIMD units. We call two SIMD units as *neighboring SIMD units* if there is an interconnection between them.

Table 1 lists the major products of SM-SIMD architecture with these characteristics.

**Table 1.** Products of SM-SIMD architecture

| Product | Institute | Year |
|---|---|---|
| MorphoSys [3] | University of California, Irvine | 2000 |
| HERA [4] | New Jersey Institute of Technology | 2005 |
| Imagine [5] | Stanford | 2004 |
| Motorola 6011 [6] | Motorola Inc. | 2003 |
| MGAP-2 [7] | Folsom Inc. | 2000 |
| Vision Chips [8] | University of Tokyo | 2004 |
| VIRAM [9] | UC Berkeley | 2004 |

Scheduling for these shared bus and interconnected architectures is difficult because the compiler must simultaneously allocate many interdependent resources: the SIMD units on which the operations take place, the register files to hold intermediate values, and the shared bus to transfer data between functional units and shared memory. These conditions put very high pressure on the optimizing algorithms of SM-SIMD architecture. Most prior VLIW scheduling algorithms, such as [17] and [18] can not deal with resource allocation. Although scheduling algorithm in [12] enables scheduling for architectures in which functional units are connected to multiple register files by shared buses and register file ports, the utilization of these resources is not considered. Optimizing algorithm in [11] solves the utilization issue of shared data bus to some extent through common sub-expressions elimination, but the locality of read-only operands is not exploited by the authors although this type of operands is very common in real multimedia applications. Scheduling algorithm in [13] is an efficiently algorithm that exploits how to improve the utilization of the resources based on the characteristics of multimedia application, but it is not presented in their works that how to exploit pipeline parallelism.

The major challenge to optimizing techniques for SM-SIMD architecture is to reduce the conflict of shared data bus and to improve the parallelism among multiple SIMD units. When there are interconnections among multiple SIMD units, some optimizations can be performed to reduce the conflict of shared data bus. If one operation executed on one SIMD unit can get its operand from the register of the neighboring SIMD unit through interconnection, it is better to get the data through interconnection rather than via shared data bus. The reason is that getting operands from neighborhood would bring no data bus conflict, which is the major motivation for the optimizing technique proposed in this paper. Data pipeline parallelism is that multiple SIMD units get data from their neighboring SIMD units and data flows among these SIMD units as in pipeline. In this paper, we present a novel algorithm, which transforms sequential multimedia programs into data pipeline forms to exploit data pipeline parallelism. While reducing the shared data bus conflict of multiple SIMD units, the algorithm also greatly improve the performance of the application programs with inherent data pipeline characteristics. This paper makes the following contributions:

- This paper presents a novel data pipeline optimization through exploiting the characteristics of read-read reuse in the multimedia applications and the interconnection characteristics in SM-SIMD.
- Based on the experimental results, this paper also gives out some advice on programming for SM-SIMD architecture.

The remaining of this paper is organized as follows. Section 2 gives out the problem overview for the pipeline scheduling. In section 3, we describe pipeline scheduling in detail. Section 4 introduces the experimental method and presents the analysis of the experimental results. And in section 5 we come to the conclusion.

## 2   Problems Overview

### 2.1   Constraint of Shared Data Bus on Parallelism

Because there are multiple SIMD units in SM-SIMD architecture, it is necessary to exploit the parallelism among SIMD instructions and map them to different SIMD units. However, many parallel SIMD instructions can not be executed in parallel because of the constraints of shared data bus. Below is an example of such condition.

```
for (i=0; i<100; i++)   // Loop1
    A[i,0:7] = B[i,0:7] + C[i,0:7];

Example code 1: A parallel code fragment.
```

The code in Example code 1 is a program after SIMD optimization. Loop1 is a parallel loop, whose different iterations can be dispatched to different SIMD units. When mapping these iterations to different SIMD units, all of them need to load their operands from the shared memory respectively. As a result, these instructions can only be executed in sequence since shared data bus can only satisfy one of their operand requirements in each cycle. Thus, it is useless to only identify the parallelism in the program to exploit the parallelism for SM-SIMD architecture. Multiple SIMD instructions can be executed in parallel only when there is no shared data bus conflict among them. Therefore it is important for SM-SIMD architecture to reduce the competition of shared data bus in order to fully utilize the computation resources.

### 2.2   Problem Overview

As analyzed in section 2.1, shared data bus would impede the parallelism among multiple SIMD units in SM-SIMD architecture. Therefore, how to reduce the conflict of shared data bus would greatly impact the parallelism among multiple SIMD units. The scheduling algorithm in [13] can reduce the conflict of shared data bus through replicating read-only data and increasing the register locality. Furthermore, the interconnections[1] among SIMD units could provide better solutions for some applications. One SIMD unit can get the data from the register of its neighboring SIMD unit. Such data-getting manner performs better than loading data from the shared memory because accessing the register of its neighborhood would provide no bus conflict. The goal of data pipeline optimization is to exploit pipeline parallelism, which can greatly reduce the conflict of shared data bus and improve the parallelism of SM-SIMD architecture.

---

[1] Transfers of values between SIMD units are accomplished through operations of explicit movements along the interconnections among SIMD units. The interconnection is assumed to have a bi-directional ring topology among SIMD units. In other words, one SIMD unit has connections with its two neighboring SIMD units. Though this assumption is not necessary, it simplifies the compiler algorithms and such topology is very popular in SM-SIMD architecture.

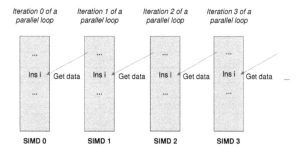

**Fig. 1.** Data pipeline

In order to exploit the parallelism among multiple SIMD units, different iterations of a parallel loop are distributed to different SIMD units. Figure 1 shows different iterations of the parallel loop which are mapped to different SIMD units. If ins i executed on SIMD unit 0 can get its operand from the register of SIMD unit 1, ins i executed on SIMD unit k can get its corresponding operand from the register of SIMD unit k+1 as well. If these iterations can be scheduled consistently, data can be transferred among different SIMD units and thus be reused. Data flows through SIMD units as in a pipeline.

The program in Example code 2 is an example of such condition.

```
for (j=0; j<4; j++) {    // Loop2
    A[j,0,0:7] = m1[0,0:7] - m2[j,0:7];
    A[j,1,0:7] = m1[1,0:7] - m2[j+1,0:7];
    A[j,2,0:7] = m1[2,0:7] - m2[j+2,0:7];
    A[j,3,0:7] = m1[3,0:7] - m2[j+3,0:7];
}
```

Example code 2: An example for data pipeline.

In order to conveniently illustrate the problem in the following parts, we assume that there are 4 SIMD units in SM-SIMD architecture and it costs one cycle to finish the computation and getting data from the shared bus. If we schedule the code with the algorithm in [13] and distribute 4 iterations of Loop2 to 4 different SIMD units, 24 cycles are needed to finish 4 iterations of Loop2 (not including the cycles for writing back the results). However, 15 cycles are enough for the same work once data pipeline characteristics are exploited. The reason is that scheduling algorithm in [13] only exploits the parallelism based on replication, therefore only array m1 is reused. As a contrast, pipeline scheduling can not only exploit the reuse of array m1, but also reuse the elements of array m2 through data pipeline. Figure 2 illustrates the part of the execution process for the program.

## 3    Optimizing Algorithm

When there is a data pipeline between neighboring SIMD units, one SIMD unit should be the owner of an operand and the other is the consumer. In other words, after the data is used by the operation in one SIMD unit, the other SIMD unit can

| Cycle | SIMD 0 | SIMD 1 | SIMD 2 | SIMD 3 |
|---|---|---|---|---|
| 1 | Load m2[0,0:7] | | | |
| 2 | | Load m2[1,0:7] | | |
| 3 | | | Load m2[2,0:7] | |
| 4 | | | | Load m2[3,0:7] |
| 5 | Replicate m1[0,0:7] | | | |
| 6 | m1[0,0:7]-m2[0,0:7] | m1[0,0:7]-m2[1,0:7] | m1[0,0:7]-m2[2,0:7] | m1[0,0:7]-m2[3,0:7] |
| 7 | Get m2[1,0:7] | Get m2[2,0:7] | Get m2[3,0:7] | Load m2[4,0:7] |
| 8 | Replicate m1[1,0:7] | | | |
| 9 | m1[1,0:7]-m2[1,0:7] | m1[0,0:7]-m2[2,0:7] | m1[0,0:7]-m2[3,0:7] | m1[0,0:7]-m2[4,0:7] |
| 10 | Get m2[2,0:7] | Get m2[3,0:7] | Get m2[4,0:7] | Load m2[5,0:7] |
| 11 | Replicate m1[2,0:7] | | | |
| 12 | m1[2,0:7]-m2[2,0:7] | m1[2,0:7]-m2[3,0:7] | m1[2,0:7]-m2[4,0:7] | m1[2,0:7]-m2[5,0:7] |
| 13 | Get m2[3,0:7] | Get m2[4,0:7] | Get m2[5,0:7] | Load m2[6,0:7] |
| 14 | Replicate m1[3,0:7] | | | |
| 15 | m1[3,0:7]-m2[3,0:7] | m1[3,0:7]-m2[4,0:7] | m1[3,0:7]-m2[5,0:7] | m1[3,0:7]-m2[6,0:7] |

**Fig. 2.** Data pipeline scheduling

get it through the interconnection and reuse it. Such relationship among multiple operations executed in multiple SIMD units leads to a data pipeline and multiple SIMD units become the stages of data pipeline. In order to optimize the programs with such method, compilers need to identify data pipeline characteristics in the programs and schedule them based on the data pipeline flow relation. We call the data that can be transferred through interconnections as **pipe-data** and the two instructions, which use the pipe-data one after the other, as **pipeline instruction pair** in data pipeline optimization.

In order to implement this optimization, data pipeline optimizing performs the following steps, which is described in detail in the remainder of this section.

1. Determine candidate loop nests that will be executed on multiple SIMD units.
2. Analyze the live data to compute pipeline instruction pairs.
3. Determine the data flow directions of pipeline instruction pairs.
4. Eliminate redundant pairs which would cause unnecessary data transfers.
5. Transform some operations to communication operations.
6. Select the parallel loop, whose different iterations will be distributed to different SIMD units.
7. Allocate the resources for the iteration of the parallel loop.
8. Schedule the codes for multiple SIMD units.

### 3.1   Preliminary Optimizations

**Code Partition.** Before our optimization, the programs have been already performed SIMD optimizations [14]. After SIMD optimizations, we use code partitioning to determine which segments of the program should be executed on

SM-SIMD architecture and which should be executed on the general purpose processor core. All sequential code, code for synchronization and controlling are mapped for execution on the general purpose processor core. The loops with SIMD operations are mapped for execution on SM-SIMD architecture.

**Computation of Data Vector Reuse.** A data vector can be represented by four parameters: the data layout direction, the vector length, the address of its first element and the coefficient. Two data vectors are equal if and only if all these four parameters are equal. For two vectors of same array, when they have the same data layout direction and belong to the same uniformly generated set [19], when there is traditional temporal reuse between their first elements, their other corresponding elements also have traditional temporal reuse opportunity. Therefore, the first elements can be used as the representative elements of the data vectors to compute the data vector reuse under the constraints that these data vectors have the same data layout direction, the same vector length and the same uniformly generated set which their references are belonging to.

## 3.2 Live Data Analysis

In order to represent the instructions in pipeline instruction pairs, each instruction should have an exclusive symbol. Therefore, we construct the dependence directed acyclic graph (dependence-DAG) for the body of each candidate loop nest mapped to SM-SIMD architecture. Each SIMD instruction is assigned a sequential number based on its topological order in its individual dependence DAG.

If two instructions from a pipeline instruction pair are mapped to two neighboring SIMD units, they can communicate through the interconnection. To calculate the parallelism and perform the scheduling conveniently, a pipeline instruction pair should associated with several properties. We use the relation $\langle$*first ins num, second ins num, dist, loop, array, subscript*$\rangle$ to represent a pipeline instruction pair.

- *first ins num* is the smaller instruction number of the instructions in a pipeline instruction pair.
- *second ins num* is the larger instruction number of the instructions in a pipeline instruction pair.
- *loop* is the loop whose different iterations the pipeline instructions belong to.
- *dist* is the distance of loop iterations that carry this pipeline instruction pair.
- *array* is the array which the pipe-data belongs to.
- *subscript* is the subscript of pipe-data.

In a pair of two instructions, there are possibly more than one pipe-data among multiply operands. We mark each pipe-data in separate pipeline instruction pair.

## 3.3 Instruction Pair Direction

After pipeline instruction pairs are recognized, the data transfer direction that the pipe-data flows in a pipeline instruction pair should be determined. In other

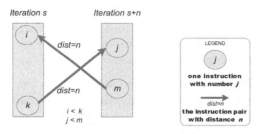

**Fig. 3.** A deadlock example

words, we need to decide which is the source of the instruction pair and which is the destination. In our algorithm, the data from a pipeline instruction pair flows from the instruction with smaller instruction number (first ins num) to the one with larger number (second ins num). The reasons are shown as follows. If data flows from an instruction with larger number to the one with smaller number, it is possible to have a cycle in the dependence DAG when a communication edge is added into the dependence DAG. Even a cycle is not involved, it is possible to lead to a deadlock when scheduling. Figure 3 is such a deadlock example (We assume the pipe-data flows along the direction of arrows. i, j, k and m are the instruction numbers of their corresponding instructions. Such representation will also be used in the following figures.). If instruction i needs the data of instruction m while instruction j is waiting for the data of instruction k, all of them would keep circular waiting and a deadlock would be formed. However, if the directions of data flow are reversed, the deadlock could be avoided. Moreover, if a data flows from an instruction with larger number to the one with smaller number, the scheduling of a lower level node in one dependence DAG depends on that of a deeper level node in the other dependence DAG. As a result, it is difficult to keep the load balance among the different DAGs when scheduling them to different SIMD units.

As a result, the direction of pipeline instruction pair flows from a smaller instruction to a larger one. It is possible to have two instructions trying to share data with each other holding the same instruction number, which means they are two instances from the same instruction. However, we do not construct pipeline instruction pair for such instructions, because the data could be reused with the replication method in [13], as the case array m1 at cycle 11 shown in Figure 2. In other words, the first ins number will be always smaller than the second one in a pipeline instruction pair.

In the following parts of this paper, we also refer to the instruction with first ins num as the **start instruction** and the instruction with second ins num as the **end instruction**.

### 3.4   Redundant Communication Elimination

While pipeline instruction pairs are used, it is possible to have some redundant pipeline instruction pairs, which would cause unnecessary data communications

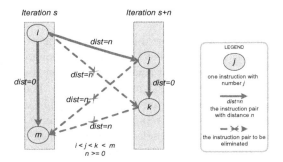

**Fig. 4.** An example of redundant pair

thus should be eliminated. Figure 4 is such an example. In this example multiple instruction pairs share the same pipe-data. Assume instruction i and instruction j are the first pipe-data requiring instructions in those two iterations. After data communication is finished between them, all other instruction pairs are redundant because the pipe-data can be saved in the local register.

Indeed, for the same reuse data, it only needs to be transferred once between the neighboring dependence DAGs. Therefore, it is enough that only the pipeline instruction pair with the smallest instruction number in the different dependence DAGs is maintained. As the redundant pairs, other data pipeline pairs using this pipe-data can be eliminated. After the elimination, we add the communication edge into the dependence DAG for each pipeline instruction pair. The weight of each edge is the distance between them.

### 3.5 Computation-Communication Transformation

Sometimes, some computing instructions can be transformed into communication operations. When two instructions satisfy the following conditions, one of the two instructions can be replicated by a communication operation. First, all operands of the two instructions are pipe-data. Second, their operations are the same. In such condition, we call the end instruction of the two instructions in the data pipeline pair as **comp-commu instruction**. A comp-commu instruction can be replicated by the operation that gets the result from the start instruction, if the cycle of executing the comp-commu instruction is less than the cycle of getting the result directly. We use the following steps to process such condition. For a comp-commu instruction $P$:

1. Get the pipe-data that would be used by other pairs that $P$ is the start instruction.
2. Compute the cycles ($cyc_{comp}$) that get all other operands (possibly no other operands need to be gotten) of $P$ and finish the operation of $P$.
3. Compute the cycles ($cyc_{comm}$) that directly get the result of $P$.
4. Compare $cyc_{comp}$ with $cyc_{comm}$. If $cyc_{comp} < cyc_{comm}$, we compute the result of $P$ through step 2. Otherwise, we transform the operation of $P$ into the operations in step 3.

## 3.6   Parallel Loop Selection

In this part, we select the loop whose different iterations would be distributed to multiple SIMD units. Before we select the loop, we compute the amounts of different distance replication data for each loop based on the algorithm in [13]. And then, a **replication weight** is assigned to each loop. The replication weight is the maximal amount value among different distance replication data. It can be represented as $<amount, rep\text{-}dist>$. rep-dist is the distance of replication data with the maximal amount. Then we select the loop, which is permutable with the innermost loop and with the maximal replication weight value, as parallel loop in order to utilize the parallelism based on replication as much as possible. If multiple loops have the same replication weights, we compute the amount of pipeline instruction pairs of these loops, whose distances are all equal to the value of rep-dist. We select the one with the maximal pipeline amount from the loops with the maximal replication weight as the **parallel distributed loop**.

Once the parallel distributed loop is selected, it is changed as the innermost parallel loop and performed loop mining optimization. The mining distance is equal to rep-dist. And only the pipeline instruction pair, which carried by parallel distributed loop and having the same distance with rep-dist, would be exploited in the scheduling algorithm.

## 3.7   Register Allocation

Once selecting the parallel distributed loop, we deal with the problem of limited register number in this section, we can allocate resource based on the requirement of the reuse data vector and average instruction parallelism in one iteration of the parallel distributed loop. We also use the interconnection characteristics in register allocation algorithm.

**Register Requirement.** Before resource allocation, we first need to compute the register requirement of one iteration, which is the number of maximally simultaneously live variables. In order to compute this value, we construct the interference graph based on the algorithm in [16]. The degree of a node in the interference graph represents the number of simultaneously live variables with this nod. Assume the degree of the interference graph is N, then the register requirement equals to N+1. Assume the total register number in $N_r$ SIMD units can finish the allocation with no live data spilled out in one iteration of the distributed loop.

**Resource Allocation.** If there does not exist instruction level parallelism in an iteration of the distributed loop, only regarding the SIMD units as register resources would waste the computation resources. Therefore we compute the average instruction parallelism of the iteration of the distributed loop for later resource allocation. Assume the value of the average SIMD instruction level parallelism is equal to $N_i$.

After computing average instruction parallelism, we allocate resources by considering both the instruction parallelism and the register requirement at the same time. We select the minimal value of $N_i$ and $N_r$ as the number for resource allocation. The main goal of our scheduling algorithm is to find as much parallelism as necessary to saturate the available hardware. Therefore, if there is instruction parallelism in an iteration with register pressure, exploiting some of them can also lower the pressure on the requirement of the registers and reduce the number of operations for spilled out. In other words, when guaranteeing the utilization of the computation resources, we also try to satisfy the register requirement of the reused data vectors because it can lower the competition for the shared data bus. Suppose $N_s$ is allocated for each iteration. After the resource allocation for the single iteration of the distributed loop, we can get the value that how many iterations ($N_p$) of the distributed loop can be executed on SM-SIMD architecture. Namely, $N_p = \lfloor NUM_{SIMD}/N_s \rfloor$.

Once $N_p$ is gotten, we do strip mining to adjust the innermost loop with only $N_p$ iterations. After the strip mining, the innermost loop would be transformed into two parts. The one with $N_p$ iterations would be the distributed loop in the innermost level, and the other part would be interchanged outside the localized vector space in order to maintain the locality in the localized vector space.

## 3.8   Scheduling Algorithm

Once the previous steps are finished, we schedule the code for SM-SIMD architecture. We use a scheduling algorithm to generate codes for SM-SIMD architecture. The scheduling algorithm itself is known to be an NP-complete problem. We propose a heuristic algorithm. According to the scheduling algorithm, the parallel distributed loop is unrolled by a factor of $N_p$ and distributed to the corresponding allocated resources. The scheduling algorithm is shown as follows.

- Construct the dependence DAG of an iteration of the parallel distributed loop and make $N_p - 1$ additional copies to form a parallel dependence DAG, whose $N_p$ sub-DAGs correspond to the DAGs of $N_p$ iterations of the parallel distributed loop.
- Mark the replication parallel point and the locality parallel point in those sub-DAGs based on the algorithm in [13].
- Add **communication node** between the instructions in the same pipeline instruction pair and connect communication nodes with the start instruction node and the end instruction node. The directions of the connecting edges are the same as the ones of the corresponding pipeline instruction pairs. When scheduling codes, we also use the communication node as the synchronization node.
- The DAG is traversed to generate code for SM-SIMD architecture. When traversing the DAG, the multiple sub-DAGs have the arbitrary scheduling sequence before reaching a synchronization point instruction. If an instruction is not marked as a synchronization point, all its instances mapped to

different SIMD units would be executed in sequence. If one of sub-DAGs reaches a synchronization point, we stop the scheduling and move to the next one until all the scheduling of the sub-DAGs reach there or no other synchronization point can be reached. Then we generate a parallel control instruction for all different instances of this synchronization instruction and execute them in parallel on different SIMD units, if the type of the synchronization point is not communication node. Otherwise, a communication VLIW instruction is generated to make the multiple SIMD units get data from their neighboring SIMD units.

– Repeat this process until the scheduling is finished.

## 4    Experimental Results

We implement a detailed performance simulator based on Morphosys[3][2] by extending Simplescalar-3.0d. Morphosys is chosen as a basic underlying hardware because of the following reasons. First, it is a typical SM-SIMD architecture and some industry SOCs are implemented using the similar techniques as in Morphosys. Second, many detailed resources about its design are available. Therefore, it can make the simulation more faithful.

Before evaluating the experiments, we first analyze the benchmarks used in [20] and [21]. Only the benchmarks with inherent data pipeline characteristics are selected because it is unnecessary to optimize the programs without such characteristics. We select *impeg2* from BMW (Berkeley Multimedia Workload) [20], *me*, *cfa* and *dct* programs in [21] as test benchmarks. However, there are some sequential optimizations in *impeg2*, which impede the exploitation for the parallelism. The program is originally programmed for general purpose processor (GPP) platforms. Due to the limited computational resource in GPP, programmers try to improve performance by reducing the proportion of computation, for example by adding extra if statement for some specific inputs and return their results in order to skip the complex computation parts. Such techniques indeed speed up those programs on GPP platforms. However, they are impeding compilers to exploit the parallelism in the programs. We rewrite a new *impeg2* version - *impeg2pa*, which remains the original application algorithm but with no extra sequential optimizations.

In the experiments, we optimize these five programs in two methods and compare the performance of the optimized programs. In order to have a uniform criteria, all speedups are computed through the results of extension architecture divided by sequential results. In order to compare the results of *impeg2* and *impeg2pa*, we compute their speedups against the same sequential program. The optimizing methods are:

---

[2] There are 8 SIMD units in Morphosys. Each SIMD unit consists of eight 32-bit processing element and the register file of each SIMD units includes 4 registers. Eight SIMD units shared one 256-bit data bus and the communication channel between two neighboring SIMD units is 128-bit.

- Automatically scheduling with *Agassiz*[3]: Agassiz converts the original programs into the optimized ones with embedded assembly codes through the algorithm in [13]. The GCC compiling tool chains of SimpleScalar can thus generate the machine codes to run on the simulator.
- Manually scheduling with data pipeline: We optimize the programs with data pipeline optimization for SM-SIMD architecture by embedding assembly instructions manually, then compile the optimized programs with GCC compiling tool chains of SimpleScalar.

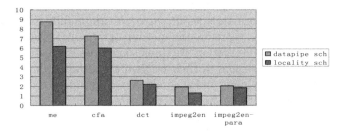

**Fig. 5.** Speedup comparison

The experimental results are shown in figure 5. There are eight SIMD units in Morphosys that we use as underlying architecture. Average utilization of the SIMD units in SM-SIMD architecture is used to illuminate the average busy ratio of eight SIMD units after scheduling. Avg P-SIMD shows how many instructions that SM-SIMD architecture can averagely finish in one cycle. First, Avg P-SIMD is computed. We gather the total cycles (C) consumed by SM-SIMD architecture not including the idle cycles and also the total number of the SIMD instructions (I) in each program. The average amount of SIMD instructions that SM-SIMD architecture can execute per cycle can be computed through the equation Avg P-SIMD = I / C. Thus the average utilization equals to (Avg P-SIMD/8)*100%. The detailed results are shown in Table 2.

From the results of speedup and average utilization, one of the observations is that data pipeline scheduling can get higher speedup and better average utilization for the applications with inherent data pipeline characteristics. The core parts of *me* and *cfa* are similar and are particularly suitable for data pipeline optimization, therefore their speedups are perfect. For the application of *dct*, its speedup is lower because the optimized proportion in its code is smaller. *me* is the core of *impeg2* algorithm. But in *impeg2* there exists many sequential optimizations which cause large obstacles to parallel optimizing. Moreover, the sequential part for controlling in *impeg2* is much more than that in *me*, thus the speedup of *impeg2* is lower than *me*.

---

[3] Agassiz is a source to source compiler tool for C programs developed by Department of Computer Science and Engineering, University of Minnesota at Twin-Cities and Parallel Processing Institute, Fudan University.

**Table 2.** The average utilization of SM-SIMD architecture

|  | cfa | me | dct | impeg2 | impeg2pa |
|---|---|---|---|---|---|
| Avg P-SIMD data pipe | 6.173 | 5.924 | 4.274 | 2.2085 | 5.130 |
| Avg P-SIMD locality sche | 2.381 | 2.267 | 3.200 | 1.580 | 1.580 |
| Avg Util data pipe | 77.2% | 74.1% | 53.4% | 27.6% | 64.1% |
| Avg Util locality sche | 29.8% | 28.3% | 40% | 19.7% | 19.7% |

Another interesting observation is that the speedup of *impeg2pa* is 14% higher than that of *impeg2*. The reason is that there are no sequential optimizations in *impeg2pa* which impede the exploitation for the parallelism in the program. The inherent data pipeline characteristics in *impeg2pa* can be fully exploited by the data pipeline optimization, therefore the speedup of *impeg2pa* is higher than that of *impeg2*. Based on this observation, we think sometimes it is better to write the application programs according to their original algorithms, which is easier for compilers to perform scheduling and generate better optimized codes. Otherwise, the codes of some applications should be re-written for higher performance.

## 5   Conclusions

The experimental results demonstrate that data pipeline optimization techniques are very effective to optimize real-life applications. Furthermore, when writing programs for SM-SIMD architecture, it is better to remain the original structure according to the application algorithms, which is much easier for compilers to exploit the parallelism in the programs and thus generate better codes.

## References

1. Diefendorff, K.; Dubey, P.K. "How multimedia workloads will change processor design" Computer, Sept., 1997, PP. 43-45
2. Rixner, S.; Dally, W.J. "Register organization for media processing", 6the International Symposium on High-Performance Computer Architecture, 2000, 375-386
3. H. Singh, M. H. Lee, N. Bagherzadeh, MorphoSys: An Integrated Reconfigurable System for Data-Parallel and Computation-Intensive Applications. IEEE Transaction on Computers, 2000, 49, 5, 465-481
4. Xiaofang Wang; Ziavras, S.G, A framework for dynamic resource assignment and scheduling on reconfigurable mixed-mode on-chip multiprocessors, IEEE International Conference on Field-Programmable Technology, 2005 51 - 58
5. K.B. Dally, W.J. Kapasi, J. Owens, J.D. Towles, B. Chang, A. Rixner, S. Imagine: media processing with streams, IEEE Micro, 2001, 21(2), pp.35-46
6. http://www.motorala.com
7. Eric S. Gayles, Thomas P. and Mary Jane Irwin. The Design of the MGAP-2: A Micro-Grained Massively Parallel Array. IEEE Transaction on Very Large Scale Integration(VLSI) Systems, Vol. 8, No. 6, Dec 2000
8. T. Komuro, M. Ishikawa. A Dynamically Reconfigurable SIMD Processor for a Vision Chip. IEEE Journal of Solid-State Circuits, Vol. 39, No. 1, Jan 2004

9. J. Gebis, S. William, C. Kozyrakis, D. Patterson, VIRAM1: A Media-Oriented Vector Processor with Embedded DRAM", 41st Design Automation Student Design Contenst, San Diego, CA, June 2004
10. H.Peter Hofstee, Power Efficient Processor Architecture and The Cell Processor, 11th International Conference on High-Performance Computer Architecture, San Francisco,USA,February 2005
11. G. Venkataramani, W. Najjar, F. Kurdahi, N. Bagherzadeh. Automatic compilation to a coarse-grained reconfigurable system-opn-chip. November 2003 ACM Transactions on Embedded Computing Systems (TECS), Vol.2 Issue 4
12. P. Mattson, W. J. Dally, S. Rixner, U. J. Kapasi, J. D. Owens Communication Scheduling, Proceedings of the ninth international conference on Architectural support for programming languages and operating systems Nov. 2000
13. W. Zhang, X. Qian, Y. Wang, B. Zang, C. Zhu, Optimizing Compiler for Shared-Memory Multiple SIMD Architecture, ACM SIGPLAN/SIGBED Conference on Languages, Compilers, and Tools for Embedded Systems 2006, Ottawa, Canada.
14. W.H Jiang, C. Mei, B. Huang, B.Y Zang, C.Q Zhu "Boosting the Performance of Multimedia Applications Using SIMD Instructions" The 15th International Conference on Compiler Construction. April 2005 Edinburgh, Scotland
15. David A. Padua and Michael J.Wolfe, Advanced Compiler optimizations for Supercomputers, Communications of the ACM, 29(1986) 1184-1201.
16. S.S. Muchnick. Advanced Compiler Design and Implementation, Mor Kaufma,1997.
17. A.Capitanio, N.Dutt, and A.Nicolau, "Partitioned register files for VLIWs: A preliminary analysis of trade-offs." Proceedings of the 25th Annual International Symposium on Microarchitecture, Dec., 1992, pp. 292-300.
18. M.Fernandes, J.Llosa, and N.Topham, Distributed modulo scheduling." Proceedings of the 5th Annual International Conference on High Performance Computer Architecture, Jan., 1999, pp. 130-134.
19. M. E.Wolf, M.S.Lam, A Data Locality Optimizing Algorithm, ACM SIGPLAN Conference on Programming Language Design and Implementation. 1991, 30-44.
20. N.T.Slingerland and A.J. Smith, Multimedia Instruction Sets for General Purpose Microprocessors : A Survey. Technical Report CSD-00-1122, Univ. of California at Berkeley Computer Science, Dec. 2000.
21. D. Talla, L.K. John, and D.C. Burger. Bottlenecks in Multimedia Processing with SIMD-Style Extensions and Architectural Enhancements, IEEE Transactions on Computers, August, 2003, 52(8), pp.1015-1031.

# Dependence-Based Code Generation for a CELL Processor

Yuan Zhao and Ken Kennedy

Computer Science Department, Rice University, Houston, TX, USA
{yzhao,ken}@cs.rice.edu

**Abstract.** Obtaining high performance on the STI CELL processor requires substantial programming effort because its architectural features must be explicitly managed, with separate codes required for two different types of cores (PPE and SPE). Research at IBM has developed a single source-image compiler for CELL that performs vectorization but uses OpenMP to specify cross-core parallelism. In this paper, we present and evaluate an alternative dependence-based compiler approach that automatically generates parallel and vector code for CELL from a single source program with no parallelism directives. In contrast to OpenMP, our approach can also handle loop nests that carry dependences. To preserve correct program semantics, we employ on-chip communication mechanisms to implement barrier and unidirectional synchronization primitives. We also implement strategies to boost performance by managing DMA data movement, improving data alignment, and exploiting memory reuse in the innermost loop.

## 1 Introduction

Computing platforms with multiple processing elements—so-called "multi-core" chips—have been embraced by many chip makers. As a strategy for increasing per-chip performance, adding more cores is an alternative to scaling up operating frequency, which has become difficult because of issues such as heat dissipation. Both Intel and AMD have released dual-core (homogeneous) microprocessors with either shared or separate secondary cache.

A second emerging trend in system design is the use of heterogeneous computing components, either on or off chip. For example, The CELL processor developed by SONY, Toshiba and IBM has $8 + 1$ (heterogeneous) processing elements. Alternatively, attached processing elements such as GPUs and FPGAs have been utilized within a single computing system to accelerate specialized applications.

One disadvantage of these multi-core approaches is that they transfer the burden of achieving high performance from the hardware to the software system or application developer. Thus, an immediate question for these platforms is: How can developers exploit the power of the parallelism? For instance, these elements can be organized by software into many different parallel computing schemes such as task parallelism and pipelined workflow. This question applies

G. Almási, C. Caşcaval, and P. Wu (Eds.): LCPC 2006, LNCS 4382, pp. 64–79, 2007.

to both developing new applications and porting existing applications. Exploring trade-offs like these makes it very difficult to develop applications for these chips, particularly if a degree of portability is desired. While advanced parallel programmers can, with great effort, use expert knowledge to exploit the advanced hardware features, ordinary users may be left out in the cold. For such users, the new generation of chips desperately need automated tools and compilers that produce code with acceptable efficiency while hiding the details of the underlying hardware.

In this paper, we focus on the CELL processor, one of the most promising heterogeneous designs. We present an automatic, dependence-based code generation scheme for this chip. Figure 1, shows the architecture of a CELL processor. A single chip contains one PowerPC Processing Element (PPE) and eight Synergistic Processing Elements (SPE) on the same chip. Each SPE supports AltiVec-like vector instructions and has a 256K-byte local store memory (LS), while the PPE is a normal PowerPC core with a two-level cache. The PPE is responsible for scheduling computation tasks onto SPEs. Computation on a SPE can only access data in its own LS; data movement in between LS and main memory is explicitly controlled by DMA requests via the Element Interconnect Bus (EIB) and Memory Interface Controller (MIC).

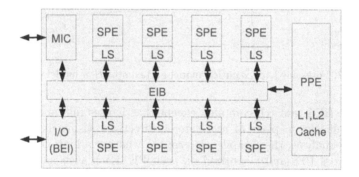

**Fig. 1.** Architecture of a CELL processor

With architecture features such as heterogeneous multi-core, parallelism at both coarse (across PEs) and fine (vector, within each PE) granularities, high data transfer bandwidth (200GB/s on chip and 25.6 GB/s off chip), and explicit local memory control through DMA, a 3.2 GHz CELL processor can, in theory, achieve a peak performance of more than 200 GFlops per second for single precision floating point computations. However, actually obtaining high performance levels requires significant programming effort because, in the distributed programming tool system, these architectural features must be explicitly managed by the programmer. This adds a significant degree of complexity to programming to conventional uniprocessors or even simple shared-memory parallel systems.

Over the years, there have been many parallel programming models developed to reduce the burden on ordinary users. They include directive-guided task parallel models such as OpenMP, data parallel models such as HPF, and programming models with language extensions such as UPC and CoArray Fortran. Recently, the DARPA HPCS program has sponsored the development of a new generation of "high-productivity" parallel programming languages such as IBM-X10, Sun-Fortress and Cray-Chapel. However, among these models, OpenMP is to date the only one supported on CELL, and that is by an IBM research compiler [9] rather than the standard distributed tool set.

In this paper, we present a dependence-based approach to automatically generating code for CELL from a high-level language. Our system performs parallelization, vectorization and data movement optimization automatically. The input program is a single source sequential program without any parallelism directives. The output is a PPE program with many SPE programs, where parallelism is realized by the PPE thread fork-and-joining the SPE threads, as shown in Figure 2. This parallelism scheme is similar to the OpenMP approach

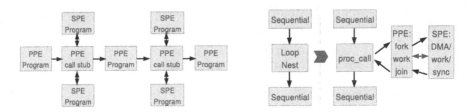

**Fig. 2.** Fork-and-join execution model and compilation model on CELL

used by the IBM research compiler, except that it uses fully automatic detection of parallelism in place of user-entered directives. Using information from dependence analysis, the compiler determines whether a loop nest can be parallelized across PEs and vectorized on each PE. Each such loop nest will be partitioned, using a technique called *procedure outlining* (the opposite of inlining), into a PPE call stub function and a SPE program, as shown in Figure 2. In contrast to the OpenMP approach, our strategy can also handle loops carrying dependences, preserving the correct semantics of the program using barrier and a uni-directional synchronization primitives we developed using the on-chip communication mechanisms.

Our dependence-based approach automatically orchestrates and optimizes data movement between the SPE local stores and main memory. For memory references in the original program, multiple data buffers are created on the SPE side and DMA transfer commands are placed accordingly in the SPE program. This strategy also handles the complications of data movement due to the data alignment constraints. In particular, loop peeling on the PPE side can help improve both data movement performance and vector data alignment.

We present the main parallelization and vectorization algorithm in Section 2, while the data movement analysis and placement algorithm is the subject of

Section 3. We discuss our preliminary performance evaluation in Section 4, review related work in Section 5, and conclude in Section 6.

## 2    Parallelization and Vectorization

In this section, we present an algorithm for determining whether a loop nest can be parallelized across PEs and vectorized on each of them. Such a loop nest will be procedure outlined into a program for the SPEs, and replaced by a call to a call stub function in the PPE program that manages fork-and-join operations for SPE threads. The SPE program will contain the vectorized loop nest with automatically generated data movement. Synchronization will be generated and placed in both the SPE and PPE programs if necessary. We refer to this loop nest as *cellized* and this process as *cellization*.

To analyze if a loop nest can be cellized, we need to determine if there exists a loop in the loop nest that can be parallelized, and a loop (the innermost loop) that can be vectorized on SPE and PPE. These two candidates can be the same, *i.e.* the innermost loop can be both parallelized and vectorized, assuming that the loop is longer that the four iterations that would fit in a single vector operation.

**Data Dependences.** The cellization analysis relies on the data dependence information. We assume that readers are familiar with the concept of true, anti-, output and input dependences, and with loop-carried and loop-independent dependences. Allen and Kennedy [4] have defined the *dependence matrix* for a loop nest to be a matrix in which each row is a dependence vector for some dependence in the nest and every such direction vector is included as a row. The columns from left to right correspond to the loops from the outermost to the innermost. A dependence is said to be *carried* by a loop if the corresponding entry is the first non-"=" entry in the dependence vector. Figure 3 gives an example of a loop nest and its dependence matrix. In the matrix, the anti-dependences in rows 1 to 3 corresponds to dependences from the first, second and third array references on the right hand side to the array reference on the left hand side. The dependence in the first row is carried by the K loop, the dependence in the second row is carried by the I loop, and the one in the third row is carried by the J loop. Rows 4 to 6 correspond to the input dependences among the right hand

```
DO K = 1, W
   DO J = 1, M
      DO I = 1, N
         A(I,J,K) = A(I,J,K+1)
                  + A(I+1,J,K)
                  + A(I+1,J+1,K)
      ENDDO
   ENDDO
ENDDO
```

$$\begin{bmatrix} K & J & I & \\ <_1 & =_0 & =_0 & anti \\ =_0 & =_0 & <_1 & anti \\ =_0 & <_1 & <_1 & anti \\ <_1 & =_0 & >_{-1} & input \\ <_1 & >_{-1} & >_{-1} & input \\ =_0 & <_1 & =_0 & input \end{bmatrix}$$

**Fig. 3.** Example of a loop nest and its dependences

side array references themselves. Note that for the purpose of parallelization and vectorization analysis, input dependences are omitted from consideration.

**Cellization Analysis.** Our cellization analysis algorithm is modified from the Allen-Kennedy loop nest vectorization algorithm [4]. As shown in Figure 4, our algorithm searches from the outermost loop towards the innermost loop for a loop that can be parallelized in the remaining dependence matrix. At each step, if no loop is found, the current outermost loop is made sequential and all dependences carried by it are removed from the dependence matrix and the search process is repeated. After a parallel loop is identified, the loop nest is cellizable if the innermost loop is vectorizable on PPE and SPE. Obviously, the algorithm can be relaxed to accommodate loop nests that can be parallelized but not vectorized.

We allow the innermost loop carrying anti-dependences to be parallelized and vectorized so long as it doesn't have a dependence cycle among different statements. As an exception, an anti-dependence cycle on a statement itself is

**procedure** *IsCellizable*(*LN*)
    // *LN*: loop nest {*L1*, *L2*, ..., *Ln*} from outermost to innermost
    obtain dependence matrix *DM* for *LN*
    initialize *ParallelFlags[1:n]* to UNMARKED
    **while** there are loops left in *LN*
        Search for *Li* in *DM* such that all entries in the *Li* column are "="
        **if** *Li* does not exist
            **if** there are no loops left in *LN*
                *ParallelFlags[n]* := PARAVEC
                **return** *IsShortVectorizable*(*Ln*, *DM*)
            **else**
                *ParallelFlags[current outermost]* := SEQUENTIAL
                remove dependences carried by the current outermost loop from *DM*
                remove the current outermost loop from *LN*
        **else**
            *ParallelFlags[i]* := PARALLEL
            **return** *IsShortVectorizable*(*Ln*, *DM*)

**procedure** *IsShortVectorizable*(*L*, *DM*)
    // *L*: the innermost loop
    // *DM*: the dependence matrix after a parallel loop is selected
    //     or all outer loops are made sequential
    **for** all dependences carried by an outer loop *Lk* in *L1* .. *Ln-1* in *DM*
        remove such dependences from *DM*
    **if** *L* carries a dependence cycle among statements
            except an anti-dependence on a statement itself
        **return** false
    **for** all array references *A* in *L*
        **if** *A* is not loop invariant to *L* and not contiguous in memory
            **return** false
    **return** true

**Fig. 4.** Cellization analysis algorithm

allowed. To preserve the semantics of a loop that has anti-dependences, we use use a post-store strategy using a uni-directional synchronization. As illustrated in Figure 5, $P1$ needs to temporarily hold the computation results in the buffer only for those writes whose main memory locations are also read by $P0$. The buffer for temporarily storing those results on $P1$ can completely remain local in LS and not appear in main memory.

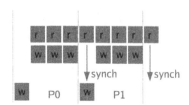

**Fig. 5.** Parallelizing a loop with anti-dependence

For the example loop nest shown in Figure 3, following the algorithm, after the first iteration of the search process, the K loop will be marked SEQUENTIAL and the dependence in row 1 will be eliminated from the dependence matrix; after the second iteration in the search process, the J loop will be marked SEQUENTIAL and the dependence in row 3 will be eliminated; after the third iteration in the search process, the I loop will be marked PARAVEC and sent to check for vectorization. Since the I loop carries an anti-dependence on the same statement and all array references are memory contiguous to the loop, the I loop is vectorizable. Hence the loop nest is cellizable.

**Parallel Code Generation.** After a loop nest is identified as cellizable, it will be procedure outlined into a SPE program and replaced with a call to a PPE call stub function which manages SPE task allocation and fork-and-joining of SPE threads. To partition $n$ iterations of the chosen parallel loop among $p$ PEs, each PE can get $(n/p + (n\%p >= id?1:0))$ iterations, where $id$ is the rank of the current PE. Other than partitioning, parallel code generation also needs to place synchronization accordingly, as shown in Figure 6.

The vector instruction sets on PPE and SPE are of short vector length (16 bytes) and support only contiguous memory accesses. Though certain patterns of strided accesses can be realized by data permutation afterward, we only consider contiguous memory accesses in this paper. Since there are many papers (see related work in Section 5) addressing loop based vectorization for SSE and AltiVec instruction sets, we will not discuss them in details.

For our example loop nest in Figure 3, the generated PPE code, PPE stub function code and the SPE code are shown in Figure 7. Note that the first element of the computed buffer is stored back after unidirectional synchronization in order to preserve the correct semantics of anti-dependences. The number of elements that need to be post-stored should be no less than the maximal distance of the anti-dependences.

**procedure** *Cellize(LN)*

    *// LN*: loop nest {*L1, L2, ..., Ln*} from outermost to innermost

    **for** loop *Li* in *LN* from outermost to innermost

        **if** *ParallelFlags[i]* is SEQUENTIAL

            output *Li* in the new loop nest

            **if** *ParallelFlags[i+1]* is not SEQUENTIAL

                output barrier synchronization

        **else if** *ParallelFlags[i]* is UNMARKED

            output *Li* in the new loop nest

        **else if** *ParallelFlags[i]* is PARALLEL or PARAVEC

            output *Li* with partitioned iterations

    vectorize *Ln*

    **if** *ParallelFlags[n]* is PARAVEC **and** *Ln* carries anti-dependence

        apply post-store to the vectorized *Ln*

        insert uni-directional synchronization

**Fig. 6.** Cellization code generation algorithm

```
                  PPEStub1(...) {          SPEmain(...) {

                  put loop invariants      dma_get(data block)
                     into data block;      for k = 1, w {
                  for(id=1; id<PEs; id++)   for j = 1, m {
                     spe_thread_fork(&block);  barrier_synch;
                                            compute my_lb, my_ub;
call PPEStub1(...)  for k = 1, w {          dma_get(b2, b3, b4);
                  for j = 1, m {            for i = my_lb, my_ub
                    barrier_synch;            b1(i)=b2(i)+b3(i)+b4(i);
                    compute my_lb, my_ub;   bt(1:1) = b1(my_lb:my_lb)
                    for i = my_lb, my_ub    dma_put(b1(my_lb+1:my_ub));
                      a(...)=a(...)+...;    uni-directional_synch;
                    uni-directional_synch;  dma_put(bt(1:1));
                  } }                       } }
                  }                         }
  (a) PPE program    (b) PPE stub            (c) SPE program
```

**Fig. 7.** Example of code generation

**Load Balancing.** Since PPE forks and joins SPE threads sequentially, a load balancing strategy should consider the cost of thread forking. Assume the cost is equal to that of executing $c$ iterations of the chosen parallel loop, to partition $n$ iterations across $p$ SPEs, the $k$-th PE will get $w_k = n/p + c(p - 2k + 1)/2$ iterations. This is derived from $w_{k+1} = w_k - c$ and $\Sigma_{k=1}^{p} w_k = n$. While $c$ could be determined by estimating the cost of each iteration with program analysis, it could also be decided with profiling information. If the measured thread forking time and total running time on one SPE are $t_f$ and $t$, respectively, assuming the parallel loop is the outermost loop, then $c = nt_f/(t - t_f)$.

**Synchronization Implementation.** The only communication mechanism on CELL other than DMA transfers that does not need special privilege is mailbox. Other mechanisms such as SPE-to-SPE signals require the executable be granted a certain capability (CAP_SYS_RAWIO). According to the linux man pages, the capability granting feature is still being developed in the Linux Kernel as of now. Therefore, we implemented the barrier and the uni-directional synchronization using mailbox as shown in Figure 8. The number associated with each arrow (mailbox send) indicates the mail sending order.

**Fig. 8.** Barrier and uni-directional synchronization using mailboxes

## 3   Data Movement and Alignment

In this section we discuss how to achieve an efficient data movement in between the SPEs' local memory and the main memory. To do this we must:

1. hide the latency of data movement by multi-buffering so that the DMA data transfer and computation are partially overlapped, if not fully, and
2. use the available bandwidth effectively, *i.e.* all data brought in should be used and repeated use of the same data should require the data be transfer as fewer times as possible.

The second issue is only briefly addressed in this paper. We will focus on multiple buffer allocation, DMA data transfer generation and placement.

Figure 9 gives an algorithm for analyzing and allocating multiple data buffers. The reference group partitioning in the algorithm is exactly the one used for scalar replacement [7]. We do not yet have a good buffer size estimation algorithm. The data buffer size depends on a set of predefined blocking sizes for the loop nest. Since the maximum size of a single DMA transfer is 16K bytes, it is desirable to allocate a size close to that limit, assuming that the combined code and data buffer fit into the SPE's 256K-byte local memory. For the generated code in Figure 7, following the algorithm, the I loop would be strip-mined and multi-buffering data buffers would be allocated.

Another factor affecting data movement performance on CELL is data alignment. It constraints data movement in three ways: vector offset, naturally aligned boundaries, and cacheline alignment.

**Vector Offset.** DMA transfer requires that the last 4 bits of the source and sink addresses be the same. Therefore, when converting an array reference in the main memory space into a local buffer reference, we need to make sure that they have same vector offsets.

**procedure** *BufferAllocation(LN)*
       // *LN*: loop nest {*L1, L2, ..., Ln*} from outermost to innermost
       perform reference group partitioning for all array references
       **for** the group generator of each reference group
              determine the innermost loop that the generator is loop variant
              determine if the generator is memory contiguous to that loop
       **for** each array reference in the loop nest
              **if** it is a group generator
                     strip-mine the innermost variant loop if memory contiguous within it
                     allocate multi-buffering buffers
                     place DMA prefetch current buffer before the loop
                     place DMA prefetch next buffer inside the loop
                     place DMA check data ready inside the loop
                     place buffer index rotation computation at the end of the loop
                     replace array reference with allocated buffer
              **else**
                     replace array reference with buffer allocated by the group generator
                     adjust subscript by the dependence distance to the generator

**Fig. 9.** Multi-buffering analysis and allocation algorithm

**Naturally Aligned Boundaries.** DMA transfer can transfer 1, 2, 4, 8, 16, $16*k$ bytes (max 16K Bytes) on naturally aligned boundaries. When the starting and ending addresses are not properly aligned, one has to issue multiple DMA instructions, as shown in Figure 10.

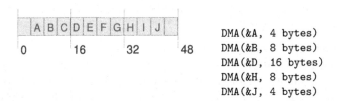

**Fig. 10.** DMA transferring unaligned data

For DMA transfers that get data from the main memory to the SPE's local memory, we can always over-fetch, *i.e.* extend the memory transfer region to naturally aligned boundaries on both ends. This is always safe as long as we are careful when allocating buffers. However, we cannot easily use this strategy for the DMA puts from SPEs to the main memory. In short, we have a false sharing problem. Over-storing would require an atomic operation to get the boundary data from main memory, merge with the local data, and put data back into the main memory on the extended boundaries. Implementing such an atomic operation would incur a significant performance penalty.

**Loop Peeling.** To reduce the performance penalty related to the unaligned DMA puts, we apply loop peeling to the innermost loop on the PPE side and only compute partitioned loop iterations as multiples of the SPE vector size. The peeled iterations are computed on PPE, while the starting address for a DMA put from an SPE is always at a vector boundary. Loop peeling on the PPE is always safe if the innermost loop is parallelized, or if a loop is chosen to parallelized only when there are no dependences left in the dependence matrix following the algorithm in Figure 4. There is a slight issue due to the different rounding modes for floating point on PPE and SPE. We leave it up to the application developers to decide if this discrepancy actually matters.

**Cache Line Alignment.** When a CELL processor performs DMA transfers, the unit data transfer is actually a cache line, *i.e.* when transferring data smaller than a cache line size, the bandwidth of an entire cache line will be consumed and the result is masked. On the other hand, when transferring a large data block that is not aligned on cache line boundaries, two whole cache lines will be transferred on the boundaries even though only a part of each cache line is requested. Loop peeling can also be used to ensure data alignment on the cache line boundaries. The wasted cache line bandwidth is relatively small when actually transferring a large data block. This is another reason why a large tile size should be used whenever possible.

# 4   Performance Evaluation

**Experimental Setup.** A dependence-based code generator for CELL (CELLizer) that includes the parallelization, vectorization, multi-buffering DMA transfer and synchronization algorithms described in Section 2 and Section 3 is implemented as an extension of our earlier tool for vectorization and code generation for short vector machines with SSE and AltiVec, which in turn was based on the D System compilation infrastructure at Rice.

CELLizer accepts a FORTRAN 90 program as source input, performs cellization, outputs a FORTRAN 90 program which will remain on PPE, a collection of PPE stub functions written in C, and a collection of corresponding SPE programs written in C, as we described in Section 1. Each SPE program corresponds to a cellized loop nest that is procedure outlined and rewritten in C.

We use the cross-platform compilers (ppuxlc and spuxlc) in the CELL software development kit version 1.1 to compile the PPE call stub functions and the SPE programs. The remaining PPE program in Fortran is translated to C using the *f2c* converter [11], and compiled with ppuxlc respectively.

The compiled executable is transferred to a 3.2 GHz Cell Blade running Linux OS for correctness verification and performance measurement. The Cell Blade has 1G bytes memory installed, while the swap disk is turned off. We use the Linux library call `gettimeofday()` to measure the time spent in either the original loop nest, or the PPE stub functions and the SPE threads combined. Each code is run 6 times and the minimum running time is kept as record. The speedup of running the generated code on various number of SPEs over running the original loop nest on PPE alone is reported. Our CELLizer has the following compiler options that can be changed.

**Table 1.** CELLizer options

| Option | Meaning |
|---|---|
| -cell \<arg\> | generate code for cell processor with \<arg\> SPEs |
| -plp | loop peeling on PPE to improve data alignment |
| -pwk \<arg\> | work on PPE (\<arg\> as a percentage to the work of a single SPE) |
| -vsr | do vectorized scalar replacement |
| -spls | do software pipelined aligned load/store |
| -novec | no vectorization, generate sequential C code |

**Test Cases.** We tested three small loop nests $LN1, LN2, ANTI$, shown in Figure 11. Each loop nest has an initialization before it and a checksum computation after it. Note that $ANTI$ carries an anti-dependence which usually requires allocating a temporary array and splitting the original loop into two so that each loop can be parallelized, as shown in $ANTITMP$. Our CELLizer, on the other hand, avoids this temporary array allocation by using post-store and uni-directional synchronization. We also tested two programs from SPEC benchmark, *swim* and *mgrid*. In all test cases, data types were converted to be single precision floating point.

The performance results are shown in Figure 12, Figure 13 and Figure 14, respectively. For $LN1$, both a small problem size $N = 7555333$ and a big problem

```
LN1:
    DO I = 1, N-2
       B(I+1) = (A(I) + A(I+2) + C(I+1)) * 0.34
    ENDDO

LN2:
    DO J = 2, M-1
       DO I = 2, N-1
          A(I,J) = A(I,J) + (B(I-1,J)+B(I+1,J)+B(I,J-1)+B(I,J+1))*0.25
       ENDDO
    ENDDO

ANTI:
    DO I = 1, N-2
       A(I+1) = (A(I+2) + B(I+1) + C(I+1)) * 0.34
    ENDDO

ANTITMP:
    DO I = 1, N-2
       D(I) = (A(I+2) + B(I+1) + C(I+1)) * 0.34
    ENDDO
    DO I = 1, N-2
       A(I+1) = D(I)
    ENDDO
```

**Fig. 11.** Testing codes

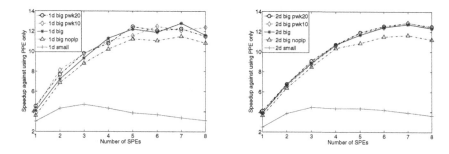

**Fig. 12.** Performance for 1D ($LN1$) and 2D ($LN2$) stencils

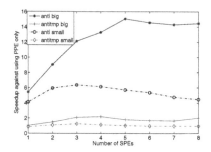

**Fig. 13.** Performance for loop ($ANTI$) with anti-dependence

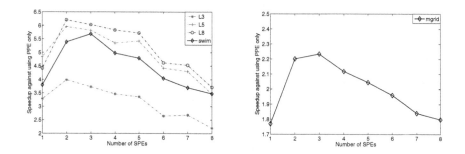

**Fig. 14.** Performance for *swim* and *mgrid*

size $N = 44222111$ are tested. Similarly, $M = N = 2955$ and $M = N = 7255$ are tested for $LN2$, $N = 7555333$ and $N = 33222111$ are tested for $ANTI$ and $ANTITMP$. For SPEC benchmark programs, the reference problem sizes are tested, *i.e.* $1335 \times 1335$ for *swim* and $128 \times 128 \times 128$ for *mgrid*.

The default set of optimizations includes parallelization across multiple PEs (-cell <arg>), multi-buffering data movement, vectorization, vectorized scalar replacement (-vsr), software pipelined load/store (-spls), and loop peeling on PPE for data alignment (-plp). In Figure 12, "pwk10" ("pwk20") assigns 10 percent (20 percent, respectively) of a single SPE's work/iterations to PPE, in an attempt to balance the load across all PEs; while "noplp" turns off the loop peeling on the PPE side.

**Performance Results.** Based on the performance data, we have the following observations:

- Programs run as much as 3 times faster on SPE than on PPE. There might be two reasons for this phenomenon. First, the latency of floating point instructions on SPE (6 cycles) is shorter than that on PPE (10-12 cycles). Second, PPE is also responsible for running the operating system.
- We do not get a linear speedup to the number of SPEs used. In fact, what we observe is a curve, *i.e.* the best speedup occurs when less than 8 SPEs are used for small problem sizes. The reason is that thread fork-and-join operations become higher in cost when more SPEs are used, compared to the computation cost on each SPE. We are still investigating the effectiveness of the load balancing strategy described in Section 2. Nevertheless, increasing the problem size can mitigate this problem by offering each SPE more work so that thread fork-and-join costs become less obvious, as illustrated in Figure 12 and Figure 13.
- Our strategy of loop peeling on the PPE side to help improve DMA data alignment works well. Compared to not performing loop peeling, our strategy achieved an average of 9 percent speed improvement for the 1D stencil and 7 percent for the 2D stencil, as shown in Figure 12. Note that for the two dimensional array in 2D stencil, the loop peeling strategy will dynamically calculate the number of "I" iterations it needs to peel within each outer "J" iteration, so that on SPEs the array reference on the left hand side is always properly aligned when entering the "J" loop.
- Comparing the performance between $ANTI$ and $ANTITMP$ in Figure 13, we can clearly see the benefits of our parallelization strategy using post-store and uni-directional synchronization to handle the anti-dependences. The extra memory traffic in $ANTITMP$ and extra thread fork-and-joining costs have caused heavy performance penalty. This result also suggests that loop fusion combined with array contraction work well for the CELL processor if the resulting loop with dependences can be parallelized with post-store strategy and proper synchronization.
- When running whole applications on CELL, we can tune each loop nest independently to determine the number of SPEs for the best speedup, instead of using the same number of SPEs for all of them. Figure 14 shows that the tuning result for three most time-consuming loop nests, $L3$, $L5$, and $L8$ in the *swim* benchmark. Unfortunately, they all achieve the best speedup with two SPEs, while the whole application achieve the best speedup with three SPEs. The discrepancy is caused by collecting timing information of $L3$, $L5$ and $L8$ for only 20 iterations, while they are iterated for 1200 iterations in *swim*, as specified by the SPEC benchmark.

– Finally, contrary to what people may think, having PPE work on partitioned workload doesn't seem to help much due to the relative slowness of the PPE, as shown in Figure 12. However, loop peeling on the PPE can help improve DMA data alignment. Load balancing across all PEs needs further investigation.

## 5    Related Work

Increased processor parallelism on chip has become a trend adopted by almost all major chip makers. The parallelism can be found at both coarse and fine level granularity. On coarse level, more and more cores (PEs) are built onto a single chip; on the fine level, vector instruction sets are included and regularly amended (*e.g.* SSE4). Research in compiling for parallelism at both levels have had a long history with many languages, tools and programming models. However, up till now, the OpenMP approach, used in an IBM research compiler [9], is only one implemented to support CELL.

The dependence-based approach presented in this paper is related to nearly two decades of work on loop nest parallelization and vectorization work done for various parallel architectures [1,3,4,2,5,8,13,10,9,21,15,16]. The data alignment problem on the CELL is very similar to that on SSE and AltiVec [10,21], except on CELL data alignment also affects data movement. Scalar replacement has been developed to improve data reuse at register level [7] and later extended to vector level [17,21]. In this paper, we use reference group partitioning to identify the array references that should share a data buffer.

Multi-buffering analysis and placement is very similar to that of software prefetching [6,14], which was designed to hide the memory latency. On the other hand, optimizing DMA transfers using multi-buffering is similar to array copying [12,18,19,20], which was proposed to eliminate conflict misses in the cache.

Effectiveness of traditional memory hierarchy optimizations for SPE's local store, *e.g.* loop tiling, is demonstrated in the IBM work [9]. Since we have not implemented these optimizations in our compiler, we have not yet achieved same amount of speedup as the IBM work for the same benchmark programs. We are currently investigating the optimizations to improve data reuse in SPE's local store.

## 6    Conclusion

In this paper, we presented a dependence-based automatic code generation strategy for the CELL processor. In contrast to approaches that use explicit parallelism directives, such as OpenMP, it doesn't require that the user perform dependence analysis manually and determine the legality of the hand-specified parallelization. Besides automatic parallelization, vectorization, and multi-buffering DMA data transfer generation, our CELLizer can also insert two kinds of synchronization automatically to preserve the correctness of a program.

Our performance study verified the correctness of our code generation strategy and the usefulness of performing loop peeling on the PPE side to help improve data alignment. However, we did not observe linear speedup in terms of the number of SPEs. In fact, the performance decreases after the number of SPEs exceeds some number. To address this issue, we must improve the amount of computation per transferred data element. One way to do this is through a more thorough use of loop fusion and tiling transformations. This is a goal of our ongoing research.

## Acknowledgments

This work is supported by the Department of Energy under Contract No. 12783-001-0549 from the Los Alamos National Laboratory to William Marsh Rice University, and the CELL development systems (including CELL blades) provided by IBM to University of Tennessee and Rice University.

## References

1. J. R. Allen. *Dependence Analysis for Subscripted Variables and its Application to Program Transformation*. PhD thesis, Rice University, Houston, Texas, 1983.
2. R. Allen, D. Callahan, and K. Kennedy. Automatic decomposition of scientific programs for parallel execution. In *POPL '87: Proceedings of the 14th ACM SIGACT-SIGPLAN symposium on Principles of programming languages*, 1987.
3. R. Allen and K. Kennedy. Vector register allocation. *IEEE Transactions on Computers*, 41(10):pp. 1290–1317, 1992.
4. R. Allen and K. Kennedy. *Optimizing Compilers for Modern Architectures*. Morgan Kauffman, October 2001.
5. A. J. C. Bik, M. Girkar, P. M. Grey, and X. Tian. Automatic intra-register vectorization for the intel architecture. *International Journal of Parallel Programming*, 30(2):pp. 65–98, 2002.
6. D. Callahan, K. Kennedy, and A. Porterfield. Software prefetching. In *Proceedings of the Fourth International Conference on Architectural Support for Programming Languages and Operating Systems*, April 1991.
7. S. Carr and K. Kennedy. Improving the ratio of memory operations to floating-point operations in loops. *ACM Transactions on Programming Languages and Systems*, 15(3):pp. 400–462, 1994.
8. Crescent Bay Software. *VAST/AltiVec*. http://www.crescentbaysoftware.com/vast_altivec.html.
9. A. E. Eichenberger, K. O'Brien, K. O'Brien, P. Wu, T. Chen, P. H. Oden, D. A. Prener, J. C. Shepherd, B. So, Z. Sura, A. Wang, T. Zhang, P. Zhao, and M. Gschwind. Optimizing compiler for a cell processor. In *PACT*, 2005.
10. A. E. Eichenberger, P. Wu, and K. O'Brien. Vectorization for SIMD architectures with alignment constraints. In *PLDI'04*, June 2004.
11. S. I. Feldman, D. M. Gay, M. W. Maimone, and N. L. Schryer. A fortran-to-C converter. Technical Report 149, AT&T Bell Laboratories, Murray Hill, NJ, 1990.
12. M. D. Lam, E. E. Rothberg, and M. E. Wolf. The cache performance and optimizations of blocked algorithms. In *ASPLOS-IV: Proceedings of the Fourth International Conference on Architectural Support for Programming Languages and Operating Systems*, April 1991.

13. S. Larsen and S. Amarasinghe. Exploiting superword level parallelism with multimedia instruction sets. In *PLDI*, 2000.
14. T. C. Mowry. *Tolerating Latency Through Software-Controlled Data Prefetching*. PhD thesis, Standford University, California, 1994.
15. D. Nuzman and R. Henderson. Multi-platform auto-vectorization. In *CGO '06: Proceedings of the International Symposium on Code Generation and Optimization*, Washington, DC, USA, 2006.
16. D. Nuzman, I. Rosen, and A. Zaks. Auto-vectorization of interleaved data for SIMD. In *PLDI*, 2006.
17. J. Shin, J. Chame, and M. W. Hall. Compiler-controlled caching in superword register files for multimeida extension architecture. In *PACT*, 2002.
18. O. Temam, E. D. Granston, and W. Jalby. To copy or not to copy: a compile-time technique for assessing when data copying should be used to eliminate cache conflicts. In *Supercomputing '93: Proceedings of the 1993 ACM/IEEE Conference on Supercomputing*, November 1993.
19. R. C. Whaley, A. Petitet, and J. Dongarra. Automated empirical optimizations of software and the ATLAS project. *Parallel Computing*, 27(1):3–25, 2001.
20. Q. Yi. Applying data copy to improve memory performance of general array computations. In *LCPC*, October 2005.
21. Y. Zhao and K. Kennedy. Scalarization on short vector machines. In *2005 IEEE International Symposium on Performance Analysis of Systems and Software (IS-PASS)*, March 20–22, 2005.

# Expression and Loop Libraries for High-Performance Code Synthesis

Christopher Mueller and Andrew Lumsdaine

Open Systems Laboratory
Indiana University
Bloomington, IN 47405
{chemuell,lums}@osl.iu.edu

**Abstract.** To simultaneously provide rapid application development and high performance, developers of scientific and multimedia applications often mix languages, using scripting languages to glue together high-performance components written in compiled languages. While this can be a useful development strategy, it distances application developers from the optimization process while adding complexity to the development tool chain. Recently, we introduced the *Synthetic Programming Environment (SPE)* for Python, a library for generating and executing machine instructions at run-time. The SPE is an effective platform for optimizing serial and parallel applications without relying on intermediate languages. In this paper, we use the SPE to develop two code generation libraries, one for scalar and vector (SIMD) expression evaluation and another for parallel and high-performance loop generation. Using these libraries, we implement two high performance kernels and demonstrate how to achieve high levels of performance by providing the appropriate abstractions to users. Our results show that scripting languages can be used to generate high-performance code and suggest that providing optimizations as user-level libraries is an effective strategy for managing the complexity of high-performance applications.

## 1 Introduction

Scripting languages have become common tools for developing many types of applications, including high-performance scientific and multimedia applications. To achieve high performance, developers often use a lower-level language such as C, C++, or FORTRAN for the performance-critical sections. While effective, this approach complicates the development process by adding new dependencies into the tool chain and requiring additional developer skills. Recently, we introduced the Synthetic Programming Environment (SPE) for Python [9]. The SPE enables the run-time synthesis of machine instructions directly from Python, without requiring an intermediate language. It exposes the full processor instruction set as a library of Python functions that can be used to construct new instruction sequences at run time and provides a library for synchronous and asynchronous execution of the generated sequences.

G. Almási, C. Caşcaval, and P. Wu (Eds.): LCPC 2006, LNCS 4382, pp. 80–95, 2007.

The SPE provides the infrastructure for generating high-performance code at run time. In this paper, we introduce two meta-programming libraries for managing the complexity of generating instruction sequences for serial and parallel applications. The first library provides abstractions for generating instruction streams for arithmetic and logical expressions on scalar and vector (SIMD) data types. The second library abstracts loop generation and provides a flexible set of tools for generating sequential and parallel loops. With these libraries, it is possible to generate high-performance computational kernels using a natural syntax, while maintaining user-level control over the final optimizations.

In the next section we introduce *synthetic programming* and provide the context for our contributions. Following that, we describe the new libraries, starting with the scalar and vector Expression library and proceeding through the Iterator library. We detail code generation techniques used by each component and illustrate their use with two examples. We conclude with a review of related techniques. A basic knowledge of Python syntax is assumed for the discussion, but more complex techniques will be described as they are introduced.

## 2    Synthetic Programming

Synthetic programming is the process of developing programs composed of computational kernels synthesized at run time using the SPE. The computational kernels, or *synthetic programs*, are generated with meta-programming routines called *synthetic components*. By using synthetic components to generate synthetic programs from a high-level language, developers can create high-performance applications without sacrificing the productivity gained from using a high-level language.

Synthetic programs are developed using three components supplied by the Synthetic Programming Environment: ISA, Processor, and InstructionStream. ISA components are collections of functions that generate binary coded machine instructions for a particular instruction set architecture. For instance, in the PowerPC ISA, the function addi(D, A, SIMM) generates the addi, or *add immediate*, machine instruction for adding a constant SIMM to the value in register A, storing the result in register D. A synthetic program is built by adding a sequence of instructions to an instance of InstructionStream. For example, the following code generates the synthetic program for the computation $r_{return} = (0 + 31) + 11$:

```
c = InstructionStream()
c.add(ppc.addi(gp_return, 0, 31))
c.add(ppc.addi(gp_return, gp_return, 11))
```

gp_return is a constant that specifies the register for integer return values. In addition to managing the user-generated instructions, InstructionStream also provides a basic register allocator that warns developers of register pressure.

Prior to execution, InstructionStream generates an ABI (application binary interface)-compliant prologue and epilogue for the synthetic program, making it a valid "function" for the current execution environment. When the sequence is ready, it is executed by a `Processor` instance:

```
proc = Processor()
result = proc.execute(c)
print result
--> 42
```

`Processor` can execute synthetic programs synchronously, blocking until completion, or asynchronously in their own threads, returning immediately.

The current implementation supports the PowerPC (scalar) and AltiVec (vector) ISAs and runs on Apple's OS X. Data is passed between the host program and the synthetic program using pointers to memory, such as native Python or Numeric Python `arrays`, and values can be passed to synthetic functions using registers following the ABI conventions. Load and store instructions move data between memory and registers, and loops and conditional code are synthesized using the branch and compare instructions.

## 3   The Expression Library

At the lowest level, all machine instructions operate on values stored in registers or on constant values encoded directly into the instruction. In a basic synthetic program, the developer refers to registers directly and explicitly manages movement of data between the processor and memory system. Arithmetic is performed by generating a sequence of instructions that operate on two or three values at a time, and it is up to the developer to ensure complex expressions are evaluated properly. Using the PowerPC `ISA`, the expression $a = a * b + a * c$ could be written as:

```
ppc.mullwx(t1, a, c)   # a, b, c are registers
ppc.mullwx(t2, a, b)   # t1, t2 are temp registers
ppc.addx(a, t1, t2)
```

While this expression was simple to convert to an instruction sequence, in a more complex expression, simple operator precedence rules and register reuse policies are difficult to enforce, leading to code that is difficult to debug and maintain.

Because expression evaluation is at the heart of most performance-critical code sections, the Expression library introduces a set of objects for managing expression evaluation for scalar and vector data types.

The main objects are illustrated in Figure 1. The base classes, `variable`, `literal`, and `expression` implement the Interpreter design pattern and manage register allocation, initialization, and expression evaluation. Python's underlying expression evaluation engine handles operator precedence. The base classes are typeless and type-specific subclasses generate instructions as the expressions are evaluated. In the diagram, the floating point class hierarchy shows how the subclasses share operator implementations, ensuring that floating point expressions

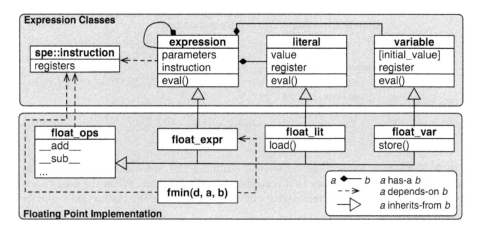

**Fig. 1.** Expression Class Hierarchy and Floating Point Implementation. The expression classes implement the Interpreter pattern for run-time code synthesis. The base classes manage evaluation and type-specific subclasses provide methods to generate code for specific operations.

are evaluated consistently. Free functions that return **expression** instances allow developers to expose operations that do not map directly to operators. These functions can be used directly in larger expression statements and may abstract sequences of instructions. This is useful for binary operators such as **fmin**, which is actually a three instruction sequence, and various ternary vector instructions.

To illustrate how the Interpreter classes work, consider the example in Figure 2 for evaluating the expression $a = a * b + a * c$. $a$, $b$, and $c$ are instances of **variable** with the $*$ and $+$ operators overloaded. When an operator is evaluated by Python, the overloaded implementation delays evaluation and returns an instance of **expression** that contains references to the operator and operands. In this example, the operands for $+$ are **expressions** and the operands for $*$ are **variables**. The root of the parse tree is the $+$ **expression**.

Up to this point, no code has been generated and registers have not been allocated. All Interpreter classes have an **eval** method. Subclasses override **eval** to generate the appropriate instructions for their data type and registers. When the **expression** tree is assigned to a **variable**, the **variable** triggers the expression evaluation, which in turn generates the instruction sequence to evaluate the expression using a depth-first traversal of the tree. Each **expression** has a register associated with its results that lives for the lifetime of the expression evaluation. After the assignment, the tree is traversed again to free up temporary resources. Note that the final **expression** uses the register from the assigned **variable**. The **variable** passes this to the **expression**'s **eval** method.

Expression evaluation is the same for scalar and vector variables of all types, but expressions cannot contain mixed type variables. As the expression tree is created, the variables are checked against each other and other expressions in the tree. An exception is thrown if there is a type error. Literals that appear in the expression are transformed into the appropriate subclass of **literal**.

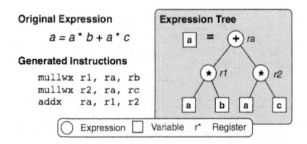

**Fig. 2.** Expression Evaluation. As Python evaluates the expression, variables return instances of expression objects that correspond to the operator. When the final tree is assigned to a variable, it is recursively evaluated, generating the instruction sequence for the expression.

`variable` instances can be used in expressions or directly with `ISA` functions. The attribute `variable.reg` contains the register assigned to the variable and is a valid argument anywhere a register is accepted. When the variable is no longer needed, registers are freed with a call to `variable.release_registers()`.

## 3.1   Scalar Types

Two scalar variable types are supplied in the Expression library. `int_var` and `float_var` implement signed integer and double-precision floating point operations, respectively. `int_var` supports $(+,-,*,/,<<,>>,\&,|,\char94)$ and `float_var` supports the standard arithmetic operations $(+,-,*,/)$.

Scalar variables are initialized using different instruction sequences, depending on the initial value. Integers use an *add immediate* instruction if the value fits into sixteen bits, otherwise they use an *add immediate* followed by a *shift/add* to load the full 32-bit value. Double-precision floating point values are loaded from an `array` backing store that contains the value as its only element. The floating point load instruction loads the value from the backing store into the register. Because the load instruction is expensive, floating point literals should be initialized outside of loops.

## 3.2   Vector Types

Vector data types support single-instruction, multiple data (SIMD) parallelism using the AltiVec instruction set. AltiVec vectors can be partitioned into a number of types, including signed and unsigned bytes, shorts, and integers and single-precision floating point numbers. The integer types support $(+,-,<<,>>,\&,|,\char94)$ and the floating point types support $(+,-,/)$. In addition, most of the AltiVec instruction set is exposed as expression functions that are type-aware. For example, the integer vector min operation has six forms, one for each integer type, `vmin[s][b,h,w]`. The type-aware expression function `vmin` abstracts the typed versions and allows the developer to use it as part of an expression. For instance,

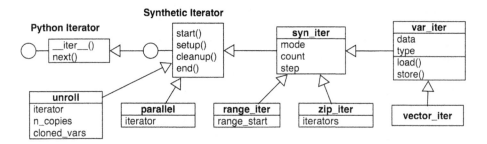

**Fig. 3.** The Iterator Hierarchy. The synthetic iterator protocol extends Python's iterator protocol to provide additional hooks into loop evaluation. **syn_iter** generates code to manage loops using the counter register or general purpose registers, as selected by the user. The subclasses override methods to implement iterator specific functionality. **unroll** and **parallel** are Proxies that restructure synthetic iterators for high-performance code generation.

```
z.v = vmin(x, y) + 4
```

adds 4 to the minimum value from the element pairs in $x$ and $y$.

Vectors are initialized from a backing store in the same way as floating point scalars. Users can also pass in an array containing the initial values. This array will continue to be used as the backing store when the **store()** method is called to save a vector back to memory.

## 4    The Iterator Library

Variables and expressions provide the foundation for developing syntactically clear high-performance synthetic programs. Synthetic iterators supply the abstractions for processing collections of variables and vectors in single or multi-threaded environments. In the same way expressions use features of Python as meta-programming constructs, the synthetic iterators are based on Python's underlying iterator protocol.

Python iterators are objects that manage element-wise iteration over sequences. The iterator protocol requires two methods, __iter__() and next(). __iter__() returns an iterator for the object, and next() is called to retrieve each element, raising StopIteration when the sequence is exhausted. All sequence iteration in Python is handled by iterators, and Python for loops expect iterators as their sequence parameter.

Synthetic iterators use the Python iterator protocol to provide a concise representation for the generation of instruction sequences for implementing machine-level loops. The synthetic iterator hierarchy is shown in Figure 3. The synthetic iterator protocol extends the Python iterator protocol with hooks for managing different aspects of code generation.

All synthetic iterators work in same basic way. To demonstrate, consider the syn_range iterator:

```
Loop code:                    Call sequence:

  sum = var(c, 0)               __iter__(): start()
  rng = syn_range(c, 20)        1st next(): setup()
                                     ... body ...
  for i in rng:                 2nd next(): cleanup()
    sum.v = sum + i                 end()
                                   raise StopIteration
```

In this example, syn_range generates integers from 0 to 19 and makes them available in the variable $i$. The pseudo-code on the above shows the Python and synthetic iterator protocols and their order of evaluation.

When the iterator is created by the for loop, start() acquires the registers, generates initialization code and returns a reference to the iterator. On the *first* iteration of the for loop, i.e. when next() is called the first time, the setup() generates the loop prologue, initializing the loop counter and branch label, and returns a variable for the current value. Then the loop body is executed, and the expression code is added to the instruction stream. Note that any instructions from the ISA can be used here, not just expressions. On the *second* iteration of the for loop, cleanup() generates the loop epilogue with the branch instruction and any loop cleanup code. It also resets the counters, in case the loop is nested. Finally, end() frees loop registers and other resources. While still at the beginning of the second iteration, the iterator raises StopIteration, ending the Python loop.

In the next few sections, we detail the design and implementation of the iterator hierarchy.

## 4.1  syn_iter

syn_iter handles the mechanics of sequential loop generation and is the base class for most other iterators. It supports three different modes of iteration: counter based (CTR), register decrement (DEC), and register increment (INC). syn_iter's constructor takes the iteration count, step size, and mode. The generated loop performs ($count \div step$) iterations of the loop body.

CTR iterators generate the most efficient loops. CTR loops use the PowerPC ctr register to hold the loop count and the bdnz (decrement counter, branch if non-zero) instruction to branch. CTR iterators do not require any general purpose registers, but only one CTR loop can be active at any time. The iterator variable (e.g., $i$ in the above example), is set to None for CTR loops.

DEC iterators work in a similar manner as CTR iterators, decrementing a value and terminating the loop when the value reaches zero. However, DEC iterators keep their counter in a general purpose register, making it available as the iterator variable for the current loop.

INC iterators are the opposite of DEC iterators, starting the counter at zero and looping until the counter reaches the stop value. This requires two registers, one for the counter and one for the stop value. The current loop count is available as the loop variable.

In all modes, syn_iter can be directed to excluded the branch instruction, allowing more complicated iterators to have fine-grained control over loop generation.

## 4.2   syn_range

syn_range is the simplest subclass of syn_iter. Its arguments follow the semantics of Python's range and support start, stop, and step keyword parameters. syn_range uses the INC mode and overloads the constructor to pass the correct count value to syn_iter. The iterator variable contains the current value from the generated sequence.

## 4.3   Scalar and Vector Iterators

var_iter and vector_iter iterate over arrays of integers or floating point values, supplying the current value as a scalar or vector variable of the appropriate type. The arrays can be native Python or Numeric Python arrays. For example, the following code implements an add/reduce operation:

```
data = array.array('I', range(100))
sum  = var(c, 0)
for value in var_iter(c, data):
   sum.v = sum + value
```

When the iterator is initialized, var_iter modifies the count and step values to conform to the length of the array and size of the data type. The first time through the Python loop, the iterator generates the code to load the next value in the array for the iterator variable. vector_iter subclasses var_iter, overloading the memory access methods to use vector instructions that handle unaligned vectors. It also adjusts the step size to account for multi-element vectors.

## 4.4   zip_iter

The previous iterators all support iteration over one sequence. Often, values for a computation are pulled from multiple sequences. Python's zip iterator pulls together multiple iterators and returns loop variables for one element from each iterator. zip_iter performs the same function on synthetic iterators. The following code uses a zip_iter to perform the element-wise operation $R = X * Y + Z$ on the floating point iterators $X$, $Y$, $Z$, and $R$:

```
for x, y, z, r in zip_iter(c, X, Y, Z, R):
   r = vmadd(x,y,z)
```

zip_iter works by disabling the branch operations for its wrapped iterators and generating its own loop using the smallest count value from the iterators. For each step of code generation, it calls the appropriate methods on each iterator in the order they are supplied.

## 4.5   The unroll Proxy

Loop unrolling is a common optimization for loop generation. An unrolled loop contains multiple copies of the loop body between the start of the loop and the branch instruction. Executing the body in rapid succession reduces the overhead from branching and gives the processor more opportunities for instruction-level parallelism. While modern branch prediction hardware has lessened the impact of loop unrolling, it is still a valuable technique for high-performance computing.

unroll is a Proxy object that unrolls synthetic loops by allowing the Python iterator to iterate over the body multiple times, generating a new set of body instructions each time. Between iterations, the the loop maintenance methods are called with the flag to exclude branches instructions. On the final iteration, a single branch instruction is generated along with the loop epilogue. The following is a simple loop and pseudo-code for the generated code:

```
Loop code:                    Generated code:

  rng = syn_range(c, N)         start()
  for i in unroll(rng, 3):        setup();  body;  cleanup();
    sum.v = sum + 2               setup();  body;  cleanup();
                                  setup();  body;  cleanup();
                                end()
```

unroll has two options that allow it to generate truly high-performance code. If the cleanup_once flag is set, the cleanup code is only generated once per unroll iteration, rather than once for each body iteration. The counter is updated appropriately by unroll. The second option allows the user to supply a list of variables that are replicated at each unrolled iteration and reduced once each actual iteration. In the above example, sum depends on itself and creates a stall in the processor pipeline. However, if the sum register is replicated for each unrolled iteration and the running sum computed at the end of an iteration, the processor can issue more instructions simultaneously to the available integer units, maximizing resource usage. The complete high-performance sum:

```
  for i in unroll(rng, 16, cleanup_once=True, vars = [sum]):
    sum.v = sum + 2
```

achieves near peak integer performance on a PowerPC 970.

## 4.6   The Parallel Proxy

Most scripting languages, Python included, are single-threaded and only ever use a single processor on multi-processor systems. However, many scientific and multimedia applications have natural parallel decompositions. To support natural parallelism, the parallel Proxy class provides an abstraction for generating instruction sequences that divide the processing task among available processors. parallel is designed for problems that divide the data among resources with little or no communication between executing threads. While communication is possible, it is better to decompose the problem into a sequence of synthetic programs, with communication handled at the Python level.

parallel works in conjunction with the ParallelInstructionStream class. ParallelInstructionStream extends InstructionStream and reserves two registers to hold the thread rank and group size parameters for the current execution group. parallel modifies the count, stop, and address values for the loops it contains to iterate through the block assigned to the current thread. The complete code sequence for a simple parallel loop is:

```
c = ParallelInstructionStream()
proc = synppc.Processor()

data = array.array('I', range(100))
rank = int_var(c, reg=code.r_rank)

for i in parallel(var_iter(c, data)):
  i.v = i + rank

if MPI:
  t1 = proc.execute(c, mode='async', params=(mpi.rank,mpi.size,0))
else:
  t1 = proc.execute(c, mode='async', params=(0,2,0))
  t2 = proc.execute(c, mode='async', params=(1,2,0))

proc.join(t1); proc.join(t2)
```

In this example, each thread adds its rank to the value in the array. Two threads are created with rank 0 and 1, respectively. The first 50 elements in data remain the same, while the second 50 elements are increased by 1. The join method blocks until the thread is complete.

## 5   Experiments

Synthetic programs are intended for small computational kernels that are executed in the context of a larger application. For compute-intensive tasks, they should provide a noticeable performance increase over a pure Python implementation and similar execution times as kernels implemented in low-level languages. Suprisingly, we have found that in most cases, because additional semantic information is available for specific optimizations, synthetic programs often outperform equivalent low-level versions.

In this section, we present two examples of synthetic programs along with performance results. The first example walks through different implementations of an array min function and compares scalar, vector, and parallel implementations against native C and Python versions. The next example implements the update function for a interactive particle system application and shows how expressions and iterators significantly simplify synthetic programs.

The timing results were obtained on a Dual 2.5 GHz PowerPC G5 with 3.5 GB RAM running Mac OS X 10.4.6. The Python version was 2.3.5 (build 1809) with Numeric Python 23.8 and PyOpenGL 2. The native extensions were built using gcc 4.0.1 (build 5250) with -03 and SWIG 1.3.25. Native versions were also tested with IBM's XLC 6.0 compiler. The results did not differ significantly between the compilers and the results for gcc are reported. Times were acquired using the Python `time` module's `time()` function.

## 5.1  Min

The `min` function iterates over an array and returns the smallest value in the array. We implemented four synthetic versions, a sequential and a parallel version for both scalar and vector arrays, and two native versions, one in Python and the other in C++. For the each example, the kernel was executed 10 times and the average time was recorded. All kernels operated on the same 10 million element array from the same Python instance.

The first two synthetic programs implement the `min` function using scalar and vector iterators and the `fmin` and `vmin` expression functions. `vmin` maps directly to a single AltiVec operation and `fmin` is implemented using one floating point compare, one branch, and two register move operations. The synthetic code for each is:

```
def var_min(c, data):              def vec_min(c, data):
  m = var(c, _max_float)             m = vector(c, _max_float)
  for x in var_iter(c, data):        for x in vector_iter(c, data):
    m.v = fmin(m, x)                   m.v = vmin(m, x)
                                     m.store()
  syn_return(c, m)                   return m
```

The scalar implementation uses the floating point return register to return the value. The vector version accumulates results in a vector and returns a four element array containing the minimum value from the four element-wise streams. The final min is computed in Python[1] and is an example of mixing Python operations with synthetic kernels to compute a result.

The parallel versions of the vector and scalar examples extend the sequential implementations by including code to store results based on the thread's rank. The code for the parallel scalar version is:

```
def par_min(c, data, result):
  min    = var(c, _max_float)
  rank   = int_var(c, reg=c.r_rank)
  offset = var(c, 0)

  for x in parallel(var_iter(c, data)):
    min.v = fmin(min, x)
```

---

[1] In all cases, any extra computation in Python was included in the execution time.

**Table 1.** Performance results for different array min implementations on a 10 million element array. The parallel speedup for vec_min is relative to var_min.

| | Time (sec) | Speedup | Parallel Speedup | M Compares/sec |
|---|---|---|---|---|
| **Python** | 1.801 | 1.0 | – | 5.6 |
| **var_min** | 0.033 | 55.2 | – | 306.6 |
| **par_min** | 0.017 | 106.4 | 1.93 | 590.9 |
| **vec_min** | 0.014 | 125.0 | *2.26* | 694.2 |
| **par_vec** | 0.010 | 177.5 | 1.42 | 986.0 |
| **C++** | 0.068 | 26.4 | – | 147.8 |

```
offset.v = rank * synppc.WORD_SIZE
min.store(address(result), r_offset=offset.reg)
return

mn = min(result) # final reduction
```

The vector version is implemented similarly, with additional space in the result array and a multiplier of 4 included in the offset. In the parallel examples, the synthetic kernels execute in two threads simultaneously and communicate results using the **result** backing store. To avoid overwriting the other thread's result, each thread calculates its index into the result array using its rank. As with vec_min, the final reduction takes place in Python.

The C++ implementation is a simple loop that uses the C++ Standard Library min function. It is directly comprable to **var_min**. The address and size of the data array are passed from Python, and the result is returned as a float using a SWIG-generated wrapper. We experimented with different approaches to dereferencing the array and computing min. In our environment, directly indexing the array and using `std::min` was the fastest technique.

The results of our timing experiments are listed in Table 1. In every case, the synthetic versions outperformed the native versions. The parallel implementations achieved good speedups over their sequential counterparts. The parallel speedup listed for vec_min is the speedup compared to the scalar implementation.

The understand the C++ results, we examined the assembly code generated for different optimization levels across both gcc and XLC for the different looping and **min** strategies. The fastest C++ version differed from **var_min** by three instructions. Instead of storing the minimum value in registers, min was updated from cache during each loop iteration, using a *pointer* to track the value rather than a register. Attempts to use the **register** keyword in C++ did not affect the compiled code. In-lined comparisons (i.e., using an **if** test instead of min) led to the worst performing C++ versions. The generated assembly used registers for results, but used an inefficient sequence of instructions of the comparison, leading to unncessary dependency stalls.

## 5.2  Particle System

In our original paper on synthetic programming, we demonstrated the technique by implementing the update function of an interactive particle system using a synthetic program. The original version was implemented using Numeric Python, and the update function limited the number of particles to approximately 20,000. The synthetic kernel improved the performance of the application to handle over 200,000 particles, at which point the graphics pipeline became the bottleneck. We reimplemented the update function using synthetic expressions and iterators to evaluate the different approaches to synthetic programming. The code for the new update loop is:

```
for vel, point in parallel(zip_iter(c, vels, points)):
  # Forces - Gravity and Air resistance
  vel.v = vel + gravity
  vel.v = vel + vmadd(vsel(one, negone, (zero > vel)), air, zero)
  point.v = point + vel

  # Bounce off the zero extents (floor and left wall)
  # and positve extents (ceiling and right wall)
  vel.v = vmadd(vel, vsel(one, floor, (zero > point)), zero)
  vel.v = vmadd(vel, vsel(one, negone, (point > extents)), zero)

  # Add a 'floor' at y = 1.0 so the points don't disappear
  point.v = vsel(point, one, (one > point))
```

To compare the synthetic and Numeric versions, we stripped out the comments and white-space and assigned each line of code to be either parameter allocation, loop and iterator management, or algorithm implementation. The results are listed in Table 2. All three versions use the same Numeric arrays to store parameters and iterators, and the Numeric version did not require any additional parameter, loop, or iterator code.

The line counts demonstrate the utility of synthetic expressions and iterators. The original synthetic kernel contained 77 lines of code, 63 of which were used for register management and manual loop maintenance. In contrast, the new synthetic kernel uses only 11 lines to manage the same operations, all of which use a clear syntax. Both the Numeric and original synthetic implementations used similar amounts of code to implement the update algorithm. The AltiVec ISA contains many instructions that have direct Numeric counterparts, and the code for both versions is similar. The synthetic expression version, on the other hand, uses only six lines of code to implement the update. While the Numeric version could have been implemented using similar syntax, Numeric's aliasing rules lead to multiple, unnecessary temporary arrays. Because the expression implementation works on registers, the cost of temporary values is kept to a minimum, allowing a more concise syntax.

**Table 2.** Lines of code allocated to parameter allocation, loop and iterator management, and the update algorithm for the three different implementations of the particle system update function

|  | Parameters | Loop/Iters | Algorithm |
|---|---|---|---|
| **Numeric** | – | – | 13 |
| **Syn. AltiVec** | 43 | 20 | 14 |
| **Syn. Expr/Iter** | 8 | 3 | 6 |

# 6   Related Work

The Expression and Template libraries are related to similar technologies for run-time code generation and user-level optimizations. Both libraries rely on object-oriented and generative programing techniques for their implementation.

The scalar and vector expressions use the Interpreter design pattern [5] to implement a domain-specific language for transforming expressions into equivalent sequences of instructions for the target architecture. This approach closely related C++ expression templates [14], and in particular Blitz++ [14]. Blitz++ uses compile-time operator overloading for transforming array expressions into more efficient source code sequences. ROSE [12], a C++ tool for generating pre-processors for domain-specific optimizations, is generalized source-to-source transformation engine that allows domain experts to design optimizations for object-oriented frameworks.

High-level systems for dynamic compilation include DyC [6], 'C (pronounced tick-C) [11], and the TaskGraph Library C++ [1]. DyC is an annotation-based system that allows users to specify sections of code that should be specialized at run time. 'C and the TaskGraph library use mini-languages that allow users to write code that is partially specialized at compile time and fully specialized at run-time. All three of these systems have compile- and run-time components and extend C or C++. The synthetic programming environment is a run-time system that uses Python directly for run-time code generation.

With the increasing in processing power on graphics cards, new domain-specific languages have emerged for generating GPU instructions from host languages. BrookGPU [2] implements a streaming language as an extension of ANSI C, and Sh [8] uses a combination of compile-time meta-programming and run-time compilation to generate GPU code. Both systems support multiple processor architectures and abstract the lowest level code from developers.

The synthetic iterators are built on Python Iterators [15] and the **parallel** and **unroll** iterators use the Proxy design pattern [5] to intercept requests. The iterators are all designed to allow the user to annotate the current operation with guidelines for generating optimal code sequences. High-performance Fortran (HPF) [4] and OpenMP [3] both use similar annotation techniques for specifying parallel sections of applications.

Finally, other systems exist for implementing high-performance code from Python. Weave [7] and PyASM [10] are code in-lining systems for C++ and x86 assembly, respectively. Psyco [13] is a run-time compiler for Python that generates efficient machine code for common Python patterns, but due to Python's high level of semantic abstraction, has difficulty finding optimal code sequences. Synthetic programming complements these systems by supplying a pure Python approach to generating high-performance code. The specialized nature of the expression library allows it to overcome the semantic challenges faced by Psyco.

## 7   Conclusion

The Expression and Iterator libraries provide an important addition to the Synthetic Programming Environment. By providing natural abstractions for common numeric and iterative operations, they allow developers to create high-performance instruction sequences using Python syntax, while at the same time removing the dependency on external tools for code synthesis.

The libraries also demonstrate how the SPE can be used to quickly develop and test optimizations for a target architecture. Whereas traditional compiler development requires extensive knowledge of the compiler framework and long build times, the SPE uses Python as the code generation infrastructure and removes the build step entirely. By exposing the code generation and optimization processes as user-level libraries, developers have more control over the generation of high-performance code.

The libraries will be made available as part of the Synthetic Programming Environment.

## Acknowledgements

This work was funded by a grant from the Lilly Endowment. Discussions with Douglas Gregor were instrumental in developing the unroll Proxy.

## References

1. Olav Beckmann, Alastair Houghton, Michael Mellor, and Paul H J Kelly. Run-time code generation in C++ as a foundation for domain-specific optimisation. In Christian Lengauer et al, editor, *Domain-Specific Program Generation*, volume 3016 of *Lecture Notes in Computer Science*. Springer-Verla.
2. Ian Buck, Tim Foley, Daniel Horn, Jeremy Sugerman, Kayvon Fatahalian, Mike Houston, and Pat Hanrahan. Brook for GPUs: stream computing on graphics hardware. *ACM Trans. Graph.*, 23(3):777–786, 2004.
3. Robit Chandra, Leonardo Dagum, Dave Kohr, Dror Maydan, Jeff McDonald, and Ramesh Menon. *Parallel programming in OpenMP*. Morgan Kaufmann Publishers Inc., San Francisco, CA, USA, 2001.
4. High Performance Fortran Forum. High performance fortran language specification. version 2.0. Technical report, Rice University, 1992.
5. Erich Gamma, Richard Helm, Ralph Johnson, and John Vlissides. *Design Patterns: Elements of Reusable Object-Oriented Software*, chapter 4-5, pages 207–219,243–257. Addison Wesley Longman, Inc., 1995.

6. Brian Grant, Markus Mock, Matthai Philipose, Craig Chambers, and Susan J. Eggers. DyC: an expressive annotation-directed dynamic compiler for C. *Theoretical Computer Science*, 248(1–2):147–199, 2000.

7. Eric Jones. *Weave User's Guide*. Enthought. Accessed May 2006.

8. Michael D. McCool, Zheng Qin, , and Tiberiu S. Popa. Shader metaprogramming. In *SIGGRAPH/Eurographics Graphics Hardware Workshop*, pages 57–68, September 2002.

9. Christopher Mueller and Andrew Lumsdaine.    Runtime synthesis of high-performance code from scripting languages. In *Dynamic Language Symposium (DLS2006)*, Portland, Orgeon, October 2006.

10. Grant Olson. *PyASM User's Guide V.0.2*. Accessed May 2006.

11. M. Poletto, W. C. Hsieh, D. R. Engler, and M. F. Kaashoek. 'C and tcc: A language and compiler for dynamic code generation. *ACM Trans. on Programming Languages and Systems*, 21(2):324–369, 1999.

12. Dan Quinlan. ROSE: Compiler support for object-oriented frameworks. *Parallel Processing Letters*, 10(2-3):215–226, 2000.

13. Armin Rigo. *The Ultimate Psyco Guide*, 1.5.1 edition, February 2005.

14. Todd L. Veldhuizen. Expression templates. *C++ Report*, 7(5):26–31, June 1995. Reprinted in C++ Gems, ed. Stanley Lippman.

15. Ka-Ping Yee and Guido van Rossum. Pep 234: Iterators. Technical report, Python Software Foundation, 2001.

# Applying Code Specialization to FFT Libraries for Integral Parameters

Minhaj Ahmad Khan and Henri-Pierre Charles

Université de Versailles Saint-Quentin en Yvelines

**Abstract.** Code specialization is an approach that can be used to improve the sequence of optimizations to be performed by the compiler. The performance of code after specialization may vary, depending upon the structure of the application. For FFT libraries, the specialization of code with different parameters may cause an increase in code size, thereby impacting overall behavior of applications executing in environment with small instruction caches.

In this article, we propose a new approach for specializing FFT code that can be effectively used to improve performance while limiting the code increase by incorporating dynamic specialization. Our approach makes use of a static compile time analysis and adapts a single version of code to multiple values through runtime specialization. This technique has been applied to different FFT libraries over Itanium IA-64 platform using icc compiler v 9.0. For highly efficient libraries, we are able to achieve speedup of more than 80% with small increase in code size.

## 1 Introduction

Modern optimizing compilers are able to trigger various optimizations if they are provided with the necessary information concerning variables used in the code. Most of the time, this information is not available until execution of the program. In this regard, code specialization can be used to expose a set of values to the program. But the impact of code specialization is diminished by the fact that specialization for a large number of values of a single variable can result in enormous code size increase.

For scientific and mathematical applications, different algorithms have been implemented in libraries that are able to calculate Discrete Fourier Transforms in $O(nlogn)$. These libraries provide support for DFT of different sizes with real and complex input data. Moreover, these code libraries are heavily dependent on integer parameters which can be fully exploited by the compiler if their values become known. However, it is difficult to specialize code with each possible value of the important parameter.

In this article, we propose an optimization technique that targets FFT libraries and makes use of code specialization in an efficient manner so that the problem related to code explosion is decreased. This technique makes an assumption that the optimizing compilers generate object code with minor differences for a large range of values of an integer variable. The basis of this assumption

G. Almási, C. Caşcaval, and P. Wu (Eds.): LCPC 2006, LNCS 4382, pp. 96–110, 2007.

is the fact that a compiler invokes a set of optimizations that is normally related to a range of values of a parameter. At static compile time, we perform a static compile time analysis to find out the instructions which are dependent on the specializing value in the object code. If these instructions fulfill the conditions required for our runtime specialization approach, a specializer is generated that modifies binary instructions for a new specializing value at runtime. This approach can therefore be acquired to limit number of versions required for specialization of code. The runtime specialization is performed with a small overhead (12 to 20 cycles per instruction) since we require specialization of only a limited set of binary instructions instead of generating complete code during execution.

The remaining part of the paper is organized as follows. Section 2 gives an example describing the behavior of specialization. The new approach of code specialization has been proposed in section 3, whereas section 4 elaborates it through description of an implementation framework. Section 5 presents the results obtained after specialization. The related work has been discussed in section 6 before concluding in section 7.

## 2   Motivating Example

The code specialization is used to reduce the number of operations to be performed by the program during its execution, however, it can also be used to facilitate compiler with necessary information required to optimize the code in an efficient manner. Different optimizations can be performed by the compiler such as loop unrolling, software pipelining, constant folding, dead-code elimination and better instruction scheduling.

For example, consider the following code:

```
void Function(int size, double * a, double * b, int dist, int stride){
    int i;
    for (i=0; i< size; i++, a+=dist, b+=dist){
        a[stride*2] = a[stride] + b[stride];
    }
}
```

Different value of specializing parameter may cause the compiler to generate different code. For a small value of loop size, loop can be fully unrolled and the loop overhead can be reduced. Similarly, if we specialize the loop size for larger value (e.g. 123), loop can be pipelined with partial unrolling depending upon the architecture for which the code is being compiled. The optimization sequence for all the specialized versions would therefore be different in all the cases depending upon the specializing value and this is the reason which impacts execution performance of an application.

Furthermore, if we specialize above given code with value of **stride**, then the compiler is able to determine the offset at static compile time and a better dependence analysis can now be performed to invoke more optimizations. For the above given example, when compiled with `icc v 9.0`, the loop is partially unrolled and software pipelining is performed with a pipeline depth of 2. For original unspecialized version, no software pipelining is performed. This makes the code execution faster for specialized version. However, keeping different versions specialized with all possible stride values would degrade performance of application. Therefore an attempt is made to keep single version and perform dynamic specialization to adapt this version to a large range of values. When we specialize the code with `stride` value being 5 and `stride` value 7, the object code produced after compilation would be similar in terms of optimizations and would differ in immediate constants that would be based on `affine` formula of the form :

$$Immediate\_value = stride * A + B. \tag{1}$$

This formula can then be used during execution to adapt single version to a large number of values, thereby taking full advantage of optimizations at static compile time instead of performing heavyweight optimizations at runtime. The task of specialization of binary instructions can be accomplished through efficient dynamic specializer as proposed in next section.

## 3  Approach for Limited Code Specialization

Existing compilers and partial evaluators [1,2] are able to perform partial evaluation if different values in the program become known. A small set of values and parameters therefore needs to be selected which should be important enough to have some impact on execution speed. Our current approach of code specialization targets only integer parameters and it fully conforms with FFT libraries where the code optimizations depend largely on integer parameters. So far our approach is restricted to positive integral values to keep the semantics of the code after specialization.

A profiling analysis can be performed to collect information regarding most frequently used functions and their parameter values. The hot parameters can then be specialized statically through insertion of wrapper (for redirection) describing the version with the parameter replaced by its value in the function body. However, for an integer parameter with n-bit size, we will require $2^n$ versions resulting in huge increase of code size. Therefore, we find a generic template specialized at static compile time and adapt it to different versions during execution through invocation of a runtime specializer. The generic template is highly optimized at static compile time since the unknown value has been made available to the compiler by providing a dummy value for the specializing parameter. This approach is different from those proposed in [2,3,4,5] which perform partial evaluation for code that has either already been specialized or suspend specialization until execution.

The main steps for our code specialization are described as follows:

1. Insert a wrapper at the start of function body containing a call to specializer and to maintain software cache. This would be used to reduce the number

of versions to be generated during execution. To define range R, initialize MINVAL to be 1 and MAXVAL with the maximum value for the type of specializing parameter.

2. Specialize the code with different positive values of the integer parameter and after compilation obtain versions (at least two) of assembly code (or dumped object code) generated with full optimizations. These versions contain the templates for which the runtime specialization will be implemented.

3. Analyze the assembly code to find the differences b/w two versions generated in previous step. The instructions will differ in immediate values which are based on the affine formula of the form $a * param + b$. Annotate all such instructions which differ in two versions. If instructions differ in any literal other than the immediate operand or they do not conform to the above given formula, go to last step.

4. Against each annotated instruction in the generated versions, solve the system of linear equations to calculate the values of $a$ and $b$ with constraints $param, a > 0$ .

5. The analysis of formulae would reveal information regarding the range of values for which the template would be valid and modify the source code (MINVAL and MAXVAL) to contain this range. The range (R) can be calculated as follows:

Let $a_i * param + b_i$ be the formula generated for i-th instruction, then we have,

$$S_i = MAX\left(1, \left\lceil \frac{1 - b_i}{a_i} \right\rceil\right), \text{ and } E_i = \left\lfloor \frac{ARCHMAX_i - b_i}{a_i} \right\rfloor,$$

where $ARCHMAX_i$ represents maximum value that can be used as immediate operand for i-th annotated instruction. The new range R for $param$ with $S = \{S_i$, for i=1 to n\} and E=\{$E_i$, for i=1 to n\}, can be represented as:

$$param \in [MINVAL, MAXVAL], \text{ where,}$$

$$MINVAL = MAX(S), \text{ and } MAXVAL = MIN(E).$$

6. Find out the exact locations where the immediate values differ in two versions, and as a consequence, the runtime specializer can be generated that will modify the binary instructions in the template. The runtime specializer requires information regarding starting location, offsets of the locations to be modified and the formulae to calculate new values. The assembly code version and the specializer generated need to be linked to make invocation of specializer possible during execution of program.

7. For the values for which the assembly code versions do not fulfill the conditions, or it is required to keep static version (through programmer directives), define a static value in the source code for the specializing parameter by generating another version of the original function code. Modify the wrapper and the range in the function code to contain the branch to redirect to static specialized code.

Let $T$ be set of values for which the static specialization needs to be performed, then, we need to modify the range R as:

$$R = R - T.$$

During execution, the wrapper inserted inside the code would cause the runtime specializer to be invoked prior to the execution of the specialized code for a particular value. When the same function code is called next time with the same value of specializing parameter, the wrapper would redirect the call to specialized code thereby avoiding the call to specializer and minimizing runtime overhead.

## 4    Implementation of Code Specialization

The low-level runtime specialization is a complex task and it would be cumbersome for programmers to manually perform specialization at binary code level. In addition, they might need to perform comparison of instructions, generation of formulae for all instructions which differ and find the valid range by taking into consideration the formats of binary instructions for that architecture. To automate this specialization technique, a small software prototype has been developed that incorporates source code modification, specializing invariants analysis and runtime specializer generation as depicted in Figure 1.

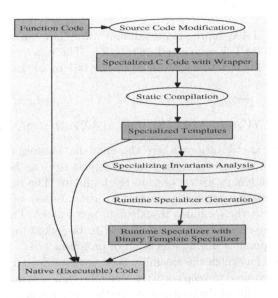

**Fig. 1.** Automation of Runtime Specialization

## 4.1    Insertion of Wrapper and Specialization

The source modification involves searching for the integer parameters in the function and replacing them with a constant value. Different functions can be specialized with different parameters. For our experiment, it is necessary to obtain the assembly code versions after specialization which resemble in terms of optimizations and differ only in a fixed set (*add/mov/cmp*) of instructions. Therefore, the prime numbers are preferred to be used as specializing value to obtain such versions of assembly code which avoid any value specific optimizations. The source code is modified to contain other versions of the candidate function specialized with an integer value. Moreover, in the function code, a wrapper is inserted containing the branch to specializer invocation only in the case when the function receives a new value. If the function receives the same value of the specializing parameter, the redirection code would cause the specialized function to be directly invoked avoiding call to specializer. The pseudo-code for the wrapper is shown in Figure 2.

```
Function (... int P2, int P3, int P4, ...)
    if P3 value in [MINVAL, MAXVAL]
        if the code was specialized with a different P3 value
            Specialize function with P3
        end if
        call Specialized function (..., P2, P4, ...)
    else
        call Standard code (... P2, P3, P4, ...)
    end if
```

**Fig. 2.** Source code after modification

The temporary values used for specialization need to be selected carefully. Usually smaller values are more suitable for specialization, and with icc compiler, the impact of specialization in terms of optimizations decreases with an increase in these values. The specialized assembly code is also the one to be linked to the client application in the final phase of static compilation. This specialized code contains templates with dummy values which would be replaced by new values and this is the task performed by automated runtime specializer.

## 4.2    Runtime Specializer Generation

The automation prototype includes a Specializing Invariants Analyzer (SIA) which performs analysis at static compile time and is used to prepare information required by runtime specializer. The analyzer finds the differences and then passes these differences to code specializer generator. Moreover, the locations of differences found will act as template holes to be filled, whereas, formulae on which these values are based, will be used to generate new values to adapt to.

The Specializer Generator takes this information and generates a specializer that will be linked to the specialized code to make modification during execution of the application.

After modification of source code, the code is compiled to either assembly code or dumped object code[1] At least two versions are generated with different values of the specializing parameter. If we compare these versions, they would differ in some instructions containing constant values as operands. For example, for the above given example, the code generated by icc v 9.0 compiler for code when specialized with the value *stride* = 5 and the one generated for *stride* = 7 would differ as shown in Figure 3.

```
//With Stride = 5                      //With Stride = 7
   { .mii                                { .mii
        sub r24=r30,r19                       sub r24=r30,r19
        add r11=40,r28                        add r11=56,r28
        nop.i 0 ;;                            nop.i 0 ;;
   }                                     }
   { .mib                                { .mib
        add r14=20,r24                        add r14=28,r24
        nop.i 0                               nop.i 0
        (p9) br.cond.dptk .b1_3;;             (p9) br.cond.dptk .b1_3;;
   }                                     }
        ....                                  ....
```

**Fig. 3.** Assembly Code generated by icc v 9.0

The comparison of the assembly code is performed by the SIA, and formulae are generated on the assumption that in both versions, these formulae are of the form:

$$Val_1 = Param_1 * a + b, \text{ and } Val_2 = Param_2 * a + b.$$

where $Val_1$ and $Val_2$ are immediate operands of binary instructions, and, $Param_1$ and $Param_2$ are the values of the parameter with which the versions are specialized. Solving these two equations provides us the values of $a$ and $b$. The formulae with known $a$ and $b$ are generated at static compile time and during execution only new value of actual specializing parameter ($Param$) is passed as shown in Figure 4. After solving equations, it is possible to find the range for which the code will be valid. For example, an adds instruction over Itanium allows a 14-bit signed immediate value to be used as operand, thereby making the above given code valid for range (i.e. $MAXVAL$) up to 1023.

For specialized code with *stride* = 8, runtime specialization will modify the immediate constants in Figure 3 with new values 64 and 32. This approach of runtime specialization is highly efficient and can be used to adapt a single version to a large range of stride values.

---

[1] Using objdump utility makes the code offset locations easy to calculate and it also facilitates to resolve different pseudo-code to actual binary instructions.

```
void Specializer_Function(long base_address, register long param)
   BinaryTemplateSpecializer( base_address, 6, 1, param * 8 + 0)
   BinaryTemplateSpecializer( base_address, 7, 0, param * 4 + 0)
   ..........
```

**Fig. 4.** Invocation of Binary Template Specializer

**Binary Template Specializer.** With the information of formulae and locations for each instruction after analysis at static compile time, a specializer is generated to invoke *Binary Template Specializer* as given in Figure 4. For Itanium where a single bundle contains 3 instructions, we also require the location of instruction within the bundle since 128-bit binary bundle contains constants at different locations of the instruction word depending upon its location in the bundle. Therefore, a different specializing strategy is adopted for each instruction location in the bundle.

**Runtime Activities.** The runtime specializer may include some initialization steps (e.g. on Itanium to make the segment of code modifiable). After the initialization, the specializer is invoked which in turn makes multiple calls to the Binary Template Specializer passing it the information regarding the location of instruction and new immediate value. This information causes the Binary Template Specializer to fill the binary templates with new values. The specializer may be invoked multiple times depending upon the number of instructions, however, it incurs a small overhead due to specialization of a limited set of instructions instead of complete function code. Finally, we also need to perform activities for cache coherence such as flushing and synchronization.

### 4.3   Static Versioning

In cases where the object code does not conform to conditions specified for dynamic specialization, we can statically specialize the code. We require the use of following directive to proceed for static specialization.

$$\#\text{defspec } param \text{ val}$$

This directive would cause the code modifier to generate a version together with the insertion of wrapper to redirect execution to this version when the *param* receives the specializing value val. The runtime overhead in this case would be reduced to single branch, but at a cost of increase in code size.

## 5   Implementation Setup and Results

Different FFT libraries including FFTW, GSL FFT, Scimark, FFT2 have been optimized through our algorithm on Itanium IA-64 processor making use of Intel compiler icc v 9.0. These libraries have been compiled with -O3 parameter for optimization. The performance measurements are made using pfmon library for computation of 1-dim DFT for complex input data.

It is to be noted that the runtime specialization is very efficient and requires 12 to 20 cycles for each binary instruction to be specialized. Most of the times, we do not require multiple invocations to amortize overhead and this makes our runtime specialization algorithm more efficient than those implemented in [2,6,7,4] where break-even point is very high (up to 100). In case where the code is already specialized for hot parameter, the runtime specialization for less effective parameter can deteriorate performance of the application.

The average specialization overhead with respect to execution time of the application and code size increase together with average speedup obtained of all executions, have been shown in table 1.

**Table 1.** Performance Summary

|  | FFTW | GSL-FFT | Scimark | FFT2 | Numutils | Kiss-FFT |
|---|---|---|---|---|---|---|
| Avg. Specialization Over-head (w.r.t exec.time) | 1.00% | 1.00% | 2.00% | 2.00% | 1.00% | 2.00% |
| Code Increase (w.r.t total li-brary size) | 10.00% | 2.00% | 19.00% | 10.00% | 12.00% | 11.00% |
| Avg. Speedup | 23.26% | 11.85% | 17.53% | 7.74% | 3.38% | 6.29% |

## 5.1   FFTW

FFTW [8,9] is one of the fastest libraries able to compute DFTs of real and complex data in $O(n \log n)$ with any size of $n$. The library contains large number of codelets which were specialized both statically and dynamically. The codelets required 4 to 20 binary instructions to be modified during execution. The FFTW wisdom was generated in `exhaustive` mode for calculating out-of-place 1-dim complex DFTs having size of powers of 2. The graph in Figure 5 shows that the large speedup occurs for small values of N (input array size) for which the codelets are invoked with small loop counter and stride values. With the known strides in smaller codelets e.g. $n1\_2$, the Initiation Interval (the number of cycles required for an iteration in stable mode of pipeline) for the specialized version was reduced. Similarly, with the small loop trip count, the compiler fully unrolled the loop to produce large speedup for 8. For large values, the codelets are

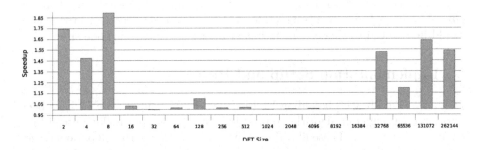

**Fig. 5.** FFTW Library Specialization Results

invoked multiple times resulting in an accumulated speedup through invocation of dynamically specialized code.

## 5.2    GSL FFT Library

The GNU Scientific Library (GSL)[10] is a numerical library containing programs able to solve different mathematical problems including FFT, BLAS, Interpolation and Numerical Differentiations etc. The figures 6 and 7 show speedup obtained with calculation of complex (forward) DFT of size of different prime numbers and those of powers of 2. The functions `fft_complex_pass_n` and `fft_complex_radix2_transform` were specialized with stride value to be one. For the function `fft_complex_pass_n`, the compiler had generated more data cache prefetch instructions and pipelined loops than those in the standard version. For the function `fft_complex_radix2_transform`, the object code generated by *icc* was almost similar for both the specialized and unspecialized versions. This shows that our specialization technique is heavily dependent on the optimizations done by the compiler at static compile time.

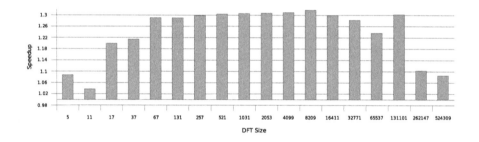

**Fig. 6.** GSL-FFT Specialization Results(Prime Numbers)

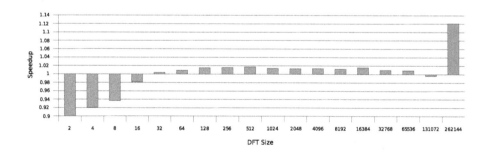

**Fig. 7.** GSL-FFT Specialization Results (Powers of 2)

## 5.3   Scimark2 Library

SciMark 2.0 [11] has been developed at the National Institute of Standards and Technology (NIST). Its C source function `fft_transform_internal` was specialized to generate a binary template that required 7 binary instructions to be specialized during execution. The small value of specializing parameter let the compiler remove the overhead of filling and draining the pipelines, however the code was restricted to a limited set of values (up to 128). In contrast to small values, the code produced by compiler after specializing with large static values did not impact performance to a large factor and resembled with the original object code.

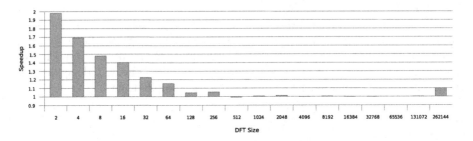

**Fig. 8.** Scimark Library Specialization Results

## 5.4   FFT2 Library

The FFT2 library[12] contains routines to perform Cooley-Tukey Fast Fourier Transform on complex and real samples. The dynamic specialization for the `join` function was performed for parameter m. The binary template was generated which contained 5 binary instructions to be modified. The static specialization was limited to 2 versions with m=1 and m=2 which are frequently called with other different values for which dynamic specializer was invoked. The Figure 9 shows speedup only for large values where the function is repeatedly called with the same value as in case of large sizes of input array. The code for static versions contained pipeline with large depth making it suitable for large executions.

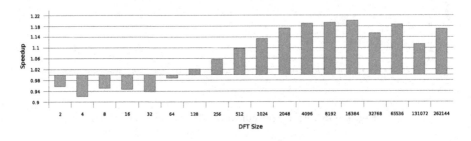

**Fig. 9.** FFT2 Library Specialization Results

Moreover, for small function calls, the performance degrades due to overhead of dynamic specialization caused by recursive calls of the same function with different input values.

## 5.5 NumUtils Library

The NumUtils library[13] contains functions to solve different mathematical problems. The results in Figure 10 show the speedup obtained through different versions of routine fft since a generic template could not be obtained after invariants analysis. The static specialized code however contained less number of loads and stores sufficient enough to produce speedup.

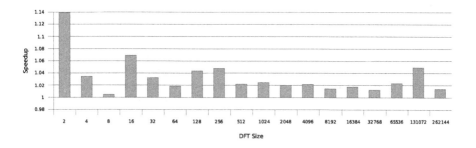

**Fig. 10.** NumUtils Library Specialization Results

## 5.6 Kiss-FFT Library

For the library Kiss-FFT[14], the functions kf_bfly2 and $kf\_bfly4$ were specialized with versions for m=1 and m=1,2,4 respectively. Moreover, the function $kf\_bfly4$ was dynamically specialized as well generating a template having 7 locations to be modified during execution. The binary template to be specialized and statically specialized versions contained very less number of memory operations as compared to unspecialized code. Moreover, the repeated invocation of these functions resulted in speedup as shown in Figure 11.

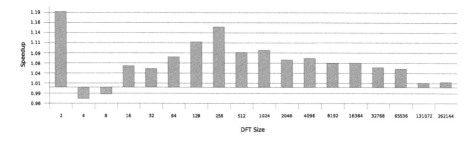

**Fig. 11.** Kiss-FFT Library Specialization Results

# 6   Related Work

The code specialization and dynamic compilation have been applied to a diverse domain of applications including the image filtering, geometrical transformations, JPEG compression, operating systems, pattern matching and DBMS Pattern Recognition [15,16,2,4,17,1,5,18,6]. Some systems (e.g. C-Mix [1]) perform source to source transformation to generate code after partial evaluation at static compile time, while others are able to perform specialization during execution of the program through runtime code generation. Most of these approaches perform specialization and optimizations in two stages. In first stage, a high level static compile time analysis is performed and optimizations are performed only for known values, thereby leaving other optimizations to be performed during execution of the code. On the contrary, our approach relies on low-level analysis of code to fulfill the required criteria. Also, these code generators perform large number of optimizations during execution at the cost of overhead, whereas our technique is able to obtain highly optimized code at static compile time.

The DCG [19] is a retargetable dynamic code generator and makes use of intermediate representation of lcc compiler to translate into machine instructions through BURS (Bottom-Up Rewrite System). For different mathematical functions, it is able to achieve large speedup (3 to 10) but at a cost of 350 instructions per generated instruction, making it suitable only for applications requiring minimum dynamic code to be generated during execution. Similarly, Tick C [7] compiler can generate code during execution and perform optimizations including loop unrolling, constant folding and dead-code elimination. With Tick C, a speedup up to 10 has been achieved for different benchmarks, but it requires multiple calls to amortize overhead. With VCODE [20] interface, optimized code is generated during execution of the program at the cost of 300 to 800 cycles per generated instruction. The optimized code is generated for single value, thereby requiring the code generation activity to be invoked again for other specializing value. In contrast, since we are constrained to apply single transformation during execution, we are able to reuse the same binary code for multiple specializations.

Fabius [21,4,22] is the system that is able to generate specialized native code at runtime for programs written in Standard ML. Although the average overhead ( 6 cycles per generated instruction) is less than that incurred through our approach, they require complete function code to be generated during execution. This is different from our specialization approach where we require only a limited number of instructions to be specialized.

Tempo [3,2] is a specializer that is able to perform offline and online partial evaluation of code. It performs a large static compile-time analysis to specialize the code during execution by keeping different versions of the same code specialized with different values. For runtime generation of code and optimizations it invokes Tick C compiler. With dynamic specialization of FFT, they are able to achieve average speedup[2] of 3.3 , with break-even point up to 8 and requiring

---

[2] Results show only 3 invocations with input size 32, 64 and 128

separate version for each size of DFT. The approach adopted by Tempo differs from ours in that if the code is not already specialized, all the optimizations will be performed during execution, whereas, our approach benefits from optimizations at static compile time by exposing constant values of specializing parameter.

## 7   Conclusion and Future Work

The exposure of values of different parameters enables the compiler to generate more efficient code. It is possible to limit the size of specialized versions through implementation of an efficient dynamic specializer which is able to specialize a fixed set of binary instructions during execution. In this way, the overhead of code generation and memory allocation is minimized, and a good speedup can therefore be obtained. For dynamic specialization, we first generate templates after a low-level analysis of code. The templates should contain instructions with immediate operands which must be dependent on the value of specializing parameter. Once a version is specialized with dynamic value, we do not require to invoke specializer for the same input value. However, if the specializer is called multiple times with different values, or the code generated at static compile time is not highly optimized, then the specialization may deteriorate the performance.

A cost analysis is being incorporated in conjunction with dependence test to automate the decision of when to apply dynamic specialization. Currently this approach makes use of specializers which are specific to Itanium architecture. So, we intend to generalize the specializer generation and template code specialization for multiple platforms.

## References

1. Makholm, H.: Specializing c- an introduction to the principles behind c-mix. Technical report, Computer Science Department, University of Copenhagen (1999)
2. Consel, C., Hornof, L., Marlet, R., Muller, G., Thibault, S., Volanschi, E.N.: Tempo: Specializing Systems Applications and Beyond. ACM Computing Surveys **30** (1998)
3. Nol, F., Hornof, L., Consel, C., Lawall, J.L.: Automatic, template-based run-time specialization: Implementation and experimental study. In: International Conference on Computer Languages (ICCL'98). (1998)
4. Leone, M., Lee, P.: Dynamic Specialization in the Fabius System. ACM Computing Surveys **30** (1998)
5. Consel, C., Hornof, L., François Noël, Noyé, J., Volanschi, N.: A uniform approach for compile-time and run-time specialization. In: Partial Evaluation. International Seminar., Dagstuhl Castle, Germany, Springer-Verlag, Berlin, Germany (1996) 54–72
6. Grant, B., Mock, M., Philipose, M., Chambers, C., Eggers, S.J.: Dyc : An expressive annotation-directed dynamic compiler for c. Technical report, Department of Computer Science and Engineering,University of Washington (1999)

7. Poletto, M., Hsieh, W.C., Engler, D.R., Kaashoek, F.M.: 'c and tcc : A language and compiler for dynamic code generation. ACM Transactions on Programming Languages and Systems **21** (1999) 324–369
8. Frigo, M., Johnson, S.G.: The design and implementation of fftw3. In: In proceedings of IEEE, Vol. 93, no. 2. (2005) 216–231
9. Frigo, M., Johnson, S.G.: FFTW: An adaptive software architecture for the FFT. In: Proc. IEEE Intl. Conf. on Acoustics, Speech, and Signal Processing. Volume 3., Seattle, WA (1998) 1381–1384
10. Galassi, M., Davies, J., Theiler, J., Gough, B., Jungman, G., Booth, M., Rossi, F.: GNU Scientific Library Reference Manual - Revised Second Edition. http://www.gnu.org/software/gsl/ (2005)
11. Gough, B.: SciMark 2.0. http://math.nist.gov/scimark2/ (2000)
12. Valkenburg, P.: FFT2 Library. http://www.jjj.de/fft/ (2006)
13. Hein, C.: Numerical Utilities. atl.external.lmco.com/projects/csim/xgraph/ numutil (2003)
14. Borgerding, M.: KissFFT v1.2.5. http://sourceforge.net/projects/kissfft/ (2006)
15. Jones, N.D., Gomard, C., Sestoft, P.: Partial Evaluation and Automatic Program Generation. Prentice Hall International, International Series in Computer Science (1993)
16. Brifault, K., Charles, H.P.: Efficient data driven run-time code generation. In: LCR '04: Proceedings of the 7th workshop on Workshop on languages, compilers, and run-time support for scalable systems, New York, NY, USA, ACM Press (2004) 1–7
17. Locanthi, B.: Fast bitblt() with asm() and cpp. In European UNIX Systems User Group Conference Proceedings (1987)
18. Grant, B., Mock, M., Philipose, M., Chambers, C., Eggers, S.J.: Annotation-Directed Run-Time Specialization in C. In: Proceedings of the ACM SIGPLAN Symposium on Partial Evaluation and Semantics-Based Program Manipulation (PEPM'97), ACM (1997) 163–178
19. Engler, D.R., Proebsting, T.A.: DCG: An efficient, retargetable dynamic code generation system. In: *Proceedings of the Sixth International Conference on Architectural Support for Programming Languages and Operating Systems*, San Jose, California (1994) 263–272
20. Engler, D.R.: Vcode : A retargetable extensible, very fast dynamic code generation system. In: In Proceedings of the SIGPLAN 96 Conference on Programming Language Design and Implementation, ACM, New York. (1996)
21. Leone, M., Lee, P.: Optimizing ml with run-time code generation. Technical report, School of Computer Science, Carnegie Mellon University (1995)
22. Leone, M., Lee, P.: A Declarative Approach to Run-Time Code Generation. In: Workshop on Compiler Support for System Software (WCSSS). (1996)

# A Characterization of Shared Data Access Patterns in UPC Programs

Christopher Barton[1], Călin Caşcaval[2], and José Nelson Amaral[1]

[1] Department of Computing Science,
University of Alberta, Edmonton, Canada
{cbarton,amaral}@cs.ualberta.ca
[2] IBM T.J. Watson Research Center
Yorktown Heights, NY, 10598
cascaval@us.ibm.com

**Abstract.** The main attraction of Partitioned Global Address Space (PGAS) languages to programmers is the ability to distribute the data to exploit the affinity of threads within shared-memory domains. Thus, PGAS languages, such as Unified Parallel C (UPC), are a promising programming paradigm for emerging parallel machines that employ hierarchical data- and task-parallelism. For example, large systems are built as distributed-shared memory architectures, where multi-core nodes access a local, coherent address space and many such nodes are interconnected in a non-coherent address space to form a high-performance system.

This paper studies the access patterns of shared data in UPC programs. By analyzing the access patterns of shared data in UPC we are able to make three major observations about the characteristics of programs written in a PGAS programming model: ($i$) there is strong evidence to support the development of automatic identification and automatic privatization of local shared data accesses; ($ii$) the ability for the programmer to specify how shared data is distributed among the executing threads can result in significant performance improvements; ($iii$) running UPC programs on a hybrid architecture will significantly increase the opportunities for automatic privatization of local shared data accesses.

## 1 Introduction

Partitioned Global Address Space (PGAS) programming languages offer an attractive, high-productivity programming model for programming large-scale parallel machines. PGAS languages, such as Unified Parallel C (UPC) [13], combine the simplicity of shared-memory programming with the efficiency of the message-passing paradigm. PGAS languages partition the application's address space into private, shared-local, and shared-remote memory. The latency of shared-remote accesses is typically much larger than that of local, private accesses, especially when the underlying hardware is a distributed-memory machine and remote accesses imply communication over a network.

In PGAS languages, such as UPC, the programmer specifies which data is shared and how it is distributed among all processors. When the data distribution is known at compile time, the compiler can distinguish between local shared data and remote shared data. This information can be used by the compiler to reduce the time to access shared data [5,12].

G. Almási, C. Caşcaval, and P. Wu (Eds.): LCPC 2006, LNCS 4382, pp. 111–125, 2007.

In this paper we report on our experience with a set of existing UPC benchmarks. We start from the premise that understanding data sharing access patterns is crucial to develop high performance parallel programs, especially in a PGAS language. We develop a set of tools to analyze memory behavior, taking advantage of our UPC compiler and runtime system. We characterize the benchmarks with respect to local and remote shared memory accesses, and based on these characteristics we make the following observations:

- Programmers are typically aware of data ownership and make an effort to compute on local data. However, since the data is declared as shared, it will incur the shared memory translation cost, unless it is copied to private memory or dereferenced through private pointers. Requiring programmers to perform both of these actions would increase the complexity of the source code and reduce the programmer's productivity. A more elegant approach is for the compiler to automatically discover which shared accesses are local and to analyze privatize them.
- PGAS languages offer data distribution directives, such as the blocking factor in UPC. Most of the time, programmers think in terms of virtual threads and processors. To develop portable code, programmers do not necessarily select the best distribution for a given platform. Again, there is an opportunity for the compiler to optimize the blocking factor to match the characteristics of the machine. In Section 3 we show several examples in which selecting the blocking factor appropriately, the number of remote accesses is reduced significantly.
- A different way to improve the latency of remote accesses, is to exploit emerging architectures that consist of multi-core chips or clusters of SMP machines – we call these machines hybrid architectures since they are a combination of shared and distributed memory. In this case, a combination of compiler and runtime support can provide an optimal grouping of threads, such that the number of local accesses is increased. In our experiments we estimate the percentage of remote accesses that can be localized.

Several programming models have been proposed for hybrid architecture. Traditionally a combination of OpenMP and MPI has been used to provide efficient communication between nodes while allowing simple distribution of work within each node [9,21]. However, presenting two very different programming models, shared memory and message passing, to the programmer makes coding of large applications very complex. Beside different data distribution requirements, there are issues of synchronization and load balancing that need to be managed across programming models.

A popular alternative have been Software Distributed Memory Systems (DSMs), such as TreadMarks [2], Nanos DSM [15], ClusterOMP [18], etc. In these systems, the user is presented with a unique programming model – shared memory, and the system takes care of maintaining the coherence between images running on distributed nodes. The coherence is typically maintained at OS page level granularity and different techniques have been developed to reduce the overhead [19]. These characteristics make workloads that have fine-grain sharing accesses and synchronization unsuitable for DSMs [18].

We believe that PGAS languages are inherently more suitable for hybrid architectures, since they are designed to make the user aware of shared data having different latencies. We have previously shown that UPC programs can scale to hundreds of thousands of nodes in a distributed machine [5]. In this work we present evidence that UPC is a suitable language for hybrid architectures, exposing a unique programming model to the user. We argue that a combination of aggressive compiler optimizations and runtime system support can efficiently map a wide range of applications to these emerging platforms.

The remainder of this paper is organized as follows: Section 2 presents an overview of the compiler and runtime system used to collect the results, as well as a description of the benchmarks studied. Section 3 presents the experimental results and discusses what are the issues and opportunities observed. In Section 4 we present the related work and we conclude in Section 5.

## 2  Environment

In this section we present the environment used for our experiments, and introduce the terminology that we are using throughout the paper. The experiments were conducted on a 32-way eServer pSeries 690 machine with 257280 MB of memory running AIX version 5.2.

### 2.1  Overview of IBM's Compiler and Runtime System

For this study, we use a development version of the IBM XL UPC compiler and UPC Runtime System (RTS). The compiler consists of a UPC front-end that transforms the UPC-specific constructs into C constructs and calls to the UPC RTS. While the compiler is capable of extensive optimizations, for the purpose of this study we did not enable them. The goal is to observe the sharing patterns in the applications and to gage the possible opportunities for optimizing shared memory accesses.

The RTS contains data structures and functions that are used during the runtime execution of a UPC program, similar to GASNet [7]. In the RTS we use the Shared Variable Directory (SVD) to manage allocation, de-allocation, and access to shared objects. The SVD provides the shared memory translation support and is designed for scalability. Every shared variable in a UPC program has a corresponding entry in the SVD. The compiler translates all accesses to shared variables into the appropriate calls in the RTS to access the values of shared variables using the Shared Variable Directory (SVD). Given that accessing a shared variable through the SVD may incur in several levels of indirection — even when the shared access is local — automatic privatization of local shared accesses by the compiler yields significant performance improvements [5].

### 2.2  Performance and Environment Monitoring (PEM)

We used the PEM infrastructure [10,22] to collect information about the shared memory behavior in UPC benchmarks.

The PEM framework consists of four components: $(i)$ an XML specification for events, $(ii)$ a tool-set to generate stubs for both event generation and event consumption, $(iii)$ an API that allows event selection and collection, and $(iv)$ a runtime that implements the API. For this study we created a new XML specification for events related to allocating and accessing UPC shared variables.

We manually instrumented the UPC RTS using the event generation stubs created by the PEM tools. These stubs track allocation of shared objects and shared memory accesses. In each run we logged the following information for each shared-array-element access: the SVD entry of the shared array being accessed, the thread that owns the array element, the thread that is accessing the array element and the type of access (load or store). By recording the thread that owns the element, rather than the shared-memory domain of the element, we are able to determine how many of the shared accesses will be local in different machine configurations. The SVD entry for each shared array provides a unique key that is used to identify each shared array. Each shared-object allocation was also monitored to record the SVD entry for every shared variable when it is allocated. This monitoring allows us to manually associate shared accesses in a trace file (each trace contains the SVD entry of the shared array being accessed) with shared variables in the source code. This monitoring step could be automated if we modified the compiler to generate calls to the PEM tools to associate shared variables with SVD entries. This compiler modification has been left for future work.

Benchmarks were compiled with the UPC compiler and linked with the instrumented RTS library. Once the benchmarks were run, the PEM runtime was able to collect a trace of the events described above. We then implemented a PEM consumer to process and analyze these traces. This tool collected statistics about the shared array accesses for each shared array and each UPC thread in a given trace.

## 2.3   Terminology

In order to facilitate understanding the discussion in the following sections of the paper, we define the terms below.

- A *thread T* refers to a UPC-declared thread of execution.
- A *processor P* is a hardware context for executing threads. Multiple threads can be executed on one processor[1].
- A *node* is a collection of processors that access a shared and coherent section of the address space.
- A *thread group* is a collection of threads that execute in the same node (the software equivalent of a node).
- A *shared-memory domain* is the shared memory in a node that is common to a thread group.
- Each element of a shared array is a *shared array element*.
- A *shared array access* is a dynamic memory access to a shared array element.
- A thread *T owns* an element of a shared array if the location of the element is in the shared memory pertaining to $T$ (*i.e.*, the element has affinity to $T$).
- The *local shared array elements* for a thread $T$ are the array elements that are located in the shared-memory domain of $T$. These elements may be owned by $T$ or may be owned by other threads that are in the thread group of $T$.

---

[1] Thus a processor may be a context in a hyper-threading processor, or it may be a core in a chip-multiprocessor architecture, or it may be a stand-alone processor.

– The *remote shared array elements* for a thread $T$ are the array elements that are outside the shared-memory domain of $T$. These are elements that are owned by threads outside of the thread group of $T$.

The shared keyword is used in UPC to identify data that is to be shared among all threads. Every shared object has affinity with one, and only one, thread. The programmer can specify the *affinity* between shared objects and threads using the blocking factor. If a shared object $O_s$ has affinity with a thread $T$ then $T$ *owns* $O_s$. In an ideal UPC program, the majority of shared data accesses are to shared data owned by the accessing thread. Such a data distribution reduces the amount of data movement between threads, thereby improving the performance of the program.

### 2.4  Overview of Current UPC Benchmarks

From the NAS suite [3,4], we selected the CG, MG and IS kernels. These benchmarks were developed by the UPC group at George Washington University based on the original MPI+FORTRAN/C implementation [17]. Each kernel comes with three versions containing different levels of user-optimized code. We used the O0 versions of the kernels because they contain the least amount of hand optimizations. Each kernel also comes with several class sizes that dictate the input size used by the benchmark. When possible, each benchmark was run with input classes S, A and B. The memory requirements for class S are the smallest and for class B are the largest that we could run. Not all the benchmarks could be run with class B.

CG is a kernel typical of unstructured grid computations. CG uses a conjugategradient method to approximate the smallest eigenvalue in a large, sparse matrix. The matrix is evenly divided between the processors.

MG uses a multigrid method to compute the solution of the 3D scalar Poisson equation. The partitioning is done by recursively halving the grid until all the processors are assigned. This benchmark must be run in $K$ processors where $K$ must be a power of 2. Communication occurs between iterations by exchanging the borders.

Integer Sort (IS) performs a parallel sort over small integers. Initially the integers are uniformly distributed.

A Sobel Edge Detection benchmark, written for this study, was also used. The Sobel operator is a discrete differentiation operator used in image processing. It computes an approximation of the gradient of the image intensity function. At each point in an image, the result of the Sobel operator is either the corresponding gradient vector or the norm of the vector [1].

The remaining UPC NAS Benchmarks have been optimized for access locality through the use of UPC block memory transfer methods (*e.g.,* upc_memget, upc _memput, upc_memcpy). These benchmark versions contain a relatively small number of accesses to shared variables and may not be representative for this study.We expect to use them as a target that our compiler should strive to achieve by analyzing naively written UPC programs. [2]

---

[2] The LU benchmark does not currently verify when compiled with our compiler and thus was not included in the study.

# 3   Results and Discussion

There are four questions that we are interested in answering in this study: $(i)$ What is the ratio of local to remote shared array accesses? $(ii)$ Of the remote accesses, what is the subset of threads that own them? $(iii)$ Are there regular patterns in accessing remote data? $(iv)$ How does the blocking factor used to distribute the shared arrays impact the ratio of local to remote accesses?

For each of these questions, we will take one of the benchmarks described above and discuss what are the characteristics that make it display a particular behavior. Given that the set of benchmarks available in UPC is quite restricted, we hope that our discussion tying program features to performance characteristics will also serve as a best-practice foundation for UPC programmers.

## 3.1   Local vs Remote Access Ratio

For the CG benchmark, more than 99.5% of the shared array accesses are to six shared arrays (independent of the number of threads used to run the benchmark): `send_start_g`, `exchange_len_g`, `reduce_threads_g`, `reduce_send_start_g`, `reduce_send_len_g`, and `reduce_recv_start_g`. The `send_start_g` and `exchange_len_g` are shared arrays with THREADS elements that are used in calls to `upc_memget` to move shared data between processors. They are created with the default (cyclic) blocking factor, where each processor is assigned one array element in a cyclic fashion. The `reduce_threads_g`, `reduce_send_start_g`, `reduce_send_len_g`, and `reduce_recv_start_g` are two-dimensional shared arrays of size THREADS*NUM_PROC_COLS, where NUM_PROC_COLS is based on the class size; the arrays use a blocking factor of NUM_PROC_COLS. These arrays are used in the conjugate-gradient computation.

Threads access only the elements they own in the `reduce_recv_start_g` and `reduce_threads_g` shared arrays. For the `reduce_send_len_g` and `exchange_len_g` shared arrays almost all accesses are to remote array elements. The local access ratios for `send_start_g` and `exchange_len_g` vary between threads. For example, for Class B run with 16 threads, threads 0, 5, 10 and 15 only access local array elements and the remaining threads access almost exclusively remote elements.

Figure 1(a) shows the distribution of array element accesses vs. ownership for accesses performed by the CG Benchmark running with Class B input. For thread $i$, we record all the threads that own elements accessed by $i$. We sort the threads in descending order of the frequency of accesses. The bars in the graph show, for each run, how many elements were accessed in one of the other threads, averaged over all threads. For example, when run with 32 threads, about 41% of accesses are local, 19% are to a remote thread (first owner), 19% to a second owner, 12% to a third owner and about 9% to a fourth. This ownership distribution indicates that most of the remote accesses are confined to a small number of remote threads: even when run with 32 threads the majority of remote accesses are to at most 4 unique threads. Almost all benchmarks that we studied exhibit this type of pattern for up to 128 threads. Of the benchmarks we analyzed, IS is the only one that does not exhibit similar behavior. In IS, approximately 40% of remote accesses are to a large number of threads.

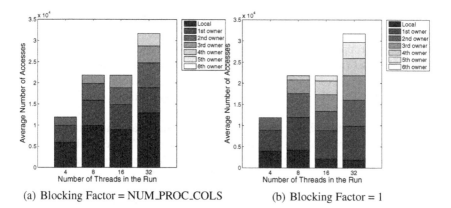

(a) Blocking Factor = NUM_PROC_COLS           (b) Blocking Factor = 1

**Fig. 1.** Threads involved in Remote Accesses for blocking factor of NUM_PROC_COLS and for a blocking factor of 1 in the CG Class B benchmark

**Table 1.** Local accesses as a percentage of total shared accesses as a function of the number of UPC threads and the number of threads per group (TpG)

| Benchmark | UPC Threads | Percentage of Local Shared Accesses | | | | |
|---|---|---|---|---|---|---|
| | | 1 TpG | 2 TpG | 4 TpG | 8 TpG | 16 TpG |
| CG Class B | 4 | 50.2 | 83.4 | - | - | - |
| | 8 | 45.6 | 72.8 | 90.9 | - | - |
| | 16 | 41.1 | 68.3 | 86.4 | 90.9 | - |
| | 32 | 40.8 | 59.5 | 78.2 | 90.6 | 93.8 |
| IS Class S | 2 | 50.0 | - | - | - | - |
| | 4 | 25.1 | 50.0 | - | - | - |
| | 8 | 13.2 | 25.2 | 50.1 | - | - |
| | 16 | 7.6 | 13.7 | 25.7 | 50.5 | - |
| | 32 | 6.2 | 9.3 | 15.2 | 27.1 | 51.4 |
| MG Class S | 2 | 74.8 | - | - | - | - |
| | 4 | 62.2 | 74.8 | - | - | - |
| | 8 | 55.4 | 62.3 | 74.9 | - | - |
| | 16 | 52.3 | 56.0 | 62.3 | 74.9 | - |
| | 32 | 50.6 | 52.9 | 56.1 | 62.5 | 75.0 |
| Sobel Easter (BF 1) | 2 | 26.68 | - | - | - | - |
| | 4 | 23.3 | 60.0 | - | - | - |
| | 8 | 21.7 | 56.7 | 76.7 | - | - |
| | 16 | 20.8 | 55.0 | 73.3 | 85.0 | - |
| | 32 | 20.4 | 54.1 | 71.7 | 81.7 | 89.2 |
| Sobel Easter (Max BF) | 2 | 93.2 | - | - | - | - |
| | 4 | 89.7 | 93.2 | - | - | - |
| | 8 | 87.7 | 89.7 | 93.2 | - | - |
| | 16 | 86.2 | 87.7 | 89.7 | 93.2 | - |
| | 32 | 84.3 | 86.2 | 87.7 | 89.7 | 93.2 |

Table 1 shows the number of local accesses as a percentage of the total number of shared accesses for each benchmark run with the number of threads and the number of threads per group (TpG) specified. In most of these benchmarks, a large number of accesses are local (more than 40%) even when there is a single thread in each thread group. From these accesses, the ones in CG, MG and Sobel are mostly easily detected by the compiler. Therefore, they can be privatized to avoid the overhead of translation through the SVD.

The results in Table 1 indicate that as the benchmarks are run with more threads per group, the percentage of local shared accesses increases. These results highlight the benefit of running UPC programs on architectures that have multiple processors in each share-memory domain. For the CG and Sobel benchmarks, an overwhelming majority (more than 90%) of the accesses become local when run with a thread group consisting of 50% of the running threads. Even the IS benchmark, which exhibits irregular shared-access patterns improves significantly as the size of the thread groups is increased. In the case the compiler fails to identify and privatize these additional local accesses, the performance will still improve because it is not necessary to send messages between the accessing thread and the owning thread in order to exchange shared data.

## 3.2   Remote Data Access Patterns

An important factor in deciding the mapping of threads to processors in a hybrid architecture is the access patterns to remote data. This pattern depends on the algorithm used for solving the problem. Here we present evidence that, for a number of algorithms used in scientific computations, regular access patterns indeed appear and these patterns are amenable to optimization.

In Figure 2 we capture the actual pattern of data exchange between threads for the CG Benchmark running the class B input. We assume the threads are cyclically distributed and we compute the *distance* between two threads as the number of threads separating them in a ring distribution (thread 0 comes after thread N-1). A distance of zero represents accesses to local data. In these error-bar plots the circles are the average number of accesses to a remote thread. The error bars are the standard deviations. For the 32-way CG, we know, from Figure 1(a), that most remote accesses occur to four other threads. In this figure, we observe that those threads are actually the immediate neighbors, that is, the threads at distances -2, -1, 1, and 2. Most of the other benchmarks show a similar behavior, except for IS, where the remote accesses are relatively uniformly spread throughout all threads. This pattern of communicating with a small number of threads increases the opportunities to, with a good thread/processor mapping, privatize local shared data accesses in hybrid architectures.

The different access distribution in IS (integer sorting) occurs because each thread owns a set of buckets and a random set of keys that need to be sorted. The behavior of the IS benchmark class S with 2 to 128 threads is shown in Figure 3.

The scatter plot in Figure 4(a) displays the distribution of local and remote accesses performed by each thread in the CG benchmark running with 16 threads and with class B input. The size of each point is proportional to the number of accesses performed by the accessing thread to shared array elements that are mapped to the owner thread. The colors highlight the local accesses.

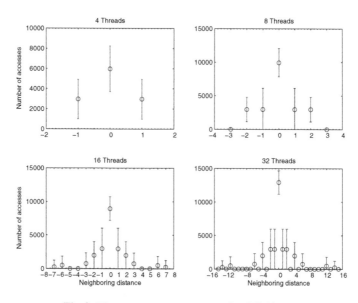

**Fig. 2.** Distance to remote accesses for CG Class B

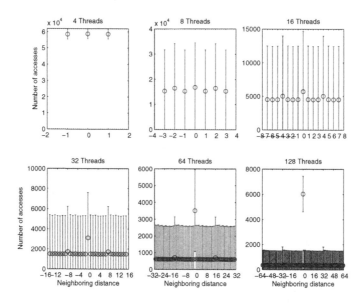

**Fig. 3.** Distance to remote accesses for IS Class S

Figure 4(a) shows that when a blocking factor of NUM_PROC_COLS is used the majority of shared memory accesses are clustered along the diagonal. Every access on the diagonal is a local access (accessing thread equals the owning thread) while accesses near the diagonal indicate the accessing and owning threads are in close proximity to each other (in terms of thread distance). This observation provides strong support for

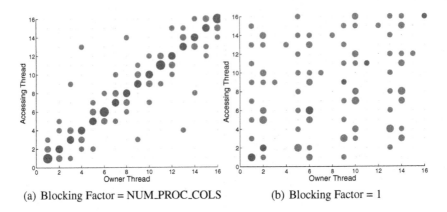

(a) Blocking Factor = NUM_PROC_COLS          (b) Blocking Factor = 1

**Fig. 4.** Distribution of shared accesses for blocking factor of NUM_PROC_COLS and for a blocking factor of 1 in the CG Class B benchmark running with 16 threads. The darker markers on the diagonal are local accesses, while the lighter colored markers are remote accesses. The size of the marker denotes the number of accesses, the larger, the more accesses.

running the benchmark on a hybrid machine where threads are mapped to thread groups based on their distance from each other. For example, on a hybrid machine with thread groups of size four, threads 0 through 3 are mapped to one node, threads 4 through 7 are mapped to a second node, *etc.,*.

### 3.3    Effects of Blocking Factor

To illustrate the effect the blocking factor, the CG benchmark was modified to create the `reduce_threads_g`, `reduce_send_start_g`, `reduce_send_len_g`, and `reduce_recv_start_g` arrays with a blocking factor of 1. Figure 1(b) shows the number of unique threads involved in remote accesses while the scatter plot in Figure 4(b) shows the distribution of local and remote accesses. These figures emphasize the importance of using an adequate blocking factor to increase the number of shared accesses that are local and thus candidates for privatization. When compared with the plot in Figure 4(a), we see the selection of blocking factor is even more important for hybrid architectures.

In the NAS MG Benchmark, we observed a high percentage of remote accesses for the two shared arrays `sh_u` and `sh_r`. These two shared arrays contain the original and residual matrices used in the multigrid computation. They are relatively small arrays (for class S their size is 6*THREADS) and they are distributed using a blocking factor of 6. Figure 5(a) shows the index frequency histogram for the `sh_u` array when run with input class S on 4 threads. The height of the bars indicate the number of accesses to a specific index. The colors denote the ownership of the shared data being accessed. From this histogram we see that the majority of accesses are to indices 20, 21, 22 and 23. However, because a blocking factor of 6 was used to distribute the array, all of these indices map to thread 3. When run with the original blocking factor there were approximately 12.5% local accesses to `sh_u`. By manually modifying the source code

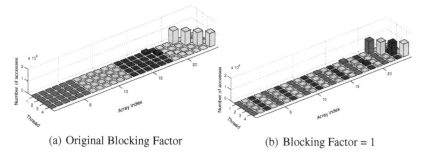

(a) Original Blocking Factor          (b) Blocking Factor = 1

**Fig. 5.** MG class S array access index frequency using original blocking factor. Color denotes ownership.

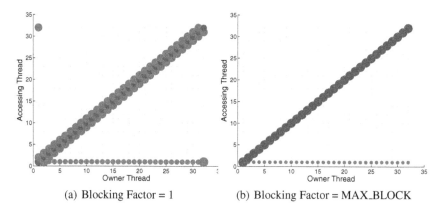

(a) Blocking Factor = 1          (b) Blocking Factor = MAX_BLOCK

**Fig. 6.** Distribution of shared accesses for blocking factor of 1 and blocking factor of MAX_BLOCK = (ROWS*COLUMNS)/THREADS for the Sobel benchmark running with 32 threads

to use the default blocking factor of 1, the number of local accesses increased to 99.4%. The index frequency histogram using a blocking factor of 1 is shown in Figure 5(b).

Figure 6 illustrates the effect of different blocking factors on the Sobel benchmark. The Sobel benchmark performs a stencil computation where the eight neighbors of an array element are used to compute a new value. Thus choosing the largest possible blocking factor, such that the eight neighbours of a give array element are local (for most array elements) proves to be the best strategy.

## 4   Related Work

This is the first performance study to provide an empirical measurement of the distribution of thread ownership of the accesses performed by each thread in UPC benchmarks. This data allows the community to both identify the opportunities for optimization of data accesses in UPC and to estimate the potential gains that such optimizations may yield.

Several research groups have investigated the performance of UPC and compared with other languages. El-Ghazawi and Cantonnet found that both the Compaq UPC 1.7 Compiler on the Compaq AlphaServer SC produced code that was slower than, but competitive with, the code produced for MPI versions of the NAS parallel benchmarks [17]. In their study the UPC codes were modified by hand to convert all local shared accesses into private accesses.

The performance study by Cantonnet *et al.* provides strong support to improving the code generation for local shared accesses in UPC[8]. Not only did they measure the high overhead of such accesses in current compilers, they also demonstrated, through hand-optimization, that significant performance gains can be obtained by privatizing such accesses. By manually privatizing local shared accesses and prefetching remote data in the Sobel Edge Detection benchmark they were able to obtain nine times speedup for a 2048×2048 image and results showing very-high parallel efficiency with speedup almost linear on the number of processors. In cluster architectures formed by many multiprocessor nodes the potential for improvement in performance may be even higher than these experiments indicate. Similarly Chen *et al.* found that if local shared accesses were privatized in the Berkeley UPC compiler, a simple vector addition application would see an order of magnitude speedup [11].

Berlin *et al.* compared the time required for a private local access and for a shared local access [6]. The smallest difference between these two accesses was in the SGI Origin 2000 (the private access was 7.4 times faster). In a 64-node Compaq AlphaServer cluster with four ES-40 processors per node with an earlier version of the Compaq UPC compiler, they found that a private access was 580 times faster than a local shared access in the same processor, and was 7200 times faster than a shared access to an address mapped to another processor in the same node. Later versions of that compiler have reduced this overhead, but these staggering numbers speak to the need to improve the identification and privatization of local-shared accesses.

In a comparative study between UPC and Co-array Fortran, Coarfa *et al.* found that in both languages, bulk communication is essential to deliver significant speedup for the NAS benchmarks [12]. They also point out that references to the local part of shared array through shared pointers is a source of inefficiency in UPC. They suggest that the way to work around this inefficiency is for UPC programmers to use private C pointers to access the local part of shared objects. We propose a more elegant two-pronged solution: (1) an optimizing UPC compiler may modify the blocking factor to improve the number of local accesses for a given machine configuration; and (2) the compiler should automatically convert shared accesses to the local part of a shared array into private local accesses.

The analysis required for the privatization of local shared accesses finds parallel in the analysis of array accesses in loop nests in the modified version of Parascope by Dwarkadas *et al.* [16]. Their goal is to inform the runtime system that it does not need to detect accesses to shared data. Their compiler-time analysis allows the runtime system to prepare for the shared accesses ahead of time. In UPC the analysis will be able to simply replace the shared access with a simple pointer-based access.

Zhang and Seidel developed the UPC STREAM benchmark [23]. Their experimental study also found the overhead of accessing local sections of a shared array through shared accesses to be significant. They also report on an empirical comparison between an implementation of UPC over MPI and Pthreads from Michigan Technological University, the first commercial UPC compiler from Hewlett-Packard, and the Berkeley UPC compiler.

Zhang and Seidel propose a model to predict the runtime performance of UPC programs [24]. Their technique uses dependence analysis to identify four types of shared memory access patterns and predict the frequency of each pattern. Microbenchmarks are used to determine the cost of each pattern on various architectures. Their results demonstrate their model is able to predict execution times within 15% of actual running times for three application benchmarks.

The issue of identifying shared accesses that are local arises in UPC because of a language design decision that makes the physical location of the memory referenced transparent to the programmer. Other languages, such as Co-Array Fortran [20] expose the distinction between local and remote accesses at the language level and thus they compilers do not have to deal with the privatization of local shared accesses.

Barton *et al.* describe a highly scalable runtime system based on the design of a shared variable directory [5]. They also describe the optimization of the upc_forall loop, local memory accesses, and remote update operations implemented in the IBM XL UPC Compiler [14].

Intel has recently announced Cluster OpenMP that support OpenMP programs running on a cluster of workstations [18]. A licensed version of TreadMarks [2] is used for the runtime system to manage the movement of shared data between nodes. The OpenMP specification has been extended to include the *sharable* directive, used to identify variables shared among threads. A sharable equivalent to malloc has also been added to support dynamic shared data.

A mixed-mode programming model for hybrid architectures has been explored by several groups. In this mixed-mode model, MPI is used to communicate between nodes while OpenMP is used to parallelize work within a node. Smith and Bull conclude that this mixed-mode programming model is well suited for some applications but warn it is not the best solution for all parallel programming problems [21]. A programmer should understand the nature of the application (load balancing characteristics, parallel granularity, memory limitations from data replication and general MPI performance) before attempting to use the mixed-mode model.

## 5  Conclusions

We started this detailed study of data access patterns in UPC from the premise that understanding these patterns will allow us to estimate the potential of several compiler optimizations. Indeed, we find that the number of local accesses that are identifiable by the compiler is quite high in the set of benchmarks that we studied. Privatizing these accesses automatically will remove a significant source of overhead while keeping the code portable and simple to understand.

In addition, we observed that, contrary to the intuition that the largest blocking factor is always better for improving locality, there are cases in which a blocking factor selected based on the access pattern provides more benefit. We are working on a solution to the problem of finding the best blocking factor for an application.

And finally, we have shown that even considering a naive mapping of threads to processors in a hybrid architecture, there is tremendous potential to increase the performance of applications because of better data locality. We are confident that through a combination of compiler and runtime optimization the performance of PGAS languages such as UPC can be on-par with traditional high performance MPI+OpenMP codes. At the same time, PGAS programming models are a more elegant solution to the problem of programming hybrid architectures when compared with mixed programming models, such as combinations of MPI with OpenMP.

# References

1. Sobel - wikipedia, the free encyclopedia. http://en.wikipedia.org/wiki/Sobel.
2. Christina Amza, Alan L. Cox, Sandhya Dwarkadas, Pete Keleher, Honghui Lu, Ramakrishnan Rajamony, Weimin Yu, and Willy Zwaenepoel. TreadMarks: Shared memory computing on networks of workstations. *IEEE Computer*, 29(2):18–28, 1996.
3. D. Bailey, E. Barszcz, J. Barton, D. Browning, R. Carter, L. Dagum, R.Fatoohi, S. Fineberg, P. Frederickson, T. Lasinski, R. Schreiber, H. Simon, V Venkatakrishnan, and S. Weeratunga. The NAS parallel benchmarks. Technical Report RNR-94-007, NASA Ames Research Center, March 1994.
4. David Bailey, Tim Harris, William Saphir, Rob van der Wijngaart, Alex Woo, and Maurice Yarrow. The NAS parallel benchmarks 2.0. Technical Report NAS-95-020, NASA Ames Research Center, December 1995.
5. Christopher Barton, Calin Cascaval, George Almasi, Yili Zhang, Montse Farreras, Siddhartha Chatterjee, and José Nelson Amaral. Shared memory programming for large scale machines. In *Programming Language Design and Implementation (PLDI)*, pages 108–117, June 2006.
6. Konstantin Berlin, Jun Huan, Mary Jacob, Garima Kochbar, Jan Prins, Bill Pugh, P. Sadayappan, Jaime Spacco, and Chau-Wen Tseng. Evaluating the impact of programming language features on the performance of parallel applications on cluster architectures. In *The 16th International Workshop on Languages and Compilers for Parallel Computing (LCPC 2003)*, Texas, USA, October 2003.
7. Dan Bonachea. GASNet specification, v1.1. Technical Report CSD-02-1207, U.C. Berkeley, November 2002.
8. François Cantonnet, Yiyi Yao, Smita Annareddy, Ahmed S. Mohamed, and Tarek A. El-Ghazawi. Performance monitoring and evaluation of a UPC implementation on a NUMA architecture. In *International Parallel and Distributed Processing Symposium (IPDPS)*, page 274, Nice, France, April 2003.
9. Franck Cappello and Daniel Etiemble. MPI versus MPI+OpenMP on the IBM SP for the NAS benchmarks. In *ACM/IEEE Supercomputing*, November 2000.
10. Calin Cascaval, Evelyn Duesterwald, Peter F. Sweeney, and Robert W. Wisniewski. Performance and environment monitoring for continuous program optimization. *IBM Journal of Research and Development*, 50(2/3), March 2006.
11. Wei-Yu Chen, Dan Bonachea, Jason Duell, Parry Husbands, Costin Iancu, and Katherine Yelick. A performance analysis of the Berkeley UPC compiler. In *Proceedings of the 17th Annual International Conference on Supercomputing (ICS'03)*, June 2003.
12. Cristian Coarfa, Yuri Dotsenko, John Mellor-Crummey, François Cantonnet, Tarek El-Ghazawi, Ashrujit Mohanti, Yiyi Yao, and Daniel Chavarría-Miranda. An evaluation of global address space languages: Co-Array Fortran and Unified Parallel C. In *Symposium on Principles and Practice of Parallel Programming(PPoPP)*, pages 36–47, Chicago, IL, June 2005.

13. UPC Consortium. *UPC Language Specification, V1.2*, May 2005.
14. IBM Corporation. IBM XL UPC compilers. `http://www.alphaworks.ibm.com/tech/upccompiler`, November 2005.
15. J.J. Costa, Tony Cortes, Xavier Martorell, Eduard Ayguadé, and Jesús Labarta. Running OpenMP applications efficiently on an everything-shared SDSM. *Journal of Parallel and Distributed Computing*, 66:647 – 658, September 2005.
16. Sandhya Dwarkadas, Alan L. Cox, and Willy Zwaenepoel. An integrated compile-time/run-time software distributed shared memory system. In *Architectural Support for Programming Languages and Operating Systems*, pages 186–197, Cambridge, MA, 1996.
17. Tarek El-Ghazawi and François Cantonnet. UPC performance and potential: a NPB experimental study. In *Proceedings of the 2002 ACM/IEEE conference on Supercomputing (SC'02)*, pages 1–26, Baltimore, Maryland, USA, November 2002.
18. Jay P. Hoeflinger. Extending OpenMP to clusters. 2006. `http://www.intel.com/cd/software/products/asmo-na/eng/compilers/285865.htm`.
19. Pete Keleher. *Distributed Shared Memory Using Lazy Release Consistency*. PhD thesis, Rice University, December 1994.
20. Robert W. Numrich and John Reid. Co-array fortran for parallel programming. *ACM SIGPLAN Fortran Forum*, 17(2):1–31, August 1998.
21. Lorna Smith and Mark Bull. Development of mixed mode mpi / openmp applications. *Scientific Programming*, 9(2-3/2001):83–98. Presented at Workshop on OpenMP Applications and Tools (WOMPAT 2000), San Diego, Calif., July 6-7, 2000.
22. Robert W. Wisniewski, Peter F. Sweeney, Kertik Sudeep, Matthias Hauswirth, Evelyn Duesterwald, Călin Caşcaval, and Reza Azimi. Performance and environment monitoring for whole-system characterization and optimization. In *PAC2 - Power Performance equals Architecture x Circuits x Compilers*, pages 15–24, Yorktown Heights, NY, October 6-8 2004.
23. Zhang Zhang and Steven Seidel. Benchmark measurements of current UPC platforms. In *International Parallel and Distributed Processing Symposium (IPDPS)*, Denver, CO, April 2005.
24. Zhang Zhang and Steven Seidel. A performance model for fine-grain accesses in UPC. In *International Parallel and Distributed Processing Symposium (IPDPS)*, Rhodes Island, Greece, April 2006.

# Exploiting Speculative Thread-Level Parallelism in Data Compression Applications

Shengyue Wang, Antonia Zhai, and Pen-Chung Yew

Department of Computer Science and Engineering
University of Minnesota
Minneapolis, MN 55455, USA
{shengyue, zhai, yew}@cs.umn.edu

**Abstract.** Although hardware support for Thread-Level Speculation (TLS) can ease the compiler's tasks in creating parallel programs by allowing the compiler to create potentially dependent parallel threads, advanced compiler optimization techniques must be developed and judiciously applied to achieve the desired performance. In this paper, we take a close examination on two data compression benchmarks, GZIP and BZIP2, propose, implement and evaluate new compiler optimization techniques to eliminate performance bottlenecks in their parallel execution and improve their performance. The proposed techniques (i) remove the critical forwarding path created by synchronizing memory-resident values; (ii) identify and categorize reduction-like variables whose intermediate results are used within loops, and propose code transformation to remove the inter-thread data dependences caused by these variables; and (iii) transform the program to eliminate stalls caused by variations in thread size. While no previous work has reported significant performance improvement on parallelizing these two benchmarks, we are able to achieve up to 36% performance improvement for GZIP and 37% for BZIP2.

## 1 Introduction

Chip Multiprocessors (CMP) have become nearly commonplace [17, 14, 2, 32]. It is relatively straightforward for explicitly multithreaded workloads to benefit from the increasing computing resources, but how would sequential programs take advantage of such resources? One natural way to speedup a sequential program is to exploit parallelism to utilize multiple processing units. Traditionally, compilers create parallel programs by identifying *independent* threads [4, 13, 33]—but this is extremely difficult, if not impossible, for many general purpose programs due to their complex data structures and control flow, as well as their use of ambiguous pointers. One promising alternative to overcome this problem is *Thread-Level Speculation* (**TLS**), which allows the compiler to create parallel threads without insisting on their independence. The underlying hardware ensures that inter-thread dependences through memory are satisfied, and re-executes any thread for which they are not. Unfortunately, despite numerous proposals on efficient hardware support [19, 1, 10, 7, 9, 29, 11, 12, 20, 24, 25, 31, 34] and compiler optimizations [39, 40, 38, 22], only moderate performance improvements have been reported from parallelizing general purpose programs. This calls for the development of

G. Almási, C. Caşcaval, and P. Wu (Eds.): LCPC 2006, LNCS 4382, pp. 126–140, 2007.

more aggressive compiler optimizations that take full advantage of profiling information to perform novel program transformations.

In this paper, we focus on one important class of general purpose applications, data compression, for which most of the previously proposed techniques are unable to claim significant performance improvement. Starting with a parallelized and optimized version of BZIP2 and GZIP—the parallel loop selection and value communication optimization algorithms are described in our previous work [39, 40, 38], we carefully studied the program behaviors. Three performance bottlenecks are identified and the corresponding optimization techniques are proposed.

1. The first performance bottleneck that we observed is the critical forwarding path introduced by forwarding *memory*-resident values between threads. In our previous work [40], we have demonstrated the importance of forwarding values between speculative threads to statisfy inter-thread data dependence of *memory*-resident values and to avoid speculation failure. However, the critical forwarding path introduced by such synchronization can serialize paralle threads. In our previous work, we have proposed a compiler optimization technique to address a similar issue—reducing the critical forwarding path introduced by communicating *register*-resident values. In this paper, we apply the same instruction scheduling technique to reduce the critical forwarding path introduced by communicating *memory*-resident values. We observe that, to reduce the critical forwarding path of a *memory*-resident value, instructions *must* be scheduled aggressively—across both control and data dependences to achieve performance improvement. On the contrary, in the case of *register*-resident value, conservative instruction scheduling provides most of the performance benefit. Details are described in Section 3.1.
2. The second performance bottleneck is also due to inter-thread value communication. This bottleneck is caused by a class of reduction-like variables: where the variable is defined in the loop body through reduction operations, but there also exist *use*s of the intermediate result of this variable, thus it is impossible to apply traditional reduction optimizations [18] to eliminate the inter-thread data dependence. We propose an aggressive speculative reduction transformation to reduce the critical forwarding path caused by reduction-like variables. Details of this technique is described in Section 3.2.
3. The third performance bottleneck is caused to complex control flow—threads can take any execution path through an iteration, and thus vary in execution time. In the example shown in Figure 1(a), there are 8 parallel threads with the following execution order $T1, T2, T3, T4, T5, T6, T7$, and $T8$. The size of long threads $T1, T4, T7$, and $T8$ contains thousands of dynamic instructions and short threads $T2, T3, T5$, and $T6$ contain only a few instructions. Assuming 4 threads are executed in parallel, little parallel overlap is possible. One way to get parallel overlap is to merge short threads with long threads and execute consecutive long threads in parallel, as shown in Figure 1(b). Unfortunately, it is impossible to statically determine the number of iterations to merge since thread sizes are not known until runtime. We propose a program transformation to *dynamically* merge multiple short threads with a long thread. The details are described in Section 3.3.

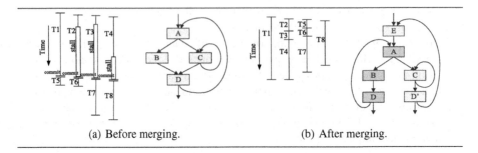

(a) Before merging.                    (b) After merging.

**Fig. 1.** Iteration merging

## 1.1 The TLS Execution Model

In TLS, the compiler partitions a program into parallel speculative threads without having to prove that they are independent, while at runtime the underlying hardware checks whether inter-thread data dependences are preserved and re-executes any thread for which they are not. This TLS execution model allows the parallelization of programs that were previously non-parallelizable as demonstrated by the following example.

In this paper, we will only experiment with parallel threads that are created by executing multiple iterations of the same loop simultaneously . However, we expect the techniques developed for improving value communication applicable to other parallel threads. The most straightforward way to parallelize a loop is to execute multiple iterations of the same loop in parallel. With TLS, loops with potential loop-carried data dependences are speculatively parallelized. A thread is allowed to commit if no inter-thread data dependence is violated. In case of a data dependence violation, the thread that contains the consumer instruction is re-executed.

**Inter-Thread Value Communication in TLS.** From the compiler's perspective, TLS supports two forms of communication and the compiler can decide which mechanism is appropriate for a particular data dependence to obtain maximum parallel overlap:

**Synchronization.** explicitly forwards a value between the source and the destination of a data dependence. It allows for partial parallel overlap and is thus suitable for frequently occurring data dependences that can be clearly identified. However, if the instructions that compute the communicating value are sparsely located in a thread, explicit synchronization could also limit performance by stalling the consumer threads more than necessary.

**Speculation.** relies on the underlying hardware to detect data dependence violations at runtime and trigger re-execution when necessary. It allows for maximum parallel overlap when speculation always succeeds, however, if speculation always fails, this mechanism would introduce a significant performance penalty. Thus, this form of value communication is suitable for data dependences that are difficult to analyze and occur rarely.

## 1.2   Related Work

Researchers have developed various compiler [39,40,6,16,8,22] and manual [26,27] optimization techniques to fully utilize the hardware support for TLS to parallelize general purpose applications. This paper extends our previous work on improving inter-thread value communication [39,40] and integrates the recover code generation mechanism to enable both inter-thread and intra-thread speculation to avoid processor stalls caused by data dependences from memory-resident values.

Existing research in parallel compilers has mainly focused on two critical performance problems: how to divide a sequential program into parallel threads [3,8,16,37, 38,22] and how to improve inter-thread value communication [21,28,35,36,39,40, 12,41,22]. These compiler optimization techniques typically start by building a probabilistic model of speculative execution first, and then estimating the amount of parallel overlap that can be achieved. However, few recognized that in real applications dependences are often inter-related and intelligent code transformations could be used to speculate on predictable dependence patterns for performance gain.

Prabhu *et al.* [26,27] have developed several advanced *manual* code transformations to improve the performance of TLS, and they expect the programmers to apply these techniques. Although some of the techniques described by Prabhu *et al.* resemble the techniques in this paper at a first glance; detailed examinations reveal significant differences: (i) both papers have observed that reduction variables can serialize program execution, but Prabhu *et al.* only applied traditional reduction variable elimination technique to remove them, while we studied the existence of a large class of reduction-like variables with complex usage patterns and develop new code transformations to prevent them from serializing execution; (ii) although both paper has proposed techniques to balance the workload that are assigned to each thread, our iteration merging technique is proposed in the context of automatic compilation and thus can be integrated in an optimizing compiler.

## 2   Compression Algorithms

The compression applications are commonly used general-purpose applications. TLS typically achieves modest speedup for those applications. In order to gain insight on the performance bottleneck and exploit more potential speculative TLP, we select two compression benchmarks BZIP2 and GZIP from SPEC2000 benchmark suite for an extensive study.

**BZIP2.** BZIP2 [5] represents one class of compression applications that uses a block-based algorithm. It divides the input data into blocks of the size $N$ ranging from 100k to 900k bytes, and processes the blocks sequentially. While it is possible to process different blocks in parallel, the huge size of the speculative data modified by each thread often exceeds the capacity of speculative buffer provided by TLS, which is typically from 16k to 32k bytes. The frequent stalls due to the buffer overflow inhibit most of the performance gains from TLS.

During the compression of each block $S$ of size $N$, the most time consuming part is Burrows-Wheeler Transform (BWT). It forms $N$ rotations of a block by cyclically shift

$S$, and sorts these rotations lexicographically. Bucket sort is used in the main sorting phase. The buckets are organized as a two-level hierarchical structure. The big bucket in the outer level contains all rotations starting with the same character, while the small bucket in the inner level contains all rotations starting with the same two characters.

Consequently, a two-level nested loop is used to traverse each bucket to sort all rotations inside. The outer loop seems an ideal target for parallel execution since sorting of big buckets can be done independently. However, in order to speedup the sequential algorithm, the information about the sorting of the current bucket is kept in the global data structures such as *quadrant* and used in the sorting of following buckets to avoid redundant computations. Also, the results of sorting the current big bucket are used to update other unsorted buckets. As a result, those optimizations for sequential algorithm introduces inter-thread dependences that are undesirable for parallel execution. On the other hand, the performance of the inner loop is mainly limited by the reduction-like variable *workDone*. Reduction elimination cannot be applied here since *workDone* is also used somewhere in the loop besides the reduction operations. The sorting of each small bucket is done by calling *qSort*. Since *qSort* is not always called in every inner loop iteration, it introduces unbalanced load among threads.

The compression algorithm also include other phases such as run-length encoding, move-to-front encoding, and Huffman encoding. The performance of the main loops in those phases are typically limited by long critical forwarding paths that are hard to optimize.

The decompression phase in BZIP2 has much lower coverage than in the compression phase. Similar to compression, decompression is performed for one block at a time. Decompression of multiple blocks cannot run in parallel due to the size limitation of the speculative buffer. Most loops in the decompression phase is sequential due to the fact that the decoding of a character is completely dependent on the previous characters.

**GZIP.** GZIP [42] represents another class of compression applications that uses a dictionary-based algorithm. The input data is scanned sequentially, once a repeated string is detected, it is replaced by a pointer to the previous string. A hash table is used for detecting a repeated string. All input strings of length three are inserted in the hash table.

Two versions of the algorithm are implemented. *Deflate_fast* is a simplified version, which is fast but with low compression ratio. The main loop iterates through all input characters. Each time a match is found, it is selected immediately. The main performance limitation is caused by the use of global variables such as *lookahead* and *strstart*. *Deflate*, a more complex and time consuming version, uses a technique called lazy evaluation in order to find a longer match. With lazy evaluation, the match is not selected immediately. Instead, it is kept and compared with the matches for the next input string for a better choice. However, the use of current match in the next matching step causes additional data dependences. Both *deflate* and *deflate_fast* call *longest_match* to find the longest match among all string with the same hash index. The average iteration size of the main loop is typically small due to the facts that most of strings do not match with the current string and a fast check is used to avoid unnecessary comparison.

Similar to BZIP2, the decompression phase in GZIP has a much lower coverage than in the compression phase. The decompression is performed sequentially since the decoding of the current character depends on the characters decoded previously. As a result, it is hard to extract TLP in the decompression phase.

## 3   TLS Optimizations

For both BZIP2 and GZIP, the main hurdle to create efficient parallel programs under TLS is data and control dependences. In this session, we propose several compiler optimization techniques to overcome these limitations.

### 3.1   Speculative Scheduling for Memory-Resident Value Communication

In order to avoid excessive failures under TLS, synchronizations are required for frequently occurring *memory* dependences. While scheduling for *register*-resident value communication has been shown effective for many benchmarks [39], the benefit of scheduling for *memory*-resident value communication is still unknown. Due to the facts that *memory* dependences are prevalent in both BZIP2 and GZIP, it is important to investigate the performance impact of scheduling techniques for *memory*-resident value. Unlike the scheduling for *register*-resident value, the scheduling of *memory*-resident value may interact with the underlying TLS support. The details of how scheduling and TLS work together need a closer examination.

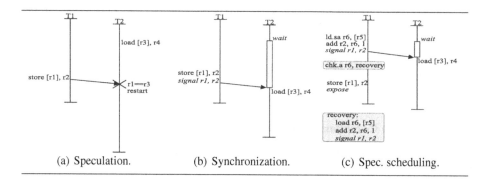

(a) Speculation.          (b) Synchronization.          (c) Spec. scheduling.

**Fig. 2.** Scheduling for memory-resident value communication

Figure 2(a) shows two threads T1 and T2 with a frequently occurring dependence between *store* and *load*. To avoid mis-speculation, synchronization is used to delay the execution of *load* until *store* finishes its execution, as shown in Figure 2(b). A *signal* instruction is inserted after *store* to explicitly forward both the address (stored in register *r1*) and the value (stored in register *r2*) to T2.

In order to reduce the waiting time of *load*, speculative scheduling is applied so that both the address (stored in register *r1*) and the value (stored in register *r2*) of *store* are computed earlier. Control and data speculation are used to overcome the dependence limitation during aggressive scheduling, and recovery code needs to be generated for possible mis-speculation as well. In our study, we support both control and data speculation similar to those on IA-64 architecture [15]. As shown in Figure 2(c), in order to compute the value of *r2* earlier, the instructions it depends on have to be scheduled. If *load r6, [r5]* in the dependence chain is scheduled across an aliasing store, it will be changed into a data speculative load (*ld.a*). If it crosses a branch, it will be changed into a control speculative load (*ld.s*). In this example, *ld.sa* is used for both data and control speculation. A check instruction *chk.a* is inserted to the home location of the speculatively scheduled load to detect possible mis-speculations. In case of a mis-speculation, the corresponding recovery code is invoked to re-compute and re-forward the value, as shown in Figure 2(c). When instructions are speculatively scheduled across a branch, a signal with NULL address is inserted to the alternative path. Execution of such signal indicates that a wrong signal from the other path has already been forwarded.

The consumer thread keeps both addresses and values in a special forwarding buffer. It is accessed by each exposed load that is not proceeded by a store to the same location in the same thread. If the address matches, the value will be used. When the consumer thread receives the same signal *twice*, it indicates a mis-speculation is detected by the producer thread, and either the address or value has been wrongly forwarded. The old address and value are replaced by the new ones. The consumer thread has to be squashed if the old value has already been consumed.

The data stored in the forwarding buffer will not be checked for inter-thread dependence violation. In Figure 2(c), if there is another store instruction *store 1* between *signal* and *store*, and it accesses the same address as *store*, it will not cause an inter-thread dependence violation since the forwarded data is invisible to *store 1*. However, if another store instruction *store 2* after *store* accesses the same address, an inter-thread dependence violation should be detected since *store 2* produces a newer value that should be used by *load*. For this purpose, we insert a new instruction *expose* immediately after *store* to inform the consumer thread to make the forwarded data exposed for the dependence checking.

## 3.2   Aggressive Reduction Transformation

A reduction operation iteratively summarizes information into a single variable called the reduction variable. The presence of reduction variables causes inter-thread dependences, and serializes parallel execution. Such serialization can become performance bottlenecks when nested loops are involved. The example in Figure 3(a)-i shows a reduction variable *sum* defined in a nested loop. During the parallel execution of the outer loop, in thread $i$, the definition in the last iteration of the inner loop is used by thread $i+1$ in the first iteration of the inner loop. This creates an inter-thread data dependence that must be synchronized as shown in Figure 3(a)-ii. However, such synchronization can potentially serialize parallel execution.

In traditional parallelizing compilers [18], reduction variables are eliminated through a process in which multiple independent variables are created and store in an array as shown in Figure 3(a)-iii. Because each thread stores reduction variable in a different location, inter-thread data dependences are eliminated, thus the threads can be parallelized. The final result of the reduction operation is computed after parallel execution ends.

Although reduction elimination is effective in removing inter-thread dependences, the application of this technique is limited due to one important constraint—intermediate results of the reduction operation cannot be used anywhere in the parallelized loop. In the example shown in Figure 3(b)-i, the intermediate result of the reduction variable $sum$ is used in the outer loop. In order to retrieve the intermediate result, the reduction valuable must be communicated between the parallel threads. Fortunately, we can perform partial reduction elimination and update the value of $sum$ only once in the outer loop, as shown in Figure 3(b)-ii, where all uses of the reduction variable $sum$ in the outer loop is replaced with $sum + sum[i]$. Although the reduction variable is not eliminated, its impact on the parallel performance is greatly reduced, as we can see that the distance between the update of $sum$ in a thread and use of it in the successor thread becomes relatively small. Another benefit of this transformation is that the summation step can be eliminated. Under TLS, because all local scalars are thread-private, we can avoid the creation of the array $sum[]$ and use a scalar to hold the partial results of the reduction operation, as shown in Figure 3(b)-iii. Just like any other values that are communicated through synchronization, the critical forwarding path of this communication can be reduced with instruction scheduling.

Unfortunately, not all usage patterns of reduction variables can be optimized as described above. In the example shown in Figure 3(c)-i, the *signal* instruction cannot be scheduled before the inner loop because it depends on the value of $sum0$ which is computed by the inner loop; and *wait* instruction cannot be scheduled after the inner loop, because it is used to guard a branch instruction. As a result, the critical forwarding path introduced by the reduction variable is very long. Fortunately, the outcome of the branch instruction guarded by the reduction variable is often predictable; and we can exploit this predictability to postpone the use of the reduction variable till after the completion of the inner loop. In the example shown in Figure 3(b)-ii, the branch is predicted as not-taken; moved across the inner loop and executed as a verification. In the original location of this branch, both $sum0$ and $x$ are saved, so that they can be used later in the verification. The use of $sum$ is delayed so that the critical forwarding path is reduced. When the value of $sum$ becomes available, and the branch is proved to be mis-predicted, the thread must be squashed and an un-optimized version of code must be executed [30]. The squash/recovery mechanism that enables this aggressive optimization is already available in TLS, thus no extra hardware support is needed.

However, this aggressive transformation does not handle all usage patterns of $sum$ within the loop: the reduction variable can be used in the inner loop, as shown in Figure 3(c)-iii. In order to reduce the critical forwarding path introduced by such usage, the branch in the inner loop has to be moved to the outer loop. Is it possible to make such a code transformation and to guarantee that all mis-predictions are detected? The answer is yes, and the key to this transformation is that most reduction operations are monotonic. If the reduction variable is monotonically increasing or decreasing and the branch is to test whether it is greater or less than a certain loop invariant, the verification can be delayed till after the inner loop is complete. In our example, if the condition $sum + sum0 > 100$ is true in the inner loop, it must also be true for the test in the outer loop. Mis-predictions can always be detected by the delayed verification in the outer loop.

```
while (cond1) {              while (cond1) {              while (cond1) {
    while (cond2) {              wait (sum);                  while (cond2) {
        sum++;                   while (cond2) {                  sum[i]++;
    }                                sum++;                   }
}                                }                            }
(i)A reduction variable          signal (sum);            while (cond1) {
                             }                                sum+=sum[i];
                             (ii)Synchronizing the        }
                             reduction variable           (iii)Traditional
                                                          reduction elimination
```

(a) Reduction elimination.

```
                         while (cond1) {              while (cond1) {
                             while (cond2) {              while (cond2) {
while (cond1) {                  sum[i]++;                   sum0++;
    while (cond2) {          }                            }
        sum++;               ...                          ...
    }                        wait (sum);                  wait (sum);
    ...                      =sum+sum[i];                 =sum+sum0;
    =sum;                    ...                          ...
    ...                      sum+=sum[i];                 sum+=sum0;
} (i)Using intermediate      signal (sum);                signal (sum);
result of reduction      }                            }
variable                 (ii)Reduction transformation (iii)Replace sum[]
                         with explicit forwarding     with sum0
```

(b) Reduction-like variable with a single use and short critical forwarding path.

```
                     while (cond1) {
while (cond1) {          sum0'=sum0;                                          while (cond1) {
    wait (sum);          x'=x;               while (cond1) {                      while (cond2) {
    if (sum+sum0>x)      work2;                  wait (sum);                          sum0++;
        work1;           ...                     while (cond2) {                       work1;
    else             while (cond2) {                  sum0++;                     }
        work2;           sum0++;                      if (sum+sum0>100)           ...
    ...              }                                    return;                 wait (sum);
    while (cond2) {   ...                                work1;                   if (sum+sum0>100)
        sum0++;       wait (sum);                   }                                 recovery;
    }                 if (sum+sum0'>x')             ...                            sum+=sum0;
    ...                   recovery;                 sum+=sum0;                     signal (sum);
    sum+=sum0;        sum+=sum0;                    signal (sum);              }
    signal (sum);     signal (sum);             }                             (iv) Predicting
}                    }                           (iii) Used in the             branch outcome
(i)Used to determine (ii) Predicting             inner loop                   then verifying
a branch outcome     branch outcome                                           in the outer loop
                     then verifying
```

(c) Using the intermediate result of a reduction variable to determine a branch outcome.

**Fig. 3.** Transformation for reduction-like variable

## 3.3  Iteration Merging for Load Balancing

In TLS, to preserve the sequential semantics, speculative threads must be committed in order. Thus, if a short thread that follows a long thread completes before the long thread, it must stall till the long thread completes. When workload is not balanced between parallel threads, the waiting time can be significant. One way to achieve more balanced workloads is to merge multiple short iterations with a long iteration, so that multiple iterations of a loop are aggregated into a single thread.

Figure 1(a) shows the Control Flow Graph (CFG) of a nested loop. Each node in the graph represents a basic block. The outer loop is selected for parallelization. The path A->B->D on the left is more likely to be taken than the path A->C->...->C->D on the right. However, the right path is much longer than the left path since an inner loop is involved. This causes the load imbalance problem. A shorter thread finishes its execution much earlier than a longer thread, but it has to wait until the previous longer thread commits its results.

The idea of using iteration merging to solve this problem is to combine multiple consecutive loop iterations to make the workload more balanced. When a short but frequent path is identified, a new inner loop is formed which only contains the part from this short path. As shown in Figure 1(b), the newly formed inner loop, which contains A, B and D from the short path, is marked by the shadowed blocks. For all basic blocks that are reached from the outside of this inner loop, tail duplications are needed in order to eliminate side entries. In this example, block D' is tail duplicated and inserted in the outer loop. A new block E is also inserted to the beginning of the outer loop, and only contains a trivial unconditional branch that transfers the control flow to A. Later a $fork$ instruction will be inserted to E in order to spawn a new thread at runtime. After this transformation, multiple short iterations are combined together with a long iteration, resulting in more balanced workloads among threads.

## 4   Evaluation

We have developed our TLS compiler based on the ORC compiler, which is an industrial-strength open-source compiler targeting Intel's Itanium Processor Family (IPF). Three phases are added to support TLS compilation. The first phase performs data dependence and edge profiling, and feeds profile information back to the compiler. The second phase selects loops that are suitable for TLS [38]. Optimizations for TLS are applied in the third phase. Both the loop selection and the optimization phases extensively use profiles obtained by using `train` input set.

For the optimization techniques proposed in this paper, we have implemented scheduling for memory-resident value communication. Both aggressive reduction transformation and iteration merging are still under development and performed manually for this study.

### 4.1   Simulation Methodology

The compiled multithreaded binary is running on a simulator that is built upon Pin [23] and models a CMP with four single-issue in-order processors. The configuration of our simulated machine model is listed in Table 1. Each of processor has a private L1 data cache, a write buffer, an address buffer, and a communication buffer. The write buffer holds the speculatively modified data within a thread [34]. The address buffer keeps all exposed memory addresses accessed by a speculative thread. The communication buffer stores data forwarded by the previous thread. All four processors share a L2 data cache.

**Table 1.** Simulation parameters

| Issue Width | | 1 | | |
|---|---|---|---|---|
| L1-Data Cache | 32KB, 2-way, 1 cycle | | Commu. Buffer | 128 entries, 1 cycle |
| L2-Data Cache | 2MB, 4-way, 10 cycle | | Commu. Delay | 10 cycles |
| Cache Line Size | | 32B | Thread Spawning | 10 cycles |
| Write Buffer | 32KB, 2-way, 1 cycle | | Thread Squashing | 10 cycles |
| Addr. Buffer | 32KB, 2-way, 1 cycle | | Main Memory Latency | 50 cycles |

**Table 2.** Benchmark statistics

| Application Name | Input Set | Number of Parallelized Loop | Average Thread Size | Average Num of Threads/Invocation | Coverage |
|---|---|---|---|---|---|
| BZIP2 | program | 11 | 147 | 3692 | 61% |
| | graphic | 11 | 153 | 3929 | 58% |
| | source | 11 | 137 | 4451 | 65% |
| GZIP | program | 5 | 865 | 1519 | 89% |
| | graphic | 5 | 231 | 2532 | 80% |
| | source | 5 | 923 | 2549 | 84% |
| | random | 5 | 180 | 61921 | 81% |
| | log | 5 | 1378 | 1303 | 79% |

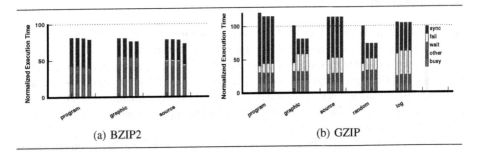

(a) BZIP2          (b) GZIP

**Fig. 4.** Program speedup compared to sequential execution. This figure shows the performance impact of the proposed optimizations on all `ref` input sets.

All simulations are performed using the `ref` input set. To save the simulation time, each parallelized loop is simulated up to 1 thousand invocations, and each invocation is simulated up to 0.1 million iterations. Overall, it allows us to simulate up to 4 billion instructions while covering all parallel loops.

## 4.2   Performance Impact

We have evaluated the proposed compiler optimizations using the simulation infrastructure described in the last section. The performance of the parallelized code is measured against a fully optimized sequential version running on a single processor. Since both GZIP and BZIP2 have multiple ref input sets, we evaluate both two benchmarks on all input sets. Benchmark statistics are listed in the Table 2 and the program speedup is shown in Figure 4.

Each bar in Figure 4 is broken down into five segments explaining what happens during all cycles. The *sync* segment represents time spent waiting for forwarded values; the *fail* segment represents time wasted executing failed threads; the *wait* segment correspond to amount of time the processor has completed execution and is waiting for previous thread to commit; the *busy* segment corresponds to time spent performing useful work; and the *other* segment corresponds to stalls due to other constraints.

The baseline performance is obtained when all existing TLS optimization techniques are applied as described in [38]. It is shown in the first bar. Three optimization techniques proposed in this paper are added on top of the baseline in the following order: scheduling for memory-resident value communication, aggressive reduction transformation, and iteration merging. Each time a new technique is applied, the *cumulative* performance is reported. They are shown in the second, third, and fourth bar respectively.

1. Scheduling for memory-resident values has a significant performance impact on GZIP. For graphic and random input sets, the program performance is improved by 24% and 36% respectively.
2. Reduction transformation that removes the critical forwarding path introduced by reduction variables benefits BZIP2 significantly. For graphic input, we saw a 7% performance improvement. This performance improvement mainly comes from the inner loop of bucket sort, as described in Section 2, whose performance is limited by a reduction-like variable *workDone*.
3. Iteration merging can further improve the performance for loops that have unbalanced workloads. The performance of BZIP2 on source input is greatly improved by 9% after this technique is applied.

### 4.3  A Sensitivity Study

The statistics for different inputs can be found in the Table 2. In the table, coverage is defined as the fraction of execution parallelized in the original sequential program. The coverage for both benchmarks is high: around 60% for BZIP2 and 80% for GZIP. Thread size is defined as the number of dynamic instructions. In BZIP2, the average thread size and the average number of threads per invocation are consistent across different input sets. However, in GZIP, graphic and random input sets have much shorter threads than others. The difference in the thread size indicates that different execution paths may be taken under different input sets.

Instruction scheduling is effective for GZIP on both graphic and random input sets. However, it is ineffective on source input set. In order to better understand this phenomenon, we examine the most time-consuming loop in *deflate* for an examination (see Section 2). There are three major paths in that loop: Path 1 is taken if no matched string is found. Path 2 is taken if a matched string is found, and it is better than the previous match. Path 3 is taken if a matched string is found, and it is not better than the previous match. The generated parallel threads are aggressively optimized along path 2, since path 2 is identified as the most frequent path based on the train input set. For the ref input set, path 2 is the frequent path for both graphic and random input sets, but it is taken less frequently for source input set. As a result, performance improvement on source input set is less significant than other two.

Reduction transformation achieves significant performance improvement for BZIP2 on the graphic input set, however, only moderate performance improvement for source and program input sets. After a close look at the loops, we find that they have more balanced workloads on graphic input set than on other two after reduction transformation. For other two input sets, load imbalance becomes the new bottleneck after reduction transformation, and their performance is greatly improved after iteration merging is applied.

## 5   Conclusions and Future Work

Researchers have found it difficult to exploit parallelism in data compression applications, even with the help of TLS. In this paper, we report the results of an extensive study on parallelizing these benchmarks, under the context of TLS. We have identified several performance bottlenecks caused by data and control dependences. To address these problems, we propose several effective compiler optimization techniques that take advantage of profiling information to remove stalls caused by such dependences. Careful evaluation of these technique reveals that, we can achieve up to 37% program speedup for BZIP2, and 36% for GZIP.

Although our techniques have only been applied to BZIP2 and GZIP, in our experience, the data and control access patterns we studied in this paper have been observed in many other integer benchmarks. We are currently integrate these applications in our compiler infrastructure so that we can evaluate the impact of the proposed techniques on a wide-range of applications. We believe, although no single optimization will enable the creation of efficient parallel programs for TLS, a compiler infrastructure that supports a general set of compiler optimization techniques, each designed to optimally manage a specific situation, can be built to create efficient parallel programs.

## References

1. AKKARY, H., AND DRISCOLL, M. A Dynamic Multithreading Processor. In *31st Annual IEEE/ACM International Symposium on Microarchitecture (Micro-31)* (December 1998).
2. AMD CORPORATION. Leading the industry: Multi-core technology & dual-core processors from amd. http://multicore.amd.com/en/Technology/, 2005.
3. BHOWMIK, A., AND FRANKLIN, M. A fast approximate interprocedural analysis for speculative multithreading compiler. In *17th Annual ACM International Conference on Supercomputing* (2003).
4. BLUME, W., DOALLO, R., EIGENMANN, R., GROUT, J., HOEFLINGER, J., LAWRENCE, T., LEE, J., PADUA, D., PAEK, Y., POTTENGER, B., RAUCHWERGER, L., AND TU, P. Parallel programming with polaris. *IEEE Computer 29*, 12 (1996), 78–82.
5. BURROW, M., AND WHEELER, D. A block-sorting lossless data compression algorithm. Tech. Rep. 124, Digital Systems Research Center, May 1994.

6. CHEN, P.-S., HUNG, M.-Y., HWANG, Y.-S., JU, R., AND LEE, J. K. Compiler support for speculative multithreading architecture with probabilistic points-to analysis. In *ACM SIGPLAN 2003 Symposium on Principles and Practice of Parallel Programming* (2003).

7. CINTRA, M., AND TORRELLAS, J. Learning cross-thread violations in speculative parallelization for multiprocessors. In *8th International Symposium on High-Performance Computer Architecture (HPCA-8)* (2002).

8. DU, Z.-H., LIM, C.-C., LI, X.-F., YANG, C., ZHAO, Q., AND NGAI, T.-F. A cost-driven compilation framework for speculative parallelization of sequential programs. In *ACM SIGPLAN 04 Conference on Programming Language Design and Implementation (PLDI'04)* (June 2004).

9. DUBEY, P., O'BRIEN, K., O'BRIEN, K., AND BARTON, C. Single-program speculative multithreading (spsm) architecture: Compiler-assisted fine-grained multithreading. In *International Conference on Parallel Architectures and Compilation Techniques (PACT 1995)* (June 1995).

10. FRANKLIN, M., AND SOHI, G. S. The expandable split window paradigm for exploiting fine-grain parallelsim. In *19th Annual International Symposium on Computer Architecture (ISCA '92)* (May 1992), pp. 58–67.

11. GUPTA, M., AND NIM, R. Techniques for Speculative Run-Time Parallelization of Loops. In *Supercomputing '98* (November 1998).

12. HAMMOND, L., WILLEY, M., AND OLUKOTUN, K. Data Speculation Support for a Chip Multiprocessor. In *8th International Conference on Architectural Support for Programming Languages and Operating Systems (ASPLOS-IIX)* (October 1998).

13. HIRANANDANI, S., KENNEDY, K., AND TSENG, C.-W. Preliminary experiences with the Fortran D compiler. In *Supercomputing '93* (1993).

14. INTEL CORPORATION. Intel's dual-core processor for desktop PCs. http://www.intel.com/personal/desktopcomputer/dual_core/index.htm 2005.

15. INTEL CORPORATION. Intel itanium architecture software developer's manual, revision 2.2. http://www.intel.com/design/itanium/manuals/iiasdmanual.htm, 2006.

16. JOHNSON, T., EIGENMANN, R., AND VIJAYKUMAR, T. Min-cut program decomposition for thread-level speculation. In *ACM SIGPLAN 04 Conference on Programming Language Design and Implementation (PLDI'04)* (June 2004).

17. KALLA, R., SINHAROY, B., AND TENDLER, J. M. IBM Power5 Chip: A Dual-Core Multithreaded Processor. *Microprocessor Forum '99* (October 1999).

18. KENNEDY, K., AND ALLEN, R. *Optimizing Compilers for Modern Architectures: A Dependence-based Approach*. Academic Press, 2002.

19. KNIGHT, T. An Architecture for Mostly Functional Languages. In *Proceedings of the ACM Lisp and Functional Programming Conference* (August 1986), pp. 500–519.

20. KRISHNAN, V., AND TORRELLAS, J. The Need for Fast Communication in Hardware-Based Speculative Chip Multiprocessors. In *International Conference on Parallel Architectures and Compilation Techniques (PACT 1999)* (October 1999).

21. LI, X.-F., DU, Z.-H., ZHAO, Q.-Y., AND NGAI, T.-F. Software value prediction for speculative parallel threaded computations. In *1st Value-Prediction Workshop (VPW 2003)* (Jun 2003).

22. LIU, W., TUCK, J., CEZE, L., AHN, W., STRAUSS, K., RENAU, J., AND TORRELLAS, J. Posh: A tls compiler that exploits program structure. In *ACM SIGPLAN 2006 Symposium on Principles and Practice of Parallel Programming* (March 2006).

23. LUK, C.-K., COHN, R., MUTH, R., PATIL, H., KLAUSER, A., LOWNEY, G., WALLACE, S., REDDI, V., AND HAZELWOOD, K. Pin: Building Customized Program Analysis Tools with Dynamic Instrumentation. In *ACM SIGPLAN 05 Conference on Programming Language Design and Implementation (PLDI'05)* (June 2005).

24. MARCUELLO, P., AND GONZALEZ, A. Clustered speculative multithreaded processors. In *13th Annual ACM International Conference on Supercomputing* (Rhodes, Greece, June 1999).
25. OPLINGER, J., HEINE, D., AND LAM, M. In search of speculative thread-level parallelism. In *Proceedings PACT 99* (October 1999).
26. PRABHU, M., AND OLUKOTUN, K. Using thread-level speculation to simplify manual parallelization. In *ACM SIGPLAN 2003 Symposium on Principles and Practice of Parallel Programming* (2003).
27. PRABHU, M., AND OLUKOTUN, K. Exposing speculative thread parallelism in spec2000. In *ACM SIGPLAN 2005 Symposium on Principles and Practice of Parallel Programming* (2005).
28. QUINONES, C. G., MADRILES, C., SANCHEZ, J., GONZALES, P. M. A., AND TULLSEN, D. M. Mitosis compiler: an infrastructure for speculative threading based on pre-computation slices. In *ACM SIGPLAN 05 Conference on Programming Language Design and Implementation (PLDI'05)* (June 2005).
29. SOHI, G. S., BREACH, S., AND VIJAYKUMAR, T. N. Multiscalar Processors. In *22nd Annual International Symposium on Computer Architecture (ISCA '95)* (June 1995), pp. 414–425.
30. STEFFAN, J. G., COLOHAN, C. B., AND MOWRY, T. C. Architectural support for thread-level data speculation. Tech. Rep. CMU-CS-97-188, School of Computer Science, Carnegie Mellon University, November 1997.
31. STEFFAN, J. G., COLOHAN, C. B., ZHAI, A., AND MOWRY, T. C. A Scalable Approach to Thread-Level Speculation. In *27th Annual International Symposium on Computer Architecture (ISCA '00)* (June 2000).
32. SUN CORPORATION. Throughput computing—niagara. http://www.sun.com/processors/throughput/, 2005.
33. TJIANG, S., WOLF, M., LAM, M., PIEPER, K., AND HENNESSY, J. *Languages and Compilers for Parallel Computing.* Springer-Verlag, Berlin, Germany, 1992, pp. 137–151.
34. TSAI, J.-Y., HUANG, J., AMLO, C., LILJA, D., AND YEW, P.-C. The Superthreaded Processor Architecture. *IEEE Transactions on Computers, Special Issue on Multithreaded Architectures 48*, 9 (September 1999).
35. TSAI, J.-Y., JIANG, Z., AND YEW, P.-C. Compiler techniques for the superthreaded architectures. *International Journal of Parallel Programming - Special Issue on Languages and Compilers for Parallel Computing* (June 1998).
36. VIJAYKUMAR, T. N., BREACH, S. E., AND SOHI, G. S. Register communication strategies for the multiscalar architecture. Tech. Rep. Technical Report 1333, Department of Computer Science, University of Wisconsin-Madison, Feb. 1997.
37. VIJAYKUMAR, T. N., AND SOHI, G. S. Task selection for a multiscalar processor. In *31st Annual IEEE/ACM International Symposium on Microarchitecture (Micro-31)* (Nov. 1998).
38. WANG, S., YELLAJYOSULA, K. S., ZHAI, A., AND YEW, P.-C. Loop selection for thread-level speculation. In *The 18th International Workshop on Languages and Compilers for Parallel Computing* (Oct 2005).
39. ZHAI, A., COLOHAN, C. B., STEFFAN, J. G., AND MOWRY, T. C. Compiler optimization of scalar value communication between speculative threads. In *10th International Conference on Architectural Support for Programming Languages and Operating Systems (ASPLOS-X)* (Oct 2002).
40. ZHAI, A., COLOHAN, C. B., STEFFAN, J. G., AND MOWRY, T. C. Compiler optimization of memory-resident value communication between speculative threads. In *The 2004 International Symposium on Code Generation and Optimization* (Mar 2004).
41. ZILLES, C., AND SOHI, G. Master/slave speculative parallelization. In *35th Annual IEEE/ACM International Symposium on Microarchitecture (Micro-35)* (Nov 2002).
42. ZIV, J., AND LEMPEL, A. A universal algorithm for sequential data compression. 337–343.

# On Control Signals for Multi-Dimensional Time[*]

DaeGon Kim[1], Gautam[1,2], and S. Rajopadhye[1]

[1] Colorado State University, Fort Collins, CO, U.S.A.
{kim,gautam}@cs.colostate.edu,
Sanjay.Rajopadhye@colostate.edu
[2] IRISA, Rennes, France

**Abstract.** Affine control loops (ACLs) comprise an important class of compute- and data-intensive computations. The theoretical framework for the automatic parallelization of ACLs is well established. However, the hardware compilation of arbitrary ACLs is still in its infancy. An important component for an efficient hardware implementation is a control mechanism that informs each processing element (PE) which computation needs to be performed and when.

We formulate this *control signal problem* in the context of compiling arbitrary ACLs parallelized with a multi-dimensional schedule into hardware. We characterize the logical time instants when PEs need a control signal indicating which particular computations need to be performed. Finally, we present an algorithm to compute the minimal set of logical time instants for these control signals.

## 1  Introduction

It is well known that loops comprise the compute-intensive kernels of many applications. An important class of statically-analyzable loops is affine control loops (ACLs). Bastoul et. al. [1] report that over 99% in 7 out of 12 programs of the widely studied benchmark suites SpecFP and PerfectClub are affine control loops. Due to their high computational complexity, considerable research has aimed at deriving application specific circuits directly and automatically from ACLs and incorporated in both academic and commercial tools [2,3]. However, these tools have been restricted to a proper subset of ACLs, specifically, those that can be systematically transformed to loops that possess a 1-dimensional *affine schedule* and with uniform dependences[1] (or slight generalizations). One-dimensional affine schedules imply that only one loop carries dependences.

This paper deals with the full generality of arbitrary ACLs. The ACL may be arbitrarily nested, have arbitrary affine dependences and may have been parallelized with a multidimensional schedule [4]. Multidimensional schedules assign a time vector to computations which is interpreted as the logical instant at which

---

[*] This research was supported in part, by the National Science Foundation, under the grant EI-030614: HiPHiPECS: High Level Programing of High Performance Embedded Computing Systems.

[1] These conditions were motivated by the need to derive systolic architectures.

G. Almási, C. Caşcaval, and P. Wu (Eds.): LCPC 2006, LNCS 4382, pp. 141–155, 2007.
© Springer-Verlag Berlin Heidelberg 2007

they are executed. These time vectors are the iteration vectors corresponding to outer sequential (time) loops in a loop nest. The total order between logical time instants is lexicographic. Multidimensional schedules present the following advantages over linear schedules (i) Some applications do not admit a linear schedule [5], and (ii) The architecture resulting from the parallelism exposed by linear schedules might not fit into the available hardware resources. With multidimensional schedules, we may limit the degree of parallelism.

The chosen parallelization is fine-grained such that the inner loops are parallel. The resulting loop nest is called an FGP-ACL. Parallel computations are mapped to distinct simple processing elements (PEs). Each PE may either be active or inactive for a certain logical time-vector. When it is active, it executes the assigned computation. The set of all valid time-vectors is called the *global time domain* of the specification and the set of all active time-vectors of a processor is called its *local time domain*.

The context of this work is the generation of custom hardware that realizes PEs, registers and memory banks local to each PE and an interconnection for data transfer across PEs. The target implementation for this custom hardware may either be an ASIC or an FPGA. Previous work [6] in this direction presents a methodology in which each PE implements a multi-dimensional counter to scan the global time domain, *i.e.*, an automaton enumerating valid time-vectors together with a test for the membership of time-vectors in the local time domain. The resource overhead for this scheme is significant.

Avoiding such an automaton involves (i) providing the control to every PE instructing it to resume or suspend its activity (start and stop are treated as special cases) and information about the statements it needs to compute at any particular time instant, and (ii) the computation of the array addresses for statements in the body of the loop nest. The related problem of developing an interconnection so that each PE can access the memory where data is stored has been addressed elsewhere [7].

This paper deals with the problem of providing the suspend and resume signals to each PE and the statements that need to be executed. In the presentation of this paper, we will specialize suspend and resume with respect to particular statements such that both these problems are solved together. We will refer to this as the *control signal problem*. The key contributions of this paper are (i) a precise formulation of control signal problem, (ii) characterization of time when control signals are necessary, and (iii) an algorithm computing an exact solution for the control signal problem.

The rest of this paper is organized as follows. The following section illustrates the control signal problem with an example. We introduce some concepts and notations for fine-grained parallel ACLs in Section 3. Section 4 precisely formulates the control signal problem, characterizes the time when PEs need to receive a control signal, and presents an algorithm to compute an exact solution for the control signal problem. Section 5 is a discussion on the propagation of the signals. Section 6 discusses related work, and finally we present our conclusions and future work in Section 7.

## 2  Illustrating Example

*Example 1.* Consider the following program.

```
for t1 = 0 to n
  for t2 = 0 to t1
    forall p1 = 0 to t2
      forall p2 = 0 to t1
      . . .
```

The first two loops are executed sequentially, and the remaining loops are parallel loops. We will interpret this program as follows: the two sequential loops represent time, and the parallel loops denote processors. For example, the processor $(0,0)$ and $(0,1)$ are active, i.e. execute statement, at time $(1,0)$. Given an iteration of the sequential loops, all the iterations of the parallel loops are executed at the same time. For instance, when $t1 = n$ and $t2 = n$, all the $n \times n$ processors are active.

Now, we would like to address the question of which processors become active and idle at a given time. For example, the processor $(0,0)$ resumes at time $(0,0)$, and both the processor $(1,0)$ and $(1,1)$ resume at time $(1,1)$.

In this program, the set of valid time coordinates for the entire program is called the *global time domain*. It is the iteration space of the time loops. Similarly, the set of all processor coordinates is called the *global processor domain*. It is the set of all the possible iterations over the global time domain. Figure 1 shows the global time and processor domain of this example for $n = 5$. Every processor is, however, not active all the time, i.e. for all the points in the global time domain. Each processor $p$ has its own active time. Similarly, the set of active processors varies over the time. Figure 1 also illustrates the time when the processor $(1,2)$ is active and the active processors at time $(2,1)$.

It is easy to see when the processor $(1,2)$ should receive a resume (or suspend) signal from Figure 1(a). For each $i$ such that $2 \leq i \leq 5$, it will become active at

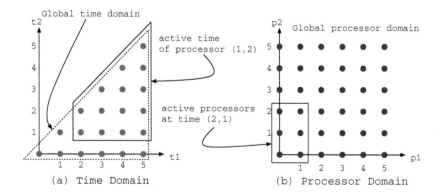

**Fig. 1.** Time and processor domain

time $(i, 1)$ and idle after $(i, i)$. However, it is not obvious which processors should receive resume (or suspend) signals at time $(2, 1)$ from Figure 1(b). For instance, the processor $(0, 0)$ need not receive a resume signal, because it was already active at the previous time step $(2, 0)$. Among the six processors in Figure 1(b), only three processors $(1, 0)$, $(1, 1)$ and $(1, 2)$ have to receive a resume signal. As shown in Figure 2, the set of time coordinates when processor $(p1, p2)$ is active is the intersection of the global time domain and $\{t1, t2 \mid p1 \leq t2; p2 \leq t1\}$. For instance, the earliest active time of processor $(1, 2)$ is $(2, 1)$. For each processor whose first coordinate is 0, it is always active at $(t1, 0)$ if the processor is active at $(t1, 1)$. So, the other three processors in Figure 1 does not need to receive a resume signal at $(2, 1)$ because these processors was active at the previous time step $(2, 0)$.

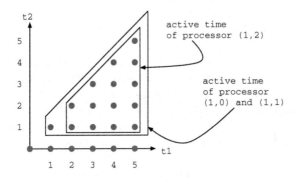

**Fig. 2.** Active time of processors $(1, 0)$, $(1, 1)$ and $(1, 2)$ in the global time domain

## 3   Problem Formulation

The following transformations are involved in the hardware compilation of ACLs. Value based dependence analysis (or exact dataflow analysis) [8,9] on ACLs transforms it to a system of recurrence equations defined over polyhedral domains. On these equations, scheduling analysis [10,11,5,12,13,14,15,16] is performed which assigns an (multidimensional) execution time to each computation so that dependences are satisfied. The schedule may be such that multiple computations are executed at the same time step. Thus, there is inherent parallelism. An intermediate code generation step generates *fine-grained parallel* (FGP) ACLs. In FGP-ACLs, the outer loops are sequential (representing multidimensional time) and the inner loops are parallel. The array access functions in the statements within the body of the loop nest are in terms of the time and processor loop indices and size parameters. Hardware compilation is the mapping of parallel computations to distinct processing elements.

We will first present ACLs and the required mathematical background of integer polyhedra. Then we will discuss FGP-ACLs and define the terminology needed for our analysis.

## 3.1   ACLs (Affine Control Loops)

ACLs are loop nests of the form defined in Figure 3. Note that **Lower** (respectively, **Upper**) is the maximum (respectively, minimum) of *a finite number of* affine functions, respectively. Kuck [17] showed that the set of iterations with such bounds can be described as (a union of) integer polyhedra. Precisely, an iteration space of ACLs is a union of integral polyhedra parameterized by the size parameters $s$.

```
                   ACL Grammar
ACL          : Stmt *
Stmt         : Loop | Assignment
Loop         : for Index=Lower ... Upper
                   ACL
Assignment : ArrayRef = Expression;
```

**Fig. 3.** ACL grammar. **Index** is an identifier; **Lower** (respectively, **Upper**) is the maximum (respectively, minimum) of affine functions of outer indices and size parameters; **ArrayRef** is a reference to a multidimensional array whose access expression is an affine function of an iteration vector and the size parameters; and **Expression** is an arbitrary expression comprising finitely many **ArrayRefs** with a strict, side-effect free function.

**Definition 1.** *An **integer polyhedron** $\mathcal{P}$ is a set of integer solutions of finitely many affine inequalities with integer coefficients. These inequalities are called constraints of $\mathcal{P}$. A **parameterized integer polyhedron** is an integer polyhedron some of whose indices are interpreted as symbolic constants.*

The iteration space of ACLs can be written in the following form:

$$\left\{ \begin{pmatrix} z \\ s \end{pmatrix} \mid (M \; M_s) \begin{pmatrix} z \\ s \end{pmatrix} \geq c, \begin{pmatrix} z \\ s \end{pmatrix} \in \mathbb{Z}^{n_z+n_s} \right\} \tag{1}$$

where $n_z$ is the depth of the loop nest and $n_s$ is the number of size parameters.

## 3.2   Fine Grained Parallel ACLs

In the fine grained parallel ACLs each statement $\mathcal{S}$ is surrounded by $k_\mathcal{S}$ sequential loops and $d_\mathcal{S}$ parallel loops. Our analysis is per each statement and we will drop the subscript $\mathcal{S}$. An iteration vector of sequential loops represents time, and the order of these $k$-vectors is defined by the lexicographic order.

**Definition 2.** *Let $u = (u_1, \ldots, u_n)^T$ and $v = (v_1, \ldots, v_n)^T$ be $n$-dimensional vectors. The **lexicographic order** $\prec$ is defined by the following rule:*
*   $u \prec v$ *if there exists $i$ such that $u_j = v_j$ for all $1 \leq j < i$, $u_i < v_i$, and $1 \leq i \leq n$.*

The remaining $d$ innermost loops represents processing elements. We distinguish time and processor indices, and throughout the paper, time and processor indices are denoted by $t$ and $p$, respectively. So, the iteration space of parallel ACLs can be written as follows:

$$\left\{ \begin{pmatrix} t \\ p \\ s \end{pmatrix} \mid (M_t \; M_p \; M_s) \begin{pmatrix} t \\ p \\ s \end{pmatrix} \geq c, \begin{pmatrix} t \\ p \\ s \end{pmatrix} \in \mathbb{Z}^{k+d+n_s} \right\} \qquad (2)$$

### 3.3    Time and Processor Domain

Here, we introduce some concepts related to fine grained parallel ACLs.

**Definition 3.** The **global time domain** $\mathcal{GT}$ is the set of all the sequential loop iterations. The **local time domain** $\mathcal{LT}(p)$ is the set of the sequential loop iterations at which a given processor $p$ is active.

**Definition 4.** A **local processor domain** $\mathcal{LP}(t)$ at a given $t \in \mathcal{GT}$ is the set of active processors at time instant $t$. The **global processor domain** $\mathcal{GP}$ is the set of $\bigcup_t \mathcal{LP}(t)$ for all $t \in \mathcal{GT}$.

In fact, these concepts have already been introduced in section 2 with our example. The global time and processor domain of Example 1 is $\{(t1, t2) \mid 0 \leq t2 \leq t1 \leq n\}$ and $\{(p1, p2) \mid 0 \leq p1 \leq n; 0 \leq p2 \leq n\}$, respectively. $\mathcal{GT}$ can be computed directly from the sequential loops, and $\mathcal{GP}$ can be derived by projecting the ACL iteration space onto processor space, i.e. elimination of time indices. The local processor domain at time instant $(t1, t2)$ is $\{(p1, p2) \mid 0 \leq p1 \leq t2; 0 \leq p2 \leq t1\}$. This can be regarded as a polyhedron parameterized by the time $t$ and size parameters $s$. In fact, $\mathcal{LP}(2, 1)$ in Figure 1 is computed by replacing $t1$ with 2 and $t2$ with 1. Similarly, the local time domain can be seen as a polyhedron parameterized by the processor $p$ and $s$. So, $\mathcal{LT}(p)$ of Example 1 is $\{(t1, t2) \mid 0 \leq p1 \leq t2 \leq n; 0 \leq p2 \leq t1 \leq n\}$.

*Property 1.* $\mathcal{LT}(p)$ and $LP(t)$ are polyhedra parameterized by $p$ and $t$, respectively. More precisely, $\mathcal{LT}(p)$ is a polyhedron in $k$-dimensional space parameterized by $p$ and $s$, and $LP(t)$ is a polyhedron in $d$-dimensional space parameterized by $t$ and $s$.

## 4    Analysis

Now, we want to characterize the set of processors that receive a *resume* and *suspend* signal, as well as the time instants expressed as a function of their coordinates, at which this happens.

**Definition 5.** The **immediate precedent**, denoted by $pre(t)$, of $t \in \mathcal{GT}$ is an element $t'$ of $\mathcal{GT}$ satisfying that (i) $t' \prec t$, and (ii) there is no element $t'' \in \mathcal{GT}$ such that $t' \prec t'' \prec t$. The **immediate successor** of $t \in \mathcal{GT}$, denoted by $next(t)$, is $t'$ such that $t = pre(t')$.

Note that $pre(t)$ and $next(t)$ are defined only in the context of $\mathcal{GT}$, not $\mathcal{LT}$.

*Property 2.* A processor $p$ must receive a resume signal at time instant $t \in \mathcal{GT}$ if either (*i*) $t \in \mathcal{LT}(p)$ and $t$ is the lexicographic minimum of $\mathcal{GT}$, or (*ii*) $t \in \mathcal{LT}(p)$ and $pre(t) \notin \mathcal{LT}(p)$. Similarly, processor $p$ must receive a suspend signal at time $t \in \mathcal{GT}$ if either (*i*) $t \in \mathcal{LT}(p)$ and $t$ is the lexicographic maximum of $\mathcal{GT}$, or (*ii*) $t \in \mathcal{LT}(p)$ and $next(t) \notin \mathcal{LT}(p)$.

The above property conceptually gives a precise time when a signal arrives at a certain processor. We now characterize this set of time instants.

**Definition 6.** *A **face** of a polyhedron $\mathcal{P}$ is an intersection of $\mathcal{P}$ with a subset of inverses of its constraints. A face $\mathcal{F}$ is called a **facet** if there is no face $\mathcal{F}'$ such that $\mathcal{F} \subset \mathcal{F}' \subset \mathcal{P}$.*

Note that a facet of an integral polyhedron may be "thick" in the sense that a single hyperplane cannot contain it. Here, we distinguish two kinds of facets.

**Definition 7.** *Let $\mathcal{P}$ be a polyhedron in $n$-dimensional space. Let $e_n$ be the $n$-th unit vector, i.e., an $n$-vector whose last element is $1$ and the other elements are $0$. A facet $\mathcal{F}$ is a **lower facet** if $p - e_n \notin \mathcal{P}$ for all $p \in \mathcal{F}$. Similarly, a facet $\mathcal{F}$ is an **upper facet** if $p + e_n \notin \mathcal{P}$ for all $p \in \mathcal{F}$. Let $\mathbb{LF}(P)$ and $\mathbb{UF}(P)$ denote the set of all the lower and upper facets of $P$, respectively.*

We illustrate these concepts with the following example.

*Example 2.* Consider the following parallel ACL.

```
for t1 = 0 to n
  for t2 = 0 to n
    forall p1 = 0 to t1+n-t2
      . . .
```

The $\mathcal{GT}$ and $\mathcal{LT}(3)$ of this example are given in Figure 4 for $n = 5$. This figure also illustrates facets of the local time domain with one lower facet and two upper facets. For each point $t \notin \mathbb{LF}(\mathcal{GT})$, its immediate precedent is simply $t - (0, 1)$. Similarly, for $t \notin \mathbb{UF}(\mathcal{GT})$, its immediate successor is $t + (0, 1)$. However, $pre(t)$ of $t \in \mathbb{LF}(\mathcal{GT})$ is found in some element of $\mathbb{UF}(\mathcal{GT})$. Similarly, $next(t)$ of $t \in \mathbb{UF}(\mathcal{GT})$ is found in some element of $\mathbb{LF}(\mathcal{GT})$.

Note that a processor receives a signal at a time instant which belongs to its local time domain. The following lemma gives the first characterization for the time when a signal arrives at a processor.

**Lemma 1.** *If a processor $p$ receives a resume (resp. suspend) signal at time $t$, $t$ is in a lower (resp. upper) facet of $\mathcal{LT}(p)$.*

*Proof.* Let $e_k \in \mathbb{Z}^k$ be $(0, \ldots, 0, 1)^T$. Note that $t \in \mathcal{LT}(p)$ and $pre(t) \notin \mathcal{LT}(p)$. So, $t - e_k \notin \mathcal{LT}(p)$. Therefore, $t$ belongs to a lower facet of $\mathcal{LT}(p)$.

The proof for a suspend signal is similar.

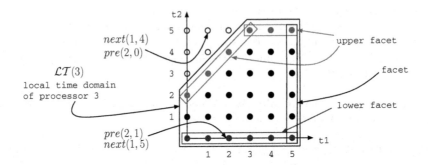

**Fig. 4.** Global and local time domain of Example 2 for $n = 5$; one lower facet and two upper facet of the local time domain

This lemma says that a processor $p$ receives a signal only if time $t$ belongs to a lower and upper facet of $\mathcal{LT}(p)$. In other words, if $t \in \mathcal{GT}$ is not in lower and upper facets of $\mathcal{LT}(p)$, the processor $p$ does not need to receive any signals. Hence, a safe solution is to generate a signal for *each point* in the lower and upper facets of $\mathcal{LT}(p)$.

*Solution 1.* A **naive** way to control a processor $p$ is to generate resume signals at all points in $\mathbb{LF}(\mathcal{LT}(p))$ and suspend signals over $\mathbb{UF}(\mathcal{LT}(p))$.

Sometimes, this naive solution might be an exact solution. For instance, processor $(1,2)$ in Figure 1 must receive signals for all the points in the lower and upper facets of its local time domain. Furthermore, in Example 1, this naive solution becomes an exact solution for all the processors except the five processors, $(0,0)$, $(0,1)$, $(0,2)$, $(0,3)$ and $(0,4)$. While processor $(1,2)$ receives the resume and suspend signals over the lower and upper facet of $\mathcal{LT}(1,2)$ respectively, processor $(0,0)$ needs to receive only two signals, a resume signal at $(0,0)$ and a suspend signal at $(5,5)$, because $\mathcal{LT}(0,0)$ is equal to $\mathcal{GT}$. With the fact that the number of suspend signals have to be the number of resume signals, the following theorem explains why the naive solution becomes an exact solution for almost all processors in Example 1.

**Theorem 1.** *Let $p \in \mathcal{GP}$.*

(a) *If $t \in \mathcal{GT}$ is in a lower facet of $\mathcal{LT}(p)$ and not in a lower facet of $\mathcal{GT}$, the processor $p$ must receive a resume signal at time $t$.*

(b) *If $t \in \mathcal{GT}$ is in an upper facet of $\mathcal{LT}(p)$ and not in an upper facet of $\mathcal{GT}$, the processor $p$ must receive a suspend signal at time $t$.*

*Proof.* (a) Suppose $t$ is in a lower facet of $\mathcal{LT}(p)$ and not in a lower facet of $\mathcal{GT}$. Let $e_k \in \mathbb{Z}^k$ be $(0,\ldots,0,1)^T$. Note that $\mathcal{GT}$ is a polyhedron in $k$-dimensional space. Since $t$ is not in a lower facet of $\mathcal{GT}$, $t - e_k \in \mathcal{GT}$. On the other hand, $t - e_k \notin \mathcal{LT}(p)$, because $t$ is in a lower facet of $\mathcal{LT}(p)$. Since $t - e_k$ is $pre(t)$, processor $p$ must receive a resume signal at time $t$.

The proof for (b) is symmetric.

Let us apply this theorem to Example 1. For a processor whose first coordinate is greater than 0, the lower facet of its local time domain shares no point with the lower facet of $\mathcal{GT}$. So, for each point in the lower facet, the processor must receive a resume signal. Also, there is a corresponding suspend signal for each resume signals. Also, note that the number of points in the lower facets is equal to that of points in the upper facets. By Lemma 1, each point in the upper facet must also receive a resume signal.

Theorem 1 proves that every point in $\mathrm{LF}(\mathcal{LT}) \setminus \mathrm{LF}(\mathcal{GT})$ and $\mathrm{UF}(\mathcal{LT}) \setminus \mathrm{UF}(\mathcal{GT})$ needs a signal. Now, we focus on the remaining part, $\mathrm{LF}(\mathcal{LT}) \cap \mathrm{LF}(\mathcal{GT})$ and $\mathrm{UF}(\mathcal{LT}) \cap \mathrm{UF}(\mathcal{GT})$. A processor need not receive a resume signal at time $t$ when $pre(t) \in \mathcal{LT}(p)$. For instance, the processor $(0, j)$ for $0 \le j \le 5$ in Example 1 needs only one resume signal because, for each point $t \in \mathrm{LF}(\mathcal{LT})$ but one, $pre(t)$ belongs to its local time domain. When a time instant $t$ is in a lower facet of $\mathcal{GT}$, $pre(t)$ is in an upper facet of $\mathcal{GT}$. So, the precise answer for the question of what point need a resume signal can be obtained from $(i)$ $\mathrm{LF}(\mathcal{LT}(p)) \cap \mathrm{LF}(\mathcal{GT})$ and $(ii)$ $\mathrm{UF}(\mathcal{LT}(p)) \cap \mathrm{UF}(\mathcal{GT})$. Algorithm 1 illustrates how the precise solution can be obtained by comparing these two sets for the 2-dimensional control signal problem. The operations in the algorithm are well supported [18,19].

Now, consider example 2 with Figure 4. Its $\mathcal{GT}$ and $\mathcal{LT}$ are $\{t1, t2 \mid 0 \le t1 \le n; 0 \le t2 \le n\}$ and $\{t1, t2 \mid 0 \le t1 \le n; 0 \le t2 \le n; t2 \le t1 + n - p1\}$, respectively. Here, we compute only the set of points that require a suspend signal, and that of a resume signal will be left as an exercise. First, there are two upper facets of $\mathcal{LT}$, $\{t1, t2 \mid 0 \le t1 \le p1 - 1; t2 = t1 + n - p1\}$ and $\{t1, t2 \mid p1 \le t1 \le n; t2 = n\}$. Note that either of them can be empty set and the point $(p1, n)$ is removed from the first set. In fact, the first set is $\mathrm{UF}(\mathcal{LT}) \setminus \mathrm{UF}(\mathcal{GT})$, and the second is $\mathrm{UF}(\mathcal{LT}) \cap \mathrm{UF}(\mathcal{GT})$. Hence, a suspend signal is needed at every point in the first set. To compute the exact points in the second set, $\mathrm{LF}(\mathcal{LT}) \cap \mathrm{LF}(\mathcal{GT})$ is required, and it is $\{t1, t2 \mid 0 \le t1 \le n; n - p1 \le t1; t2 = 0\}$. Adding a ray $(1, 0)$ yields $\{t1, t2 \mid 0 \le t1 \le n; n - p1 \le t1; t2 > 0\}$, and shifting it by $(-1, 0)$ yields $\{t1, t2 \mid -1 \le t1 \le n - 1; n - p1 - 1 \le t1; t2 > 0\}$. From subtracting this from $\mathrm{UF}(\mathcal{LT}) \setminus \mathrm{UF}(\mathcal{GT})$, we get $\{t1, t2 \mid 0 \le t1 \le p1 - 1; t2 = t1 + n - p1\}$ and $\{t1, t2 \mid t1 = n; t2 = n\}$ if this point $(n, n)$ belongs to $\mathcal{LT}$. The main intuition is that $pre(t)$ of $t \in \mathrm{UF}(\mathcal{GT})$ lies in $\mathrm{LF}(\mathcal{GT})$, and consequently, $next(t)$ of $t \in \mathrm{LF}(\mathcal{GT})$ lies in $\mathrm{UF}(\mathcal{GT})$.

We now introduce another example that has non-trivial behavior, and will help understand the algorithm for the general case.

*Example 3.* Consider the following simple extension of Example 2 with a third time loop.

```
for t1 = 0 to n
  for t2 = 0 to n
    for t3 = 0 to n
      forall p1 = 0 to t1+t2+n-t3
        . . .
```

**Algorithm 1.** Algorithm for 2-dimensional time

INPUT : $\mathcal{LT}$ - local time domain, $\mathcal{GT}$ - global time domain
OUTPUT : $\mathcal{R}$ - the set of points requiring resume signals, $\mathcal{S}$ - the set of points requiring suspend signals
1: compute $\mathrm{LF}(\mathcal{LT})$, $\mathrm{UF}(\mathcal{LT})$, $\mathrm{LF}(\mathcal{GT})$ and $\mathrm{UF}(\mathcal{GT})$
2: $\mathcal{R} \leftarrow \mathrm{LF}(\mathcal{LT}) \setminus \mathrm{LF}(\mathcal{GT})$; $\mathcal{S} \leftarrow \mathrm{UF}(\mathcal{LT}) \setminus \mathrm{UF}(\mathcal{GT})$
3: compute $\mathrm{LF}(\mathcal{LT}) \cap \mathrm{LF}(\mathcal{GT})$ and $\mathrm{UF}(\mathcal{LT}) \cap \mathrm{UF}(\mathcal{GT})$
4: add a ray $(0, -1)$ to $\mathrm{UF}(\mathcal{LT}) \cap \mathrm{UF}(\mathcal{GT})$, shift it by $(1, 0)$, and subtract it from $\mathrm{LF}(\mathcal{LT}) \cap \mathrm{LF}(\mathcal{GT})$
5: add a ray $(0, 1)$ to $\mathrm{LF}(\mathcal{LT}) \cap \mathrm{LF}(\mathcal{GT})$, shift it by $(-1, 0)$, and subtract it from $\mathrm{UF}(\mathcal{LT}) \cap \mathrm{UF}(\mathcal{GT})$
6: add the result of step 4 to $\mathcal{R}$; add the result of step 5 to $\mathcal{S}$
7: return $\mathcal{R}$ and $\mathcal{S}$

Figure 5(a) shows the $\mathcal{GT}$ of this example for $n = 10$, as well as $\mathcal{LT}(3)$ and $\mathcal{LT}(12)$. First, consider the times when processor 3 needs a resume signal. As shown in Figure 5(a), $\mathrm{LF}(\mathcal{LT}(3)) \cap \mathrm{LF}(\mathcal{GT})$ is the entire bottom square $\{t1, t2, t3 \mid t3 = 0; 0 \le t1, t2 \le 10\}$. Figure 5(b) visualizes the $3D$ generalization of step 5 in the algorithm 1. For every point $t$ in $\mathrm{LF}(\mathcal{LT}(3)) \cap \mathrm{LF}(\mathcal{GT})$ except its lower facet, $pre(t)$ is "directly above" $t$ after shifting. However, $pre(t)$ of the point $t$ on the line segment between $(0, 0, 0)$ and $(10, 0, 0)$ is on the line segment between $(0, 0, 0)$ and $(10, 0, 0)$. The first line segment can be seen as a lower facet of a lower facet of $\mathcal{GT}$ (we call this the second lower facet of $\mathcal{GT}$). Similarly, the line segment between $(0, 0, 0)$ and $(10, 0, 0)$ is the second upper facet of $\mathcal{GT}$. This explains why the algorithm for general case recurses on the dimensions of the polyhedra it manipulates. So, processor 3 needs a resume signal at the following set $\{t1, t2, t3 \mid t3 = 0; 0 \le t1; 1 \le t2; t1 + t2 \le 4\} \cup \{(0, 0, 0)\}$.

Now, consider the processor 12. The intersection of $\mathrm{LF}(\mathcal{LT}(12))$ and $\mathrm{LF}(\mathcal{GT})$ is $\mathrm{LF}(\mathcal{LT}(12))$ itself, $\{t1, t2, t3 \mid 0 \le t1, t2 \le 10; t1 + t2 \ge 2; t3 = 0\}$. The intersection of $\mathrm{UF}(\mathcal{LT}(12))$ and $\mathrm{UF}(\mathcal{GT})$ is $\{t1, t2, t3 \mid t1 \le 10; t2 \le 10; t1 + t2 \ge 12; t3 = 10\}$.

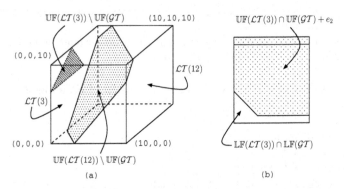

**Fig. 5.** (a) Global time domain of Example 3; $\mathcal{LT}(3)$ contains $\mathcal{LT}(11)$ (b)and $\mathrm{LF}(\mathcal{LT}(3)) \cap \mathrm{LF}(\mathcal{GT})$ and shifted $\mathrm{UF}(\mathcal{LT}(3)) \cap \mathrm{UF}(\mathcal{GT})$ by $(0, 1, 0)$

---

**Algorithm 2.** Algorithm for $k$-dimensional time domain (general case)

---

INPUT : $\mathcal{LT}$ - local time domain, $\mathcal{GT}$ - global time domain
OUTPUT : $\mathcal{R}$ - the set requiring resume signals, $\mathcal{S}$ - the set requiring suspend signals
1: compute $\mathrm{LF}(\mathcal{LT})$, $\mathrm{UF}(\mathcal{LT})$, $\mathrm{LF}(\mathcal{GT})$ and $\mathrm{UF}(\mathcal{GT})$
2: $\mathcal{R} \leftarrow \mathrm{LF}(\mathcal{LT}) \setminus \mathrm{LF}(\mathcal{GT})$; $\mathcal{S} \leftarrow \mathrm{UF}(\mathcal{LT}) \setminus \mathrm{UF}(\mathcal{GT})$
3: compute $\mathrm{LF}(\mathcal{LT}) \cap \mathrm{LF}(\mathcal{GT})$ and $\mathrm{UF}(\mathcal{LT}) \cap \mathrm{UF}(\mathcal{GT})$
4: $R'$ and $S' \leftarrow$ Boundary($\mathrm{LF}(\mathcal{LT}) \cap \mathrm{LF}(\mathcal{GT})$,$\mathrm{UF}(\mathcal{LT}) \cap \mathrm{UF}(\mathcal{GT})$,$\mathrm{LF}(\mathcal{GT})$,$\mathrm{UF}(\mathcal{GT})$,$k$,$k$)
5: $R \leftarrow R \cup R'$; $S \leftarrow S \cup S'$
6: return $\mathcal{R}$ and $\mathcal{S}$
Procedure: Boundary
INPUT : $L,U,GL$ and $GU$ - unions of polyhedra, $d$ - an integer, $k$ - total dimensions
OUTPUT : $R$ and $S$ - unions of polyhedra
1: if $d = 1$
2:    return $L$ and $U$
3: else $- d > 1$
4:    $L' \leftarrow \mathrm{LF}(L) \cap \mathrm{LF}(GL)$; $U' \leftarrow \mathrm{UF}(U) \cap \mathrm{UF}(GU)$
5:    $R \leftarrow \{L \setminus shift(addray(U, -e_i, \forall d \le i \le k), e_{d-1})\} \setminus L'$
6:    $S \leftarrow \{U \setminus shift(addray(L, e_i, \forall d \le i \le k), -e_{d-1})\} \setminus U'$
7:    $R'$ and $S' \leftarrow$ Boundary($L'$, $U'$,$\mathrm{LF}(GL)$, $\mathrm{UF}(GU)$, $d - 1$, $k$)
8:    $R \leftarrow R \cup R'$; $S \leftarrow S \cup S'$
9:    return $R$ and $S$

---

Step 5 in algorithm 1 tells us that a resume signal is needed in $\{t1, t2, t3 \mid 0 \le t1 \le 10; 1 \le t2 \le 10; t1 + t2 \ge 2; t1 + t2 \le 12; t3 = 0\}$. We emphasize that *only the intersection of the second lower facets of $\mathcal{LT}$ and $\mathcal{GT}$ is compared with only the intersection of the second upper facets of $\mathcal{LT}$ and $\mathcal{GT}$* although there are the two second lower facets of $\mathcal{LT}$. The final result is $\{t1, t2, t3 \mid 0 \le t1 \le 10; 1 \le t2 \le 10; t1 + t2 \ge 2; t1 + t2 \le 12; t3 = 0\} \cup \{(2, 0, 0)\}$.

The general case is addressed in algorithm 2. The difference from algorithm 1 is a recursive function for computing the exact points in $\mathrm{LF}(\mathcal{LT}) \cap \mathrm{LF}(\mathcal{GT})$ and $\mathrm{UF}(\mathcal{LT}) \cap \mathrm{UF}(\mathcal{GT})$. However, depending on which face of $\mathcal{GT}$ that $t$ belongs to, $pre(t)$ or $next(t)$ is in a different face of $\mathcal{GT}$.

**Theorem 2.** *Algorithm 2 is (i) correct and (ii) exact:*

*(i) Correctness: If a processor $p$ needs a resume (resp. suspend) signal at $t \in \mathcal{GT}$, then $t$ belongs to the set $R$ (resp. $S$).*

*(ii) Exactness: If $t \in \mathcal{GT}$ belongs to the set $R$ (resp. $S$), then a processor $p$ needs a resume (resp. suspend) signal at time $t$.*

*Proof. (i) Correctness:* Suppose that a processor $p$ needs a resume signal at time $t \in \mathcal{GT}$. Then, $t \in \mathcal{LT}(p)$ and $pre(t) \notin \mathcal{LT}(p)$. By lemma 1, $t \in \mathrm{LF}(\mathcal{LT})$. If $t \notin \mathrm{LF}(\mathcal{GT})$, then $t \in \mathrm{LF}(\mathcal{LT}) \setminus \mathrm{LF}(\mathcal{GT})$. In this case, $t$ is taken into $R$ by step 3. Otherwise, $t \in \mathrm{LF}(\mathcal{GT})$. First, consider the case that $t$ is not the lexicographic minimum of $\mathcal{GT}$. Then, $pre(t)$ exists, and let $t = (t_1, \ldots, t_k)$ and $pre(t) = (t'_1, \ldots, t'_k)$. By the definition of $pre(t)$, there exists an integer $f \ge 1$ such that (i) $t_i = t'_i$ for all $1 \le i \le f - 1$, (ii) $t_f - 1 = t'_f$, and (iii) $t' + e_i \notin \mathcal{GT}$

for all $f < i \leq k$. Now, consider when $t$ is determined to be taken or not, i.e. the face that $t$ belongs to. By the condition $(iii)$, it belongs to $(k - f)$-th upper facet of $\mathcal{GT}$. That is, the $f$-th recursive call determines whether $t$ is taken or not. By $pre(t) \notin \mathcal{LT}$ and the fact that $pre(t) + e_f$ and $t$ have the common elements up to $f$-th element, $t$ is taken into $R$. This is the only operation that affects the determination of $t$. Finally, consider the case when $t$ is the lexicographic minimum of $\mathcal{GT}$. In this case, $t$ belongs to the last lower facet of $\mathcal{GT}$. This is the base case. So $t$ is taken into $R$. Therefore, Algorithm 2 is correct.

$(ii)$ *Exactness:* Suppose that Algorithm 2 picks time $t \in \mathcal{GT}$ into $R$. By the construction of $R$, it is easy to see that every element of $R$ belongs to $\mathbb{LF}(\mathcal{LT})$. Now, let $t \in R$ be $(t_1, t_2, \ldots, t_k)$.

Case 1: $t$ is picked at step 2. Then, $t \notin \mathbb{LF}(\mathcal{GT})$. So, $t - e_k \in \mathcal{GT}$, i.e., $pre(t) = t - e_k$. Since $t \in \mathbb{LF}(\mathcal{LT})$, $t - e_k \notin \mathcal{LT}$. Hence, $pre(t) \notin \mathcal{LT}$.

Case 2: $t$ is picked at step 2 of **Boundary**. Then, $t$ is the lexicographic minimum of $\mathcal{GT}$. Therefore, a processor $p$ needs a resume signal.

Case 3: $t$ is picked at step 5 of **Boundary**. Suppose that $t$ is picked at the $f$-th recursive call. Then, $t$ is in the $f$-th lower facet of both $\mathcal{LT}$ and $\mathcal{GT}$. Since $t$ is in the $f$-th lower facet of $\mathcal{GT}$, i.e., $t$ belongs to the $i$-th lower facet of $\mathcal{GT}$ for all $1 \leq i \leq f$, $t - e_i \notin \mathcal{GT}$ for all $k - f + 1 \leq i \leq k$. Also, $t$ is not in $(f + 1)$-th lower facet of $\mathcal{GT}$. So, there exists a point $(t_1, \ldots t_{k-f+1} - 1, t'_{k-f}, \ldots t'_k)$ in $\mathcal{GT}$. Hence, $pre(t)$ is the form of $(t_1, \ldots t_{k-f+1} - 1, t''_{k-f}, \ldots t''_k)$. By the definition of $pre(t)$, $pre(t) + e_i \notin \mathcal{GT}$ for all $k - f + 1 \leq i \leq k$. So, $pre(t)$ is in the $f$-th upper facet of $\mathcal{GT}$. Since $t$ is picked, $pre(t)$ is not in the $f$-th facet of $LT$. Since $pre(t)$ is in the $f$-th upper facet of $\mathcal{GT}$, the only possibility is that $pre(t) \notin \mathcal{LT}$.

A proof for the suspend signal is symmetric.

## 4.1 Extension

For the sake of explanation, we had presented our analysis with the view that $\mathcal{LT}$ is a single polyhedron. However, our analysis and algorithm are more general and are valid for the case when $\mathcal{LT}$ is a union of polyhedra. When $\mathcal{GT}$ is a union of polyhedra, the algorithm can be applied to the convex hull $C(\mathcal{GT})$ of $\mathcal{GT}$. In this case, the algorithm may not be exact and return a superset of required signals. Precisely, it will always return the points that belong to $\mathbb{LF}(\mathcal{GT}) \setminus \mathbb{LF}(C(\mathcal{GT}))$ and $\mathbb{UF}(\mathcal{GT}) \setminus \mathbb{UF}(C(\mathcal{GT}))$.

## 5   Discussion on Propagation of Control

In our analysis, we have characterized the precise set of time vectors at which the resume (or suspend) signal is needed. Here, we will discuss, with the help of an example a possible mechanism to propagate these signals to the desired PE.

*Example 4.* Consider the following ACL and its corresponding FGP-ACL for matrix multiplication obtained by the parallelization presented in [6].

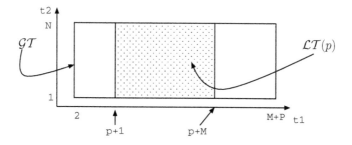

**Fig. 6.** Global and Local time domains for matrix multiplication

```
for i = 1 to M                    for t1 = 2 to M+P
  for j = 1 to P                    forall p = max(1,t1-M)
    C[i,j] = 0;                                to min(P,t1-1)
    for k = 1 to N                     C[t1-p,p]=0;
      C[i,j] += A[i,k]*B[k,j];         for t2 = 1 to N
                                         forall p = max(1,t1-M)
                                                   to min(P,t1-1)
                                           C[t1-p,p]+=A[t1-p,t2]*B[t2,p];
```

The global time domain is enumerated by the loop nest in the FGP-ACL given above. It is shown in figure 6 along with the local time domain for the PE, $p$.

This is a simple design, and by our analysis, there is only one resume and one suspend signal for every PE. These are precisely for starting and stopping the processing element and are needed at the time instants $(p+1,1)$ and $(p+M,N)$ respectively. From the figure, one may verify that the mapping, $\omega$, of logical times to concrete time, denoted by $t^c$ say, is $\omega(t_1,t_2)^T = N(t_1 - 2) + t_2$ such that the processing commences at the concrete time instant $t^c = 1$.

A possible mechanism to *create* and *convey* signals to the relevant PEs would be with the help of a controller connected to the first PE ($p = 1$) and propagation through intermediate PEs. For the first PE, the resume (start) signal is needed at $t^c = 1$ which is received directly from the controller. The next PE needs this signal at $t^c = N + 1$. This too is created by the controller, however, it is propagated through the first PE. If the latency involved with this propagation is a single time instant, the signal is created by the controller at the concrete time instant $t^c = N$. Below, we have given the concrete time instants when the controller creates resume and suspend signals for the PE $p$.

$$\text{Resume}(p) = 1 + (N - 1)(p - 1)$$
$$\text{Suspend}(p) = MN + (N - 1)(p - 1)$$

The validity requirement for such a scheme is that an unbounded number of signals are not created at the same concrete time. Any further discussion on the validity is beyond the scope of this paper.

## 6    Related Work

In the context of hardware synthesis, the control signal issue in multidimensional time was recently addressed by Guillou et. al. [6]. They proposed an solution where each PE has a clock enumerating all the points in the global time domain. The clock is an automaton [20] scanning the global time domain. Although it provides a complete solution for control signals and memory addresses, it also introduces a significant overhead to each PE. Although matrix multiplication requires each PE only one adder and multiplier, each PE intrinsically has a loop scanning the global time domain (and possibly some guards).

Bowden et. al. [21] proposed a control signal distribution scheme in linear systolic array. They assumed that a solution for the control signal problem is given as a quadratic function of the processor coordinate. The basic idea is that architecture itself, not each PE, enumerates the global time domain as a whole. They did not address the question of how to derive the quadratic function.

## 7    Conclusions

The theory and techniques for automatic derivation of systolic architectures has a long and rich history. Although systolic arrays are impractical, much of this theory had an impact in the context of automatic parallelization. Several extensions were proposed, notably those that manipulated more general specifications (ACLs), and towards multidimensional schedules. Yet, the hardware compilation of these general specifications has remained an open problem. The contribution of this paper is aimed at the completion of this circle and provides required results for compiling arbitrary ACLs directly to silicon.

In this paper, we formulated the control signal problem; characterized the time instants when a control signal is necessary; and proposed an algorithm to compute exact solution of the control signal problem. Finally, we discussed possible ways to incorporate a solution into hardware so that each PE receives a correct signal at the correct time.

Future work involves devising efficient distribution schemes for control, leading to the automatic generation of the "optimal" control mechanism for multidimensional schedules. The generation of array access functions is also an open problem.

## References

1. Bastoul, C., Cohen, A., Girbal, S., Sharma, S., Temam, O.: Putting polyhedral loop transformations to work. In: LCPC 2003. (2003) 209–225
2. Schreiber, R., Aditya, S., Mahlke, S., Kathail, V., Ramakrishna-Rau, B., Conquist, D., Sivaraman, M.: Pico-npa: High level synthesis of nonprogrammable hardware accelerators. Journal of VLSI SIgnal Processing (2001) (to appear) (preliminary version presented at ASAP 2000.
3. Guillou, A.C., Quilleré, F., Quinton, P., Rajopadhye, S., Risset., T.: Hardware design methodology with the alpha language. In: FDL'01. (2001)

4. Feautrier, P.: Some efficient solutions to the affine scheduling problem: Part II. multidimensional time. Int. J. of Parallel Program. **21**(6) (1992) 389–420
5. Feautrier, P.: Some efficient solutions to the affine scheduling problem: Part i. one-dimensional time. Int. J. of Parallel Program. **21**(5) (1992) 313–348
6. Guillou, A.C., Quinton, P., Risset, T.: Hardware synthesis for multi-dimensional time. In: ASAP 2003. (2003) 40–50
7. Gautam, Renganarayana, L., Rajopadhye, S.: GRAIL: A generic reconfigurable affine interconnection lattice. submitted (2006)
8. Feautrier, P.: Dataflow analysis of array and scalar references. Int. J. of Parallel Programming **20**(1) (1991) 23–53
9. Pugh, W.: A practical algorithm for exact array dependence analysis. Communications of the ACM **35**(8) (1992) 102–114
10. Karp, R.M., Miller, R.E., Winograd, S.V.: The organization of computations for uniform recurrence equations. JACM **14**(3) (1967) 563–590
11. Lamport, L.: The parallel execution of DO loops. Communications of the ACM (1974) 83–93
12. Darte, A., Robert, Y., Vivien, F.: Scheduling and Automatic Parallelization. Birkhäuser (2000)
13. Rajopadhye, S.V., Purushothaman, S., Fujimoto, R.: On synthesizing systolic arrays from recurrence equations with linear dependencies. In: Foundations of Software Technology and Theoretical Computer Science. Volume 241. (1986) 488–503 Later appeared in Parallel Computing, June 1990.
14. Quinton, P., Dongen, V.V.: The mapping of linear equations on regular arrays. J. of VLSI Signal Processing **1**(2) (1989) 95–113
15. Gautam, Rajopadhye, S., Quinton, P.: Scheduling reductions on realistic machines. In: SPAA '02: Symposium on Parallel algorithms and architectures. (2002) 117–126
16. Lim, A.W., Cheong, G.I., Lam, M.S.: An affine partitioning algorithm to maximize parallelism and minimize communication. In: Int. Conf. on Supercomputing. (1999) 228–237
17. Kuck, D.L.: Structure of Computers and Computations. John Wiley & Sons, Inc., New York, NY, USA (1978)
18. Bagnara, R., Hill, P.M., Zaffanella, E.: The Parma Polyhedra Library User's Manual. Dept of Mathematics, University of Parma, Prama,Italy. version 0.9 edn. (2006) Available at http://www.cs.unipr.it/ppl/.
19. Wilde, D.: A library for doing polyhedral operations. Technical Report PI-785, IRISA (1993)
20. Boulet, P., Feautrier, P.: Scanning polyhedra without do-loops. In: PACT'1998. (1998) 4–11
21. Bowden, S., Wilde, D., Rajopadhye, S.V.: Quadratic control signals in linear systolic arrays. In: ASAP 2000. (2000) 268–275

# The Berkeley View: A New Framework and a New Platform for Parallel Research

David Patterson

UC Berkeley

**Abstract.** The recent switch to parallel microprocessors is a milestone in history of computing. Industry has laid out a roadmap for multi-core designs that preserve the programming paradigm of the past via binary-compatibility and cache-coherence. Conventional wisdom is now to double the number of cores on a chip with each silicon generation. A multidisciplinary group of Berkeley researchers met for 18 months to discuss this change. Our investigations into the future opportunities in led to the follow recommendations which are more revolutionary what industry plans to do:

- The target should be 1000s of cores per chip, as this hardware is the most efficient in MIPS per watt, MIPS per area of silicon, and MIPS per development dollar.
- To maximize application efficiency, programming models should support a wide range of data types and successful models of parallelism: data-level parallelism, independent task parallelism, and instruction-level parallelism.
- Should play a larger role than conventional compilers in translating parallel programs.

The conventional path to architecture innovation is to study a benchmark suite like SPEC or Splash to guide and evaluate innovation. A problem for innovation in parallelism iit best. Hence, it seems unwise to let a set of old programs from the past drive an investigation into parallel computing of the future.

Phil Colella identified 7 numerical methods that he believed will be important for science and engineering for at least next decade. The idea is that programs that implement these numerical methods may change, but the methods themselves will remain important. After examining how well these "7 dwarfs" of high performance computing capture the computation and communication of a much broader range of computing including embedded computing, computer graphics and games, data bases, and machine learningwe doubled them yielding "14 dwarfs." Those interested in our perspective on parallelism should take a look at the wiki: http://view.eecs.berkeley.edu.

To rapidly evaluate all the possible alternatives in parallel architectures and programming systems, we need a flexible, scalable, and economical platform that is fast enough to run extensive applications and operating systems.

Today, one to two dozen processor cores can be programmed into a single FPGA. With multiple FPGAs on a board and multiple boards in

G. Almási, C. Caşcaval, and P. Wu (Eds.): LCPC 2006, LNCS 4382, pp. 156–157, 2007.

a system, 1000 processor architectures can be explored. Such a system will not just invigorate multiprocessors research in the architecture community, but since processors cores can run at 100 to 200 MHz, a large scale multiprocessor would be fast enough to run operating systems and large programs at speeds sufficient to support software research. Hence, we believe such a system will accelerate research across all the fields that touch multiple processors: operating systems, compilers, debuggers, programming languages, scientific libraries, and so on. Thus the acronym RAMP, for Research Accelerator for Multiple Processors.

A group of 10 investigators from 6 universities (Berkeley, CMU, MIT, Stanford Texas Washington) have volunteered to create th RAMP "gateware" (logic to go into the FPGAs) and have the boards fabricated and available at cost . It will run industrial standard instruction sets (Power, SPARC, ...) and operating systems (Linux, Solaris, ...) We hope to have a system that can scale to 1000 processors in late 2007 that costs universities about $100 per processor. I'll report on our results for the initial RAMP implementations at the meeting. Those interested learning more should take a look at: `http://view.eecs.berkeley.edu`.

# An Effective Heuristic for Simple Offset Assignment with Variable Coalescing

Hassan Salamy and J. Ramanujam

Department of Electrical and Computer Engineering
and Center for Computation and Technology
Louisiana State University, Baton Rouge, LA 70803, USA
{hsalam1,jxr}@ece.lsu.edu

**Abstract.** In many Digital Signal Processors (DSPs) with limited memory, programs are loaded in the ROM and thus it is very important to optimize the size of the code to reduce the memory requirement. Many DSP processors include address generation units (AGUs) that can perform address arithmetic (auto-increment and auto-decrement) in parallel to instruction execution, and without the need for extra instructions. Much research has been conducted to optimize the layout of the variables in memory to get the most benefit from auto-increment and auto-decrement. The simple offset assignment (SOA) problem concerns the layout of variables for machines with one address register and the general offset assignment (GOA) deals with multiple address registers. Both these problems assume that each variable needs to be allocated for the entire duration of a program. Both SOA and GOA are NP-complete. In this paper, we present a heuristic for SOA that considers coalescing two or more non-interfering variables into the same memory location. SOA with variable coalescing is intended to decrease the cost of address arithmetic instructions as well as to decrease the memory requirement for variables by maximizing the number of variables mapped to the same memory slot. Results on several benchmarks show the significant improvement of our solution compared to other heuristics. In addition, we have adapted simulated annealing to further improve the solution from our heuristic.

## 1   Introduction

Embedded processors are found in many electronic devices such as telephones, cameras, and calculators. Due to the tight constraints on the design of embedded systems, memory is usually limited. In contrast, the memory requirement for the execution of digital signal processing and video processing codes on an embedded system is significant. Moreover, since the program code resides in the on-chip ROM, the size of the code directly translates into silicon. So code minimization becomes a substantial goal in order to optimize the amount of memory needed.

Many Digital Signal Processors (DSPs) such as the TI C2x/C5x, Motorola 56xxx, Analog Devices 210x and ST D950 have address generation units (AGUs)

G. Almási, C. Caşcaval, and P. Wu (Eds.): LCPC 2006, LNCS 4382, pp. 158–172, 2007.

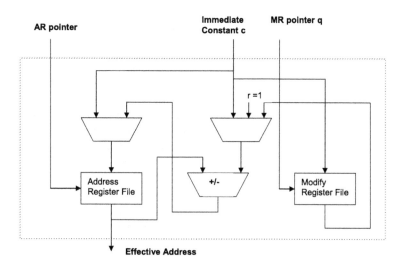

**Fig. 1.** A typical Address Generation Unit (AGU) contains a modify register file, address register file and ALU

[5]. The AGU is responsible for calculating the effective address. A typical AGU consists of an address register file and a modify register file as shown in Figure 1. The architectures of such DSPs support only indirect memory addressing. Since the base-plus-offset addressing mode is not supported, an extra instruction is needed, in general, to add (subtract) an offset to (from) the current address in the address register to compute the new address. However, such architectures support auto-increment and auto-decrement of the address register. When there is a need to add an offset of 1 or subtract an offset of 1 from the current address, this can be done in parallel with the same LOAD/STORE instruction using auto-increment or auto-decrement; and this does not require an extra address arithmetic instruction in the code. Exploiting this characteristic will lead to code compaction and thus less memory used since the length of the code in DSP directly translates into required silicon area. One method for minimizing the instructions needed for address computation is to perform *offset assignment* of the variables. Offset assignment refers to the problem of placing the variables in the memory to maximally utilize auto-increment/decrement and thus reduce code size.

Simple offset assignment (SOA) refers to the case where there is only one address register (AR), whereas general offset assignment (GOA) refers to the case where there are multiple address registers [12]. In both SOA and GOA considered in this paper, the value of auto-increment/decrement is 1; SOA and GOA are NP-complete [12]. Several researchers have studied the offset assignment problem and have proposed different heuristics.

In this paper, we present an effective heuristic for the simple offset assignment problem with *variable coalescing*. Coalescing allows two or more variables to share the same memory location provided that their live ranges do not overlap. Based on the live ranges of all the variables, an interference graph (IG) is constructed in which an edge $(a, b)$ indicates that variables $a$ and $b$ interfere and thus they can not be mapped into the same memory location. Variable coalescing improves the results by decreasing the number of address arithmetic instructions needed as well as the memory requirement for storing the variables.

The remainder of the paper is organized as follows. Section 2 presents related work in this area. Section 3 presents our algorithm for simple offset assignment with variable coalescing. Section 4 gives an example that shows how our algorithm works. Section 5 presents the simulated annealing algorithm to further improve the results. Section 6 summarizes the results. Finally Section 7 presents our conclusions.

## 2   Related Work

The problem of simple offset assignment was first discussed by Bartley [2]. Then Liao et al. [12] showed that the SOA problem is NP-complete and that it is equivalent to the Maximum Weight Path Cover (MWPC) problem. They proposed heuristics for both SOA and GOA. Given an access sequence of the variables, the access graph has a node for each variable with an edge of weight $w$ between nodes $a$ and $b$ meaning that variables $a$ and $b$ appear consecutively $w$ times in the access sequence. In this greedy heuristic, edges are selected in decreasing order of their weights provided that choosing an edge does not introduce a cycle and it does not result in a node of degree more than two. Finally, the access graph considering only the selected edges will determine the placement of the variables in the memory. One possible result of applying Liao's heuristic to the access sequence in Figure 2(a) is shown in Figure 2(c), where the bold edges are the selected edges and the final offset assignment is [e b a c d]. The cost of a solution is the sum of the weights of all unselected edges (i.e., non-bold edges). For the example in Figure 2(a), the cost is 1 which represents the non-bold edge that refers to the one address arithmetic operation needed to go from $a$ to $e$ in the access sequence since variables $a$ and $e$ are mapped to non-consecutive memory locations.

Leupers and Marwedel [9] extended Liao's work by proposing a tie-break heuristic for the SOA problem. Liao et al. [12] did not state what happens if two edges have equal weight. Leupers and Marwedel used the following tie-break function: if two edges have the same weight, they pick the edge with the smaller value of the tie-break function $T_2(a, b)$ defined for an edge $(a, b)$ as in equation 5.

Atri et al. [1] solved the SOA problem using an incremental approach. They tried to overcome some of the problems with Liao's algorithm, mainly in the case of equal weight edges as well as the greedy approach of always selecting the maximum weight edges. Starting with an initial offset assignment (which could be the result of any SOA heuristic), their incremental-SOA tries to explore more points in the solution space by considering the effect of selecting currently unselected edges.

Leupers [7] compared several algorithms for simple offset assignment. Ottoni et al. [13] studied the simple offset assignment problem with variable coalescing (CSOA). Their algorithm uses liveness information to construct the interference graph. In the interference graph, the nodes represent variables and an edge between two variables means that they interfere and thus they can not be coalesced. The authors used the SOA heuristic proposed by Liao et al. [12] enhanced with the tie-break in [9], with the difference that at each step the algorithm chooses between (i) coalescing two variables; and (ii) selecting the edge with the maximum weight as in Liao's algorithm. Their algorithm finds the pair of nodes that can be coalesced with maximum *csave* where *csave* represents the actual saving from coalescing this pair of nodes. At the same time, it finds the edge with the maximum weight $w$ that can be selected using Liao's algorithm. If there are candidates for both coalescing and selection, then it will use coalescing if *csave* is larger than $w$, otherwise use selection.

(a)The access sequence:  d c a e b a b

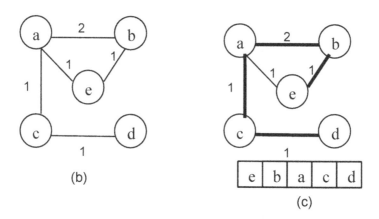

(b)

(c)

**Fig. 2.** (a) Access sequence. (b) Access graph corresponding to the access sequence. (c) Offset assignment where bold edges represent the selected edges and the cost of such assignment is 1.

In [21], the authors studied the cases of SOA with variable coalescing at the same time as [13]. Their coalescing algorithm first separates values into atomic units called webs by applying variable renaming. Their proposed heuristic starts by applying pre-iteration coalescing rules. Then the algorithm picks the two variables (i.e., nodes) with maximum saving for coalescing provided that they respect the validity conditions. If the saving is positive, then the two nodes are coalesced. Liao's SOA will then be applied to the new access graph. This process will continue as long as there are two variables that can be coalesced. Several others [10], [15], [16], [17], [19], [20] have addressed problems related to offset assignment.

# 3   CSOA: Offset Assignment with Variable Coalescing

In simple offset assignment (SOA), each memory location or slot is assigned only one variable. Simple offset assignment with variable coalescing (CSOA) refers to the case where more than one variable can be mapped into the same memory location. Variable coalescing is intended to decrease the memory requirement by further decreasing the number of address arithmetic instructions as well as by decreasing the memory requirements for storing the variables. Two variables can be coalesced if their live ranges do not overlap at any time which means that at any time, those two variables are not needed to be simultaneously live.

In CSOA, an interference graph (IG) is constructed by examining the live ranges of all the variables. Each node in the graph represents a variable, and an edge between two nodes means they interfere and thus they cannot be coalesced. Two variables can be coalesced if they meet all the following conditions:

- the two variables do not interfere;
- after coalescing, no node in the access graph has more than two selected edges incident at it; (and)
- the resulting access graph is still acyclic considering only the selected edges.

So instead of always selecting an edge as in SOA, CSOA can either select an edge or coalesce two variables that meet the three conditions listed above.

Our algorithm presented in Figure 3 integrates both selection and coalescing options in a way to minimize the total cost, which is represented by the number of address arithmetic instructions, as well as to decrease the memory requirement for storing the variables in memory. The algorithm takes as an input, the interference graph (IG) and the access sequence, and outputs the mapping of the variables to memory locations possibly with coalescing. From the access sequence, it constructs the access graph (AG) which captures the frequency of consecutive occurrence of any two variables in the access sequence. Then it sorts the edges whose end-point vertices interfere in decreasing order of their weights as a guide for selection. Since one of the purposes of the heuristic is to decrease the memory requirement for storing the variables, an edge $(a, b)$ such that $(a, b) \notin$ IG will not be considered for selection. Such an edge will be a candidate for coalescing which means that fewer edges will be considered for selection and thus more variables will probably be coalesced. Note that the selection of an edge may prevent variable coalescing opportunities in the future. So only those edges whose endpoints interfere will be considered as candidates for selection in each iteration of the algorithm.

Any two variables that do not interfere are considered as candidates for coalescing. In each iteration, all pairs of variables that meet the three conditions for variable coalescing (mentioned earlier) are candidates for coalescing. We define the following values:

$$Gain(a, b) = \frac{Actual\_Gain(a, b)}{Possible\_Loss(a, b)} \qquad (1)$$

$$
\begin{aligned}
Actual\_Gain(a,b) = \quad & W(a,b) \\
+ & \sum_{\substack{x \in Adj(a) \cap Adj(b) \\ (b,x) \in Selected\_Edges \\ (a,x) \notin Selected\_Edges}} W(a,x) \\
+ & \sum_{\substack{y \in Adj(a) \cap Adj(b) \\ (b,y) \notin Selected\_Edges \\ (a,y) \in Selected\_Edges}} W(b,y) \quad (2)
\end{aligned}
$$

$$
\begin{aligned}
Possible\_Loss(a,b) = \quad & 1 + \sum_{\substack{(a,x) \notin IG, (b,x) \in IG \\ (b,x) \notin Selected\_Edges}} (a,x) \\
+ & \sum_{\substack{(b,y) \notin IG, (a,y) \in IG \\ (a,y) \notin Selected\_Edges}} (b,y) \quad (3)
\end{aligned}
$$

A *Gain* value for each of these candidate pairs is calculated that captures the benefit of coalescing as well as the possible loss of future opportunities for coalescing. The value $Gain(a,b)$ is defined as the actual saving that results from coalescing variables $a$ and $b$ divided by the possible loss of future coalescing opportunities due to coalescing $a$ and $b$. When variables $a$ and $b$ are coalesced, all edges incident at $a$ and $b$ of the form $(a,x)$ and $(b,x)$ will be merged, and if edge $(a,b)$ exists, it will be deleted. When edges $(a,x)$ and $(b,x)$ are merged into edge $(ab,x)$, if at least one of the edges was already selected, then $(ab,x)$ is also considered to be selected. The value $Gain(a,b)$ is defined as shown in Equation 1 and the value $Actual\_Gain(a,b)$ is defined in Equation 2. The value $Actual\_Gain(a,b)$ is basically the sum of the weights of the edges incident at $a$ or $b$ that were not selected before and became selected after being merged with a selected edge plus the weight of the edge $(a,b)$.

The value $Possible\_Loss(a,b)$ is defined in Equation 3 as the sum of the edges $(a,x)$ such that $(a,x) \notin$ IG, $(b,x)$ is not selected, and $(b,x) \in$ IG plus the sum of the edges $(b,y)$ such that $(b,y) \notin$ IG, $(a,y)$ is not selected, and $(a,y) \in$ IG. As depicted in equation 3, $Possible\_Loss(a,b)$ considers only vertices that are neighbors to $a$ or $b$. Although other definitions of the loss can be used, we found that our definition captures the possible effect of coalescing on solutions that can be constructed. Even though coalescing involves vertices and not edges, using the number of edges as the essence for the loss in Equation 3 leads to better results. The rationale behind this is that an edge whose corresponding vertices interfere will probably end up as a selected edge and thus it may prevent some coalescing opportunities and as a result it may degrade the quality of the final solution.

It is worth noting that although our heuristic integrates both selection and coalescing, it gives priority to coalescing, which can be clearly deduced from the definition of loss. We believe this is one of the main reasons for our improvements in terms of the cost as well as the memory requirement for storing the variables.

We divide the value $Actual\_Gain(a,b)$ with the value $Possible\_Loss(a,b)$ to account for the number of edges whose corresponding variables were interference-free and now interfere as a result from coalescing $a$ and $b$. The reason behind this is that coalescing two variables with a larger $Possible\_Loss$ value may prevent more future coalescing opportunities and thus may prevent achieving smaller cost compared to coalescing two variables with a smaller $Possible\_Loss$ value.

Among all the pairs that are candidates for coalescing, our algorithm picks the pair with the maximum $Gain$. If the algorithm is able to find a pair for coalescing as well as an edge for selection, then it will coalesce if the $Actual\_Gain$ from coalescing is greater than or equal to the weight of the edge considered for selection; otherwise, it will select the edge. One way our heuristic attempts to maximize the number of variables mapped to each memory location is to allow the coalescing of pairs of variables with zero $Gain$ value (if possible) after no more variables with positive $Gain$ can be coalesced.

Coalescing variables without a good guide may prevent possible improvements over the standard SOA solution. Consider the example in Figure 4. Figure 4(b) shows Liao's greedy solution. The cost of this offset assignment is 4. Figure 4(c) shows the solution using the algorithm in [13] whose cost is also 4. Although there is potential for improvement through variable coalescing, the algorithm in [13] fails to capture the improvement over Liao's solution. This is because the algorithm in [13] first chooses to coalesce vertices $b$ and $e$ since they have the maximum $csave$. However, this choice will prevent any future coalescing opportunities. Our algorithm alleviates this shortcoming by calculating the $Possible\_Loss(b,e) = 5$ and thus $Gain(b,e) = 3/5$. So our algorithm first picks $a$ and $b$ for coalescing since $Gain(a,b) = 1$; edge $(b,e)$ will not be considered for selection since $b$ and $e$ do not interfere. The cost of the final solution of our algorithm is zero, as shown in Figure 4(d). For selection, we used two tie-break functions $T_1$ and $T_2$ defined below,

$$T_1(a,b) = degree(a) + degree(b) \tag{4}$$

$$T_2(a,b) = \sum_{x \in Adj(a)} W(a,x) + \sum_{y \in Adj(b)} W(b,y), \tag{5}$$

where $T_1(a,b)$ is the sum of the degree of $a$ and degree of $b$ in the access graph. $T_2(a,b)$ is the Leupers tie-break function defined as the sum of the weights of the edges that are incident at $a$ plus the sum of the weights of the edges that are incident at $b$. If two edges that are candidates for selection have the same weight then we try to tie break using the function $T_1$; if $T_1$ cannot break the tie, we use $T_2$. An edge with smaller $T_1$ or $T_2$ will win the tie. If two pairs of variables $(a,b)$ and $(c,d)$ that are candidates for coalescing are such that $Gain(a,b)= Gain(c,d)$, then we first try to break the tie using $T_0$ which is the $Actual\_Gain$ such that we choose the pair with the bigger $Actual\_Gain$. If both candidate pairs have the same actual gain, then we tie break using $T_1$ followed by $T_2$, if needed.

---

Coalescence SOA Algorithm
Input: the Access sequence.
          the Interference graph IG.
Output: Offset assignment.

Build the access graph (AG) from the access sequence.
L = list of edges (x,y) such that (x,y) ∈ IG in decreasing order of their weights using
$T_1$ then $T_2$ for tie break.
Coalesce = false.
Select = false.
Do
          Find a pair of nodes (a,b) for coalescing that satisfy:
              1. (a, b) ∉ IG.
              2. AG will still be acyclic after a and b are coalesced considering
                  selected edges.
              3. No node will end up with degree > 2 considering selected edges.
              4. (a,b) has max Gain where Gain is calculated as in equation (1).
              where $T_0, T_1$, and $T_2$ are the three tie break functions used in that order.
          If such a pair of nodes is found, then Coalesce = true.

          Among the edges that belong to L pick the first edge (c,d) such that:
              1. Selecting (c,d) will not result in a cyclic AG considering selected edges.
              2. Selecting (c,d) will not result in a node with degree > 2 considering
                  selected edges.
          If such an edge is found, then Select = true; remove (c,d) from L.

          If (Coalesce && Select)
              If (Actual_Gain(a, b) = Weight(c, d))
                  Update access graph AG with (a, b) coalesced.
                  Update interference graph IG with (a, b) coalesced.
                  Update list L
              Else
                  Select edge (c,d)
          Else
              if (Coalesce)
                  Update access graph AG with (a,b) coalesced
                  Update interference graph IG with (a,b) coalesced
                  Update list L
              Else if (Select)
                  Select edge (c,d)
While (Coalesce || Select)
Return offset assignment

---

**Fig. 3.** Our algorithm for Simple Offset Assignment with variable coalescing

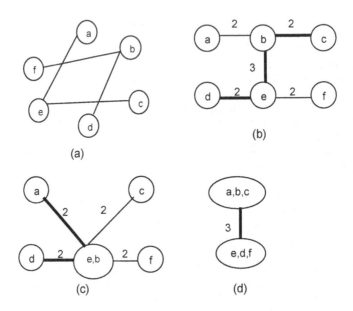

**Fig. 4.** (a) Interference Graph. (b) Liao's SOA greedy solution where the cost = 4. (c) The solution from the algorithm in [13] of cost 4 where it fails to capture the potential improvements from coalescing. (d) The optimal solution from our algorithm with cost = 0.

## 4   An Example

For the sake of clarity, consider the example in Figure 5 where Figure 5(a) shows the interference graph (IG) and Figure 5(b) shows the original access graph (AG). Figures 5(c)–(h) show how the access graph is updated when our heuristic is applied to this example. Although not shown, whenever two nodes are coalesced, the interference graph (IG) will be updated to reflect the coalescing of the nodes as well as to update the interference edges accordingly. Table 1 shows the step-by-step execution of our algorithm and the criteria used for choosing the candidates for selection and for coalescing. Note that in Table 1 we do not show coalescing candidates with zero *Gain*. Figure 5(i) shows the final solution with zero cost. If we run the algorithm in [13] on the same example presented in Figure 5, the cost of a possible final solution, shown in Figure 6, is 4.

## 5   Simulated Annealing

Since the offset assignment problem is NP complete, the heuristic presented in Section 3 will very likely produce a suboptimal solution. So in order to further improve the results, we used a simulated annealing approach. Simulated Annealing (SA) [3] is a global stochastic method that is used to generate approximate solutions to very large combinatorial problems. The technique originates from

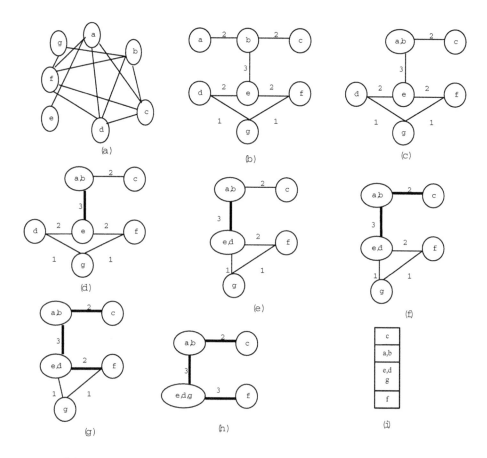

**Fig. 5.** (a) The Interference Graph. (b) Original Access Graph. (c)-(h) The access graphs after each iteration of our algorithm. (i) The final offset assignment, which incurs zero cost.

the theory of statistical mechanics, and is based on the analogy between the annealing process of solids and the solution procedure for large combinatorial optimization problems. The annealing algorithm begins with an initial feasible configuration, and then a neighbor configuration is created by perturbing the current solution. If the cost of the neighboring solution is less than that of the current solution, the neighboring solution is accepted; otherwise, it is accepted or rejected with some probability. The probability of accepting inferior solutions is a function of a parameter, called the temperature T, and the change in cost between the neighboring solution and the current solution. The temperature is decreased during the optimization process, and the probability of accepting an inferior solution decreases with the reduction of the temperature value. The set of parameters controlling the initial temperature, stopping criterion, temperature decrement between successive stages, and number of iterations for each temperature is called the *cooling schedule* [3]. Typically, at the beginning of the

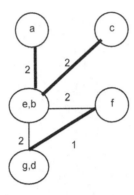

**Fig. 6.** One possible final solution for the example shown in Figure 5 using the algorithm in [13]

**Table 1.** A step by step run of our algorithm on the example in Figure 5

| Iteration | Coalesce Candidate | | | | Selection | | Decision |
|---|---|---|---|---|---|---|---|
| | Vertices | ActualGain | PossibleLoss | Gain | edge | Weight | |
| 1 | a,b | 2 | 2 | 1 | | | Coalesce(a,b) |
| | b,e | 3 | 4 | 3/4 | (b,c) | 2 | Tie-break $T_0$ |
| | d,e | 2 | 3 | 2/3 | (g,f) | 1 | |
| | g,d | 1 | 1 | 1 | | | |
| | f,e | 2 | 3 | 2/3 | | | |
| 2 | d,e | 2 | 2 | 1 | (ab,e) | 3 | |
| | g,d | 1 | 1 | 1 | (ab,c) | 2 | Select (ab,e) |
| | f,e | 2 | 2 | 1 | (g,f) | 1 | |
| 3 | d,e | 2 | 2 | 1 | | | |
| | g,d | 1 | 1 | 1 | (ab,c) | 2 | Coalesce (d,e) |
| | f,e | 2 | 2 | 1 | (g,f) | 1 | Tie-break $T_0$ |
| | c,e | 2 | 3 | 2/3 | | | |
| 4 | ed,g | 1 | 1 | 1 | (ab,c) | 2 | Select (ab,c) |
| | | | | | (ed,f) | 2 | Tie-break $T_1$ |
| | | | | | (g,f) | 1 | |
| 5 | ed,g | 1 | 1 | 1 | (ed,f) | 2 | Select (ed,f) |
| | | | | | (g,f) | 1 | |
| 6 | ed,g | 2 | 1 | 2 | (g,f) | 1 | Coalesce (ed,g) |

algorithm, the temperature T is large and an inferior solution has a high probability of being accepted. During this period, the algorithm. acts as a random search to find a promising region in the solution space. As the optimization progresses, the temperature decreases and there is a lower probability of accepting an inferior solution. The algorithm then behaves like a down hill algorithm for finding the local optimum of the current region.

Since simulated annealing requires a significant amount of time in order to converge to a good solution, we decided to use the final solution from our heuristic as the initial solution for SA and then ran SA for a short period of time with a low probability of accepting a bad solution. The neighbor function can perform one of the following operations: (i) exchange the content of two memory locations; (ii) move the content of one memory location; (iii) uncoalesce a coalesced node into two or more nodes; or (iv) coalesce two memory locations.

# 6   Results

We implemented our techniques in the *OffsetStone* toolset [14] and we tested our algorithms on the *MediaBench* benchmarks [4]. In Table 2, we compare our results with four different techniques used to solve the SOA problem, mainly Leupers' tie-break [9], incremental with Leupers' tie-break INC-TB[9][7], Genetic algorithm GA[8], and Ottoni's CSOA [13]. We measure the percentage of the number of address arithmetic instructions compared to Liao's algorithm [12]. Our heuristic drastically reduces the cost of simple offset assignment when compared to heuristics that do not allow variable coalescing since variable coalescing increases the proximity between variables in memory, thus it reduces the number of update instructions. Column 6 shows that our heuristic was able to outperform the CSOA heuristic [13] (results of which are shown in Column 5) in all the cases except for one benchmark. This improvement is due to the guide used in our choice between candidates for coalescing where we not only consider the actual saving but also an estimate of the possible loss in future coalescing opportunities. Also the idea of just considering edges whose endpoints interfere for selection increases the opportunity for coalescing nodes with maximum *Gain* as defined in Equation 1. The ability to coalesce depends on the selected edges and vice-versa. So an algorithm that can choose the right candidates for selection and coalescing, at the right iteration and decide between them, should consider the influence of such a decision on future solutions. This is accounted for in our algorithm by defining the possible loss as a guide for the possible effect of coalescing on future solutions. The three tie-break functions $T_0$, $T_1$, and $T_2$ play a role in achieving the clear improvements to the final solution. We do not show the comparison to the technique in [21] since the authors reported an average cost reduction of 33.3% when compared to [9] which is worse than the results achieved in [13].

Our simulated annealing (SA) algorithm further improved the results by searching the feasible region for better solutions starting from the final solution of our heuristic. Results in Table 2 column 6 shows that the SA further improved the results in all the cases in a short CPU time.

In Table 3, we show the reduction in memory slots needed to store the variables using our algorithm compared to that of using the algorithm presented in [13]. Results show that our algorithm drastically reduces the memory requirement by maximizing the number of variables that are assigned to the same memory location and it outperforms the CSOA algorithm [13] in all the cases. The reason behind this reduction is that we defined the *Gain* from coalescing in terms of possible loss in coalescing opportunities as well as due to the fact that we did

**Table 2.** Comparison between different techniques for solving the SOA problem where column 1 shows different benchmarks, column 2 shows the results by applying Liao's + Tie-break [9], column 3 shows the results of the GA in [8], column 4 shows the results if the Tie-break [9] is combined with the incremental SOA in [1], and column 5 show the results in the case of SOA with variable coalescing [13], column 6 shows our results when applying our algorithm, column 7 shows the results using simulated annealing

| Benchmarks | TB (%) [9] | GA(%) [8] | INC-TB(%) [9][7] | CSOA(%) [13] | Our algorithm (%) | SA (%) |
|---|---|---|---|---|---|---|
| adpcm | 89.1 | 89.1 | 89.1 | 45.6 | 42.1 | 39.1 |
| epic | 96.8 | 96.6 | 96.6 | 50.2 | 47 | 44.9 |
| g721 | 96.2 | 96.2 | 96.2 | 27.9 | 26.2 | 23.2 |
| gsm | 96.3 | 96.3 | 96.3 | 19.4 | 14.8 | 13.5 |
| jpeg | 96.9 | 96.7 | 96.7 | 32.2 | 31 | 29.1 |
| mpeg2 | 97.3 | 97.1 | 97.2 | 34.3 | 31.2 | 29.9 |
| pegwit | 91.1 | 90.7 | 90.7 | 38.8 | 39.5 | 36.1 |
| pgp | 94.9 | 94.8 | 94.8 | 32.2 | 29.8 | 27.4 |
| rasta | 98.6 | 98.5 | 98.5 | 21.1 | 19.9 | 19.5 |

**Table 3.** The number of memory slots needed using our algorithm to the algorithm presented in [13]

| Benchmarks | #Variables | #Memory slots [13] | #Memory slots our algorithm |
|---|---|---|---|
| adpcm | 198 | 55 | 43 |
| epic | 4163 | 1125 | 767 |
| g721 | 1152 | 289 | 199 |
| gsm | 4817 | 1048 | 433 |
| jpeg | 13690 | 4778 | 2555 |
| mpeg2 | 8828 | 2815 | 1503 |
| pegwit | 4122 | 1454 | 910 |
| pgp | 9451 | 2989 | 1730 |
| rasta | 4040 | 1056 | 557 |

not consider the edges $(a, b)$ such that $(a, b) \notin IG$ as candidates for selection and this will result in more opportunities for coalescing. However, the main reason for this improvement is that our heuristic allows zero $Gain$ coalescing between nodes in the final AG. That is, we coalesce pairs of vertices $(a, b)$ (if possible) such that $Gain(a, b) = 0$. This zero $Gain$ coalescing will not reduce the cost in terms of the number of address arithmetic instructions but it will contribute to maximizing the number of variables mapped to a memory location. This explains the huge difference between the improvements in Table 2 and Table 3. Although a heuristic designed just to decrease the memory requirement for storing the variables can get better results than those in Table 3, it will be detrimental to the quality of the final solution in terms of the number of address arithmetic instructions. So our heuristic not only decreases the cost (which is defined as the reduction in the number of address arithmetic instructions), but also decreases the number of memory locations needed to store the variables.

## 7 Conclusions

The problem of offset assignment has received a lot of attention from researchers due to its great impact on code size reduction for DSPs. Reducing the code size is beneficial in the case of DSPs since the code is directly transformed into silicon area. Statistics show that codes for DSPs can have up to 50% address arithmetic instructions [18]. So the main idea of the ongoing research in this field is to decrease the number of address arithmetic instructions and thus the code size. The problem is studied as simple offset assignment (SOA) and as general offset assignment (GOA), where different techniques and algorithms are used to tackle these problems with different modifications such as the inclusion of the modify-registers [9] as well as the case where the offset range is greater than 1. In this paper we presented a heuristic to solve the simple offset assignment with variable coalescing that chooses between selection and coalescing in each iteration by calculating the *Actual_Gain* and *Possible_Loss* for each pair of coalescing candidates. Results show that our algorithm not only decreases the number of address arithmetic instructions, but also drastically decreases the memory requirement for storing the variables by maximizing the number of variables that are mapped to the same memory slot. Simulated annealing further improved the final solution from our heuristic.

**Acknowledgments.** We are indebted to Sam Midkiff for a careful reading of this paper which has resulted in a significant improvement in the presentation of the paper. In addition, we thank the referees for their comments. The work presented in this paper is supported in part by NSF grants 0541409, 0509442, 0508245, and 0121706.

## References

1. S. Atri, J. Ramanujam, and M. Kandemir. Improving Offset Assignment for Embedded Processors. In *Languages and Compilers for High-Performance Computing,* S. Midkiff et al. (eds.), Lecture Notes in Computer Science, Springer-Verlag, 2001.
2. D.H. Bartley. Optimizing Stack Frame Accesses for Processors with Restricted Addressing Modes. *Software-Practice and Experience,* 22(2):102–111, 1992.
3. S. Kirkpatrick, C. D. Gelatt Jr., and M. P. Vecchi. Optimization by Simulated Annealing. *Science,* 220(4598):671–680, 1983.
4. C. Lee, M. Potkonjak, and W. Mangione-Smith. MediaBench: A Tool for Evaluating and Synthesizing Multimedia and Communications Systems. In *Proc. IEEE International Symposium on Microarchitecture,* pp. 330–335, 1997.
5. R. Leupers. Code Generation for Embedded Processors. In *Proc. 13th International System Synthesis Symposium (ISSS),* 2000.
6. R. Leupers. *Code Optimization Techniques for Embedded Processors.* Kluwer Academic Publishers, 2000.

7. R. Leupers. Offset Assignment Showdown: Evaluation of DSP Address Code Optimization Algorithms. In *Proc. 12th International Conference on Compiler Construction (CC)*, Warsaw, Poland, Springer LNCS 2622, 2003.

8. R. Leupers and F. David. A Uniform Optimization Technique for Offset Assignment Problems. In *Proc. 11th International System Synthesis Symposium (ISSS)*, 1998.

9. R. Leupers and P. Marwedel. Algorithms for Address Assignment in DSP Code Generation. In *Proc. International Conference on Computer-Aided Design (ICCAD)*, 1996.

10. B. Li and R. Gupta. Simple Offset Assignment in Presence of Subword Data. In *Proc. International Conference on Compilers, Architectures and Synthesis for Embedded Systems (CASES 2003)*, pp. 12–23, 2003.

11. S. Liao. *Code Generation and Optimization for Embedded Digital Signal Processors*. Ph.D. Thesis, Dept. of Electrical Engineering and Computer Science, Massachusetts Institute of Technology, 1996.

12. S. Liao, S. Devadas, K. Keutzer, S. Tjiang, and A. Wang. Storage Assignment to Decrease Code Size. In *Proc. ACM SIGPLAN Conference on Programming Language Design and Implementation (PLDI)*, 1995.

13. D. Ottoni, G. Ottoni, G. Araujo, R. Leupers. Improving Offset Assignment through simultaneous Variable Coalescing. In *Proc. 7th International Workshop on Software and Compilers for Embedded Systems (SCOPES'03)*, Springer LNCS 2826, pp. 285–297, Vienna, Austria, September 2003.

14. *OffsetStone*. http://www.address-code-optimization.org.

15. G. Ottoni, S. Rigo, G. Araujo, S. Rajagopalan, and S. Malik. Optimal Live Range Merge for Address Register Allocation in Embedded Programs. In *Proc. 10th International Conference on Compiler Construction, CC 2001*, LNCS 2027, pp. 274–288. Springer, April 2001.

16. A. Rao and S. Pande. Storage Assignment Optimizations to Generate Compact and Efficient Code on Embedded DSPs. In *Proc. ACM SIGPLAN Conference on Programming Language Design and Implementation (PLDI)*, pp. 128–138, 1999.

17. A. Sudarsanam, S. Liao, and S. Devadas. Analysis and Evaluation of Address Arithmetic Capabilities in Custom DSP Architectures. In *Proc. Design Automation Conference*, pp. 287–292, 1997.

18. S. Udayanarayanan and C. Chakrabarti: Address Code Generation for Digital Signal Processors. In *Proc. 38th Design Automation Conference (DAC)*, 2001.

19. B. Wess and M. Gotschlich. Optimal DSP Memory Layout Generation as a Quadratic Assignment Problem. In *Proc, International Symposium on Circuits and Systems (ISCAS)*, 1997.

20. B. Wess and T. Zeitlhofer. Optimum Address pointer Assignment for Digital Signal Processors. In *International Conference on Acoustics, Speech and Signal Processing (ICASSP)*, 2004.

21. X. Zhuang, C. Lau, and S. Pande. Storage Assignment Optimizations Through Variable Coalescence for Embedded Processors. In *Proc. ACM SIGPLAN Conference on Language, Compiler, and Tool Support for Embedded Systems (LCTES)*, pp. 220–231, 2003.

# Iterative Compilation with Kernel Exploration

D. Barthou[2], S. Donadio[1,2], A. Duchateau[2], W. Jalby[2], and E. Courtois[3]

[1] Bull SA Company, France
[2] Université de Versailles, France
[3] CAPS Entreprise, France

**Abstract.** The increasing complexity of hardware mechanisms for recent processors makes high performance code generation very challenging. One of the main issue for high performance is the optimization of memory accesses. General purpose compilers, with no knowledge of the application context and approximate memory model, seem inappropriate for this task. Combining application-dependent optimizations on the source code and exploration of optimization parameters as it is achieved with ATLAS, has been shown as one way to improve performance. Yet, hand-tuned codes such as in the MKL library still outperform ATLAS with an important speed-up and some effort has to be done in order to bridge the gap between performance obtained by automatic and manual optimizations.

In this paper, a new iterative compilation approach for the generation of high performance codes is proposed. This approach is not application-dependent, compared to ATLAS. The idea is to separate the memory optimization phase from the computation optimization phase. The first step automatically finds all possible decompositions of the code into kernels. With datasets that fit into the cache and simplified memory accesses, these kernels are simpler to optimize, either with the compiler, at source level, or with a dedicated code generator. The best decomposition is then found by a model-guided approach, performing on the source code the required memory optimizations.

Exploration of optimization sequences and their parameters is achieved with a meta-compilation language, X language. The first results on linear algebra codes for Itanium show that the performance obtained reduce the gap with those of highly optimized hand-tuned codes.

## 1 Introduction

The increasing complexity of hardware mechanisms incorporated in modern processors makes high performance code generation very challenging. One of the key difficulty in the code optimization process is that several issues have to be simultaneously addressed/optimized: for example maximizing instruction level parallelism (ILP) and optimizing data reuse across multilevel memory hierarchies. Moreover, very often, a code transformation will be beneficial to one aspect while it will be detrimental for the other one. The whole problem worsens because the issues are tackled by different levels of the compiler chain: most of the

G. Almási, C. Caşcaval, and P. Wu (Eds.): LCPC 2006, LNCS 4382, pp. 173–189, 2007.

ILP is optimized by the backend while data locality optimization is performed at a higher level.

A good example for highlighting all of these problems is the simple matrix multiply operation. Although the code is fairly simple, none of the recent compilers is really able to generate performance close to hand coded routines. For dealing with this problem, Dongarra et. al.[18] have developed a specialized code generator (ATLAS) combining iterative techniques and experimentation. ATLAS is a very good progress in the right direction (it outperforms most of the compilers) but very often it still lags behind hand coded routines. Recently, ATLAS has been improved by replacing the iterative search by an adapted cost model enable to generate code with nearly the same performance [21]. But even with these recent improvements, vendor [8,16] or hand-tuned BLAS3 [11] still outperforms ATLAS compiled codes and, up to now, such libraries are the only ones capable of reaching near-peak performance on linear algebra kernels. So what is ATLAS and more generally compilers still missing in order to reach this level of performance ?

In this paper we propose an automated process (i.e. no hand coding) which allows to close this gap. The starting point is to decouple the two issues (ILP and data locality optimizations) and then to solve them separately. For the matrix multiply operation, blocking is performed to produce a primitive which will operate on subarrays fitting in cache. This blocking does not provide us with a single solution but rather with constraints on block sizes. Then for optimizing the primitive which is still a matrix multiply, we use a bottom up approach combined with systematic exploration. In general, the triply nested loop will be too complex to be correctly optimized by a compiler even if the operands are in cache (i.e. no blocking for cache has to be performed). Therefore, from the triply nested loop, several kernels (using interchange, strip mine, partial unroll) are generated. These kernels are one up to three dimensional loops, loop bodies containing several statements resulting from the unrolling. Additionally, to simplify compiler's task, loop trip count is set to a constant. The rationale for such kernels is to be simple enough so that a decent compiler can generate optimal code. Then all of these kernels are systematically tested to determine their performance. As a result of this process, a set of kernels reaching close to peak performance is produced. From these kernels, the primitives can be easily rebuilt. And finally, taking into account block size constraints, a primitive is selected and the whole code is produced.

As we will demonstrate in this paper, such an approach offers several key advantages: first it generates very high performance codes competitive with existing libraries and hand tuned codes, second it relies on existing compilers, and third it is extremely flexible i.e. capable of accommodating arbitrary rectangular matrices (not only the classical square matrix operation).

The approach proposed is demonstrated on BLAS kernels but it does not depend upon any specifics of the matrix multiply and it can be applied to other codes. In contrast to ATLAS, we did not a priori select a given primitive which is further tuned. On the contrary, a large number of primitives which are automatically produced, is considered and analyzed. Each of these primitives correspond to the application of a given set of transformations/optimization. Generation and exploration of these optimization sequences and their parameters is achieved with a meta-compilation language, X language.

The approach described in this paper applies to regular linear algebra codes. More specifically, the codes considered are static control programs[9]: loop bounds can only depend linearly on other loop iteration counters or on variables that are readonly in the code. Array indices depend linearly on loop indices.

The paper is organized as follows: Section 2 describes the iterative kernel decomposition and their optimization, Section 3 briefly gives the main features of the X Language, Section 4 gives experimental results performed on various matrix shapes comparing our approach with ATLAS and MKL, Section 5 describes related work and Section 5 gives some future directions.

## Motivating Example

Consider the standard code for matrix vector product given in Figure 1. We will assume that the matrix sizes $M, N$ are such that both matrix and vector fit in cache.

```
for (i = 0; i < M; i++)
  ML = &M[i][0]; b = B[i];
  // DAXPY code
  for( j = 0 ; j < N ; j++)
    A[j] += b * ML[j];
```

**Fig. 1.** Dgemv with daxpy

```
for (i = 0; i < M; i+=2)
  ML1 = &M[i][0]  ; b1 = B[i];
  ML2 = &M[i+1][0]; b2 = B[i+1];
  // DAXPY2 code
  for( j = 0 ; j < N ; j++)
    A[j] += b1 * ML1[j];
    A[j] += b2 * ML2[j];
```

**Fig. 2.** Dgemv with daxpy2

The same code is transformed into the code of Figure 2 by unrolling two times the outer loop (tail code is not presented). The inner loop is no longer a simple daxpy but a variant called daxpy2. The transformation process can be applied with different unrolling degree values 3, 4,... resulting in similar inner loops called daxpy3, daxpy4,... Therefore, for the same original matrix vector routine, different decompositions can be obtained using different kernels daxpy2, daxpy3,...

For this experiment, as for all others presented in this paper, the platform used is a Novascale Bull server featuring two 1.6Ghz Itanium 2 processors, with a 256KB level 2 cache and a 9MB level 3 cache. All codes are compiled using the Intel C compiler (icc) version 9.0 with -O3 -fno-aliases flags. For each of the unrolling factor of the outer loop resulting in the different kernels daxpy2, daxpy3, ..., the $j$ loop was also unrolled 1, 2, 3 and 4 times (resp. U1, U2, U3 and U4). Performance of the resulting kernels (i.e. the $j$ loop only) for

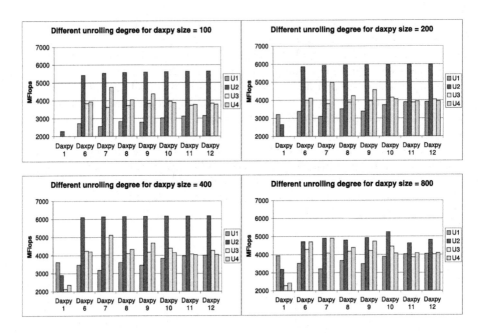

**Fig. 3.** Performance of daxpy with different sizes and unrolling degrees

$N$=100, 200, 400, 800 is displayed in Figure 3. Results below 2000MFlops do not appear in the figures. Due to lack of space, performance numbers of the whole matrix vector primitive are not shown but they have been generated and they are strictly equivalent to the performance number of the primitive they are using.

This shows several points:

- The compiler is able to generate near peak performance with a daxpy12 unrolled 2 times, of size 400 (peak performance for this machine is 6300MFlops). Even if this is obtained through a vendor compiler, this shows that compiler technology is able to produce high performance codes, without the help of hand-tuned assembly code;
- There is a speed-up of 3.13 between the slowest version (daxpy 1, unroll factor of 3) and the fastest one, among the versions that are displayed. This speedup is worth the effort but the optimization parameters to use in order to obtain the fastest version are far from obvious. This advocates for an iterative method relying on search;
- Selecting the right vector length is essential to reach peak performance. Vector length 100 is too short, while vector length 400 is optimal. Vector length 800 examplifies a typical performance problem of Itanium L2 cache banking system: since $800 = 25x32$ all of the vectors ML1, ML2, etc ... start in the same L2 bank.

This illustrates the fact that micro-optimization of loop can bring substantial performance improvement, even when resorting only to compilers. The rest of the paper shows how to use this idea in order to generate automatically high-performance linear algebra codes.

## 2    Iterative Kernel Decomposition

The principle of the approach described in this paper is the following: the code is first tiled for memory reuse. Then each tile is tiled again to create computational kernels. The performance of these kernels is evaluated, for different tile sizes and for different memory alignments, independently of the application context. The most efficient kernels are then put back into the memory reuse tile, according to the different possible sizes of the tile and the performance of the tile is evaluated. The data layout transformations (copies, transpositions) required by the computational kernels are also evaluated by microbenchmarking. From there, a decision tree builds up, for all loop sizes, the best decomposition into memory reuse tiles and computational tiles, according to the cost previously evaluated. All the steps concerning kernel optimization are new contributions for high performance compilation approach and are illustrated in Figure 4.

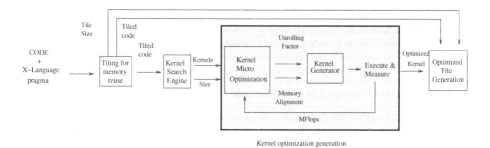

**Fig. 4.** Steps of iterative kernel decomposition

Each step is presented in details in the following sections. Figure 5 represents a matrix multiplication that will illustrate each step of the approach.

```
for (i = 0; i < N ; i++)
  for (j = 0; j < N ; j++)
    for (k = 0; k < N ; k++)
      c[i][j] += a[i][k] * b[k][j];
```

**Fig. 5.** Naive DGEMM

```
// copy B into b by blocks of width NJ
for (i = 0; i < N ; i += NI)
  // copy A into a by block of width NK
  for (j = 0; j < N ; j += NJ)
    // copy C into c
    for (k = 0; k < N ; k += NK)
      // Tile for memory reuse
      for (ii = 0; ii < NI; ii++)
        for (jj = 0; jj < NJ; jj++)
          for (kk = 0; kk < NK; kk++ )
            c[ii][jj] += a[ii][kk] * b[kk][jj];
```

**Fig. 6.** Tiled DGEMM

## 2.1  Loop Tiling

The goal of loop tiling[19,4,14,13] is to reduce memory traffic by enhancing data reuse. Tiling also enables memory layout optimizations, such as copies or scalar promotions to exhibit locality for instance. Given the cache size, the tile sizes must be such that the working set used in the tile fits into the cache. Moreover, we impose that tiles are rectangular. Indeed, even for a non rectangular initial iteration domain, it is always possible to tile most of the computation with rectangular bounds. The remaining iterations represent then a negligible amount of computation. Then, rectangular tiles are easier to optimize (possible to unroll with no remainder loop, more regular address streams for prefetching,... ). Due to the fact that the global iteration space may not permit all tile sizes, a set of tile sizes that enable the partition of any outer iteration domain is considered.

The tiling is obtained through strip mine of all loops, followed by a search using loop permutation, skewing, reversal and loop distribution. Tile sizes are parametric and will be determined later in the method. The exact evaluation of the working set may lead in general to complex results, difficult to handle[3]. We choose to use for each array the min, max interval index value used in the tile as an over-approximation of the array elements accessed. Other methods, more sophisticated, can later be used.

The tiling applyied on DGEMM is presented Figure 6. The tiled code corresponds to a mini-MMM according to ATLAS terminology. The copy-out of c is not included.

## 2.2  Tiling for Computation Kernels

The code of the previously obtained tiles is then micro-optimized. It is important to stress the fact that a part of the overall code performance can only be obtained at this level. Further optimizations with scheduling among tiles or with higher level in memory hierarchy optimization may only degrade performance obtained in this level. The optimization of the tile code is in two steps: (i) we create inside the tile a simpler computation tile. Note that usually, this level of tiling corresponds to a level of blocking for register file. Here we create instead a new tile containing one loop (1D tile) up to the dimension of the surrounding tile loops. (ii) the computation tile is optimized and evaluated in an iterative process.

The goal is to partition data reuse tiles into tiles that are simpler for a code generator (basically the compiler) to optimize. Compiler technology has a long history on low-level, low-complexity optimizations. Even if affine schedules and complex array data dependence analysis have existed since a long time, few are really implemented in vendor compilers and a large part of performance, when all the dataset is in cache, comes from the backend optimizations anyway. Simplifying source code by giving simple kernels once at a time is a method to take advantage of a code generator high quality backend (constant loop bounds enable accurate prefetching distances, opportunities for better unrolling or software pipelining).

The search for computation kernels relies on application of stripmine and loop permutations. The resulting kernels come from a selection of this inner tile.

After these simple transformations, partial unroll is applied to the loops not in the kernel, generating many variations of the same family of kernel. In order to bound the search, range of unrolling factor is defined by the user with a pragma annotation in the source code. The data structures are then simplified, such that all iteration counters not in the kernel are considered as constants and projected out. A memory copy, transposition or another data layout transformation may be necessary to simplify the data layout.

The search is exhaustive, therefore a bound of the search space has to be given: for perfect loop nests, of depth $n$, there are $\binom{p}{n}$ possible kernels with $p$ loops (considering any loop order, less if some dependences prevent some permutations). For each kernel with $p$ loops, there are at most $n - p$ loops to unroll, therefore an upper bound of the number of kernels, including all versions obtained by unrolling, is $\mathcal{O}(n.2^n)$ where $n$ is the depth of the initial loop nest. This not an issue since the maximum loop depth is usually lower than 4.

Concerning the mini-MMM code for DGEMM, searching for kernels leads to 5 different kernels, 4 of them are presented in Figures 7, 8, 9, 10. The remaining 3D kernel is the DGEMM itself. The values $n$, $m$ correspond to the unrolling factor of the surrounding loops.

```
for( i = 0 ; i < ni ; i++)
    c11 += V1[i] * W1[i];
    . . .
    c1n += V1[i] * Wn[i];
    c21 += V2[i] * W1[i];
    . . .
    cmn += Vm[i] * Wn[i];
```

**Fig. 7.** 1D Kernel: dot product nm

```
for( i = 0 ; i < ni ; i++){
    V1[i] += a11 * W1[i];
    . . .
    V1[i] += a1n * Wn[i];
    V2[i] += a2n * W1[i];
    . . .
    Vm[i] += amn * Wn[i];
```

**Fig. 8.** 1D Kernel: daxpy mn

```
for (i = 0; i < ni ; i++)
    for (j = 0; j < nj ; j++)
        c1[j] += a1[j] * b[i][j];
        . . .
        cn[j] += an[j] * b[i][j];
```

**Fig. 9.** 2D Kernel: dgemv

```
for (i = 0; i < ni ; i++)
    for (j = 0; j < nj ; j++)
        c[i][j] += a1[i] * b1[j];
        . . .
        c[i][j] += an[i] * bn[j];
```

**Fig. 10.** 2D Kernel: outer product n

### 2.3  Kernel Micro-optimization

Once kernels have been selected, their optimization is achieved. As stated before, this step mainly relies on the optimization capacity of some code generator. However, some optimizations and optimization parameters are still searched for:

– Loop bound sampling: different values of loop bounds are tested. The reason is that the loop bound impact directly the working set, using other levels of cache that the outer data-reuse tile. Moreover, mechanisms such as prefetching may be influenced by the actual value of the bound and loop overheads, pipelines with large MAKESPAN or large unrolling factors can take advantage of larger iteration counts. The span of the sampling can be user-defined through X language pragmas.

- Array alignments: the code generated may be unstable w.r.t. the alignment of the arrays starting addresses. Important performance gains can be obtained by finding the best alignment[12]. Testing the different possible alignments reveals performance stability. If stability is an issue, it is then possible to copy part of the arrays necessary for the tile with the specific alignments that enable the best performance.
- Loop transformations: interchange for kernels that have more than one loop, and unrolling (sometimes taken care of by the compiler) generate new versions of the kernel and increase parallelism. Optimizations such as software pipeline are performed by some compilers.

All experimental results are presented in Section 4. Note that as the data structures have been simplified and do no longer depend on the surrounding loops, it is quite possible to optimize the kernels in-vitro: out of the application context. The advantage of such approach is that kernel optimizations and micro-benchmarkings can be easily reused from one code to the other. The idea of using a database of highly optimized kernels is already used by CAPS with codes generated by XLG [20].

This suggests another method for kernel micro-optimization: with high performance libraries or kernels, matching the source kernel with an existing library function (source interface) would avoid completely the iterative optimization step. The kernel can then be replaced by the assembly version of the library function. Pattern-matching based techniques have been applied for instance by Bodin[2] for vectorized kernels. In general, recognizing codes even after data structure and loop transformations boils down to algorithm recognition techniques[1,15].

Finally, exploration space can be limited by static evaluation and comparison of the assembly codes. Tools such as MAQAO[6] potentially detects inefficient codes from the assembly and compare different versions. Indeed, the compiler sometimes generates the same assembly code from two different source codes.

## 2.4   Putting Kernels to Work

The final step consists of reassembling the code from the available kernels. This bottom-up phase first builds the data reuse tiles with kernels, according to the tile size. For a sampling of tile sizes, each decomposition in kernels is evaluated. In particular very thin tiles are studied because they necessitate special computation kernels to tile them. Then copies and other data layout transformations necessary for the kernels to work are added.

For the matrix multiplication, tiles considered are denoted by formula such as $(k \times N)X(N \times k)$: this denotes the multiplication of a matrix of size $k \times N$

where $k << N$, by a matrix $N \times k$. In these formula, $k$ denotes an integer much smaller than $N$. The tile size studied are: $(k \times N)X(N \times N),(N \times k)X(k \times N)$, $(k \times N)X(N \times k)$ and $(N \times N)X(N \times N)$.

Figures 11 and 12 present two mini-MMM tiled with a kernel of daxpy 10,1 unrolled 2 times (this unrolling factor concerns the loop inside the daxpy) and a kernel of dot product 1,1 unrolled 10 times. The later requires that the block b is transposed. The code of Figure 11 would be a good kernel for a matrix product of the form $(k \times N)X(N \times N)$ but is not adequate for a matrix product $(N \times k)X(k \times N)$ with $k < 10$ for instance. Another kernel decomposition is then needed.

```
for (ii = 0; ii < NI; ii++)
  for (jj = 0; jj < NJ; jj+=nj)
    for (kk = 0; kk < NK; kk+=10 )    // transpose b into bt
        daxpy_10_u2(nj,c[ii],          for( ii = 0 ; ii < NI; ii++)
          a[ii][kk],..,a[ii][kk+9],      for( jj = 0 ; jj < NJ; jj++)
          b[kk],..,b[kk+9]);               for (kk = 0; kk < NK; kk+=nk)
                                             dotproduct_u10(nk,c[ii][jj],a[ii],bt[jj]);
```

**Fig. 11.** Tile using daxpy 10,1 unrolled 2 times

**Fig. 12.** Tile using dotproduct 1,1 unrolled 10 times

Finally, according to the external loop sizes, the best performing combination of tile and memory copies is selected. Evaluation of the fastest combination requires that the memory operations are also evaluated. As a matter of fact, they are considered as kernels and are micro-optimized as well. A decision tree selects the right version.

## 3  X Language

X Language[7] is a language of pragmas used for meta-compilation: with the help of pragmas, a user can:

- Specify fragments of codes for which X Language transformations apply, using #pragma xlang begin and #pragma xlang end directives around selected code;
- Trigger some source to source transformations on the specified code using specific pragma directives, such as

```
#pragma xlang transform tile(i,II,STRIDE)
#pragma xlang transform unroll(i,UNROLL)
```

to first tile the loop i with a stride STRIDE into a new loop II and then unroll this new loop by a factor of UNROLL. Available transformations include unrolling, tiling, fission, fusion, interchange, scalar promote,... The transformation engine is in Prolog and transformations can easily be added to the language.

– Generate multiple versions by defining search intervals, such as

```
#pragma xlang parameter STRIDE [16:128:32]
#pragma xlang parameter UNROLL [1:8:1]
```

These directives define that STRIDE can take any value multiple of 32 between 16 and 128. X Language then generates automatically all versions of the code fragment with these optimization parameters.
– Trigger a search for the decomposition of a code fragment into kernels:

```
#pragma xlang decompose i
```

This directive decomposes loop i into kernels. This step corresponds to the tiling into computation kernels. X Language generates as many files as different kernels found.

Compared to the version presented in [7], this version of X Language is based on a C99 front-end parser (tiny C compiler), relies on a Prolog engine for the source to source transformations and finds kernels that compose a code fragment. Micro optimization of these kernels still requires now another compilation step using X Language. Testing stability w.r.t. array alignment is achieved by another tool, Kerbe, which is not yet linked to X language. Further automation of the method presented in this paper is planned for future work.

## 4    Experimental Results

We study in this section different kernels to do a matrix-matrix multiplication (DGEMM) and a convolution function. We compare these results with those of the functions of library like Atlas and the Intel library MKL. As for all experiments, after the kernel decomposition, each kernel is evaluated separately and then inside the data reuse tile.

### 4.1    Micro-optimization of DGEMM Kernels

All kernels are presented in previous sections.

For 1D kernels, daxpy $n, 1$ kernels ($m = 1$) have been evaluated and the results of the experiments are presented in Figure 3. All experiments have measured the impact of array alignment. Only the best results are presented. For 2D kernels,

**Table 1.** Matrix-Vector multiply

| N | cycles | cycles/fma | MFlops |
|---|---|---|---|
| 96 | 50166,7 | 0,544 | 5863,970 |
| 128 | 88332,9 | 0,539 | 5918,367 |
| 160 | 137900,5 | 0,538 | 5929,368 |
| 192 | 226383,5 | 0,614 | 5195,439 |

performance of matrix-vector product are presented in the following table: The Figure 13 sums up performances of the outer product kernel. The 3D kernel represents a complete matrix matrix multiplication. Its performance are shown in Figure 18 and prove that this is not an adequate kernel.

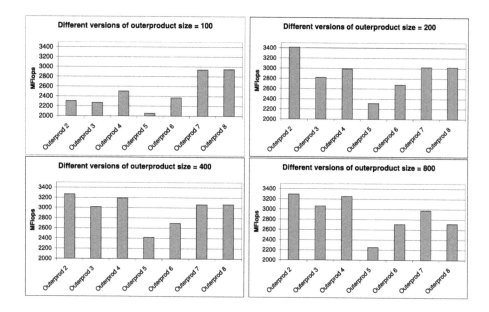

**Fig. 13.** Outer product performance for different versions and sizes

## 4.2    Results on DGEMM Operation

We present the best results of dgemm according to the size of the tile or of the matrices. The decomposition is automatically performed by our tool, given the detected kernels. The limit sizes (values of $k << N$) are determined by the user in X language. Here, we choose $k = 1, 2, 4, 8$ and $N$ ranges from 100 to 1500. Results for Atlas, MKL and our method are presented for the same tile sizes.

**Type $(k \times N)X(N \times N)$:** This type of tile corresponds to a 2D kernel, performing $k$ vector-matrix products (named Dgemv). For this type of tile, the fastest dgemm uses a kernel of dotproduct 1,1 unrolled 10 times, requiring a matrix transposition of **b**. Performance results are displayed in Figure 14 and following. A 50% speedup is obtained w.r.t. ATLAS and performance follows those of the MKL library. Performance drops around $N = 800$ because the tile size exceeds the cache size. At this point the outer tiling or the use of another kernel of our library can correct this degradation.

**Type $(N \times k)X(k \times N)$:** This type of tile corresponds to a 1D kernel, performing $k$ outer products. For this type of tile where the common dimension if

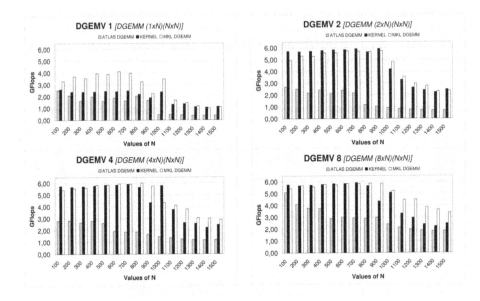

**Fig. 14.** DGEMM (kxN) X (NxN) with k=1,2,4,8

much lower than the others, the fastest dgemm uses the kernels of daxpy $k, 1$. Therefore each value of $k$ requires a different kernel. Performance results are displayed in Figure 15 and following. The results outperform those of ATLAS by more than a factor of 2 and MKL is better by 50%. For $N > 900$, performance drops since the tile size exceeds the cache size, which is out of bounds for the kernel execution.

**Type $(k \times N)X(N \times k)$:** This type of tile corresponds to a 1D kernel, performing $k$ independent dot products. For this type of tile, the fastest dgemm uses the kernel of dot product $6, 6$. Performance results are displayed in Figure 16 and following. The results outperforms those of ATLAS by a factor of at least 3 and of MKL by a factor of at least 2. The dataset still fits into the cache for large values of $N$, since the resulting matrix is very small. Note that the performance of our product is very unstable w.r.t. the array alignment. Array copies when entering inside the tile prevents such unpredictability.

**Type $(N \times N)X(N \times N)$:** Finally, we build the code of a complete matrix product. As this step is not yet automated (construction of the decision tree), we consider only square matrices. Taking only into consideration the previous experimental results for various tile sizes, we choose to tile the matrices with rectangular matrices of the type $(k \times N)X(N \times k)$ with $k = 6$ (best performance) resorting to a kernel of daxpy $10, 1$ unrolled twice. Performance surprisingly enough matches those of the MKL, using only the compiler and source to source transformations. The performance of the naive code are shown in Figure 18 for comparison.

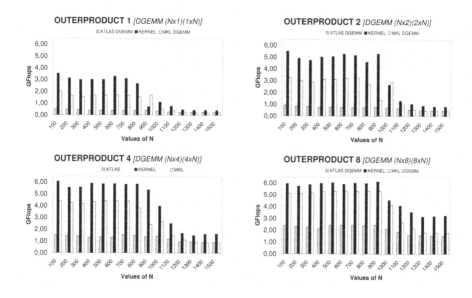

**Fig. 15.** DGEMM (Nxk) X (kxN) with k=1,2,4,8

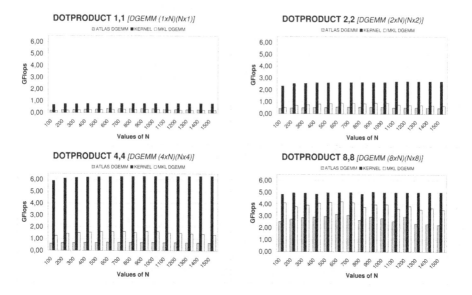

**Fig. 16.** DGEMM (kxN) X (Nxk) with k=1,2,4,8

## 4.3   1D Convolution

This code presented in Figure 19 is an example of how to reuse kernel micro-optimization for other codes. Indeed, this code can be decomposed, after tiling,

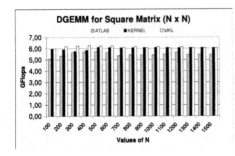
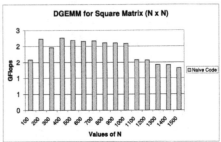

**Fig. 17.** Optimized DGEMM          **Fig. 18.** Naive DGEMM

```
for(i=0;i<N-n;i++)
  for(j=0;j<2*n;j++)
    a[i] += b[j] * c[i-j+n];
```

**Fig. 19.** Code of 1D convolution    **Fig. 20.** Results of 1D convolution with daxpy 5,1 unrolled twice

into daxpy and dot product kernels again. Using one of the previously optimized kernels leads to a 66% performance improvement.

## 5  Related Works

Among related works, many works have been dedicated to iteration exploration of optimization search:

Atlas[18] explores tile sizes and performs some simple micro-optimization (software pipeline, scalar promotion,...), but it relies mainly on only one kernel. This kernel was chosen according to its good ratio memory accesses/computations, not according to its performance on the target architecture. It is however possible to introduce new high performance kernels into Atlas, since there is an add-on mechanism that enable Atlas to use external, possibly hand-tuned assembly, codes. Compared with Atlas, the approach described in the paper is not limited to specific application and performs quite extensive search for the micro-optimizations, having the opportunity to find better kernels. This shows up on the performance results of previous section, where our approach compares to vendor library performance and outperforms Atlas. On the other hand, our method does not resort to exhaustive search and poor performance may result from the selected parameters. For example the exploration of tile sizes might generate unexpected results such as the poor performance numbers reported for vector length 800 in the motivating example.

For model-based Atlas[21], the model targets essentially cache behavior. Our approach focuses more on micro-mmm optimization, and resorts to simple model based tiling and then iterative search for finding tile sizes, guided by the user. The use of more complex models ([10] for instance) is still possible.

Extensive search among optimizations[5] shows that it is difficult to understand the links between optimization parameters, optimization sequence and performance. The exploration proposed by the authors is very time consuming and yet does not include many optimizations. In comparison, our method resorts to a very small number of transformations and relies on existing compiler to perform adapted optimizations.

The compiler optimization space exploration proposed by [17] changes the heuristic guiding optimizations by a search. This search is not exhaustive and is guided by some cost function. The goal is mostly to improve the optimization step of the compiler but does not seem to be aggressive enough to apply to library optimization.

Finally, [11] describes a methodology for hand-tuned optimization, applied to BLAS optimization. The authors propose a decomposition of micro kernel similar to ours, according to different tile sizes. The main focus of this work is to compact the data layout (making copies or transpositions of arrays) in order to improve TLB hit ratio. All the fine-tuning of micro kernels is however performed by hand. In comparison, our approach is automatic, at the expense of a small performance degradation, and is not specific to matrix matrix multiplication.

## 6   Conclusions/Future Directions

In this paper, we introduced a new automated approach for generating highly optimized code addressing simultaneously ILP issues as well as data locality issues. This approach relies on state of the art compiler and does not require any hand coding. This approach has been successfully validated on Itanium and BLAS3/BLAS2 routines, outperforming ATLAS and being very competitive with MKL highly tuned routines.

To be successful, this approach requires a state of the art compiler capable of generating kernels with performance close to peak. We performed experiments replacing icc with gcc; unfortunately gcc is far from being able to generate good code even on simple DAXPY like kernels and the overall performance results were pretty low. Now, when looking further at the exact requirements of our approach, what is essential is the ability to compile simple code structure, i.e. one dimensionnal loops with a loop body containing regular array access. Such capabilities are provided for example by XLG[20] code Tuner developed at CAPS Entreprise which is using specific code optimization techniques for well structured vector loops. Experiments were also performed replacing icc by XLG code Tuner: the results in terms of overall performance were similar at least for medium and large matrix sizes. However, XLG Caps Tuner was much easier to drive than icc (requiring less tuning parameters) and for small matrix sizes, XLG Caps Tuner also is capable of generating better code.

Finally, two directions are the main focus for future works: (i) More codes and libraries need to be tested with this approach, (ii) More architectures need to be tested besides Itanium. It includes not only testing other uniprocessor but also tackling the multicore/multithread case.

# References

1. C. Alias and D. Barthou. On Domain Specific Languages Re-Engineering. In *ACM Int. Conf. on Generative Programming and Component Engineering*, pages 63–77, Tallinn, Estonia, September 2005. LNCS 3676, Springer-Verlag.
2. F. Bodin, Y. Mevel, and R. Quiniou. A user level program transformation tool. In *ACM Int. Conf. on Supercomputing*, pages 180–187, New York, NY, USA, 1998. ACM Press.
3. P. Clauss. Counting solutions to linear and nonlinear constraints through Ehrhart polynomials: Applications to analyze and transform scientific programs. In *ACM Int. Conf. on Supercomputing*, pages 278–295. ACM Press, 1996.
4. S. Coleman and K. S. McKinley. Tile size selection using cache organization and data layout. In *ACM Conf. on Programming Language Design and Implementation*, pages 279–290, New York, NY, USA, 1995. ACM Press.
5. K. D. Cooper and T. Waterman. Investigating Adaptive Compilation using the MIPSPro Compiler. In *Symp. of the Los Alamos Computer Science Institute*, October 2003.
6. L. Djoudi, D. Barthou, P. Carribault, C. Lemuet, J.-T. Acquaviva, and W.Jalby. Exploring application performance: a new tool for a static/dynamic approach. In *Symp. of the Los Alamos Computer Science Institute*, Santa Fe, NM, October 2005.
7. S. Donadio, J. Brodman, K.Yotov, T. Roeder, D. Barthou, A. Cohen, M. Garzaran, D. Padua, and K. Pingali. A language for the Compact Representation of Multiple Program Versions. In *Languages and Compilers for Parallel Computing*, Hawthorne, New York, October 2005.
8. Engineering and scientific subroutine library. Guide and Reference. IBM.
9. P. Feautrier. Dataflow analysis of scalar and array references. *Int. J. of Parallel Programming*, 20(1):23–53, February 1991.
10. B. Fraguela, R. Doallo, and E. Zapata. Automatic analytical modeling for the estimation of cache misses. In *Int. Conf. on Parallel Architectures and Compilation Techniques*, page 221, Washington, DC, USA, 1999. IEEE Computer Society.
11. K. Goto and R. van de Geijn. On reducing tlb misses in matrix multiplication. Technical report, The University of Texas at Austin, Department of Computer Sciences, 2002.
12. W. Jalby, C. Lemuet, and X. Le Pasteur. Wbtk: a new set of microbenchmarks to explore memory system performance for scientific computing. *Int. J. High Perform. Comput. Appl.*, 18(2):211–224, 2004.
13. I. Kodukula, N. Ahmed, and K. Pingali. Data-centric multi-level blocking. In *ACM Conf. on Programming Language Design and Implementation*, pages 346–357, 1997.
14. I. Kodukula and K. Pingali. Transformations for imperfectly nested loops. In *ACM Int. Conf. on Supercomputing*, page 12, Washington, DC, USA, 1996. IEEE Computer Society.

15. R. Metzger and Z. Wen. *Automatic Algorithm Recognition: A New Approach to Program Optimization.* MIT Press, 2000.
16. Intel math kernel library (intel mkl). Intel.
17. S. Triantafyllis, M. Vachharajani, and D. I. August. Compiler Optimization-Space Exploration. *Journal of Instruction-level Parallelism*, 2005.
18. R. Whaley and J. Dongarra. Automatically tuned linear algebra software, 1997.
19. M. Wolfe. Iteration space tiling for memory hierarchies. In *Conf. on Parallel Processing for Scientific Computing*, pages 357–361, Philadelphia, PA, USA, 1989. Society for Industrial and Applied Mathematics.
20. Caps entreprise. http://www.caps-entreprise.com.
21. K. Yotov, X. Li, G. Ren, M. Garzaran, D. Padua, K. Pingali, and P. Stodghill. Is search really necessary to generate high-performance blas, 2005.

# Quantifying Uncertainty in Points-To Relations*

Constantino G. Ribeiro and Marcelo Cintra

School of Informatics, University of Edinburgh
c.g.ribeiro@sms.ed.ac.uk, mc@inf.ed.ac.uk

**Abstract.** For programs that make extensive use of pointers, pointer analysis is often critical for the effectiveness of optimizing compilers and tools for reasoning about program behavior and correctness. Static pointer analysis has been extensively studied and several algorithms have been proposed, but these only provide approximate solutions. As such inaccuracy may hinder further optimizations, it is important to understand how short these algorithms come of providing accurate information about the points-to relations.

This paper attempts to quantify the amount of uncertainty of the points-to relations that remains after a state-of-the-art context- and flow-sensitive pointer analysis algorithm is applied to a collection of programs from two well-known benchmark suites: SPEC integer and MediaBench. This remaining static uncertainty is then compared to the run-time behavior. Unlike previous work that compared run-time behavior against less accurate context- and flow-insensitive algorithms, the goal of this work is to quantify the amount of uncertainty that is intrinsic to the applications and that defeat even the most accurate static analyses.

Experimental results show that often the static pointer analysis is very accurate, but for some benchmarks a significant fraction, up to 25%, of their accesses via pointer de-references cannot be statically fully disambiguated. We find that some 27% of these de-references turn out to access a single memory location at run time, but many do access several different memory locations. We find that the main reasons for this are the use of pointer arithmetic and the fact that some control paths are not taken. The latter is an example of a source of uncertainty that is intrinsic to the application.

## 1 Introduction

For programs that make extensive use of pointers, pointer analysis is often critical for the effectiveness of optimizing compilers and tools for reasoning about program behavior and correctness. Without accurate pointer analysis, data accesses through pointer de-references must be assumed to be directed to almost any program data, thus, making it impossible to accurately establish the flow of data. Pointer analysis has been extensively studied and several algorithms have been proposed (e.g., [5,18,21,24,25], see [9] for a comprehensive list). Completely accurate pointer analysis (i.e., uniquely identifying the target of every pointer

---

* This work was supported in part by EPSRC under grants GR/R65169/01 and GR/S79572/01.

G. Almási, C. Caşcaval, and P. Wu (Eds.): LCPC 2006, LNCS 4382, pp. 190–204, 2007.

at every program point) is, in general, undecidable [11]. Thus, such algorithms are only approximate, and usually trade-off efficiency and accuracy. There is no consensus on what the best class of algorithm is and, in fact, many algorithms that theoretically vary significantly in accuracy actually perform very similarly in practice. Nevertheless, it is commonly accepted that context-sensitive and flow-sensitive algorithms are the most accurate ones.

Considering that context- and flow-sensitive pointer analysis represents the best that can be achieved with "general purpose" pointer analysis [1], it is important to understand how short these algorithms come of providing accurate information about the points-to relations. An understanding of the sources of such uncertainty is critical for devising new heuristics that lead to unsafe but often accurate pointer analyses, such as probabilistic static pointer analyses [10]. Also, an understanding of the inaccuracy of pointer analysis is necessary in order to assess the performance impact that such inaccuracy may have on program optimization (e.g., [3,4,7]).

The main contribution of this paper is to systematically quantify the amount of uncertainty in the static may-alias points-to relations for two well-known classes of benchmarks and to compare this to the run-time behavior to quantify what fraction of this uncertainty is actually observed at run time. This paper also attempts to characterize the reasons for the differences between the static and the run-time results. Note that, unlike previous works [13,15], the goal of this paper is not to quantify the amount of uncertainty arising from analyses that trade-off reduced precision for increased scalability. Instead, the goal of this paper is to quantify the amount of uncertainty that is intrinsic to the applications. By intrinsic we mean uncertainty that comes from the program structure and that would defeat any static analysis technique. For such an study we use, unlike previous work, a flow- and control-sensitive pointer analysis, which is the closest to the limit of what is possible with static analyses only.

More specifically, in this paper we quantitatively evaluate the uncertainty of the points-to relations that remains after a state-of-the-art context- and flow-sensitive pointer analysis algorithm [21] is applied to a collection of benchmarks from the well-known SPEC integer [23] and the MediaBench [12] suites. The static pointer de-references that exhibit uncertain points-to behavior are then instrumented and the actual run-time behavior is quantified. Experimental results show that for most of the benchmarks this static pointer analysis is very accurate, but for some benchmarks a significant fraction, up to 25%, of their accesses via pointer de-references cannot be statically fully disambiguated. We find that some 27% of these de-references turn out to access a single memory location at run time, but many do access several different memory locations. Further analysis shows that the main reasons for this are the use of pointer arithmetic and the fact that some control paths are not taken. The latter is an example of a source of uncertainty that is intrinsic to the application.

---

[1] Other types of analyses, such as shape analysis (e.g., [6,22]) may give further information about the behavior of pointers, but they only work for certain classes of applications.

The rest of the paper is organized as follows: Section 2 briefly overviews pointer analysis and the sources of uncertainty; Section 3 describes our methodology for quantifying uncertainty at compile and run time; Section 4 describes our empirical evaluation methodology; Section 5 presents the experimental results; Section 6 discusses related work; and Section 7 concludes the paper.

# 2   Pointer Analysis

In this section we present a very brief and informal overview of pointer analysis. The sole goal is to provide a minimal understanding of the problems and, more importantly, the sources of uncertainty.

## 2.1   Basics

The goal of pointer analysis is to compute for every *program point* the set of memory objects that each pointer may be pointing to. For some simple algorithms there is a one-to-one correspondence between a program point and a source code line, while for context- and flow-sensitive analyses a program point is a source code line augmented with the context and flow information, so that, for instance, the same source code line if reached by two different paths can be treated as two different program points.

The granularity of individual memory objects may vary depending on the capability of the particular algorithm. Powerful algorithms can handle individual scalar variables and individual fields of complex data structures, and can also handle dynamically created memory objects. However, most algorithms treat whole arrays as a single memory object. Following the notation in [21], memory objects that can be individually named are associated with *location sets*, or *locsets* for short.

A common representation for pointers and their target memory locations is based on the notion of *points-to relations*, which are formed by tuples of the form $(p, v)$, where $p$ is a pointer and $v$ is some location set. These tuples are sometimes referred to as a *points-to relationship* between $p$ and $v$. More formally, if $P$ and $V$ are the set of pointers and location sets, respectively, then $R \subset P \times V$ is a points-to relation and every tuple $(p, v) \in R$ implies that pointer $p$ may point to location set $v$, which is represented by $p \rightarrow v$. Note that in languages that allow multiple levels of pointers (i.e., a pointer to a pointer, such as int **p in C) pointers can be themselves location sets and $P \subset V$. A common representation for a points-to relation is a *points-to graph*, which is a tuple $G = (N, E)$ of $N = P \cup V$ nodes and $E = R$ edges.

With this representation, the pointer analysis problem then results in computing the points-to graph for every program point. This is done by solving a set of dataflow equations using a fixed point algorithm. The dataflow equations are derived from the pointer manipulation operations allowed in the language. For instance, the algorithm in [21] assumes the following four *basic pointer assignment operations*:

```
p1 = &p2;  // Address-of assignment
p1 = p2;   // Copy assignment
p1 = *p2;  // Load assignment
*p1 = p2;  // Store assignment
```

where p1 and p2 are pointer variables. Note that these do not include pointer arithmetic, which is allowed in some languages such as C, but is not usually supported in existing pointer analysis frameworks.

After the dataflow equations have been solved, the resulting points-to graphs at all program points contain points-to relationships of two types: *definitely* points-to relationships (also known as *must alias*) and *possibly* points-to relationships (also known as *may alias*). A definitely points-to relationship $(p, v)$ at some program point means that at this point $p$ is for certain pointing to location set $v$. This implies that there is no edge leaving node $p$ in the points-to graph other than the edge $(p, v)$, or, equivalently, that there is no tuple $(p, u)$ in the points-to relation where $u \neq v$. A possibly points-to relationship $(p, v)$ at some program point means that at this point $p$ may point to location set $v$, but may also point to at least another different location set $u$. In this case we say that there is some *uncertainty* or *ambiguity* in the points-to relation.

Finally, changes in the points-to graph after processing some program point can be of two types: *strong updates* and *weak updates*. Strong updates are those that delete all the existing outgoing edges from a pointer $p$, while weak updates are those that simply add new edges without deleting any of the existing edges. For instance, the update at a program point that contains the assignment p = &v is strong as it deletes all edges $(p, u)$ that may have existed before this program point. Note that the assignment p1 = p2, where both $p1$ and $p2$ are pointers, is by this definition a strong update (all previous edges from $p1$ are deleted) even if $p1$ is left with several possibly points-to relationships because of the possibly points-to relationships of $p2$. As explained in the next section, weak updates are the source of possibly points-to relationships and they appear due to a few different reasons.

## 2.2   Uncertainty in Pointer Analysis

Context- and flow-sensitive pointer analysis provides the most accurate static results, but it still cannot fully disambiguate all pointer de-references in many practical situations. Some of the most common reasons for this uncertainty are:

*Control Flow:* A problem occurs when different control paths perform different updates to pointer variables. In this case, without dynamic knowledge of the actual program behavior, the static analysis can only assume that both updates are possible and at the merge point both targets are possible.

*Pointer Arithmetic:* A problem occurs when the value of a pointer is updated through some arithmetic operation. In this case, even if the original target of the pointer is well-known, the final target can only be known if the pointer analysis algorithm has an accurate knowledge of the layout of objects in virtual memory.

*Unavailable Procedure Code:* A problem occurs when the original source code of a procedure is not available to the pointer analysis algorithm and the procedure takes a pointer as a parameter. In this case, unless the pointer analysis algorithm has some prior knowledge about the side-effects (or lack thereof) of the called procedure, the static analysis can only assume that after returning from the procedure the pointer may be pointing to any memory object.

*Recursive Data Structures:* A problem occurs when pointers are used to link objects from recursive data structures. Usually these form well structured forms such as lists, trees, circular queues, etc. However, traditional pointer analysis is not designed to recognize such structures and end up collapsing several objects into a single memory target. Shape analysis (e.g., [6,22]) has been specially designed to handle such cases. This paper's goal is to investigate the accuracy of "general-purpose" pointer analyses and a study of the effects of shape analysis is beyond its scope.

*Aggregates:* A problem occurs when pointers are used to access internal parts of an aggregate (e.g., an array or a structure) but the pointer analysis assigns a single name for the whole aggregate. In this case, the pointer analysis cannot disambiguate accesses to different parts of the aggregate.

*Dynamically Allocated Objects:* A problem occurs when pointers are assigned to dynamically allocated objects that are allocated at the same static code site. In this case most pointer analyses will simply assign a single name to the static memory allocation site and will not be able to disambiguate accesses to the (possibly) multiple objects that are allocated at the site. In fact, many pointer analyses tools are even less accurate and simply assign a single name to the whole heap area, so that even memory objects that are allocated at different static code sites end up being aliased.

## 3    Quantification Methodology

### 3.1    Source Code Analysis

To collect the static points-to statistics we modify a context- and flow-sensitive pointer analysis algorithm [21] to count the number of accesses *through a pointer de-reference*, and for each access to count the number of possible target locsets as identified by the points-to graph immediately before the access. When analyzing the source code we count the number of locsets accessed (used or modified) through a pointer de-reference as follows. In these examples assume that $p$ is a pointer variable and that $*^n$ represents $n$ levels of indirection (e.g., $*^2p$ is equivalent to $**p$).

*Indirect use of a variable through a pointer de-reference* (e.g., ...=*p;):
This is counted as one *use* via pointer.

*Indirect modification of a variable through a pointer de-reference*
(e.g., *p=...;):
This is counted as one *modification* via pointer.

*Multi-level indirect use of variable through a pointer de-reference*
(e.g., ...=*$^n$p;):
This is counted as $n$ *uses* via pointers. The number of possible target locsets is counted for each de-reference. For instance, in ...=**p; if p may only point to a single target locset, but *p may point to two target locsets, then we count one use with a single target and one use with two targets.

*Multi-level indirect modification of variable through a pointer de-reference*
(e.g., *$^n$p=...;):
This is counted as $n-1$ *uses* via pointers plus one *modification* via pointer. The number of possible target locsets is counted for each de-reference, as described above.

*Procedure call* (e.g., foo(..., *p, ...);):
This is counted as one *use* via pointer. Multi-level indirect uses are counted as described above.

*Loops:*
Accesses within loops are treated as *one* instance of one of the cases above.

*Procedures:*
Accesses within procedures are treated as *one* instance *per calling context.*

Also, languages like C allow right-hand-side expressions and boolean expressions to contain assignments, such as while(*p=a) or if(a==(*p=b)). Obviously, in this case we must appropriately account for the embedded modification.

## 3.2 Run-Time Statistics Collection

To collect the dynamic points-to statistics we further modify the context- and flow-sensitive pointer analysis of [21] to insert additional profiling code just before accesses through a pointer de-reference that are identified as having multiple target locsets. When compiled, this profiling code will record all different run-time memory addresses touched via these pointer de-references and count the number of accesses to each different address.

Each run-time access profiled is given a unique identifier that contains the source code number, so that we can match the run-time accesses with their static access. Note, however, that two mismatches between static and dynamic statistics can happen. First, multiple static accesses identified by the pointer analysis algorithm may map to the same source code line and, thus, to the same run-time counter. This happens because the pointer analysis algorithm separates static accesses according to their context. Second, not all static accesses may appear at run time if that portion of the code is not executed with the given input data.

# 4    Evaluation Setup

## 4.1    Applications

To quantify the uncertainty that is intrinsic to static context- and flow-sensitive pointer analysis, we use a subset of the SPEC2000 integer benchmarks [23] and of the MediaBench benchmarks [12] that are written in C [2] These applications are representative of the workloads typical of workstations and desktop computing and are well-known for their intense use of pointers in many cases. For the run-time experiments the input sets used are the standard ones provided with each suite (*ref* for SPEC2000). Table 1 shows, for each application, the total number of lines of C code, the total number of location sets and of pointer location sets, the number of source code expressions that are uses through pointer de-references, and the number of source code expressions that are modifications through pointer de-references.

**Table 1.** Application characteristics

| Application | Suite | Lines of Code (KLOC) | Total (Pointer) Location Sets | Pointer Uses | Pointer Modifications |
|---|---|---|---|---|---|
| 164.gzip | | 9.1 | 1,750 (246) | 113 | 43 |
| 175.vpr | | 17 | 3,959 (649) | 960 | 428 |
| 181.mcf | | 1.9 | 506 (194) | 16 | 13 |
| 186.crafty | SPEC | 12 | 4,920 (469) | 4,716 | 672 |
| 197.parser | int | 12 | 3,631 (917) | 10,587 | 83 |
| 256.bzip2 | | 2.9 | 887 (85) | 4 | 0 |
| 300.twolf | | 17.5 | 5,262 (950) | 751 | 79 |
| epic | | 7.6 | 397 (105) | 37 | 13 |
| unepic | | 7.6 | 531(242) | 18 | 6 |
| mpeg2enc | | 8.5 | 2,179 (455) | 116 | 276 |
| mpeg2dec | MediaBench | 4.9 | 1,605 (295) | 140 | 85 |
| g721-enc | | 1 | 393 (68) | 2 | 0 |
| g721-dec | | 1 | 122 (36) | 4 | 2 |
| gsmencode | | 5.8 | 448 (133) | 22 | 0 |
| gsmdecode | | 5.8 | 1566 (599) | 168 | 31 |

## 4.2    Static Analysis

The statistics collection methodology described in Section 3 was implemented on the SPAN tool [20], which is an add-on to the SUIF compiler [8] that implements the pointer analysis algorithm of [21]. We modified SPAN to record all instances of pointer de-references along with the number of possible targets as identified

---

[2] The benchmarks not included from the suites are those either written in Fortran or C++, which are incompatible with SUIF, or those written in C that did not work with the *original* SPAN package (see Section 4.2 for details on the compilation infrastructure).

by SPAN and with the source code line number. The source code line number is useful for identifying instances where SPAN is able to distinguish the different calling contexts of the same source line. Uses and modifications via pointer de-references were counted separately.

Uses and modifications through pointer de-references that may find the pointer uninitialized (according to the SPAN analysis) result in SPAN adding a special location set, called unk, to the target set. We decided to count these cases separately. For instance, a pointer de-reference with two possible targets where one of them is unk is counted separately from other pointer de-references with two possible targets where both targets are well-defined user objects. The reason for highlighting the ambiguous points-to sets that include unk is because this is an important special case that may be treated differently by optimizing compilers and program understanding tools. For instance, an optimizing compiler may choose to ignore the unk target when performing an aggressive (possibly unsafe) optimization under the assumption that an actual occurrence of the unk target is highly unlikely. On the other hand, a program understanding tool would likely especially flag de-references with possible unk targets as they may suggest a bug in the code.

Finally, SPAN creates a single locset *per context* for each dynamic memory allocation call site, and calls these locsets heap.X, where X is a number that identifies the context. However, it cannot disambiguate further the accesses to different parts of the memory object. Again, we decided to count these cases separately because this is also an important special case. In fact, dynamically allocated memory objects seem to often require specialized analyses [1,17].

### 4.3   Profiling Environment

To monitor the actual run-time behavior of static pointer de-references with multiple possible targets we further modified the SPAN tool to add the necessary profiling code. More specifically, at each static de-reference where the pointer may have multiple targets the tool inserts code to record the actual address accessed and to increment a counter per address seen so far. The resulting instrumented code is converted from the SUIF file format (.spd) to C code and this code is then compiled for the Intel x86 platform using gcc 3.4.4 and using the -O2 optimization level.

## 5   Experimental Results

### 5.1   Static Pointer Analysis Statistics

We start our study by measuring the amount of uncertainty resulting from the static pointer analysis. Table 2 shows the breakdown of the static accesses through pointer de-references according to the number of possible target memory locations, as given by SPAN. The table presents separate results for uses and modifications. The number of uses and modifications through pointer de-references in this table are often larger than those in Table 1 because of the context-sensitivity of the analysis. This can also be seen from the often great disparity between the number of accesses and the number of source code lines in Table 2. Note that in most cases the number of accesses through pointer de-references is only a small fraction of all static program references.

From this table we can see that the result of the context- and flow-sensitive static analysis of SPAN is fairly accurate and can unambiguously identify the target of the pointer de-references in all accesses for most applications and in more than 90% of the accesses for all but 3 applications. Across the whole suite 81% of all the accesses have a single unambiguously identified target. Nevertheless, for some benchmarks the amount of uncertainty is non-negligible, reaching up to 25% of the accesses for *197.parser*.

Another observation from these results is that often a large fraction of the accesses with multiple possible targets have unk as one of the targets (meaning that the pointer may be uninitialized at this point). The exception is *197.parser*. As previously explained, these represent a special case of uncertainty that may be treated differently by an optimizing compiler or a program understanding tool. We do not expect any of these unk targets to actually occur at run-time (Section 5.2).

Finally, we also note from these results that there are often many fewer modifications through pointer de-references than there are uses (1731 modifications versus 47230 uses). However, per application these modifications have a relatively larger amount of uncertainty than uses: e.g., 76% of modifications in *197.parser* have multiple possible targets versus 24% of uses.

## 5.2   Profiling Results

**Run-Time Uncertainty.** The first step in quantifying the run-time behavior of the ambiguous pointer de-references is to measure the number of different location sets actually touched by each static reference. Such results can be directly compared to those of Table 2 as these references correspond to those in white text with grey background in that table. Note that since the profiling framework annotates source code lines the run-time accesses reported here correspond to those reported *per source code line* in Table 2. Table 3 shows the breakdown of only those static accesses through pointer de-references that have 2 or more possible target memory locations according to the number of actual target memory locations touched. Again, the two sections of the table correspond to uses and modifications, respectively. Note that some of the static references are not actually executed with the input sets used. Finally, note that in this experiment a static reference is said to touch two or more target memory locations as long as at least two of more of its dynamic instances touch different memory locations.

From this table we can see that some (27% of the executed accesses) of the uncertainty of the static analysis disappears at run time and actually a single memory location is accessed. Nevertheless, a significant fraction of the accesses indeed turn out to point to more than one different memory location at run time. The next section discusses is more detail the reasons for the differences between static and dynamic results.

**Table 2.** Breakdown of static accesses according to the number of possible target memory locations. Results for the source code analysis. The first number (top-left) in each entry is the *total* number of accesses in that category. The numbers in parenthesis are: the number of accesses that have **unk** as one of the targets, the number of accesses that have **heap** as one of the targets, and the number of static source code accesses (as opposed to per-context). For instance, *186.crafty* has 542 uses through pointer dereferences with two possible targets; of these, 534 have **unk** as one of the targets, 67 have **heap** as one of the targets; and these 542 uses appear in only 59 source code lines. The entries in white text with grey background are those that reflect ambiguity in the static analysis and are instrumented for the run-time statistics collection.

| Application | Uses (u) and Modifications (m) with N possible targets (including **unk** target, including **heap** target, number of source code lines) | | | |
|---|---|---|---|---|
| | $N = 1$ | $N = 2$ | $N = 3$ | $N > 3$ |
| gzip | u: 277<br>m: 43 | 0 (0,0,0)<br>0 (0,0,0) | 0 (0,0,0)<br>0 (0,0,0) | 0 (0,0,0)<br>0 (0,0,0) |
| vpr | u: 2488<br>m: 428 | 0 (0,0,0)<br>0 (0,0,0) | 0 (0,0,0)<br>0 (0,0,0) | 0 (0,0,0)<br>0 (0,0,0) |
| mcf | u: 67<br>m: 13 | 0 (0,0,0)<br>0 (0,0,0) | 0 (0,0,0)<br>0 (0,0,0) | 6 (0,0,3)<br>0 (0,0,0) |
| crafty | u: 4970<br>m: 479 | 542 (534,67,59)<br>47 (45,11,9) | 2 (2,2,1)<br>146 (146,66,13) | 119 (0,26,24)<br>0 (0, 0, 0) |
| parser | u: 25178<br>m: 20 | 241 (241,241,35)<br>32 (32,32,6) | 36 (0,0,11)<br>0 (0,0,0) | 7841 (181,230,259)<br>31 (9,4,9) |
| bzip2 | u: 119<br>m: 0 | 0 (0,0,0)<br>0 (0,0,0) | 0 (0,0,0)<br>0 (0,0,0) | 0 (0,0,0)<br>0 (0,0,0) |
| twolf | u: 3687<br>m: 77 | 6 (6,0,6)<br>2 (2,0,2) | 0 (0,0,0)<br>0 (0,0,0) | 0 (0,0,0)<br>0 (0,0,0) |
| epic | u: 156<br>m: 13 | 0 (0,0,0)<br>0 (0,0,0) | 0 (0,0,0)<br>0 (0,0,0) | 0 (0,0,0)<br>0 (0,0,0) |
| unepic | u: 59<br>m: 6 | 0 (0,0,0)<br>0 (0,0,0) | 0 (0,0,0)<br>0 (0,0,0) | 0 (0,0,0)<br>0 (0,0,0) |
| mpeg2enc | u: 395<br>m: 276 | 0 (0,0,0)<br>0 (0,0,0) | 0 (0,0,0)<br>0 (0,0,0) | 0 (0,0,0)<br>0 (0,0,0) |
| mpeg2dec | u: 499<br>m: 75 | 8 (8,8,2)<br>0 (0,0,0) | 0 (0,0,0)<br>0 (0,0,0) | 6 (6,6,1)<br>10 (10,10,2) |
| g721-enc | u: 22<br>m: 0 | 0 (0,0,0)<br>0 (0,0,0) | 0 (0,0,0)<br>0 (0,0,0) | 0 (0,0,0)<br>0 (0,0,0) |
| g721-dec | u: 6<br>m: 2 | 0 (0,0,0)<br>0 (0,0,0) | 0 (0,0,0)<br>0 (0,0,0) | 0 (0,0,0)<br>0 (0,0,0) |
| gsmencode | u: 154<br>m: 0 | 0 (0,0,0)<br>0 (0,0,0) | 0 (0,0,0)<br>0 (0,0,0) | 0 (0,0,0)<br>0 (0,0,0) |
| gsmdecode | u: 346<br>m: 31 | 0 (0,0,0)<br>0 (0,0,0) | 0 (0,0,0)<br>0 (0,0,0) | 9 (0,0,9)<br>0 (0,0,0) |

**Table 3.** Breakdown of static accesses with 2 or more possible target memory locations (Table 2) according to the number of actual target memory locations. Results for the profile analysis. NE stands for static accesses that are not executed. For instance, of the 59+1+24=84 source code lines with pointer de-references with two or more possible targets in *186.crafty* (Table 2), 59 are not executed, 1 has only a single target at run time, 1 has two targets at run time, and 23 have three or more targets at run time. The entries in white text with grey background are those that reflect actual ambiguity at run time. The entries with light grey background are those were the static ambiguity disappears at run time.

| Application | Uses with N actual targets | | | | Modifications with N actual targets | | | |
|---|---|---|---|---|---|---|---|---|
| | NE | N = 1 | N = 2 | N > 2 | NE | N = 1 | N = 2 | N > 2 |
| mcf | 1 | 2 | 0 | 0 | - | - | - | - |
| crafty | 59 | 1 | 1 | 23 | 17 | 0 | 0 | 5 |
| parser | 193 | 27 | 0 | 85 | 6 | 1 | 0 | 8 |
| twolf | 1 | 5 | 0 | 0 | 2 | 0 | 0 | 0 |
| mpeg2dec | 2 | 0 | 0 | 1 | 1 | 0 | 0 | 1 |
| gsmdecode | 0 | 9 | 0 | 0 | - | - | - | - |

**Table 4.** Classification of dynamic accesses according to the difference with respect to the static behavior and according to the cause for the difference

| Behavior difference | | Cause | Number of cases |
|---|---|---|---|
| Static | Actual | | |
| 2 or more targets | Not executed | - | 282 |
| 2 targets (inclusive *unk*) | Single target | Pointer turns out to be always initialized | 6 |
| 2 targets | 3 or more targets | Pointer arithmetic to index into array-like object | 22 |
| | | Use of arrays | 2 |
| | | Use of recursive data structures | 5 |
| 3 or more targets | Single target | Use of structure fields | 2 |
| | | Pointer arithmetic to index into array-like object | 9 |
| | | Control path alternative never taken | 28 |
| No change | - | - | 95 |

**Causes of Uncertainty.** A closer inspection at the actual outcomes of the ambiguous static references reveals that several factors contribute to the difference between the static and dynamic behaviors. Table 4 shows the causes for this difference and the number of instances of each cause. The references here correspond to all of those in Table 3.

From this table we can see two directions of variation: from fewer possible targets of the static analysis to more actual targets at run time, and from more possible targets of the static analysis to fewer actual targets at run time. There are two major factors affecting those variations. One is the use of pointer arithmetic, which, interestingly, turns out to produce variations in both directions. Another is the fact that some control paths are simply not taken at run time. We also note that many variations come from the use of structures and arrays, which may trow off the static analysis.

**Variations with Input Sets.** Finally, to assess the sensitivity of the run-time results with respect to input data we repeated some of the experiments with the SPEC benchmarks with the *train* input sets. Significant variability in the run-time points-to behavior with different input data would indicate that techniques that rely on profiling to refine the results of the static analysis are likely to fail. Naturally, the converse is not necessarily true: little variability in the run-time points-to behavior does not guarantee that profiling will work well for all types of feedback-directed analysis. This occurs when the profile-directed analysis is not directly driven by the points-to behavior, but by some other run-time behavior. For instance, probabilistic pointer analysis [10] uses the frequency of path execution to estimate the probability of points-to relations. Nevertheless, little variability in the run-time points-to behavior is a good indication that profile-directed analyses are likely to often work well.

Our experiments show very little to no variability in the run-time behavior of the points-to relations between executions with the *ref* and *train* input sets. A similar result was obtained in [15].

# 6 Related Work

Pointer analysis has been extensively studied and several algorithms have been proposed. A comprehensive list of pointer analysis research and some discussion on open problems can be found in [9]. The work in [21] introduced the flow- and context-sensitive pointer analysis algorithm that is implemented in the tool we used to gather the static points-to information. Despite not being as fast and efficient as more recent summary-based pointer analysis algorithms (e.g., [18]), it is still reasonably fast and can handle non-trivial programs in practice. Works that propose and evaluate new pointer analysis algorithms usually present a quantitative breakdown of the number of possible target memory locations. However, this often consists of only the static statistics (quite often just average points-to set sizes) and does not include a quantification of the actual run-time behavior.

Recently, a few works have attempted to investigate the impact of pointer analysis on overall compiler optimization [3,4,7]. These works show that pointer analysis is often critical to enable a large number of optimizations. They also indirectly quantify the amount of run-time uncertainty and its impact on optimizations, but they do not provide a full quantification of such run-time uncertainty.

Researchers have since long attempted to extend static analysis with information that better reflects the actual run-time behavior. One such approach is probabilistic static analyses. The work in [19] developed a framework to integrate frequency, or probability, into a class of static dataflow analyses. The framework uses control flow frequencies to compute the probabilities of execution of all possible control flow paths and then uses this information to assign frequencies of occurrence to dataflow facts. This framework has been extended and applied to the problem of pointer analysis in [10], in which case the dataflow facts of interest, for which a frequency of occurrence is sought, are the points-to relationships. That work also quantitatively compared the static points-to results against run-time behavior, but this evaluation was limited to only portions of a few simple benchmarks.

The closest work to ours is [15], which also systematically attempted to quantify the run-time behavior of points-to sets. Our work differs from that work in that we are interested in measuring the gap between the run-time behavior and the best static analysis in order to assess the limitations of purely static analysis and the potential benefits of different extended approaches (e.g., probabilistic points-to heuristics). For this reason we use a context- and flow-sensitive algorithm as the baseline for comparisons, instead of the scalable algorithms used in that work, and we concentrate our evaluation on those references where the static analysis computes points-to sets with more than one element. The work in [13] is similar to [15], but in the context of reference analysis for Java programs, and also used a variation for Java of a context- and flow-insensitive pointer analysis algorithm.

Finally, there has been recently a significant interest in speculative compiler optimizations based on imprecise dataflow and pointer analyses. The cost analyses of such optimizations require a good knowledge of the expected run-time behavior of dataflow and points-to relationships. Our work attempts to systematically evaluate the run-time behavior of points-to relationships and is an important step in the way of developing effective cost analyses for speculative compiler optimizations. Examples of speculative compiler optimizations requiring knowledge of run-time behavior of points-to relationships include: [14], which performs speculative partial redundancy elimination in EPIC architectures with speculative loads; [2], which performs speculative parallelization; and [16], which performs program slicing for a program understanding tool.

# 7   Conclusions

In this paper we attempted to systematically quantify the amount of uncertainty due to may-alias points-to relations for two well-known classes of benchmarks. Unlike previous works [13,15] that consider pointer analysis algorithms that trade-off reduced precision for increased scalability, in this paper we are interested in the amount of uncertainty that is intrinsic to the applications and that defeat even flow- and control-sensitive pointer analysis.

We performed our evaluation applying a state-of-the-art context- and flow-sensitive pointer analysis algorithm [21] to a collection of benchmarks from the well-known SPEC integer [23] and the MediaBench [12] suites. Experimental results show that for most of the benchmarks this static pointer analysis is very accurate, but for some benchmarks a significant fraction, up to 25%, of their accesses via pointer de-references cannot be statically fully disambiguated. We find that some 27% of these de-references turn out to access a single memory location at run time, but many do access several different memory locations. Further analysis shows that the main reasons for this are the use of pointer arithmetic and the fact that some control paths are not taken. These results suggest that some further compiler optimizations may be possible by exploiting the cases where the uncertainty does not appear at run time, but for this to happen it is necessary to improve the handling of pointer arithmetic and to develop probabilistic approaches that capture the actual control flow behavior.

# References

1. R. Z. Altucher and W. Landi. "An Extended Form of Must Alias Analysis for Dynamic Allocation." *Symp. on Principles of Programming Languages*, pages 74-84, January 1995.
2. P.-S. Chen, M.-Y. Hung, Y.-S. Hwang, R. D.-C. Ju, and J. K. Lee. "Compiler Support for Speculative Multithreading Architecture with Probabilistic Points-to Analysis." *Symp. on Principles and Practice of Parallel Programming*, pages 25-36, June 2003.
3. B. Cheng and W.-M. Hwu. "Modular Interprocedural Pointer Analysis using Access Paths: Design, Implementation, and Evaluation." *Conf. on Programming Language Design and Implementation*, pages 57-69, June 2000.
4. M. Das, B. Liblit, M. Fähndrich, and J. Rehof. "Estimating the Impact of Scalable Pointer Analysis on Optimization." *Intl. Static Analysis Symp.*, pages 260-278, July 2001.
5. M. Emami, R. Ghiya, and L. J. Hendren. "Context-Sensitive Interprocedural Points-to Analysis in the Presence of Function Pointers." *Conf. on Programming Language Design and Implementation*, pages 242-256, June 1994.
6. R. Ghiya and L. J. Hendren. "Is it a Tree, a DAG, or a Cyclic Graph? A Shape Analysis for Heap-Directed Pointers in C." *Symp. on Principles of Programming Languages*, pages 1-15, January 1996.
7. R. Ghiya, D. Lavery, and D. Sehr. "On the Importance of Points-To Analysis and Other Memory Disambiguation Methods for C Programs." *Conf. on Programming Language Design and Implementation*, pages 47-58, June 2001.
8. M. Hall, J. Anderson, S. Amarasinghe, B. Murphy, S-W. Liao, E. Bugnion, and M. Lam. "Maximizing Multiprocessor Performance with the SUIF Compiler." *IEEE Computer*, Vol. 29, No. 12, pages 84-89, December 1996.
9. M. Hind. "Pointer Analysis: Haven't We Solved This Problem Yet?" *Wksp. on Program Analysis for Software Tools and Engineering*, pages 54-61, June 2001.
10. Y.-S. Hwang, P.-S. Chen, J. K. Lee, and R. D.-C. Ju. "Probabilistic Points-to Analysis." *Intl. Wksp on Languages and Compilers for Parallel Computing*, pages 290-305, August 2001.
11. W. Landi. "Undecidability of Static Analysis." *ACM Letters on Programming Languages and Systems*, Vol. 1, No. 4, pages 323-337, December 1992.
12. C. Lee, M. Potkonjak, W. H. Mangione-Smith. "MediaBench: A Tool for Evaluating and Synthesizing Multimedia and Communications Systems." *Intl. Symp. on Microarchitecture*, pages 330-335, December 1997.

13. D. Liang, M. Pennings, and M. J. Harrold. "Evaluating the Precision of Static Reference Analysis Using Profiling." *Intl. Symp. on Software Testing and Analysis*, pages 22-32, July 2002.

14. J. Lin, T. Chen, W.-C. Hsu, P.-C. Yew, R. D.-C. Ju, T.-F. Ngai, and S. Chan. "A Compiler Framework for Speculative Analysis and Optimizations." *Conf. on Programming Language Design and Implementation*, pages 289-299, June 2003.

15. M. Mock, M. Das, C. Chambers, and S. J. Eggers. "Dynamic Points-to Sets: A Comparison with Static Analyses and Potential Applications in Program Understanding and Optimization." *Wksp. on Program Analysis for Software Tools and Engineering*, pages 66-72, June 2001.

16. M. Mock, D. C. Atkinson, C. Chambers, and S. J. Eggers. "Improving Program Slicing with Dynamic Points-to Data." *Intl. Symp. on Foundations of Software Engineering*, pages 71-80, November 2002.

17. E. M. Nystrom, H.-S. Kim, and W.-M. Hwu. "Importance of Heap Specialization in Pointer Analysis." *Wksp. on Program Analysis for Software Tools and Engineering*, pages 43-48, June 2004.

18. E. M. Nystrom, H.-S. Kim, and W.-M. Hwu. "Bottom-Up and Top-Down Context-Sensitive Summary-Based Pointer Analysis." *Intl. Static Analysis Symp.*, pages 165-180, August 2004.

19. G. Ramalingam. "Data Flow Frequency Analysis." *Conf. on Programming Language Design and Implementation*, pages 267-277, May 1996.

20. R. Rugina and M. Rinard. "Span: A shape and Pointer Analysis Package." Technical report, M.I.T. LCSTM-581, June 1998.

21. R. Rugina and M. Rinard. "Pointer Analysis for Multithreaded Programs." *Conf. on Programming Language Design and Implementation*, pages 77-90, May 1999.

22. M. Sagiv, T. Reps, and R. Wilhelm. "Parametric Shape Analysis via 3-valued Logic." *Symp. on Principles of Programming Languages*, pages 105-118, January 1999.

23. Standard Performance Evaluation Corporation. www.spec.org/cpu2000

24. B. Steensgaard. "Points-to Analysis in Almost Linear Time." *Symp. on Principles of Programming Languages*, pages 32-41, January 1996.

25. R. P. Wilson and M. S. Lam. "Efficient Context-Sensitive Pointer Analysis for C Programs." *Conf. on Programming Language Design and Implementation*, pages 1-12, June 1995.

# Cache Behavior Modelling for Codes Involving Banded Matrices*

Diego Andrade, Basilio B. Fraguela, and Ramón Doallo

Universidade da Coruña
Dept. de Electrónica e Sistemas
Facultade de Informática
Campus de Elviña, 15071 A Coruña, Spain
{dcanosa,basilio,doallo}@udc.es

**Abstract.** Understanding and improving the memory hierarchy behavior is one of the most important challenges in current architectures. Analytical models are a good approach for this, but they have been traditionally limited by either their restricted scope of application or their lack of accuracy. Most models can only predict the cache behavior of codes that generate regular access patterns. The Probabilistic Miss Equation(PME) model is able nevertheless to model accurately the cache behavior for codes with irregular access patterns due to data-dependent conditionals or indirections. Its main limitation is that it only considers irregular access patterns that exhibit an uniform distribution of the accesses. In this work, we extend the PME model to enable to analyze more realistic and complex irregular accesses. Namely, we consider indirections due to the compressed storage of most real banded matrices.

## 1 Introduction

Memory hierarchies are essential in current architectures, since they cushion the gap between memory and processor speed. Understanding and improving the usage of caches is therefore absolutely necessary for obtaining good performance both in sequential and parallel computers. There are several methods to study the cache behavior. For example, trace-driven simulations [1] provide accurate estimations of the cache behavior but the required simulations have a high computational cost. Hardware counters [2] yield also accurate estimations but the execution of the real code is needed and their use is limited to the architectures where such registers exist. Both techniques provide a summarized characterization of the cache behavior and little insight about the observed behavior is obtained. As a result, it is difficult to benefit from the information generated in order to improve the cache performance.

---

* This work has been supported in part by the Ministry of Science and Technology of Spain under contract TIN 2004-07797-C02-02 and Xunta de Galicia under contract PGIDIT 03TIC10502PR.

G. Almási, C. Caşcaval, and P. Wu (Eds.): LCPC 2006, LNCS 4382, pp. 205–219, 2007.
© Springer-Verlag Berlin Heidelberg 2007

Analytical models of the source code [3,4] are the best suited approach to enable compilers to extract the behavior of the memory hierarchy and guide optimizations based in this understanding. Models can obtain an accurate prediction of the cache behavior based in the analysis of the source code to execute. Their main drawback is their limited scope of application. Most of them are restricted to codes with regular access patterns. There have been few attempts to model irregular codes but they are either non-automatable [5] or quite imprecise [6]. The Probabilistic Miss Equation (PME) model is nevertheless able to analyze automatically codes with irregular access patterns originated by data-dependent conditionals [7] or indirections [8] with a reasonable accuracy. In the case of irregular codes due to indirections, some knowledge about the distribution of the values contained in the structure that produces the indirection is required in order to achieve certain precision in the predictions. Until now the PME model could only model with a reasonable accuracy indirect accesses that follow an uniform distribution, that is, access patterns in which every position of the dimension affected by the indirection has the same probability of being accessed. This model extension was fully automated and integrated in a compiler in [9]. In the present work the PME model is extended to be able to model automatically and precisely an important class of non-uniform irregular access patterns. Namely, we consider the indirections generated by the compressed storage of realistic banded matrices, a very common distribution in sparse matrices [10]. Most banded matrices are composed of a series of diagonals with different densities of nonzeros. This way, we have developed a more general model that considers this kind of distribution. The accuracy of this new extension will be evaluated using well-known matrix collections.

The rest of the paper is organized as follows. Section 2 introduces the basics of the PME model. Then, Section 3 discusses the extended scope of the model and the problems that the modeling of non-uniformly distributed irregular accesses implies. The extension of the model to cover indirections using realistic banded matrices is described in Section 4. Section 5 is devoted to the experimental results. Section 6 briefly reviews the related work. Finally, in Section 7 the conclusions of our work are established.

## 2    Introduction to the Probabilistic Miss Equations (PME) Model

Our model estimates the number of misses generated by a code studying the behavior of each static reference $R$ separately. Its strategy lies in detecting the accesses of $R$ that cannot exploit reuse in the cache, and the potential reuse distances for those that can. The reuse distance is the interval in the execution between two consecutive accesses to a same line. During the reuse distance other data structures of the program can be accessed that can interfere in the cache with the studied data structure. These reuse distances are measured in terms of iterations of the loops that enclose the reference, and they generate interference miss probabilities that depend on the cache footprint of the regions accessed during their execution. The estimation of the number of misses generated by the reference is thus a summatory of its first-time accesses to lines (cold misses) and the number of potential reuses it gives place to, multiplied by the interference miss probability associated to their reuse distance (capacity and conflict misses). This summatory is what we call a Probabilistic Miss Equation (PME), and it is built analyzing the behavior of the reference in each nesting level $i$ that encloses it, beginning in the innermost one and proceeding outwards. In each level the model builds a partial PME $F_{Ri}$ that captures the information on the reuses with reuse distances associated to this loop. Namely, the model calculates the number of different sets of lines (SOLs) that the reference may access during the execution of the loop, the potential reuses for those SOLs, with their correspond- ing reuse distance, and also the probability those reuses actually take place. A SOL is the set of lines that $R$ can access during one iteration of the loop. In the innermost loop that contains $R$, each SOL consists of one line. In outer loops, it consists of the set of lines that $R$ can access during a whole execution of the immediately inner loop. Obviously, the first-time accesses to each SOL during the execution of the loop $i$ cannot exploit the reuse within the loop that $F_{Ri}$ captures, but this does not necessarily turn them into misses. These accesses could enjoy reuses with reuse distances associated to outer loops, or to previous loops, when non-perfectly nested loops are considered. As a result, every PME $F_{Ri}$ needs as input for its evaluation a representation $Reg$ of the memory region accessed since the immediately previous access to any of the SOLs that $R$ refer- ences in loop $i$. Notice that given this reasoning, the number of misses generated by each first access to a SOL found in nesting level $i$ is given by the evalua- tion of $F_{R(i+1)}$, the PME for the immediately inner level, providing as input the memory region $Reg$. Similarly, the number of misses generated by the attempts to reuse SOLs in level $i$ will be given by the evaluation of $F_{R(i+1)}$ providing as input the memory region for the reuse distance that $F_{Ri}$ estimates. This way, $F_{Ri}$ is built recursively in terms of $F_{R(i+1)}$.

The calculation of the memory regions accessed during a reuse distance is not covered in this paper due to space limitations (see [8] for more information). Still, it is worth to comment that the PME model maps the regions into a mathematical representation consisting of a vector $V$ of $k+1$ probabilities, where $k$ is the associativity of the cache, called area vector. The first element of this vector, $V_0$ is the probability a cache set has received $k$ or more lines from the region. Each element $V_s$ of the remaining $k - 1$ elements of the area vector contains the probability a given cache set has received exactly $k - s$ lines. In the calculation of this area vector the total cache size $C_s$, line size $L_s$ and degree of associativity $K$ of the cache are taken into account.

In the innermost loop that contains a reference, the recurrence of PMEs fin- ishes defining $F_{R(i+1)}(Reg)$ as the first component of the area vector associated to $Reg$. The reason is that in the innermost loop containing $R$, $Reg$ is the set of regions accessed since the latest access to the line, and if the cache has a LRU replacement policy, the condition for the attempt of reuse to fail is that $k$ or

```
DO I_0 =1, N_0
  DO I_1 =1, N_1
    ...
    DO I_Z =1, N_Z
      ...
      A(f_A1(I_A1), ..., f_Aj(B(f_B1(I_B1))), ...)
      ...
    END DO
  ...
  END DO
END DO
```

**Fig. 1.** Nested loops with structures accessed using indirections

more different lines have been mapped to the set during the reuse distance. This is exactly the probability represented by the first element of the area vector.

On the other hand, the PME for the outermost loop is evaluated using an area vector such that its component 0 is one. The reason is that this vector will only affect those accesses that cannot exploit any reuse within the code, which means that they are the cold misses. Using an area vector $V$ with $V_0 = 1$ for them ensures that the model will predict these accesses result in misses.

## 3   Scope of Application of the PME Model

Figure 1 shows the kind of codes covered by the PME model extended to cope with irregular access patterns due to indirections [8]. It is a set of perfectly or non-perfectly nested loops in which the number of iterations of the loops must be known at compile-time and the indexing of the data structures must be done using either affine functions of the loop indexes or across indirections. In [8] the values generated by the indirection had to follow an uniform distribution, that is, every position along the indexed dimension had to have the same probability of being accessed. Unfortunately this situation is not very common. In this work we relax this restriction for an important class of codes, namely those that operate with sparse banded matrices, by means of new PMEs.

As for the hardware, the PME model is oriented to caches with LRU replacement policy, allowing arbitrary sizes, block sizes and associativities.

### 3.1   Complexity of PMEs for Irregular Access Patterns

The equations for references with regular access patterns are relatively simple because all the accesses that can result in a cold miss have an unique interference probability, and a different unique interference probability is applied for the accesses that can result in an interference miss, as all the reuses have the same constant reuse distance.

```
DO I=1,M
  REG=0
  DO J=R(I), R(I+1) - 1
    REG = REG + A(J) * X(C(J))
  ENDDO
  D(I)=REG
ENDDO
```

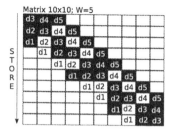

Matrix 10x10; W=5

**Fig. 2.** Sparse matrix-vector product       **Fig. 3.** Banded sparse matrix

In an irregular pattern, every access has a set of different possible reuse distances, each with an associated interference probability. PMEs weight the prediction of misses for each potential reuse distance with the probability that the considered reuse attempt happens. If the distribution of the accesses is uniform, the same set of interference regions can be used for all the accessed lines and they all have the same probability of reuse associated to each reuse distance. When this is not the case, that is, when different lines have different probabilities of being accessed, a different set of interference regions must be calculated for each accessed line, and different lines will have different probabilities of reuse for the same reuse distance.

We will illustrate these ideas with the code in Figure 2, which performs the product between a sparse matrix stored in CRS format [11] and a vector, and which is part of SPARSKIT [12]. The CRS (compressed row storage) format stores sparse matrices by rows in a compressed way using three vectors. One vector stores the nonzeros of the sparse matrix ordered by rows, another vector stores the column indexes of the corresponding nonzeros, and finally another vector stores the position in the other two vectors in which the data of the nonzeros of each row begins. In our codes we always call these vector A, C and R respectively. The innermost loop of the code in Figure 2 performs the product between vector X and row I of the sparse matrix. In this code reference X(C(J)) performs an irregular access on vector X only in the positions in which the matrix row contains nonzeros. Let us suppose that the sparse matrix that is being multiplied is a banded matrix like the one shown in Figure 3, in which the $W = 5$ diagonals that constitute its band have been labeled. During the processing of each row of the sparse matrix, a maximum of $W$ different elements of X will be accessed. Each one of these $W$ elements has a different probability of being accessed that depends on the density of the corresponding diagonal in the banded matrix. The set of elements eligible for access is displaced one position in the processing of each new row. Also, each element of X will be accessed a maximum of $W$ times during the execution of the code, as a maximum of $W$ rows may have nonzeros in the corresponding column. Interestingly, the probability of access is not uniform along those $W$ rows. For example, every first potential access during the processing of this matrix in this code will take place for sure, while every second potential access to an element of X will happen with a probability of 30%.

This is because all the positions in the fifth diagonal ($d_5$) keep nonzeros, while in the fourth diagonal ($d_4$) of the band 3 out of its 9 positions keep nonzeros, which is a density of nonzeros of 30%

The situation depicted in our example is clearly more common than the one modeled in our previous work [8], in which we only considered irregular access patterns which had an uniform probability of access for each element of the dereferenced data structure, and in which such probability did not change during the execution of the code. It is very usual that the diagonals of banded matrices have different densities, with the distribution of the nonzeros within each diagonal being relatively uniform. As a result, we have extended our model to cope with this important class of matrices, which enables to model automatically and accurately the cache behavior of codes with irregular access patterns in the presence of a large number of real sparse matrices, as the evaluation proves. We will characterize the distribution of nonzeros in these matrices by a vector $\vec{d}$ of $W$ probabilities where $d_i$ contains the density of the $i - th$ diagonal, that is, the probability a position belonging to the $i - th$ diagonal of the band contains a nonzero. This extension can be automated using a compiler framework that satisfies its information requirements, such as the one used in [9]. The vector $\vec{d}$ of diagonal densities is the only additional information we need in this work with respect to [9]. These values are obtained from an analysis of the input data that can be provided by the user, or obtained by means of runtime profiling.

## 4   PME Model Extension for Non-uniform Banded Matrices

As explained in Section 2, the PME model derives an equation $F_{Ri}$ that calculates the number of misses for each reference $R$ and nesting level $i$. This PME is a function of input memory regions calculated in outer or preceding loops that are associated to the reuses of the sets of lines (SOLs) accessed by $R$ in loop $i$ whose immediately preceding access took place before the loop began its execution. The uniformity of the accesses in all our previous works allowed to use a single region $Reg$ for this purpose, that is, all the SOLs had the same reuse distance whenever a loop began. This happened because all the considered lines had uniform probabilities of access, and thus they also enjoyed equal average reuse distances and miss probabilities. The lack of uniformity of the accesses makes it necessary to consider a separate region of interference for each SOL. Thus we extend the PMEs to receive as input a vector $\vec{Reg}$ of memory regions. The element $Reg_l$ of this vector is the memory region accessed during the reuse distance for what in this level of the nest happen to be first access to the $l$-th SOL that $R$ can access. Another way to express it is that $Reg_l$ is the set of memory regions that could generate interferences with an attempt to reuse the $l$-th SOL right when the loop begins its execution. This way, $\vec{Reg}$ has as many elements as SOLs defines $R$ during the execution of the considered loop.

The shape of PME $F_{Ri}$ depends on the access pattern followed by $R$ in loop $i$. The PME formulas for references following a regular access pattern and references following irregular access patterns due to indirections with a uniform distribution have been presented in [8]. A simple extension was also proposed in [8] to support accesses generated by the processing of banded matrices with an uniform distribution of the entries inside the band by applying small modifications to the formulas of indirections with uniform distributions. This section contains a description of the formulas we have developed for references with irregular access patterns generated by indirections due to the compressed storage of banded matrices in which the distribution of non-zeros within the band is not uniform. In the remaining, the array accessed using an indirection will be known as the base array while the array that is used to generate the values of the index of the indirection will be known as the index array. A different formula will be applied depending on whether the values read from the index array are known to be monotonic or not. They are monotonic when, given two iterations of the current loop $i$ and $j$ and being $f(i)$ and $f(j)$ the values generated by the index array in these iterations, for all $i \leq j$ then $f(i) \leq f(j)$ or for all $i \leq j$ then $f(i) \geq f(j)$. When the index values are known to be monotonic a more accurate estimation can be obtained because we known that if our reference $R$ reuses a SOL of the base array in a given iteration, this SOL is necessarily the one accessed in the previous iteration of the loop.

## 4.1 PME for Irregular Monotonic Access with Non-uniform Band Distribution

If we assume that the nonzeros within each row have been stored ordered by their column index in our sparse matrix in CRS format, reference X(C(J)) generates a monotonic irregular access on the base array X during the execution of the innermost loop in Figure 2. Let us remember that the index array C stores the column indexes of the nonzeros of the row of the sparse matrix that is being multiplied by X in this loop.

The general formula that estimates the number of misses generated by a reference $R$ in nesting level $i$ that exhibits an irregular monotonic access with a non-uniform band distribution is

$$F_{Ri}(\vec{Reg}) = \left( \sum_{l=0}^{L_{Ri}-1} p_{i(lG_{Ri})} F_{R(i+1)}(Reg_l) \right) +$$
$$\left( \sum_{l=1}^{W} d_l - \sum_{l=0}^{L_{Ri}-1} p_{i(lG_{Ri})} \right) F_{R(i+1)}(IntReg_{Ri}(1)) \tag{1}$$

The interference region from the outer level is different for each set of lines (SOL) accessed and it is represented as a vector $\vec{Reg}$ of $L_{Ri}$ different components, where $L_{Ri}$ is the total number of different SOLs of the base array A that $R$ can access in this nesting level. $L_{Ri}$ is calculated as $\lceil W/G_{Ri} \rceil$ being $W$ the band size and $G_{Ri}$ is the average number of positions in the band that give place to accesses of $R$ to a same SOL of the base array A. This value is calculated as $\lceil L_s/S_{Ri} \rceil$, being $S_{Ri} = \alpha_{Rj} \cdot d_{Aj}$ where $j$ is the dimension whose index depends on the loop variable $I_i$ through the indirection; $L_s$ is the cache line size; $\alpha_{Rj}$ is the scalar that multiplies the index array in the indexing of A, and $d_{Aj}$ is the cumulative size[1] of the $j$-th dimension of the array A referenced by $R$.

If we consider reference $X(C(J))$ in Figure 2, while processing the matrix in Figure 3, with a cache line size $L_s = 2$, in the innermost level $d_{A1} = 1$ and $\alpha_{R1} = 1$. Each $G_{Ri} = 2$ consecutive positions in the band give place to accesses to the same SOL of X. Consequently, since $W = 5$, the number of different SOLs of X accessed would be $L_{Ri} = \lceil 5/2 \rceil = 3$.

The vector of probabilities $\vec{p_i}$ has $W$ positions. Position $s$ of this vector keeps the probability that at least one of the diagonals $s$ to $s + G_{Ri} - 1$ has a nonzero, that is, it is the probability they generate at least one access to the SOL of the base array that would be accessed if there were nonzeros in any of these $G_{Ri}$ diagonals. Each component of this vector is computed as :

$$p_{is} = 1 - \prod_{l=s}^{min(W,s+G_{Ri}-1)} (1 - d_l) \qquad (2)$$

Let us remember that $\vec{d}$ is a vector of $W$ probabilities, $d_s$ being the density of the $s - th$ diagonal in the band as it is reflected in Figure 3.

In Formula 1 each SOL $l$ of the base array that R can access in nesting level $i$ has a probability $p_{i(lG_{Ri})}$ of being accessed, where $lG_{Ri}$ is the first band that can generate accesses to the $l-th$ SOL. The miss probability in the first access to each SOL $l$ depends on the interference region from the outer level associated to that SOL $Reg_l$. The remaining accesses are non-first accesses during the execution of the loop, and because the access is monotonic, their reuse distance is necessarily on iteration of the loop. As a result, the interference region will be $IntReg_{Ri}(1)$, the memory region accessed during one iteration of loop $i$ that can interfere with the reuses of $R$. The number of potential reuses of SOLs by R in the loop is calculated as $\sum_{l=1}^{W} d_l - \sum_{l=0}^{L_{Ri}-1} p_{i(lG_{Ri})}$, where the first term estimates the number of different accesses generated by R during the processing of a row or a column of a band while the second term is the average number of different SOLs that R accesses during this processing.

## 4.2 PME for Irregular Non-monotonic Access with Non-uniform Band Distribution

A data structure stored in a compressed format, such as CRS [11], is typically accessed using an offset and length construction [13]. In this situation, very common in sparse matrix computations, the knowledge that the values accessed across the indirection follow a banded distribution can be used to increase the accuracy of the prediction using a specific formula. For example, in the code of Figure 2 the reference $X(C(J))$ accesses the structure X using an offset and length construction. The values generated by the index array C in the innermost loop

---

[1] Let A be an $N$-dimensional array of size $D_{A1} \times D_{A2} \times \ldots D_{AN}$, we define the cumulative size for its $j$-th dimension as $d_{Aj} = \prod_{i=1}^{j-1} D_{Ai}$

are monotonic but the values read across different iterations of the outermost loop are non-monotonic because a different row is processed in each iteration of this loop. When this situation is detected and we are in the presence of a banded matrix, the behavior of the reference in the outer loop can be estimated as

$$F_{Ri}(RegIn) = N_i F_{R(i+1)}(\vec{Reg}(RegIn)) \tag{3}$$

In this formula the $N_i$ iterations in the current nesting level are considered to repeat the same behavior. Although the $W-1$ first and last iterations have a different behavior than the others as for example their band is not $W$ positions wide, we have checked experimentally that the lost of accuracy incurred when not considering this is not significant. This is expected, as usually the band size $W$ is much smaller than $N_i$, which is the number of rows or columns of the sparse matrix.

An average interference region for each one of the $L_{Ri}$ SOLs accessed in the inner level must be calculated. This average interference region takes account of all the possible reuses that can take place with respect to a previous iteration of the current loop depending on the different possible combinations of accesses to the studied base array. The interference region associated with each possible reuse distance must be weighted with the probability an attempt of reuse with this reuse distance happens before being added in the computation of the average interference region. The expression that estimates the average interference region associated to the $l-th$ SOL that $R$ can access in this loop is,

$$Reg_l(RegIn) = \prod_{z=lG_{Ri}+1}^{W} (1 - p_{iz})(RegIn \cup IntReg_{Ri}(W - lG_{Ri} - 1) +$$
$$\sum_{s=lG_{Ri}+1}^{W} p_{is} \left( \prod_{z=lG_{Ri}+1}^{s-1} (1 - p_{iz}) \right) IntReg_{Ri}(s - lG_{Ri}) \tag{4}$$

In the previous section we saw that $lG_{Ri}$ is the first diagonal that could generate an access to the $l$-th SOL in a given iteration and $p_{i(lG_{Ri})}$ the probability of accessing that SOL during the processing of a row or column of the matrix. As the band is shifted one position to the right every row, in general, the probability that the same SOL of the base array is accessed by $R$ $m$ iterations before the current iteration is $p_{i(lG_{Ri}+m)}$. As a result, $\prod_{z=lG_{Ri}+1}^{W}(1 - p_{iz})$ calculates the probability that the $l-th$ SOL has not been accessed in any previous iteration of this loop. In this case the interference region is equal to the union of the input region from the outer level and the region associated to the accesses that take place in the $W - lG_{Ri} - 1$ previous iterations. The union of two regions is performed as the union of their associated area vectors. The addition of a region to the average region weighted by its corresponding probability is performed adding the area vector of the region weighted by the corresponding probability to the vector that represents the average region. Regarding the reuses within loop $i$, the probability that the last access to a SOL took place exactly $m$ iterations ago is calculated multiplying the probability of being accessed in that iteration $p_{i(lG_{Ri}+m)}$ by the product of the probabilities of not being accessed in any of the

```
DO I= 1,M
  DO K= R(I), R(I+1) - 1
    REG0=A(K)
    REG1=C(K)
    DO J= 1,H
      D(I,J)=D(I,J)+REG0*B(REG1,J)
    ENDDO
  ENDDO
ENDDO
```

**Fig. 4.** Sparse Matrix - Dense Matrix (IKJ)

iterations between that iteration and the current iteration $\prod_{z=lG_{Ri}+1}^{lG_{Ri}+m-1}(1-p_{iz})$. The interference region associated to this attempt of reuse will be the region covered by the accesses that take place in those $m$ iterations of the current loop. In this equation $L_{Ri} = L_{Rj}$, $G_{Ri} = G_{Rj}$ and the vector $\vec{p_i} = \vec{p_j}$, being j the innermost nesting level of the offset and length construction.

## 5    Experimental Results

The validation was done applying by hand the PME model to 5 kernels of increasing complexity : an sparse-matrix vector product, see Figure 2, an sparse-matrix dense-matrix product with IKJ (see Figure 4), IJK and JIK order, and a sparse-matrix transposition (omitted due to space limitations). The three sparse-matrix dense-matrix products contain an access to a bidimensional array that contains an indirection in the first dimension, thus they illustrate the correctness of our model when conflicts between columns appear. The sparse-matrix transposition code exhibits particularly complex access patterns, as it has several loop nests with several nesting levels, and it involves references with up to 4 levels of indirection.

The model was validated comparing its predictions with the results of trace-driven simulations. The input data set were the 177 matrices from the Harwell-Boeing [14] and the NEP [15] sets that we found to be banded or mostly banded (a few nonzeros could be outside the band). These matrices represent 52% of the total number of matrices contained in these collections.

The matrices tested are a heterogeneous test set of input data. Some matrices have all their entries uniformly spread along a band, like the AF23560 matrix in Figure 5(a). The LNSP3937 matrix shown in Figure 5(b), has all its values spread along a band of the matrix but not uniformly. Finally, there are some matrices like CURTIS54, shown in Figure 5(c), where not all the values are spread along a band but a significant percentage of them are limited to this area.

Table 1 summarizes data giving an idea of the accuracy of the model. The results were obtained for the benchmarks performing 1770 tests considering 10 different cache configurations of each one of the 177 matrices of the Harwell-Boeing and the NEP sets. For each matrix and cache configuration 10 different

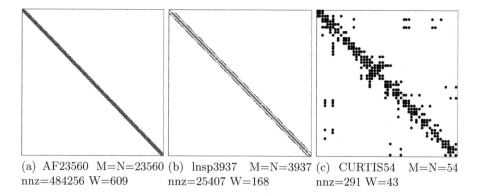

(a) AF23560  M=N=23560    (b) lnsp3937   M=N=3937    (c) CURTIS54   M=N=54
nnz=484256 W=609                nnz=25407 W=168                nnz=291 W=43

**Fig. 5.** Examples of matrices in the Harwell-Boeing set, M and N stands for the matrix dimension, nnz is the number of nonzeros and W is the band size

**Table 1.** Average measured ($\overline{MR_{\text{Sim}}}$) miss rate, average typical deviation ($\overline{\sigma_{\text{Sim}}}$) of the measured miss rate, average predicted ($\overline{MR_{\text{Mod}}}$) miss rate and the average value $\overline{\Delta_{MR}}$ of the absolute difference between the predicted and the measured miss rate in each experiment

| Code | $\overline{MR_{\text{Sim}}}$ | $\overline{\sigma_{\text{Sim}}}$ | Uniform Bands Model | | Non-Uniform Bands Model | |
|---|---|---|---|---|---|---|
| | | | $\overline{MR_{\text{Mod}}}$ | $\overline{\Delta_{MR}}$ | $\overline{MR_{\text{Mod}}}$ | $\overline{\Delta_{MR}}$ |
| SPMXV | 14.00% | 0.08% | 15.57% | 1.80% | 14.45% | 0.70% |
| SPMXDMIKJ | 27.66% | 2.02% | 45.62% | 26.81% | 28.85% | 4.19% |
| SPMXDMIJK | 8.62% | 0.29% | 27.48% | 17.23% | 10.91% | 3.10% |
| SPMXDMJIK | 7.87% | 0.43% | 10.63% | 3.23% | 8.36% | 0.78% |
| TRANSPOSE | 10.31% | 0.33% | 11.38% | 3.55% | 9.52% | 3.23% |

simulations were performed changing the base address of the data structures involved in each code. In the case of the three orderings of the sparse-matrix dense-matrix product the number of columns of the dense matrix is always a half of its number of rows. The cache configurations have cache sizes ($C_s$) from 16 KBytes to 2 MBytes, line sizes ($L_s$) from 16 to 64 bytes and associativity degrees ($K$) 1, 2, 4 and 8. Column $\overline{MR_{\text{Sim}}}$ contains the average value of the miss rate simulated in the set of experiments. Column $\overline{\sigma_{\text{Sim}}}$ is the average typical deviation of the miss rate obtained in the 10 simulations performed changing the base address of the data structures. The table compares the precision of the predictions achieved using the simple model for banded matrices assuming an uniform distribution of nonzeros introduced in [8] and the improved model presented in this paper. The table shows for each model, $\overline{MR_{\text{Mod}}}$ the average value of the miss rated predicted, and $\overline{\Delta_{MR}}$ the average value of the absolute value $\Delta_{MR}$ of the difference between the predicted and the measured miss rates for each experiment. We use absolute values, so that negative errors are not compensated with positive errors. These results show that the improved model

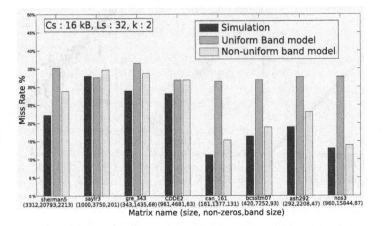

(a) Simulation and modeling for a typical level 1 cache configuration

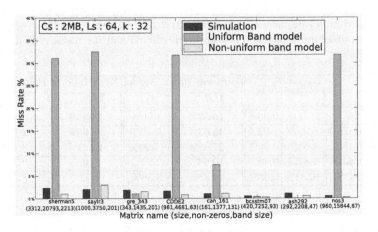

(b) Simulation and modeling for a typical level 2 cache configuration

**Fig. 6.** Comparison of the miss rates obtained by the simulation, the uniform bands model and the non-uniform bands model during the execution of the sparse matrix-dense matrix product with IJK ordering for several real matrices

is much mode accurate in the presence of real heterogeneous input banded matrices than the original model. The small values of $\overline{\sigma_{\text{Sim}}}$ point out that the base addresses of the data structures play a minor role in the cache behavior.

Figure 6 contains a comparison of the miss rate obtained in the simulation, the miss rate obtained by the uniform bands model and the miss rate obtained by the non-uniform bands model during the execution of the sparse matrix-dense matrix product with IJK ordering using some matrices from the Harwell-Boeing and the NEP collections. The number of columns of the dense matrix used in the multiplication was always one half of the number of rows of the sparse

**Table 2.** Memory hierarchy parameters in the architectures used (sizes in Bytes)

| Architecture | L1 Parameters $(C_{s_1}, L_{s_1}, K_1, \text{Cost}_1)$ | L2 Parameters $(C_{s_2}, L_{s_2}, K_2, \text{Cost}_2)$ | L3 Parameters $(C_{s_3}, L_{s_3}, K_3, \text{Cost}_3)$ |
|---|---|---|---|
| Itanium 2 | (16K,64,4,8) | (256K,128,8,24) | (6MB,128,24,120) |
| PowerPC 7447A | (32K,32,8,9) | (512K,64,8,150) | - |

matrix. Figure 6(a) shows the results obtained using a typical level 1 cache configuration, while a typical level 2 cache configuration is used in Figure 6(b). The cache configuration parameters are: $C_s$ the total cache size, $L_s$ the line size and $K$ the associativity degree. The non-uniform bands model almost always estimates more accurately the miss rate. The difference is bigger in the level 2 cache configuration. The reason for the poor estimations obtained using the uniform bands model is that in matrices with wide bands but in which most of the values are concentrated in a few diagonals, there is a lot of reuse that is not captured by the uniform bands model, as it assumes that the entries are uniformly spread along all the diagonals in the band.

The accuracy of the model and its low computational cost, always less than 1 second in a 2GHz Athlon, makes it very suitable for driving compiler optimizations. As a simple experiment aimed to prove its ability to help optimize codes with irregular access patterns due to indirections, we used its predictions to choose the best loop ordering for the sparse matrix-dense matrix product in terms of the lowest number of CPU detention cycles caused by misses in the memory hierarchy. The prediction is based on a cost function consisting of the addition of the number of misses predicted in each cache level of a real system, weighted by the miss latency for that level. Two very different systems were used for this experiment: an Itanium 2 at 1.5GHz and a PowerPC 7447A at 1.5GHz. Table 2 contains the configurations of the different cache levels in the considered architectures, using the notation $(C_s, L_s, K)$ presented in Figure 6. A new parameter, $\text{Cost}_i$ the cost in CPU cycles of a miss in the level $i$, is also taken into account. Notice that the first level cache of the Itanium 2 does not store floating point data; so it is only used for the study of the behavior of the references to arrays of integers. Also, the PowerPC does not have a third level cache.

Our model always chose the JIK order (see Table 1) in both architectures. The tests were performed using all the banded matrices from the Harwell-Boeing and the NEP collections, in multiplications with dense matrices with 1500 columns. These tests agreed with the predictions of the model: the JIK version was the fastest one in 95.9% and 99.7% of the experiments in both architectures. The codes were compiled using g77 3.4.3 with -O3 optimization level.

# 6    Related Work

Most of the analytical models found in the bibliography are limited to codes with regular access patterns [4,3,16].

The modeling of codes with irregular access patterns has been developed ad-hoc for specific pieces of code. For example, Fraguela et al. [5] proposed a model that obtained a very accurate estimation with a low computation cost but the proposed model was not automatable. In [17], an ad-hoc approach was proposed but it was limited to direct mapped caches and it did not consider the interaction between different interleaved access patterns.

Some approaches tried to model this kind of codes automatically. Cascaval's indirect accesses model [6] is integrated in a compiler framework, but it is a simple heuristic that estimates the number of cache lines accessed rather than the real number of misses. For example, it does not take into account the distribution of the irregular accesses and it does not account for conflict misses, since it assumes a fully-associative cache. As a result it suffers from limited accuracy in many situations. The modal model of memory [18] requires not only static analysis but also runtime experimentation (potentially thousands of experiments) in order to generate performance formulas. Such formulas can guide code transformation decisions by means of relative performance predictions, but they cannot predict code performance in terms of miss rates or execution time. The validation uses two very simple codes and no information is given on how long it takes to generate the corresponding predictions.

## 7    Conclusions

We have proposed an automatable extension for the modeling of indirect accesses due to the compressed storage of banded matrices. The model has been validated using codes of increasing complexity and real matrices from the NEP [15] and the Harwell-Boeing [14] collections. Our experiments show that the model reflects correctly the cache behavior of the codes with irregular access patterns due to the operation on banded matrices found in these collections. Such matrices account for 52% of the matrices that these collections contain. This extension achieves higher degrees of accuracy than a previous model of the authors which considered only banded matrices with an uniform distribution of nonzero entries. Besides, the time required to apply the model was less than 1 second in all the performed experiments.

It has been shown that our model can be used as a powerful tool for guiding optimization processes, performing successful experiments in two very different architectures, an EPIC processor Itanium 2 and a superscalar PowerPC 7447A. As future work, we plan to apply the model automatically over a wider range of different codes and to use the model as a guide in more optimization processes.

## References

1. Uhlig, R., Mudge, T.N.: Trace-driven memory simulation: A survey. ACM Comput. Surv. **29** (1997) 128–170
2. Ammons, G., Ball, T., Larus, J.R.: Exploiting Hardware Performance Counters with Flow and Context Sensitive Profiling. In: SIGPLAN Conf. on Programming Language Design and Implementation. (1997) 85–96

3. Ghosh, S., Martonosi, M., Malik, S.: Cache Miss Equations: A Compiler Framework for Analyzing and Tuning Memory Behavior. ACM Transactions on Programming Languages and Systems **21** (1999) 702–745
4. Chatterjee, S., Parker, E., Hanlon, P., Lebeck, A.: Exact Analysis of the Cache Behavior of Nested Loops. In: In Proceedings of the ACM SIGPLAN'01 Conf. on Programming Language Design and Implementation. (2001) 286–297
5. Doallo, R., Fraguela, B.B., Zapata, E.L.: Cache probabilistic modeling for basic sparse algebra kernels involving matrices with a non uniform distribution. In: In Proceedings of EUROMICRO Conference, Engineering Systems and Software for the Next Decade. (1998) 345–348
6. Cascaval, C.: Compile-time Performance Prediction of Scientific Programs. PhD thesis, Dept. of Computer Science, University of Illinois at Urbana-Champaign (2000)
7. Andrade, D., Fraguela, B.B., Doallo, R.: Analytical modeling of codes with arbitrary data-dependent conditional structures. Journal of Systems Architecture **52** (2006) 394–410
8. Andrade, D., Fraguela, B.B., Doallo, R.: Precise automatable analytical modeling of the cache behavior of codes with indirections. ACM Transactions on Architecture and Code Optimization (2006) Accepted for publication.
9. Andrade, D., Arenaz, M., Fraguela, B.B., Touriño, J., Doallo, R.: Automated and accurate cache behavior analysis for codes with irregular access patterns. In: In Proceedings of Workshop on Compilers for Parallel Computers, A Coruña, Spain (2006) 179–193
10. Duff, I., Erisman, A., Reid, J.: Direct Methods for Sparse Matrices. Oxford Science Publications (1986)
11. Barrett, R., Berry, M., Chan, T.F., Demmel, J., Donato, J.M., Dongarra, J., Eijkhout, V., Pozo, R., Romine, C., der Vorst, H.V.: Templates for the Solution of Linear Systems: Building Blocks for Iterative Methods. Philadalphia: Society for Industrial and Applied Mathematics. (1994)
12. Chow, E., Saad, Y.: Tools and Libraries for Parallel Sparse Matrix Computations. (1995)
13. Lin, Y., Padua, D.: On the automatic parallelization of sparse and irregular fortran programs. In: Languages, Compilers, and Run-Time Systems for Scalable Computers, Pittsburgh (1998) 41–56
14. Duff, I.S., Grimes, R.G., Lewis, J.G.: Users' guide for the Harwell-Boeing sparse matrix collection (Release I). Technical Report CERFACS TR-PA-92-96 (1992)
15. Bai, Z., Day, D., Demmel, J., Dongarra, J.: A test matrix collection for non-Hermitian eigenvalue problems, release 1.0 (1996)
16. Vera, X., Xue, J.: Efficient and accurate analytical modeling of whole-program data cache behavior. IEEE Transactions on Computers **53** (2004) 547–566
17. Ladner, R.E., Fix, J.D., LaMarca, A.: Cache performance analysis of traversals and random accesses. In: In Proceeding of the annual ACM-SIAM Symposium on Discrete Algorithms, Philadelphia, PA, USA, Society for Industrial and Applied Mathematics (1999) 613–622
18. Mitchell, N., Carter, L., Ferrante, J.: A modal model of memory. In: ICCS '01: Proc. of the Int'l. Conf. on Computational Sciences-Part I. Volume 2073 of Lecture Notes in Computer Science., Springer-Verlag (2001) 81–96

# Tree-Traversal Orientation Analysis

Kevin Andrusky, Stephen Curial, and José Nelson Amaral

Department of Computing Science
University of Alberta
Edmonton, Alberta, Canada
{andrusky, curial, amaral}@cs.ualberta.ca

**Abstract.** This paper presents a profiling-based analysis to determine
the traversal orientation of link-based tree data structures. Given the
very-high memory-hierarchy latencies in modern computers, once the
compiler has identified that a pointer-based data structure represents
a tree, it would be useful to determine the predominant orientation of
traversal for the tree. Optimizing compilers can implement the static
shape analysis proposed by Ghiya and Hendren to determine if a linked
data structure is a tree [10]. However no techniques have been reported
to enable an optimizing compiler to determine the predominant traversal
orientation of a tree. This paper describes an analysis that collects data
during an instrumented run to determine if the traversal is predominantly
breadth-first or depth-first. The analysis determined, with high accuracy,
the predominant orientation of traversal of trees in programs written by
us as well as in the Olden benchmark suite. This profile-based analysis is
storage efficient — it uses only 7% additional memory in comparison with
the non-instrumented version of the code. Determining the predominant
orientation of traversal of a tree data structure will enable several client
optimizations such as improved software-based prefetching, data-storage
remapping and better memory allocators.

## 1   Introduction

Data locality is critical for performance in modern computers. A fast processor's time is wasted when programs with poor data locality spend a significant
amount of time waiting for data to be fetched from memory [1,12]. Although
optimal cache-conscious data placement is NP-hard and difficult to approximate
well [17], researchers have developed many techniques that reduce memory stalls
in pointer-chasing programs [2,6,7,8,9,14]. Some improvements to data locality
require changes to the source code [7,11,18,16]. An alternative is for an optimizing compiler to automatically perform data transformations that improve
locality [2,9,14,20].

Most published pointer-chasing optimizations do not specifically address the
problem of improving data locality when the pointer-based data structure represents a tree. This paper presents a profile-based tree-traversal orientation analysis that determines the primary orientation of traversal for each pointer-based

G. Almási, C. Caşcaval, and P. Wu (Eds.): LCPC 2006, LNCS 4382, pp. 220–234, 2007.
© Springer-Verlag Berlin Heidelberg 2007

tree in a program. The results of this analysis can be used by several client optimizations to improve locality beyond what is possible with current techniques. This analysis neither requires changes to the source code nor requires significant alterations to existing compilers.

Often, dynamically allocated structures are not allocated in the same order in which they are referenced. For instance the allocation order may be determined by the organization of a data file while the traversal order is determined by the algorithm that uses the data. Data structures may exhibit poor locality due to the structure's design or due to an initial implementation that does not consider locality [11,16]. As a result, the nodes of a linked data structure may be scattered throughout the heap. For example, assume an application containing a binary tree with 15 nodes, allocated into consecutive memory locations with a breadth-first orientation as shown in Figure 1.

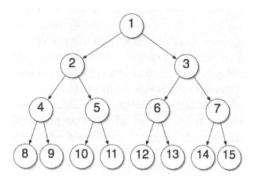

**Fig. 1.** A binary tree with 15 nodes. The node number indicates the order in which the node was allocated.

If the application accesses these nodes in a depth-first orientation[1] it will exhibit relatively poor spatial locality and likely result in degraded performance. On the other hand, if the data had been allocated in a depth-first fashion, then the traversal would have been a series of accesses to adjacent locations in memory. A regular access pattern would enable latency-hiding techniques, such as prefetching, to greatly reduce the number of memory stalls.

Optimizing compilers are better able to transform programs to improve data locality when enough information about the data access pattern is available. For instance, if a compiler could determine the traversal order of the tree in the example above, it could automatically replace a standard memory allocator with a custom memory allocator that would place tree nodes with strong reference affinity close to each other in memory.

There are many ways of traversing and accessing data stored in trees. Most of these fall into two general categories: *breadth-first* and *depth-first* traversals.

---

[1] Two possible depth-first access sequences are ⟨1, 2, 4, 8, 9, 5, 10, 11, 3, 6 ,12, 13, 7, 14, 15⟩ and ⟨1, 3, 7, 15, 14, 6, 13, 12, 2, 5, 11, 10, 4, 9, 8⟩.

If the predominant traversal orientation of a tree-based data structure is known, the compiler can reduce memory stalls caused by poor data locality. Sections 2 and 3 of this paper present a method to determine the types of traversals taking place in a program, while minimizing the amount of memory used to make this determination. This profile-based analysis compiles an instrumented version of an application, and executes the profiled code. After the program execution is finished, a value in the range $[-1, 1]$ is returned for each tree-based structure, which indicates the primary orientation of the tree traversal in the profiled code.

In order to determine the effectiveness of this analysis, we wrote several programs containing tree-based data structures with known traversal orientations. We also ran the analysis for several of the programs that comprise the Olden benchmark suite. The results of these tests are presented in Section 4. For all the tests performed, the analysis successfully identified the predominant orientation of traversal of the tree-based data structured. In addition, the amount of memory used by the profiled code, and the runtime of the code, were evaluated. In general, the instrumentation required only 7% more memory on top of the program's normal memory requirements. The instrumented application require approximately six times longer to execute than the non-instrumented version of the program. Given that training runs are typically executed once and offline, the longer execution time is acceptable in most domains.

A large number of client optimizations, in existing compilers or proposed in recent literature, could make use of the information provided by our analysis. In addition to the custom-memory allocator mentioned above, this analysis would be useful with many prefetching and structure-field reordering techniques. Section 5 surveys techniques that are possible clients to our analysis.

## 2    Overview of the Tree-Traversal Orientation Analysis

The tree-traversal orientation analysis uses an optimizing compiler to automatically instrument a program at each dereference of a tree node. For modularity, this instrumentation is a single function call to a library, linked with the compiled code. Each memory access is classified and used to create a *orientation score* for the tree.

In the context of this work, a *tree* is any linked data structure where there is at most one path between any two nodes. A *traversal* is any method for visiting all the nodes of a tree.

In a *breadth-first traversal*, all of the nodes on one level of a tree are visited before the traversal moves to the next level. Any memory access deemed to be part of a breadth-first traversal is referred to as a *breadth-first access*. Breadth-first traversals are often implemented using queues that contain the nodes that still need to be visited. As a node is processed, its children are added to the queue of nodes to be processed, ensuring that one level of the tree is traversed in its entirety before any nodes on the next level are visited. Conversely, in a *depth-first* traversal once a node is visited, one of its children is selected and the traversal continues from that child. Only when the subtree rooted by that child is fully processed is another child of the original node processed. Any memory access deemed to be part of a depth-first traversal is referred to as a *depth-first access*.

The instrumentation function updates an orientation score of the corresponding tree at each access. If the access is characterized as a breadth-first access, $-1$ is added to the orientation score. When a depth-first access occurs, $+1$ is added to the orientation score. Linked list traversals can be considered both depth- and breadth-first. To ensure that list traversals are identified, we classify accesses from a 1-ary node to its only child as depth-first [2]. A breadth-first traversal over a tree containing nodes with only one child will still appear breadth-first, as the traversal will still move among the nodes on every level of the tree, and not directly to the child of a 1-ary node. Finally, an access which cannot be classified as either breadth- or depth-first will force the score closer to 0 by either adding or subtracting 1 from the score. After all accesses have been analyzed, the orientation score is divided by the number of accesses, and returns a *traversal orientation score* in the range $[-1, 1]$ for each tree. A tree with orientation score of $-1$ is always traversed in breadth-first order. A score of $+1$ indicates pure depth-first traversal, and a score of 0 indicates that there is no predominant order of traversal.

## 3   Implementation of the Tree-Traversal Orientation Analysis

The implementation of this analysis has two primary objectives: (1) require no additional effort on the part of the programmer; (2) require minimal alterations to the compiler using the analysis. We modified the Open Research Compiler (ORC) [5] to instrument programs with calls to our Tree Analysis Library (TAL). The TAL performs all of the analysis, using the memory access information passed to it by the instrumented program. All of the computation required for the analysis is done within the instrumented code.

The TAL only analyzes trees that are represented by recursive data structures which are referenced by pointers and where pointers to children are in separate fields. For instance, TAL does not handle (1) trees where the children of a node are stored in a dynamically allocated array of pointers; and (2) trees in which the pointers to children are in fields that are unions or of type void.

In order to analyze the traversal orientation of trees, the compiler has to be able to identify the structures that represent trees in the first place. Fortunately, Ghiya and Hendren [10] have devised a static shape analysis that can determine if a pointer points to a tree data structure. Ghiya and Hendren's analysis would also allow the compiler to identify disjoint data structures using the interference matrix created by their algorithm.Ghiya and Hendren's analysis may prove conservative and not identify all possible tree-like data structures. Thus, the programmer can supplement Ghiya and Hendren's analysis with annotations. Either

---

[2] Double-linked lists are considered 1-ary nodes because one of the pointers will be identified as a parent pointer.

the interference matrix in Ghiya and Hendren's analysis or Lattner and Adve's Data Structure Analysis can be used to identify disjoint data structures [13]. Once Ghiya and Hendren's algorithm has been run, the symbol table can be annotated with the correct information as to whether or not a pointer points to a tree-like data structure. In the interest of time, for the experimental evaluation presented in this paper instead of implementing Ghiya and Hendren's analysis, we annotated the source code of the benchmarks with a special label to identify the data structures that represent trees.

Our modified version of the ORC adds instrumentation for each dereference to a tree structure, $t$, that calls the analysis function in the TAL with (1) the address of $t$, (2) all of the recursive fields of $t$ linking node $t$ to nodes $c_1 \ldots c_n$ and (3) a unique number to identify disjoint data structures. The TAL keeps a stack of choice-points for each tree. These choice-points are used to determine if a memory access can be considered part of a depth-first traversal. A choice-point structure contains the memory address of a node in the tree, $t$, and the memory addresses of all $n$ children, $c_1 \ldots c_n$.

Let $cp_{top}$ be the address of the choice-point on top of the choice-point stack; $cp_{low}$ be the address of a choice point below $cp_{top}$ in the choice-point stack; and $t$ be athe current memory access to a tree node. $t$ is considered depth-first if and only if:

1. $cp_{top}$ is equal to $t$; OR
2. a child $c_i$ of $cp_{top}$ is equal to $t$; OR
3. there exists a lower choice point in the stack, $cp_{low}$, such that $cp_{low}$ or a child of $cp_{low}$ is equal $t$ AND all of the choice-points on the stack above $cp_{low}$ have been visited.

If case (2) identifies a depth-first access then a new choice-point, representing node $t$ having all of the children $c_1 \ldots c_n$ of $t$, is pushed onto the stack. If a new choice-point is to be added to the stack, special care must be taken when copying the addresses of child pointers into the new choice-point. Tree structures often contain pointers to parent nodes. The addresses in these pointers must not be added to the new choice-point as children of the tree node $t$. To identify parent pointers the TAL compares the addresses of each possible child $c_i$ in $t$, with the addresses stored in the choice points on the stack. If case (3) identifies a depth first access then all of the choice-points up to $cp_{low}$ are popped off the stack and we leave the number of accesses and score unchanged.

To identify breadth-first searches the TAL maintains an *open list* and a *next list*. Both lists are implemented as double-ended bit vectors. When a memory access $m$ occurs, if $m$ is in the open list, then $m$ is a breadth-first access. The children of $m$ are added to the next list, and $m$ is removed from the open list. When the open list is exhausted, the next list becomes the open list and the next list is emptied. The initial entry in the list is set at bit 0. Each bit in the bit vector represents a byte in the address space. Each new entry is added to the vector based upon its distance from the initial entry. If the points-to analysis can identify that all of the objects pointed to by the pointer are of the same type, Lattner and Adve refer to this as being *type-homogeneous*, then size of the bit representation of the open list may be further reduced by using a bit to represent each structure instead of each byte.

A program may have more than one traversal of the same tree occurring simultaneously, or the orientation of traversal of a tree may change during execution. To deal with this situation, the TAL maintains a list of active data structures. This list contains multiple choice-point stacks and pairs of open and next lists. For instance, if a memory access $m$ is not considered depth-first for any active choice-point stack, a new choice-point stack is created representing a depth-first traversal rooted at $m$. New choice-point stacks are created even if the access was classified as being breadth-first.

The data structures in the active list are either choice-point stacks or pairs of open/next lists. An access *matches* a choice-point stack if it is deemed to be a depth-first access by that choice-point stack. Conversely, the access matches a pair of open/next lists if it is deemed to be breadth first by those lists.

Whenever a memory access to a tree node occurs, this access is checked against all the data structures in the active list. A reference counter is associated with each data structure. If the access does not match a data structure, the reference counter of that structure is incremented. When the access matches a data structure, the data structure reference counter is reset to zero. If the reference counter of an structure reaches a threshold (16 in our implementation) the structure is removed from the active list and its space is reclaimed.

## 3.1   Time and Space Complexity

In the interest of readability, the analysis for the identification of depth-first and breadth-first accesses will be considered separately. In this analysis, we consider a tree containing $V$ nodes.

First we consider the space and time complexity of identifying a depth-first memory access, assuming tree nodes have a minimum degree of $b$. The number of entries in a choice-point stack is bounded by $O(\log_b V)$. The bound on the number of nodes in the choice-point stack stems from the fact that before a choice-point representing node $t$ is pushed onto the stack, the choice-point representing the parent of $t$ is on the top of the stack. To consider the time complexity of determining if a memory access is a depth-first access we let $cp_{top}$ be the node on the top of the choice-point stack. In the worst case, a memory access is not to $cp_{top}$, not to any children of $cp_{top}$, nor is it to an ancestor of $cp_{top}$ and thus all entries in the stack have to be checked. It takes $O(b)$ operations to check the children of $cp_{top}$, and $O(\log_b V)$ operations to check all ancestors of $cp_{top}$ on the stack. In addition, for an access, a new choice-point may be added, or several may be removed from the stack, which also is $O(b)$ or $O(\log_b V)$ depending on which of those values is larger. Thus, the worst case total time complexity is $O(b + \log_b V)$ per memory access.

In the breadth-first analysis, the size of a double-ended vector used is largely determined by the arrangement of the nodes in memory. We assume that nodes are located relatively close together in memory, and thus the size of the vector is not significant. This assumption was confirmed in the experimental results performed on the system. If the memory allocator packs the structures contiguously then the breadth-first traversal uses $O(V)$ memory because both the open list and the next list may grow proportionally to the number of nodes in the largest level of the tree data structure being profiled. A lookup in the double-ended vector takes $O(1)$ time. Insertions into the vector may require growing the vector, which will take time proportional to the new size of the vector.

Several active lists and stacks may be maintained during the analysis. The maximum value that the reference counters for the choice point stacks and open and next lists are allowed to grow to will limit the number of active structures in the system at any point in time. Thus, the maximum number of active structures can be considered constant, and is independent of the size of the tree. As a result, the fact that multiple lists and stacks are maintained does not affect the order complexity of the analysis.

## 4   Experimentation

To evaluate the accuracy of the analysis we ran a series of experiments on programs we designed to test the tree-orientation analysis as well as on the Olden benchmark suite. Our analysis was able to correctly identify the expected traversal orientation in all the benchmarks and required only 7% additional memory on average.

### 4.1   Experimental Setup

In order to determine both the accuracy of the tree-orientation analysis, and its use of both memory and time, tests were run on fifteen tree-based programs. We created a collection of programs to determine if the analysis correctly identifies standard tree traversals. In addition, we applied the tree-traversal orientation analysis to several of the Olden benchmarks.

For each program tested, the code was compiled both with and without the profiling code inserted. The maximum amount of memory used, and the execution times of both the instrumented and non-instrumented programs were calculated. The value(s) returned by the analysis inside the profiled code were also recorded. Using these values, it is possible to demonstrate the effectiveness of the analysis in properly determining tree traversals while demonstrating that the profiled code does not use significantly more memory than the original code.

All of the experiments were performed using the Open Research Compiler version 2.1. Instrumentation was added to the code by making minor modifications to the ORC to add function calls to the program wherever a tree pointer was dereferenced. The analysis library described in Section 3 was then linked with the instrumented code. The machine used for the experiments had a 1.3 GHz Itanium2 processor with 1 GB of RAM.

### 4.2   Programs with Known Traversal Orientation

Seven programs were written to test the effectiveness of the analysis. Each of these programs has specific properties that allowed the accuracy of the orientation analysis to be evaluated. In the context of this work, a *search* in a tree is a traversal that ends before exhausting all the nodes in the tree.

- RandomDepth: A binary tree is traversed using a depth-first oriented traversal. At each node, the order in which the children are visited is chosen at random.
- BreadthFirst: A breadth-first traversal is made over a binary tree.
- DepthBreadth: A depth-first traversal is performed over a binary tree, followed by a breadth-first traversal over the same tree.
- NonStandard: A non-standard traversal of a binary tree is performed. This traversal progresses in the following order: (1) data in the current node $n$ and the right child of $n$ are processed (2) the traversal is recursively performed on the left child of $n$; (3) the traversal is recursively performed on the right child of the right child of $n$; and (4) the traversal is recursively performed on the left child of the right child of $n$. This traversal would produce the following node access sequence for the tree of Figure 1: $\langle 1, 3, 2, 5, 4, 9, 8, 11, 10, 7, 15, 14, 6, 13, 12 \rangle$. This traversal is neither depth- nor breadth-first, and should be recognized as such.
- MultiDepth: Several depth-first traversals of a binary tree are performed by this program, varying the point at which the data in each node is accessed. *i.e.* The data field(s) in the tree node are accessed either before the recursive calls to the traversal function, in between the recursive calls (if the structure has more then 1 child), or after the recursive calls to the children have been completed.
- BreadthSearch: A tree with a random branching factor for each node (with 2 to 6 children per node) is searched, breadth-first, several times.
- BinarySearch: Several tree searches are performed on a binary search tree.

### 4.3   Results of the Tree-Traversal Orientation Analysis

The tree-traversal orientation analysis was able to correctly identify the expected traversal orientation for all of the programs that we created as well as for all of the Olden benchmarks.

Table 1 gives the value computed by the tree-traversal orientation analysis for each of the programs created to test the analysis, along with the expected value. Each program has a single tree, thus Table 1 reports the score for the program.

The original Olden benchmarks were designed for multi-processor machines [4]. We used a version of the Olden benchmarks specifically converted for use with uniprocessor machines [15]. We used the following Olden benchmarks in our evaluation: BH, Bisort, Health, MST, Perimeter, Power, Treeadd and TSP [3]. Four of the Olden benchmark programs, Bisort, Perimeter, Power, and Treeadd, use a single binary tree. MST does not use a proper tree; rather it uses linked lists to deal with collisions inside a hash table. BH, Health, and TSP use a mixture of trees and linked lists connected as a single structure. In these benchmarks, linked

---

[3] Benchmarks em3d and Voronoi are omitted from this study because they could not be correctly converted to use 64 bit pointers.

**Table 1.** Analysis results on the synthetic and Olden benchmarks

| Synthetic | Analysis Result | | Olden | Analysis Result | |
|---|---|---|---|---|---|
| Benchmark | Expected | Experimental | Benchmark | Expected | Experimental |
| RandomDepth | 1.0 | 1.000000 | BH | 0.0 | 0.010266 |
| BreadthFirst | -1.0 | -0.999992 | Bisort | 0.0 | -0.001014 |
| DepthBreadth | 0.0 | 0.000000 | Health | 1.0 | 0.807330 |
| NonStandard | Close to 0.0 | 0.136381 | MST | low positive | 0.335852 |
| MultiDepth | 1.0 | 0.999974 | Perimeter | low positive | 0.195177 |
| BreadthSearch | -1.0 | -0.995669 | Power | 1.0 | 0.991617 |
| BinarySearch | 1.0 | 0.941225 | Treeadd | 1.0 | 1.000000 |
| | | | TSP | low positive | 0.173267 |

lists hang off the nodes of trees, and traversals frequently start with depth-first access to the tree nodes and continue with accesses to the linked lists.

We will examine each of the Olden benchmark programs in turn:

- BH contains tree nodes which contain both pointers to the children of a node, as well as pointers to nodes which are not considered children. As a result, even though the program performs several depth-first traversals of the tree, it cannot be classified as depth-first because many of the children of nodes are not traversed. A score of 0 is expected, as the traversal is not truly depth-first, and is definitely not breadth-first.
- Bisort performs two operations. A depth-first traversal of the tree is performed to manipulate the values stored in the tree. A merge operation routinely manipulates both children of a single node at once, which is a breadth-first way of accessing nodes. Other merge operations are neither breadth- nor depth-first. As we have competing breadth- and depth-first accesses, as well as many non-standard accesses, a score close to 0 is expected.
- Health consists of a relatively small 4-ary tree, where each node in that tree contains several linked lists. During simulations, a depth-first traversal of the tree is performed, however, at each node, the linked lists are traversed. As both linked-list and depth-first traversals are scored the same, a score close to one is expected.
- MST is based around hash tables. The tree data structure used is a linked list for chaining collisions in the hash table. Since MST performs many short linked-list traversals, a small positive value is expected.
- Perimeter uses a quad tree with a parent pointer to compute the perimeter of a region in an image. The program recursively traverses the tree, but, during the depth-first traversal, uses parent pointers to find adjacent nodes in the tree. This access pattern exhibits a mostly depth-first traversal strategy but the deviations from this pattern lead us to expect a score close to 0.
- Power repeatedly traverses a binary tree that consists of a two different types of structures. The tree traversal is depth-first and implemented via recursion. We therefore expect the TAL to calculate a score close to 1 for this program.

**Table 2.** The maximum amount of memory used in kilobytes

| Synthetic Benchmark | Memory Usage (kbytes) | | Olden Benchmark | Memory Usage (kbytes) | |
|---|---|---|---|---|---|
| | Original | Instrumented | | Original | Instrumented |
| RandomDepth | 854 976 | 855 040 | BH | 3 520 | 3 520 |
| BreadthFirst | 424 928 | 441 328 | Bisort | 3 008 | 3 040 |
| DepthBreadth | 220 112 | 252 896 | Health | 8 448 | 8 624 |
| NonStandard | 420 800 | 420 912 | MST | 4 752 | 6 272 |
| MultiDepth | 529 344 | 652 288 | Perimeter | 6 064 | 6 528 |
| BreadthSearch | 30 192 | 47 408 | Power | 3 648 | 3 712 |
| BinarySearch | 224 192 | 224 320 | Treeadd | 3 008 | 3 008 |
| | | | TSP | 3 024 | 3 040 |

– Treeadd performs a single depth-first traversal of a tree, while the program recursively computes the sum of the nodes. As this traversal is purely depth-first we expect a score close to 1.
– TSP combines a linked list and a tree into a single data structure. Each node has two pointers that indicate its position in a double-linked list, and two pointers pointing to children in a binary tree. Both list traversals and depth-first tree traversals are performed on this structure, however neither traversal visits all the children of a node (as all the children would comprise the two real children of the node, and the next and previous nodes in the list). The expected result is a very low positive score for the traversal.

### 4.4 Memory Usage

Despite the fact that the TAL creates and manipulates many data structures, it only increase memory usage by a modest amount. Code profiled with TAL requires, on average, 7% more memory than the original version of the program.

Table 2 compares the amount of memory used by the profiled and non-profiled versions of the code. In every case, the maximum amount of memory used by the program during its execution is given. The worst memory performance of the Olden benchmark comes from MST, where memory use increased by 32% during profiling. In contrast, several of the programs - BH, Power, Treeadd and TSP - only required about 1% more memory than the non-instrumented code.

### 4.5 Timing Results

Our instrumentation increases the runtime of the profiled code by an average of 5.9 times over the non-profiled code. Given that the instrumented version is typically executed once and offline, the additional runtime is acceptable.

Table 3 shows the runtime overhead introduced by the offline tree-orientation analysis. For the test programs, the profiled code runs 6.7 times slower than the non-profiled code on average. Execution time of the Olden benchmarks increased by an average of 5.5 times during profiled runs.

**Table 3.** Execution time in seconds

| Synthetic | Execution Time (seconds) | | Olden | Execution Time (seconds) | |
|---|---|---|---|---|---|
| Benchmark | Original | Instrumented | Benchmark | Original | Instrumented |
| RandomDepth | 0.90 | 10.72 | BH | 0.45 | 6.88 |
| BreadthFirst | 1.09 | 1.81 | Bisort | 0.03 | 1.01 |
| DepthBreadth | 1.33 | 7.84 | Health | 0.05 | 12.06 |
| NonStandard | 0.36 | 2.68 | MST | 5.71 | 11.42 |
| MultiDepth | 0.47 | 3.94 | Perimeter | 0.02 | 1.55 |
| BreadthSearch | 0.36 | 1.83 | Power | 1.35 | 1.60 |
| BinarySearch | 0.20 | 2.75 | Treeadd | 0.13 | 6.35 |
| | | | TSP | 0.01 | 1.40 |

Although the instrumented code takes longer to run, the performance degradation caused by profiling is acceptable for three reasons. First, this analysis can be run infrequently, for final compilations of code, or when major changes have been made to the data structures or the associated traversals. Second, the analysis can correctly determine traversal order in a relatively short period of program execution. The size of the tree considered is unimportant, as long as a representative traversal is performed on it. A proper selection of a representative input to profiling could help ensure that the analysis does not take too long. Finally, the analysis performs all the necessary calculations during the profiled run of the code. Additional work need not be performed by the compiler in order to determine the orientation of the tree traversal.

## 5   Related Work

### 5.1   Analysis of Pointer-Based Structures

Ghiya and Hendren provide a context-sensitive inter-procedural shape analysis for C that identifies the shape of data structures [10]. Their analysis differentiates structures where the shape is a cyclic graph, a directed acyclic graph, or a tree. This work allows a compiler to automatically identify tree-like data structures and the pointers to those data structures, both of which are necessary for our profiling framework.

Lattner and Adve develop a framework that partitions distinct instances of heap-based data structures [13]. The partitioning is performed by allocating the disjoint structures into independent allocation pools. Their algorithm uses a context-sensitive unification-based pointer analysis to identify disjoint data structures for their memory allocator. Compile time incurred at most 3% additional overhead. Lattner and Adve's analysis can be used to identify disjoint instances of trees but does not provide a shape analysis.

### 5.2   Potential Clients of the Tree-Orientation Analysis

**Prefetching.** Luk and Mowry propose three software prefetching schemes for recursive data structures [14]. The first prefetching scheme, known as greedy prefetching, prefetches all of the children of a structure when that structure is accessed. Greedy prefetching was implemented in the SUIF research compiler and obtained up to a 45% improvement in runtime on the Olden benchmarks. The prefetch distance is not adjustable with this technique and thus it is not able to hide the considerable memory access latency experienced in modern processors. To allow the compiler to control the prefetch distance, Luk and Mowry propose two other prefetching schemes, history-pointer prefetching and data-linearization prefetching. When the application is running, history-pointer prefetching records the access pattern via a history-pointer in each structure during the first tree traversal. Once all of the history pointers have been initialized, the system can use them to prefetch data. History-pointer prefetching was implemented by hand, and in spite of the runtime and space overhead, this technique can obtain up to a 40% speedup compared with greedy prefetching. Data-linearization prefetching allocates nodes with high access affinity near each other to increase spatial locality. Data-linearization prefetching is both implicit, through the use of spatial locality, and explicit, through the use of prefetches to incremental memory locations. Data-linearization prefetching was implemented by hand and resulted in up to a 18% speedup over greedy prefetching.

Cahoon and McKinley use compile-time data flow analysis to develop a software prefetching scheme for linked data structures in Java [2]. Traversals of linked data structures are identified through the use of a recurrent update to a pointer that is placed within a loop or recursive call related to the traversal of the linked data structure. A jump pointer, similar to Luk and Mowry's history pointer, is added to each structure that is updated recurrently and jump pointers are used for prefetching when the application is traversing the data structure. The prefetching scheme results in performance improvements as large as 48% but Cahoon and McKinley note that "... consistent improvements are difficult to obtain."

Our analysis could be used with Luk and Mowry's history-pointer prefetching or Cahoon and McKinley's jump-pointer prefetching to reduce the overhead of computing the history pointers and increase the benefit from prefetching. In both schemes, the first traversal of the tree is used to calculate the history pointer. Unless the structure is traversed many times this initial overhead may not be amortized out, and performance degradation could result. If the traversal pattern of the tree is known, a custom allocator could be used to linearize the subtrees that are allocated and prefetching could be performed in the same fashion as Luk and Mowry's data-linearization prefetching during the first tree traversal or used to set the jump pointers before they can be initialized by the first tree traversal. This would also allow hardware prefetchers, which are commonly found on modern processors, to retrieve the data and eliminate much of the latency caused by compulsory misses.

**Modifying Data Layout.** Calder *et al.* present a framework that uses profiling to find the temporal relationship between objects and to modify the data placement of the objects to reduce the number of cache misses [3]. A profiling phase creates a temporal relationship graph between objects where edges connect those objects likely to be in the cache together. To reduce the number of conflict misses, objects with high temporal locality are placed in memory locations that will not be mapped to the same cache blocks. Field reordering is used to place objects in memory to maximize locality and reduce capacity misses by reducing the size of the working set. Finally, Calder *et al.* reduce compulsory misses by allowing blocks of data to be efficiently prefetched. These techniques are applied to both statically- and dynamically-allocated data. For dynamically-allocated data, the data placement is accomplished using a custom memory allocator that places allocated objects into a specific allocation bin based on information about the object traversal pattern. Experimentation showed that the data cache miss rate could be reduced by 24% on average, with some reductions as high as 74%.

Chilimbi, Hill and Larus describe techniques to improve the locality of linked data structures while reducing conflict misses, namely cache-conscious allocation and cache-conscious reorganization [7]. Two semi-automatic tools are created to allow the programmer to use cache-conscious allocation, ccmalloc, and cache-conscious reorganization, ccmorph, for their data structures. The main idea behind the tools are clustering, packing data with high affinity into a cache block, and coloring, using k-coloring to represent a k-way set-associative cache to reduce cache-conflicts. Their memory allocator, ccmalloc, takes a memory address of an element that is likely to be accessed at the same time as the newly allocated object and allocates them near one another in memory. The tree reorganizer, ccmorph, copies subtrees and lays them out linearly. After tree reorganization, any references to nodes in the tree must be updated. Chilimbi, Hill and Larus obtained speedups of 28-138% using their cache-conscious allocation techniques.

The work by Calder *et al.* and Chilimbi, Hill and Larus both aim to improve cache-hit rates by modifying where data is allocated. The profiling used by Calder *et al.* could be combined with our tree-traversal analysis to allow more information to be given to the compiler. A custom allocator could be created that can be given hints by the compiler based on information in the profile that was collected. The allocator could use Calder *et al.*'s or Chilimbi, Hill and Larus' techniques to arrange data to avoid cache conflicts while increasing the locality of tree nodes by allocating the nodes based on the profile information.

**Structure Reorganization.** Truong, Bodin and Seznec use semi-automatic techniques to improve the locality of dynamically allocated data structures based on field reorganization and instance interleaving [19]. *Field reorganization* groups fields of a data structure that are referenced together into the same cache line, while *instance interleaving* groups identical fields of different instances of a structure into a common area in memory. They present a memory allocator, ialloc, that allocates structures, or chunks of structures, into arenas to increase locality.

Chilimbi, Davidson and Larus used field reordering and structure splitting to improve the behavior of structures that are larger then a cache line [6]. Field reordering groups the fields of a structure that are accessed together into sets which will fit into a cache line. Chilimbi, Davidson and Larus also group the fields of structures into hot (frequently accessed) and cold (infrequently accessed) fields. These techniques can increase the number of hot fields that can fit in the cache and they improved execution time by 6 - 18% over other co-allocation schemes by reducing cache miss rates by 10 - 27%.

It would be possible to combine Truong, Bodin and Seznec's `ialloc` memory allocator and the idea of allocation arenas with compiler technology to perform structure splitting similar to that performed by Zhao *et al.* [20], to apply this technique to recursive data-structures instead of arrays.

# 6   Conclusions

This work presents an analysis that accurately identifies the predominant traversal orientation of trees in a program. The analysis gives a floating point value for each tree, representing how close to a pure breadth- or depth-first orientation the traversal of that tree is. This value can be used by many client optimizations inside a compiler or may be used by programmers to improve the data structure layout. Most of the work is performed by a static library used to profile instrumented code which only slightly increases memory use. The tree-traversal orientation analysis requires no work on the part of the programmer, and requires only minor modifications to a compiler.

# Acknowledgments

This research is supported by grants from the Natural Sciences and Engineering Research Council of Canada (NSERC), and by IBM Corporation.

# References

1. A. Ailamaki, D. J. DeWitt, M. D. Hill, and D. A. Wood. DBMSs on a modern processor: Where does time go? In *25th Very Large Data Base (VLDB) Conference*, Edinburgh, Scotland, 1999.
2. B. Cahoon and K. S. McKinley. Data flow analysis for software prefetching linked data structures in Java. In *10th International Conference on Parallel Architectures and Compilation Techniques (PACT '01)*, pages 280–291, Los Alamitos, CA, USA, 2001. IEEE Computer Society.
3. B. Calder, C. Krintz, S. John, and T. Austin. Cache-conscious data placement. In *Proceedings of the Eighth International Conference on Architectural Support for Programming Languages and Operating Systems (ASPLOS-VIII)*, San Jose, 1998.
4. M. Carlisle and A. Rogers. Olden web page. http://www.cs.princeton.edu/~mcc/olden.html.
5. S. Chan, Z. H. Du, R. Ju, and C. Y. Wu. Web page: Open research compiler - aurora. http://sourceforge.net/projects/ipf-orc.
6. T. M. Chilimbi, B. Davidson, and J. R. Larus. Cache-conscious structure definition. In *PLDI '99: Proceedings of the ACM SIGPLAN 1999 conference on Programming Language Design and Implementation*, pages 13–24, 1999.
7. T. M. Chilimbi, M. D. Hill, and J. R. Larus. Cache-conscious structure layout. In *PLDI '99: Proceedings of the ACM SIGPLAN 1999 conference on Programming Language Design and Implementation*, pages 1–12, 1999.

8. T. M. Chilimbi and M. Hirzel. Dynamic hot data stream prefetching for general-purpose programs. In *PLDI '02: Proceedings of the ACM SIGPLAN 2002 conference on Programming Language Design and Implementation*, page 1990209, Berlin, Germany, 2002.

9. S. Choi, N. Kohout, S. Pamnani, D. Kim, and D. Yeung. A general framework for prefetch scheduling in linked data structures and its application to multi-chain prefetching. *ACM Transactions on Computer Systems*, 22(2):214–280, 2004.

10. R. Ghiya and L. J. Hendren. Is it a tree, a DAG, or a cyclic graph? A shape analysis for heap-directed pointers in C. In *Symposium on Principles of Programming Languages (POPL)*, pages 1–15, St. Petersburg, Florida, January 1996.

11. A. Ghoting, G. Buehrer, S. Parthasarathy, D. Kim, A. Nguyen, Y. Chen, and P. Dubey. Cache-conscious frequent pattern mining on a modern processor. In *VLDB '05: Proceedings of the 31st international conference on Very large data bases*, pages 577–588. VLDB Endowment, 2005.

12. M. Itzkowitz, B. J. N. Wylie, C. Aoki, and N. Kosche. Memory profiling using hardware counters. In *SC '03: Proceedings of the 2003 ACM/IEEE conference on Supercomputing*, 2003.

13. C. Lattner and V. Adve. Automatic pool allocation: Improving performance by controlling data structure layout in the heap. In *PLDI '05: Proceedings of the 2005 ACM SIGPLAN conference on Programming language design and implementation*, pages 129–142, 2005.

14. C. K. Luk and T. C. Mowry. Compiler-based prefetching for recursive data structures. In *ACM SIGOPS Operating Systems Review*, 1996.

15. C.K. Luk. Web resource: Uniprocessor olden tarball. http://www.cs.cmu.edu/~luk/software/olden_SGI.tar.gz.

16. R. Niewiadomski, J. N. Amaral, and R. C. Holte. A performance study of data layout techniques for improving data locality in refinement-based pathfinding. *ACM Journal of Experimental Algorithmics*, 9(1.4):1–28, October 2004.

17. E. Petrank and D. Rawitz. The hardness of cache conscious data placement. In *POPL '02: Proceedings of the 29th ACM SIGPLAN-SIGACT symposium on Principles of programming languages*, pages 101–112, Portland, Oregon, Jan. 2002.

18. J. Rao and K. A. Ross. Making B+ Trees cache conscious in main memory. In *SIGMOD '00: Proceedings of the 2000 ACM SIGMOD International Conference on Management of Data*, pages 475–486, 2000.

19. D. N. Truong, F. Bodin, and A. Seznec. Improving cache behavior of dynamically allocated data structures. In *Seventh International Conference on Parallel Architectures and Compilation Techniques (PACT'98)*, pages 322–329, 1998.

20. P. Zhao, S. Cui, Y. Gao, R. Silvera, and J. N. Amaral. *Forma*: A framework for safe automatic array reshaping. *ACM Transactions on Programming Languages and Systems*, To Appear.

# UTS: An Unbalanced Tree Search Benchmark[*]

Stephen Olivier[1], Jun Huan[1], Jinze Liu[1], Jan Prins[1], James Dinan[2],
P. Sadayappan[2], and Chau-Wen Tseng[3]

[1] Dept. of Computer Science, Univ. of North Carolina at Chapel Hill
{olivier, huan, liuj, prins}@cs.unc.edu
[2] Dept. of Computer Science and Engineering, The Ohio State Univ.
{dinan, saday}@cse.ohio-state.edu
[3] Dept. of Computer Science, Univ. of Maryland at College Park
tseng@cs.umd.edu

**Abstract.** This paper presents an unbalanced tree search (UTS) benchmark designed to evaluate the performance and ease of programming for parallel applications requiring dynamic load balancing. We describe algorithms for building a variety of unbalanced search trees to simulate different forms of load imbalance. We created versions of UTS in two parallel languages, OpenMP and Unified Parallel C (UPC), using work stealing as the mechanism for reducing load imbalance. We benchmarked the performance of UTS on various parallel architectures, including shared-memory systems and PC clusters. We found it simple to implement UTS in both UPC and OpenMP, due to UPC's shared-memory abstractions. Results show that both UPC and OpenMP can support efficient dynamic load balancing on shared-memory architectures. However, UPC cannot alleviate the underlying communication costs of distributed-memory systems. Since dynamic load balancing requires intensive communication, performance portability remains difficult for applications such as UTS and performance degrades on PC clusters. By varying key work stealing parameters, we expose important tradeoffs between the granularity of load balance, the degree of parallelism, and communication costs.

## 1 Introduction

From multicore microprocessors to large clusters of powerful yet inexpensive PCs, parallelism is becoming increasingly available. In turn, exploiting the power of parallel processing is becoming essential to solving many computationally challenging problems. However, the wide variety of parallel programming paradigms (e.g., OpenMP, MPI, UPC) and parallel architectures (e.g., SMPs, PC clusters, IBM BlueGene) make choosing an appropriate parallelization approach difficult. Benchmark suites for high-performance computing (e.g., SPECfp, NAS, SPLASH, SPEComp) are thus important in providing users a way to evaluate how various computations perform using a particular combination of programming paradigm, system software, and hardware architecture.

---

[*] This work was supported by the U.S. Department of Defense.

G. Almási, C. Cașcaval, and P. Wu (Eds.): LCPC 2006, LNCS 4382, pp. 235–250, 2007.
© Springer-Verlag Berlin Heidelberg 2007

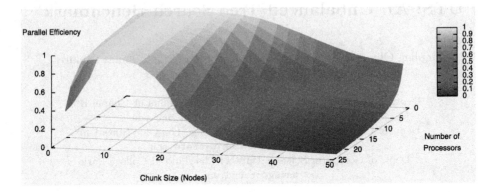

**Fig. 1.** Tree T1 has about 4.1 million nodes, and a depth of 10. The degree of each node varies according to a geometric distribution with mean 4. The parallel efficiency of the UPC implementation using 2 to 24 processors of an SGI Origin 2000 is shown relative to the sequential traversal of the tree. Work is stolen in chunks of $k$ nodes at a time from the depth-first stack of processors actively exploring a portion of the tree. When $k$ is small, the communication and synchronization overheads in work stealing start to dominate performance and lower the efficiency. As $k$ increases, it becomes increasingly difficult to find processors with $k$ nodes on their stack (the expected maximum number of nodes on the stack is 40), hence efficiency suffers from lack of load balance.

One class of applications not well represented in existing high-performance benchmarking suites are ones that require substantial dynamic load balance. Most benchmarking suites either exhibit balanced parallel computations with regular data access (e.g. solvers communicating boundary data such as SWM, TOMCATV, APPSP), or balanced computations with irregular data access and communication patterns (e.g. sparse solvers, FFT, Integer Sort, APPLU). Existing benchmarks that do utilize dynamic load balancing do so only at specific points in the application (e.g. Barnes-Hut n-body simulation, or solvers using adaptive mesh refinement).

We introduce a simple problem – parallel exploration of an unbalanced tree – as a means to study the expression and performance of applications requiring continuous dynamic load balance. Applications that fit in this category include many search and optimization problems that must enumerate a large state space of unknown or unpredictable structure.

The unbalanced tree search (UTS) problem is to count the number of nodes in an implicitly constructed tree that is parameterized in shape, depth, size, and imbalance. Implicit construction means that each node contains all information necessary to construct its children. Thus, starting from the root, the tree can be traversed in parallel in any order as long as each parent is visited before its children. The imbalance of a tree is a measure of the variation in the size of its subtrees. Highly unbalanced trees pose significant challenges for parallel traversal because the work required for different subtrees may vary greatly. Consequently, an effective and efficient dynamic load balancing strategy is required to achieve good performance.

In this paper we describe OpenMP and UPC implementations of the UTS problem and evaluate their performance on a number of parallel architectures and for a number of different tree shapes and sizes. The implementations use a work-stealing strategy for dynamic load balancing. Threads traverse the portion of the tree residing on their local stack depth first, while stealing between threads adds a breadth first dimension to the search. Figure 1 illustrates the performance of the UPC implementation on a shared memory machine as a function of number of processors and the granularity of load balancing. We are particularly interested in how well a single UPC implementation performs across shared and distributed memory architectures, since UPC is a locality-aware parallel programming paradigm that is intended to extend to both memory models.

The remainder of the paper is organized as follows. Section 2 describes the class of unbalanced trees, and some of their properties. Section 3 describes the benchmark programs that were developed to implement parallel unbalanced tree search. Section 4 provides a detailed performance analysis of the implementations on a variety of shared and distributed memory architectures, comparing absolute performance, processor and work scaling. Section 5 has the conclusions.

## 2    Generating Unbalanced Trees

We describe a class of synthetic search trees whose shape, size, and imbalance are controlled through a small number of parameters. The class includes trees representing characteristics of various parallel unbalanced search applications.

The trees are generated using a Galton-Watson process [1], in which the number of children of a node is a random variable with a given distribution. To create deterministic results, each node is described by a 20-byte descriptor. The child node descriptor is obtained by application of the SHA-1 cryptographic hash [2] on the pair (parent descriptor, child index). The node descriptor also is the random variable used to determine the number of children of the node. Consequently the work in generating a tree with $n$ nodes is $n$ SHA-1 evaluations.

To count the total number of nodes in a tree requires all nodes to be generated; a shortcut is unlikely as it requires the ability to predict a digest's value from an input without executing the SHA-1 algorithm. Success on this task would call into question the cryptographic utility of SHA-1. Carefully validated implementations of SHA-1 exist which ensure that identical trees are generated from the same parameters on different architectures.

The overall shape of the tree is determined by the *tree type*. Each of these generates the children of its nodes based on a different probability distribution: binomial or geometric. One of the parameters of a tree is the value $r$ of the root node. Multiple instances of a tree type can be generated by varying this parameter, hence providing a check on the validity of an implementation.

We examined a variety of tree shapes and choose to report on two representative shapes due to space limits.

## 2.1  Binomial Trees

A node in a *binomial tree* has $m$ children with probability $q$ and has no children with probability $1 - q$, where $m$ and $q$ are parameters of the class of binomial trees. When $qm < 1$, this process generates a finite tree with expected size $\frac{1}{1-qm}$. Since all nodes follow the same distribution, the trees generated are self-similar and the distribution of tree sizes and depths follow a power law [3]. The variation of subtree sizes increases dramatically as $qm$ approaches 1. This is the source of the tree's imbalance. A binomial tree is an optimal adversary for load balancing strategies, since there is no advantage to be gained by choosing to move one node over another for load balance: the expected work at all nodes is identical.

The root-specific branching factor $b_0$ can be set sufficiently high to generate an interesting variety of subtree sizes below the root according to the power law. Alternatively, $b_0$ can be set to 1, and a specific value of $r$ chosen to generate a tree of a desired size and imbalance.

## 2.2  Geometric Trees

The nodes in a *geometric tree* have a branching factor that follows a geometric distribution with an expected value that is specified by the parameter $b_0 > 1$. Since the geometric distribution has a long tail, some nodes will have significantly more than $b_0$ children, yielding unbalanced trees. The parameter $d$ specifies the maximum, beyond which the tree is not allowed to grow. Unlike binomial trees, the expected size of the subtree rooted at a node increases with proximity to the root.

Geometric trees have a depth of at most $d$, and have an $O((b_0)^d)$ expected size. The depth-first traversal of a geometric tree resembles a stage of an iterative deepening depth-first search, a common search technique for potentially intractable search spaces.

# 3    Implementation

Our implementations perform a depth-first traversal of an implicit tree as described in the previous section. Since there is no need to retain a description of a node once its children have been generated, a depth-first stack can be used. A node is explored by popping it off the stack and pushing its children onto the stack. Parallel traversals can proceed by moving one or more node(s) from a non-empty stack of one processor to the empty stack of an idle processor.

Several strategies have been proposed to dynamically balance load in such a parallel traversal. Of these, work-stealing strategies place the burden of finding and moving tasks to idle processors on the idle processors themselves, minimizing the overhead to processors that are making progress. Work-stealing strategies have been investigated theoretically and in a number of experimental settings, and have been shown to be optimal for a broad class of problems requiring dynamic load balance [4]. Work-sharing strategies place the burden of moving work to idle processors on the busy processors. A thorough analysis of load balancing strategies for parallel depth-first search can be found in [5] and [6].

One key question concerns the number of nodes that are moved between processors at a time. The larger this chunk size $k$, the lower the overhead to both work stealing and work sharing strategies when amortized over the expected work in the exploration of the $k$ nodes. This argues for a larger value of $k$. However, the likelihood that a depth first search of one of our trees has $k$ nodes on the stack at a given time is proportional to $\frac{1}{k}$, hence it may be difficult to find large amounts of work to move. Indeed it was our goal to construct a problem that challenges all load balancing strategies, since such a benchmark can be used to assess some key characteristics of the implementation language, runtime environment, and computing system. For example, distributed-memory systems that require coarse-grain communication to achieve high performance may be fundamentally disadvantaged on this problem.

## 3.1   Work Stealing in UPC and OpenMP

UPC (Unified Parallel C) is a shared-memory programming model based on a version of C extended with global pointers and data distribution declarations for shared data [7]. The model can be compiled for shared memory or distributed memory execution. For execution on distributed memory, it is the compilers responsibility to translate memory addresses and insert inter-processor communication. A distinguishing feature of UPC is that global pointers with affinity to one particular thread may be cast into local pointers for efficient local access by that thread. Explicit one-sided communication is also supported in the UPC run-time library via routines such as *upc_memput()* and *upc_memget()*.

We implemented work stealing in OpenMP for shared memory machines and UPC for shared and distributed memory machines. Instead of trying to steal procedure continuations as would be done in Cilk [8], which requires cooperation from the compiler, in our implementation idle threads steal nodes from another thread's depth-first stack. Initially, the first thread holds the root node. As enough nodes are generated from the root and its descendants, other threads steal chunks of nodes to add to their stacks. Each thread performs a depth-first traversal of some part of the tree using its own stack of nodes. A thread that empties its stack tries to steal one or more nodes from some other thread's nonempty stack. On completion, the total number of nodes traversed in each thread can be combined to yield the size of the complete tree.

## 3.2   Manipulating the Steal Stack

We now consider the design of the stack. In addition to the usual push and pop operations, the stack must also support concurrent stealing operations performed by other threads, which requires the stacks to be allocated in the shared address space and that locks be used to synchronize accesses. We must eliminate overheads to the depth-first traversal performed by a working thread as much as possible. Thus each thread must be able to perform push and pop operations at stack top without incurring shared address translation overheads in UPC or requiring locking operations. Figure 2 shows the stack partitioned into two regions.

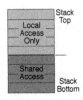

**Fig. 2.** A thread's
steal stack

**Table 1.** Sample trees, with parameters and their resulting depths and sizes in millions of nodes

| Tree | Type | $b_0$ | $d$ | $q$ | $m$ | $r$ | Depth | MNodes |
|------|------|-------|-----|-----|-----|-----|-------|--------|
| T1 | Geometric | 4 | 10 | – | – | 19 | 10 | 4.130 |
| T2 | Geometric | 1.014 | 508 | – | – | 0 | 508 | 4.120 |
| T3 | Binomial | 2000 | – | 0.124875 | 8 | 42 | 1572 | 4.113 |

The region that includes the stack top can be accessed directly by the thread with affinity to the stack using a local pointer. The remaining area is subject to concurrent access and operations must be serialized through a lock. To amortize the manipulation overheads, nodes can only move in chunks of size $k$ between the local and shared regions or between shared areas in different stacks.

Using this data structure, the local push operation, for example, does not involve any shared address references in UPC or any lock operations. The *release* operation can be used to move a chunk of $k$ nodes from the local to the shared region, when the local region has built up a comfortable stack depth (at least $2k$ in our implementation). The chunk then becomes eligible to be stolen. A matching *acquire* operation is used to move nodes from the shared region back onto the local stack when the local stack becomes empty.

When there are no more chunks to reacquire locally, the thread must find and steal work from another thread. A pseudo-random probe order is used to examine other stacks for available work. Since these probes may introduce significant contention when many threads are looking for work, the count of available work on a stack is examined without locking. Hence a subsequent steal operation performed under lock may not succeed if in the interim the state has changed. In this case the probe proceeds to the next victim. If the chunk is available to be stolen, it is reserved under lock and then transferred outside of the critical region. This is to minimize the time the stack is locked.

When a thread out of work is unable to find any available work in any other stack, it enters a barrier. When all threads have reached the barrier, the traversal is complete. A thread releasing work sets a global variable which in turn releases an idle thread waiting at the barrier.

### 3.3 Data Distribution in OpenMP

Unlike UPC, the OpenMP standard does not provide a way to specify the distribution of an array across the memories of processors [9]. Generally this distribution is accomplished by allocating page frames to memories local to the processor which generated the page fault [10]. However this strategy is prone to false sharing when a large number of processors share a relatively small array of per-processor data structures that are being updated. The symptom of such false sharing is poor scaling to large processor counts.

**Table 2.** Sequential performance for all trees (Thousands of nodes per second)

| System | Processor | Compiler | T1 | T2 | T3 |
|---|---|---|---|---|---|
| Cray X1 | Vector (800 MHz) | Cray 5.5.0.4 | 29 | 29 | 31 |
| SGI Origin 2000 | MIPS (300 MHz) | GCC 3.2.2 | 158 | 156 | 170 |
| SGI Origin 2000 | MIPS (300 MHz) | Mipspro 7.3 | 169 | 166 | 183 |
| Sun SunFire 6800 | Sparc9 (750 MHz) | Sun C 5.5 | 260 | 165 | 384 |
| P4 Xeon Cluster (OSC) | P4 Xeon (2.4GHz) | Intel 8.0 | 717 | 940 | 1354 |
| Mac Powerbook | PPC G4 (1.33GHz) | GCC 4.0 | 774 | 672 | 1117 |
| SGI Altix 3800 | Itanium2 (1.6GHz) | GCC 3.4.4 | 951 | 902 | 1171 |
| SGI Altix 3800 | Itanium2 (1.6GHz) | Intel 8.1 | 1160 | 1106 | 1477 |
| Dell Blade Cluster (UNC) | P4 Xeon (3.6GHz) | Intel 8.0 | 1273 | 1165 | 1866 |

The Irix-specific *distribute_reshape* directive provided compiler-mediated distribution of the array across processor memories, improving performance on the SGI Origin. However we found that on the Intel compiler on the SGI Altix, this directive was not operative.

As a result, we replaced the array of per-thread data with an array of pointers to dynamically allocated structures. During parallel execution, each thread dynamically allocates memory for its own structure with affinity to the thread performing the allocation. This adjustment eliminated false sharing, but was unnecessary for UPC. The facilities for explicit distribution of data in OpenMP are weaker than those of UPC.

# 4   Performance Evaluation

The UTS program reports detailed statistics about load balance, performance, and the tree that is generated. We have examined data on several different parallel machines and discovered some meaningful trends, which are presented in this section.

Three sample trees were used for most of the experiments. Two of these are geometric trees and one is a binomial tree. All trees are approximately the same size (4.1 million nodes, ±1%). However, they vary greatly in depth. The parameters, depth, and size of each tree are given in Table 1.

## 4.1   Sequential Performance

Before examining parallel execution, we ran the benchmark sequentially on a variety of systems. The performance results are given in Fig. 2. Unless otherwise noted, all performance measures are the average of the best eight out of ten executions. Note that some systems were tested with both their native compilers and GCC. This establishes a helpful baseline for the parallel performance results presented later. When compiling UTS with OpenMP, the native compilers were used. The Intrepid UPC compiler, based on GCC, was used to compile UTS with UPC on the shared memory systems. The *-O3* optimization flag was used when

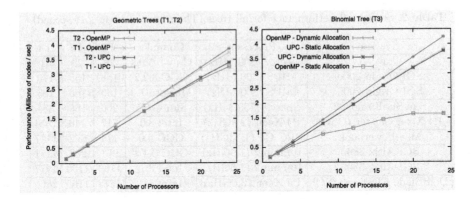

**Fig. 3.** Parallel performance on the Origin 2000 using OpenMP and UPC. On the left, results for geometric trees T1 and T2. On the right, results for T3 with static versus dynamic data allocation for the steals stacks. The chunk size used in each run is chosen to optimize performance for the tree type.

compiling on the shared memory machines. On the Pentium 4 and Dell blade clusters, the Berkeley UPC compiler was used. The Berkeley compiler translates UPC to C for final compilation on the native compiler. An experimental set of optimizations offered by Berkeley UPC was not used in the results reported here, but will be used shortly.

Despite the similar sizes of the trees, most systems showed significant and systematic differences in performance due to differences in cache locality. Ideally, a node will remain in cache between the time it is generated and the time it is visited. The long tail of the geometric distribution results in some nodes generating a large number of children, flushing the L1 cache. In the binomial tree T3, nodes generate only 8 children, if any, keeping L1 cache locality intact for faster execution. The impact of this difference in sequential exploration rate will be seen in the parallel results given in the next section, where we will show that the parallel performance also varies by tree type.

### 4.2    Parallel Performance on Shared Memory Machines

Performance using UPC and OpenMP on the SGI Origin 2000 is given in the left graph of Fig. 3. The OpenMP results for T1 and T2 are from the modified version of the benchmark discussed in Section 3.3. The results for T3 in the right graph of Fig. 3 quantify the performance change between OpenMP implementations using static and dynamic allocation of per-thread data structures. OpenMP performance is dramatically improved using dynamic allocation. UPC performance is slightly decreased using dynamic allocation version, as the extra shared pointer dereference adds to overhead costs. (The two are nearly indistinguishable in the graph.)

The UPC version runs more slowly than the OpenMP version due to the increased overheads of UPC. The variations in runtimes by tree type seen in

Section 4.1 are also present in the parallel runs. Absolute performance on T3 is higher, though all scale well.

### 4.3    Parallel Performance on Distributed Memory

Using the same UPC code, we compiled and ran UTS on a Dell blade cluster at UNC. The cluster's interconnect is Infiniband, and we configured the Berkeley UPC runtime system to run over VAPI drivers, as opposed to UDP or MPI. Still, performance was markedly poor. Figure 4 shows the overall performance of the sample trees and a comparison of parallel efficiency between the SGI Origin and the Dell blade cluster for trees T1 and T3. Note each plotted value represents the best of 100 runs per chunk size on the cluster at that processor count. We have found that the performance varies as much as one order of magnitude even between runs using identical settings. While the efficiency on the Origin is consistently above 0.9, the program's efficiency on the cluster falls off sharply as more processors are used. Poor scaling was also seen on the P4 Xeon Cluster at Ohio Supercomputer Center (OSC).

Poor performance on distributed memory is consistent with previous UPC evaluation [11]. Program designs that assume efficient access of shared variables do not scale well in systems with higher latency.

Key factors contributing to the poor peak performance and high variability are the work-stealing mechanism and termination detection, neither of which create performance bottlenecks on shared memory machines. Each attempted steal involves several communication steps: check whether work is available at the victim, reserve the nodes, and then actually transfer them. Failed steal attempts add additional communication. The termination detection uses a simple cancelable barrier consisting of three shared variables: a cancellation flag, a count of nodes at the barrier, and a completion flag. It is a classic shared variable solution that uses local spinning when implemented in a shared memory machines. We speculate that the distributed memory runtime has a different coherence protocol that is a poor match to algorithms that rely on local spinning.

### 4.4    Visualization for Detailed Analysis

When tracing is enabled, each thread keeps records of when it is working, searching for work, or idle. It also records the victim, the thief, and the time of each steal. Since some systems, in particular distributed memory machines, do not have synchronized clocks, the records kept by the threads are adjusted by an offset. This offset is found by recording the time following the completion of a OpenMP or UPC barrier. This gives millisecond precision on the clusters we tested, but more sophisticated methods could likely do better.

The PARAVER (PARallel Visualization and Events Representation) tool[12] is used to visualize the data. PARAVER displays a series of horizontal bars, one for each thread. There is a time axis below, and the color of each bar at each time value corresponds to that thread's state. Yellow vertical lines drawn between the bars represent the thief and victim threads at the time of each steal.

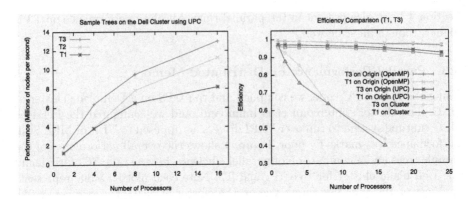

**Fig. 4.** Performance on the Dell blade cluster (left); Parallel efficiency on the Dell cluster versus the Origin 2000 (right)

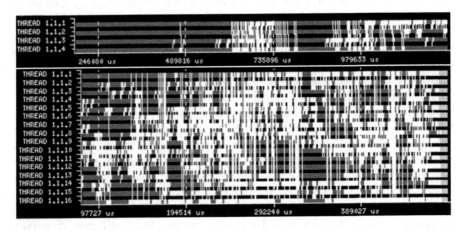

**Fig. 5.** PARAVER time charts for T3 on 4 vs. 16 processors of OSC's P4 cluster

Figure 5 shows PARAVER time charts for two runs on OSC's P4 Xeon cluster at chunk size 64. The bars on the top trace (4 threads) are mostly dark blue, indicating that the threads are at work. The second trace (16 threads) shows a considerable amount of white, showing that much of the time threads are searching for work. There is also noticeable idle time (shown in light blue) in the termination phase. The behavior of the Origin with 16 threads, shown in Fig. 6, is much better, with all threads working almost all of the time.

## 4.5    Work Stealing Granularity

The most important parameter in performance is chunk size, which sets the granularity of work stealing. A thread initiates a steal from another thread only when at least two chunks have accumulated in that thread's steal stack. If the

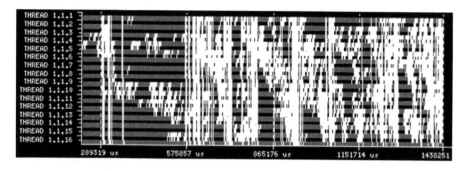

**Fig. 6.** PARAVER time chart for T3 exploration on 16 processors of the Origin 2000

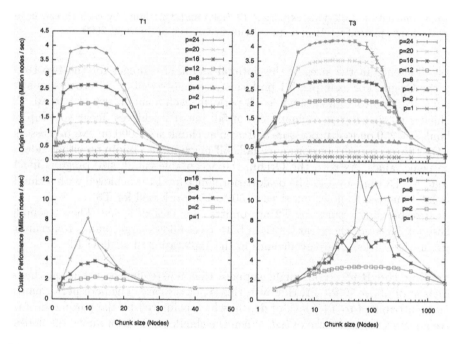

**Fig. 7.** Performance of UTS at various chunk sizes on the SGI Origin 2000 (top) and Dell blade cluster (bottom). For the cluster, the best performance out of 100 executions at each setting is shown.

chunk size is set too small, the threads will be too busy stealing (or trying to steal) to get any work done. If the chunk size is too large, nodes will remain on the stacks where they were generated and too few steals will occur.

**Optimal Ranges for Chunk Size.** Figure 7 shows the performance of UTS at various chunk sizes for trees T1 and T3 on the Origin 2000 using OpenMP and on the Dell blade cluster using UPC. Results for UPC on the Origin were nearly identical to those for OpenMP, and results on the Altix were similar. Note the

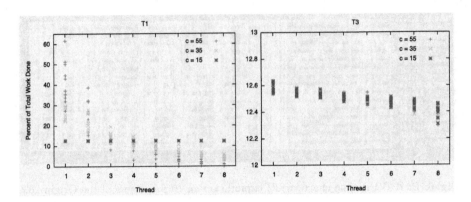

**Fig. 8.** Percent of work done exploring T1 (left) and T3 (right) by each thread in an 8-thread run, plotted for 10 runs per chunk size on the SGI Origin 2000

vast difference in the sizes of the optimal chunk size ranges for the two trees on the Origin. For example, T1 performs reasonably well on 24 processors at a chunk size of 5 to 15 nodes, while T3 performs well a chunk size of 8 to 80. T1 achieves no speedup at a chunk size of 50, but T3 achieves linear speedup at chunk size 250 on four processors and even at chunk size 1000 on two processors.

On the cluster, the performance falls off much more rapidly on either side of the peak values. As with the Origin, the acceptable chunk size range is much larger for T3 than for T1. The peak performance for T1 is achieved with a chunk size of 10 nodes, while chunk sizes of 50 to 150 work well for T3.

Corresponding results for T2 are omitted for lack of space. They resemble those for T3, since the great depth of both trees allows large chunks to accumulate on the stacks, a rare occurrence in the exploration of shallow T1.

**Stealing the Root.** One might suppose that no stealing occurs when chunk size is at or above 50 for T1. However, this is not the case. The poor performance can be attributed to T1's lack of depth, which is limited by the parameter $d$ to give an expected stack size of $b_0 d$. When the chunk size is at or above $\frac{b_0 d}{2}$ nodes, we expect that a chunk will only be released on the infrequent occasion that a node generates more than $b_0$ children, due to the long tail of the geometric distribution. The chunk that is released, and possibly stolen, in such a case will contain the older nodes from the bottom of the stack, i.e. the higher nodes in the tree. The nodes which were generated most recently and are deeper in the tree will be at the top of the stack for the local thread to continue working on.

Now suppose the chunk in the shared stack is stolen. The thief will then hold nodes which are high in the tree and be able to generate some amount of work before reaching the depth limitation. Meanwhile, the victim will quickly, if not immediately, run out of work, because it holds nodes which are already at or near the cutoff depth for the tree. Once the thief generates another chunk of work in the lower portion of the tree, it in turn becomes the victim, giving up the higher nodes. In this way, execution is effectively serialized. The number of

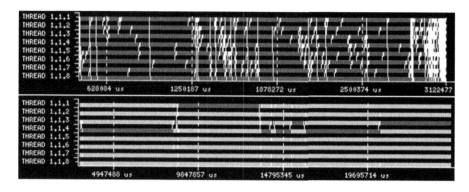

**Fig. 9.** PARAVER time charts for T1 exploration at chunk sizes of 10 nodes (top) and 60 nodes (bottom) on the Origin 2000. Note that when the higher chunk size is used, the work becomes serialized.

steals that occur over the course of the run is in fact a good indication of how many times a value much higher than the expected branching factor was drawn from the binomial distribution.

On the Origin, the root is most often passed back and forth between just two threads. This is a consequence of the non-uniform memory access architecture, in which some threads see shared variable modifications earlier than other threads.

Figure 8 shows ten runs at different chunk sizes for T1 and T3 on the Origin 2000. Note that for chunk sizes of 15 to 55 nodes, the work for T3 is spread evenly among the eight threads, about 12.5% each. The work for T1 is also evenly distributed when the chunk size is 15. With a chunk size of 35, a disproportionate amount of work is done by just a few threads. When chunk size is increased to 55 nodes, work distribution is even more biased. Figure 9 shows PARAVER time charts for runs for T1 with chunk sizes 10 (ideal) and 60 (pathological).

Recall from Table 1 that T1 has a depth limitation $d = 10$ and a constant expected branching factor $b = 4$, yielding an expected stack size of 40 nodes. For any chunk size greater than 20 nodes, the stack rarely accumulates the two-chunks worth of work needed to enable a release. In contrast, binomial trees like T3 have no depth limitation, allowing the stack to grow very deep and facilitating many chunk releases and subsequent steals, even at a large chunk size. This is also the case for deep geometric trees such as T2, which has a much lower branching factor than T1 and a less restrictive depth limitation. The example illustrates well the subtle interactions between the tree shape and the load balance strategy.

### 4.6   Comparing Absolute Performance of Various Machines

UPC is supported by a great variety of shared memory and distributed memory machines. In Fig. 10, a performance comparison for T3 on a variety of shared memory and distributed memory machines running the UPC version of UTS on 16 processors is shown. The OpenMP version is used for the SunFire 6800.

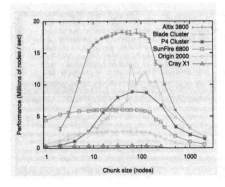
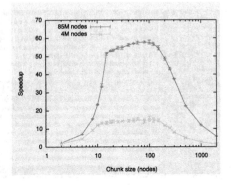

**Fig. 10.** Performance for T3 on 16 processors on various machines. Except on the SunFire, the UPC version was used.

**Fig. 11.** Speedup on the SGI Altix 3800 using 64 processors for T3 and another, much larger, binomial tree

In terms of absolute performance, the Altix is the fastest and the Dell cluster is the second-fastest. If scaling on the cluster were 65% or better, it would overtake the Altix in this UPC comparison.

### 4.7   Larger Trees for More Processors

When running UTS on a large number of processors, the tree must be large enough to produce work for all the threads. Figure 11 shows the speedup of the UPC version of UTS on the Altix 3800 for binomial trees of different sizes using 64 processors. The smallest, T3, is 4.1 million nodes. The other is 85 million nodes in size. The speedup of T3 never approaches that of the larger tree. However, the Altix achieves a near-linear parallel speedup of nearly 60 on the 85M node tree, searching over 67M nodes/sec. Larger trees are able to generate large chunks of work more often. Running at a higher chunk size further amortizes the cost of stealing, as more work is procured per steal than at lower chunk sizes. Thus, a greater number of processors can be effectively utilized.

## 5   Conclusions and Future Work

The primary contributions of our work are twofold: First, we have introduced a novel and challenging benchmark to measure a parallel system's ability to perform substantial dynamic load balancing. Second, we have used the benchmark to investigate the performance portability of shared memory programming models to distributed memory systems. Comparison of the OpenMP and UPC versions showed that both of these easily-programmed implementations exhibit near-ideal scaling and comparable absolute performance on shared memory systems, but the UPC implementation scaled poorly on distributed memory systems. While UPC, with its shared memory abstractions, can simplify programming for clusters, severe performance penalties can be incurred by the implicit communication costs of a dynamic load-balancing implementation based upon liberal shared variable accesses. We have also presented analysis of situations in which data locality, horizon effects, granularity of load balance, and problem size can dramatically impact the effectiveness of distributed load balancing.

One of our early versions of UTS, *psearch*, was one of several benchmarks used to test recent communications optimizations for UPC [13]. We encourage testing of our implementations with different optimization schemes and on a variety of systems, as well as the development of new implementations. In some future implementations, we will seek to improve performance on distributed memory machines without degrading the performance on shared memory. We will be turning the tables to ask whether a program designed for efficiency on distributed memory can compete with our shared memory implementation on shared memory machines in terms of scaling and absolute performance. In that scenario, just as in those presented in this paper, the UTS benchmark's dynamic load balancing makes it a daunting task for performance portability.

## Acknowledgements

The authors would like to thank the European Center for Parallelism in Barcelona for the use of their PARAVER visualization tool. We thank the Ohio Supercomputer Center for use of their Pentium cluster and the University of North Carolina at Chapel Hill for the use of their Dell blade cluster and Altix. We would also like to thank William Pugh for his involvement in the early stages of the UTS project.

## References

1. T. Harris, *The Theory of Branching Processes.* Springer, 1963.
2. D. Eastlake and P. Jones, "US secure hash algorithm 1 (SHA-1)," Internet Engineering Task Force, RFC 3174, Sept. 2001. [Online]. Available: http://www.rfc-editor.org/rfc/rfc3174.txt
3. J. Leskovec, J. Kleinberg, and C. Faloutsos, "Graphs over time: densification laws, shrinking diameters and possible explanations," in *Proc. 11th ACM SIGKDD Int'l Conf. Know. Disc. Data Mining (KDD '05)*, 2005, pp. 177–187.
4. R. Blumofe and C. Leiserson, "Scheduling multithreaded computations by work stealing," in *Proc. 35th Ann. Symp. Found. Comp. Sci.*, Nov. 1994, pp. 356–368.
5. V. Kumar, A. Y. Grama, and N. R. Vempaty, "Scalable load balancing techniques for parallel computers," *J. Par. Dist. Comp.*, vol. 22, no. 1, pp. 60–79, 1994.
6. V. Kumar and V. N. Rao, "Parallel depth first search. part ii. analysis," *Int'l J. Par. Prog.*, vol. 16, no. 6, pp. 501–519, 1987.
7. UPC Consortium, "UPC language specifications, v1.2," Lawrence Berkeley National Lab, Tech. Rep. LBNL-59208, 2005.
8. M. Frigo, C. E. Leiserson, and K. H. Randall, "The implementation of the Cilk-5 multithreaded language," in *Proc. 1998 SIGPLAN Conf. Prog. Lang. Design Impl. (PLDI '98)*, 1998, pp. 212–223.

9. A. Marowka, "Analytic comparison of two advanced c language-based parallel programming models." in *Proc. Third Int'l Symp. Par. and Dist. Comp./Int'l Workshop Algorithms, Models and Tools for Par. Comp. Hetero. Nets. (IS-PDC/HeteroPar'04)*, 2004, pp. 284–291.

10. J. Marathe and F. Mueller, "Hardware profile-guided automatic page placement for ccnuma systems," in *Proc. 11th ACM SIGPLAN Symp. Princ. Pract. Par. Prog. (PPoPP '06)*, 2006, pp. 90–99.

11. K. Berlin, J. Huan, M. Jacob, G. Kochhar, J. Prins, W. Pugh, P. Sadayappan, J. Spacco, and C.-W. Tseng, "Evaluating the impact of programming language features on the performance of parallel applications on cluster architectures." in *Proc. LCPC 2003*, ser. LNCS, L. Rauchwerger, Ed., vol. 2958, 2003, pp. 194–208.

12. European Center for Parallelism, "PARAVER," 2006. [Online]. Available: http://www.cepba.upc.edu/paraver/

13. W. Chen, C. Iancu, and K. A. Yelick, "Communication optimizations for fine-grained UPC applications." in *Proc. Int'l Conf. Par. Arch. Compilation Tech. (PACT 2005)*, 2005, pp. 267–278.

14. J. Prins, J. Huan, B. Pugh, C. Tseng, and P. Sadayappan, "UPC implementation of an unbalanced tree search benchmark," Univ. North Carolina at Chapel Hill, Tech. Rep. TR03-034, Oct. 2003.

# Copy Propagation Optimizations for VLIW DSP Processors with Distributed Register Files*

Chung-Ju Wu, Sheng-Yuan Chen, and Jenq-Kuen Lee

Department of Computer Science
National Tsing-Hua University
Hsinchu 300, Taiwan
{jasonwu, sychen, jklee}@pllab.cs.nthu.edu.tw

**Abstract.** High-performance and low-power VLIW DSP processors are increasingly deployed on embedded devices to process video and multimedia applications. For reducing power and cost in designs of VLIW DSP processors, distributed register files and multi-bank register architectures are being adopted to eliminate the amount of read/write ports in register files. This presents new challenges for devising compiler optimization schemes for such architectures. In our research work, we address the compiler optimization issues for PAC architecture, which is a 5-way issue DSP processor with distributed register files. We show how to support an important class of compiler optimization problems, known as copy propagations, for such architecture. We illustrate that a naive deployment of copy propagations in embedded VLIW DSP processors with distributed register files might result in performance anomaly. In our proposed scheme, we derive a communication cost model by cluster distance, register port pressures, and the movement type of register sets. This cost model is used to guide the data flow analysis for supporting copy propagations over PAC architecture. Experimental results show that our schemes are effective to prevent performance anomaly with copy propagations over embedded VLIW DSP processors with distributed files.

## 1   Introduction

Digital signal processors (DSPs) have been found widely used in an increasing number of computationally intensive applications in the fields such as mobile systems. As the communication applications are moving towards the conflicting requirements of high-performance and low-power consumption, DSPs have evolved into a style of large computation resources combined with restricted and/or specialized data paths and register storages. In modern VLIW DSPs,

---

* This paper is submitted to *LCPC 2006*. The correspondence author is Jenq Kuen Lee. His e-mail is jklee@cs.nthu.edu.tw, phone number is 886-3-5715131 EXT. 33519, FAX number is 886-3-5723694. His postal address is Prof. Jenq- Kuen Lee, Department of Computer Science, National Tsing-Hua Univ., Hsinchu, Taiwan.

G. Almási, C. Caşcaval, and P. Wu (Eds.): LCPC 2006, LNCS 4382, pp. 251–266, 2007.

computation resources are divided into clusters with its own local register files to reduce the hardware complexity.

In cluster-based architectures, the compiler plays an important role to generate proper codes over multiple clusters to work around the restrictions of the hardware. Data flow analysis is an important compiler optimization technique. Available expressions, live variables, copy propagations, reaching definitions, or other useful sets of properties can be computed for all points in a program using a generic algorithmic framework. Current research results in compiler optimizations for cluster-based architectures have focused on partitioning register files to work with instruction scheduling [13] [16]. However, it remains open how the conventional data flow analysis scheme can be incorporated into optimizations over embedded VLIW DSP processors with distributed files by taking communication costs into account.

In this paper, we present a case study to illustrate how to address this register communication issue for an important class of compiler optimization problems, known as copy propagations, for PAC architectures. Parallel Architecture Core (PAC) is a 5-way VLIW DSP processors with distributed register cluster files and multi-bank register architectures (known as ping-pong architectures) [1] [8] [9]. Copy propagation is in the family of data flow equations and traditionally known as an effective method used as a compiler phase to combine with common available expression elimination and dead code elimination schemes. We illustrate that a naive deployment of copy propagations in embedded VLIW DSP processors with distributed files might result in performance anomaly, a reversal effect of performance optimizations. In our proposed scheme, we derive a communication cost model by the cluster distance, register port pressures, and the distance among different type of register banks. The profits of copy propagations are also modeled among program graphs. We then use this cost model to guide the data flow analysis for supporting copy propagations for PAC architectures. The algorithm is modeled with a flavor of shortest path problem with the considerations of shared edges in program graphs. Our model will avoid performance anomaly produced by conventional copy propagations over distributed register file architectures. Our compiler infrastructure is based on ORC/Open-64 compiler infrastructure and with our efforts to retarget them in a VLIW DSP environments with multi-cluster and distributed register architectures. We also present experimental results with DSPstone benchmark to show our schemes are effective to support copy propagations over embedded VLIW DSP processors with distributed register files.

The remainders of this paper are organized as follows. In Section 2, we will introduce the processor architecture and register file organizations of PAC VLIW DSP processors. Section 3 presents motivating examples to point out performance anomaly phenomenon with copy propagations over embedded VLIW DSP processors with irregular register files. Section 4 then presents our algorithm and solution to this problem. Next, Section 5 gives experimental results. Finally, Section 6 presents the related work and discussions, and Section 7 concludes this paper.

## 2   PAC DSP Architecture

The Parallel Architecture Core (PAC) is a 32bit, fixed-point, clustered digital signal processor with five way VLIW pipeline. PAC DSP has two Arithmetic Logic Units (ALU), two Load/Store Units (LSU), and one single Scalar unit. The ALU and LSU are organized into two clusters, each containing a pair of both functional unit (FU) types and one distinct partitioned register file set. The Scalar unit can deal with branch operations, and is also capable of load/store and address arithmetic operations. The architecture is illustrated in Figure 1.

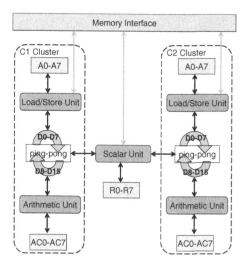

**Fig. 1.** The PAC DSP architecture illustration

As in Figure 1, the register file structure in each cluster is highly partitioned and distributed. PAC DSP contains four distinct register files. The A, AC, and R register files are private registers, directly attached to and only accessible by each LSU, ALU, and Scalar unit, respectively. The D register files are shared within one cluster and can be used to communicate across clusters. Each of the D-register files have only 3 read ports and 2 write ports (3R/2W). Among them, 1R/1W are dedicated to the Scalar Unit, leaving only 2R/1W for the cluster FUs to use. The remaining set of 2R/1W ports are not enough to connect to both cluster FUs simultaneously. Instead, they are switched between the LSU/ALU: during each cycle, the access ports of each of the two D-register files (in a single cluster) may be connected to the LSU or ALU, but not both. This means that access of the two D-register files are mutually-exclusive for each FU, and each LSU/ALU can access only one of them during each cycle. For one individual public register sub-block, we can't perform reading and writing on it in two different FUs at the same time. Due to this back-and-forth style of register file access, we call this a 'ping-pong' register file structure. We believe this special register file design can help us achieve low-power consumption because it retains an effective way of data communication with less wire connections between FUs and registers. Note that the public register files are shared register but can only be accessible by either LSU or ALU at one time. PAC DSP processor [1] is currently developed at ITRI STC, and our laboratory is currently collaborating with ITRI STC under MOEA projects for the challenging work to develop high-performance and low-power toolkits for embedded systems under PAC platforms [12], [16], [18], [19], and [20].

## 3   Motivating Examples

This section gives examples to motivate the needs of our optimization schemes. Consider the code fragment below:

Code Fragment 1
```
    (1)    x := t3;
    (2)    a[t2] := t5;
    (3)    a[t4] := x + t6;
    (4)    a[t7] := x + t8;
```

The traditional technique for compilers to optimize the above code is to use t3 for x, wherever possible after the copy statement x := t3. The related work in optimizing this code sequence by the copy propagation technique can be found in Aho's book [4]. Following the common data flow analysis and copy propagation applied to Code Fragment 1, we have the optimized code below:

Code Fragment 2
```
    (1)    x := t3;
    (2)    a[t2] := t5;
    (3)    a[t4] := t3 + t6;
    (4)    a[t7] := t3 + t8;
```

This propagation can remove all data dependency produced by x := t3, providing the compiler with possibility to eliminate the assignment x := t3. However, the scheme above is not appropriate for the design of PAC DSP architecture. Due to this specific-architecture design with clustering and distributed register files , extra intercluster-communication code needs to be inserted if there occurs the data flow across clusters. Suppose t3 is allocated to a different cluster from t6,t8, and x, the insertion of intercluster-communication code will then need to be done if applying conventional copy propagation. Such overhead of communication code increases the total cycles of the optimized code compared with non-optimized one. Figure 2 is an example of VLIW code fragment. Code bundle at the left-hand side represents one propagation path exists from Cluster 2 to Cluster 1, i.e. TN2 (Temporary Name, which is referred as a virtual register representation) can be propagated from Cluster 2 to Cluster 1. Code bundle at the right-hand side shows extra inter-communication costs needed after propagation.

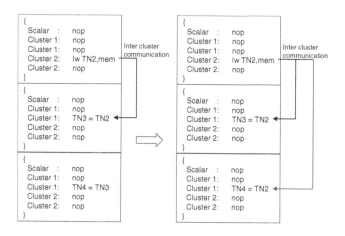

**Fig. 2.** A VLIW Code Example for Inter Cluster Communication

Not only does the clustered design make data flow across clusters an additional issue, but also compiler needs to take the distributed register file structure into consideration. The private access nature of A and AC registers makes data flows more difficult. For the convenience to trace the properties of private register access, Code Fragment 3 lists assembly code generated from Code Fragment 1. Assume that D register d2, and private registers a1, ac1, ac2 are allocated to the variables x, t3, t6 and t8, respectively.

Code Fragment 3

```
(1)  MOV  d2, a1
(2)  MOV  d3, a3
(3)  ADD  d4, d2, ac1
(4)  SW   d4, d0, 24
(5)  ADD  d6, d2, ac2
(6)  SW   d6, d0, 28
```

Note that the operation MOV d2, a1 reaches the use of d2 in line 3 and line 5. However it is impossible to replace all the uses of d2 with a1 directly, for the reason that A register files are only attached to LSU and AC register files are also only attached to ALU. If d2 is replaced with a1, compiler must insert extra copy instructions for private register access properties. This insertion of extra copy instructions also brings the penalty and occupies additional computing resources, and therefore needs to be considered for performing copy propagations.

In addition, the reduced wire connection is another important issue. Referring to the short Code Fragment 4 and Code Fragment 5, the left part of Figure 3 illustrates how Code Fragment 4 being scheduled into bundles and also shows read/write ports attached to D register files, and the right part of Figure 3 shows Code Fragment 5. Note that we arrange all the instructions into cluster 1 to avoid the cross-interference between port pressure and clustered design because we want to focus on the port pressure issue.

Code Fragment 4
```
    (1)   LW     d2,   a0,   16
    (2)   COPY   ac2,  d3
    (3)   SW     d4,   a0,   40
    (4)   ADD    d5,   ac2,  d2
```

After propagating d3 to ac2, the resulted code is as follows:

Code Fragment 5
```
    (1)   LW     d2,   a0,   16
    (2)   COPY   ac2,  d3
    (3)   SW     d4,   a0,   40
    (4)   ADD    d5,   d3,   d2
```

We observe that there are 3 read ports needed in the second bundle, but our architecture only has 2 available read ports and 1 available write port. Due to the port constraint, the bundle must be separated. Figure 4 illustrates the final bundles of Code Fragment 5.

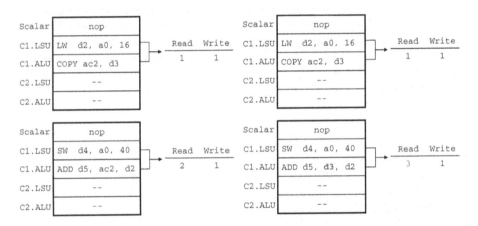

**Fig. 3.** The bundles of Code Fragment 4

In summary, Figure 2 illustrates a scenario that there might be data flows from one cluster to another cluster. In Code Fragment 3, due to private registers can only be accessible by the corresponding function units, compiler has to allocate a new temporary register first and then move data from one register to the temporary register. Propagation makes access between two different private register file types increases register pressure. In Code Fragment 4 and 5, compiler does not need to spend extra registers or communications through memory. However, due to the reduced wire connections with global register files, the instruction scheduler can only schedule them into two different bundles and fill the empty slots with nops. We name the above three behaviors as 'performance anomaly'. In the following section, this problem is solved by deriving cost models and using the cost models to guide the copy propagation process for performance benefits.

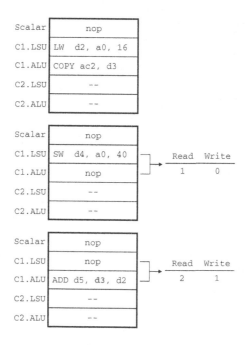

**Fig. 4.** Schedule of Code Fragment 5 according to the register ports constraint

# 4   Enhanced Data Flow Analysis on PAC Architecture

## 4.1   Cost Model and Algorithm

As mentioned in section 3, a naive application of data flow analysis scheme to programs on PAC DSP actually increases execution cycles because of memory interface access, register pressure, and separated bundles. In the following discussions, we will first introduce our cost models, and we will then develop an algorithm based on our cost models to guide the analysis process to avoid performance anomaly.

Our cost models for data flow analysis are to model the total weights we spend and the total gains we get. We have defined several attributes for evaluating the costs and gains of data propagation. The total weights of data flow path are the costs of propagation from the TN $n$ of instruction $p$ to the TN $m$ of instruction $q$. Note that one TN (Temporary Name) of register type is referred as a virtual register required to be allocated to a physical register in the machine level IR used in compilers.

We also build equations to evaluate the extra communication costs of data propagations from variable $n$ to variable $m$, i.e. the three performance anomaly effects mentioned in section 3. We define our cost equation as follows:

$$Cost(n, m) = PP(n, m) + RP(n, m) + CBC(n, m), \tag{1}$$

where $PP(n, m)$ shows the port pressure caused by data flows from variable $n$ to variable $m$. And $PP(n, m)$ is the extra cycles caused by the separation of bundles. We rewrite $PP(n, m)$ as

$$PP(n, m) = \lceil \frac{k_r - p_r}{p_r} \rceil + \lceil \frac{k_w - p_w}{p_w} \rceil, \tag{2}$$

where $k_r/k_w$ is the number of read/write ports needed after data flows from variable $n$ to variable $m$, and $p_r/p_w$ is the number of read/write port constraint we have mentioned in section 2. $k_r$, $k_w$, $p_r$, and $p_w$ need to be calculated according to the instructions in $n$ and $m$, respectively.

$RP(n, m)$ represents the register pressure caused by data access between two different private register file types. Due to the distributed register file constraint, one extra copy instruction must be inserted to move data from one private register to a temporary register. $RP(n, m)$ returns the number of extra copy instructions. $CBC(n, m)$ returns the cost of memory access cycles when propagating across clusters. PAC DSP provides a special instruction pair (BDT and BDR) to broadcast data from one cluster to another.

Table 1 shows the corresponding cost functions used in each kind of data flow path. Note that we have local register A for data movement units, local register AC for ALU unit, register D as a ping-pong register to be interleaved between ALU and load/store units.

**Table 1.** Costs in each data flow path

| Data Flow | Cluster1.D | Cluster1.A | Cluster1.AC | Cluster2.D | Cluster2.A | Cluster2.AC |
|---|---|---|---|---|---|---|
| Cluster1.D | – | PP | PP | CBC | CBC | CBC |
| Cluster1.A | – | – | RP | CBC | CBC | CBC |
| Cluster1.AC | – | RP | – | CBC | CBC | CBC |
| Cluster2.D | CBC | CBC | CBC | – | PP | PP |
| Cluster2.A | CBC | CBC | CBC | – | – | RP |
| Cluster2.AC | CBC | CBC | CBC | – | RP | – |

The total gains are the reduced communication codes and the reduced copy assignments from propagations between TN $n$ of instruction $p$ to TN $m$ of instruction $q$. We define the total gains as

$$Gain(n, m) = RCC(n, m) + \sum_{j \in path(n,m)} ACA(c[j]), \tag{3}$$

where $RCC(n, m)$ represents the original communication cost on this $n$-$m$ path, and the communication cost can possibly be reduced if the assignment is done directly instead of going through a sequence of copy propagations. $ACA(c[j])$ is to calculate the number of all available copy assignments which can be reduced along this $n - m$ data flow path. $c[j]$ is the intermediate copy assignment on

$n - m$ path, and $path(n, m)$ represents the set of intermediate nodes in the flow path from $n$ to $m$.

We view each variable as a node, and the data flows between those nodes form an acyclic DFG. Our analysis algorithm mainly comprise 2 procedures. In the first procedure, we perform the ordinary copy propagation algorithm illustrated in Figure 5. Let $U$ be the 'universal' set of all copy statements in the program. Define $c\_gen[B]$ to be the set of all copies generated in block $B$ and $c\_kill[b]$ to be the set of copies in $U$ that are killed in $B$ [4]. The conventional copy propagation algorithm can be stated with the following equation.

$$out[B] = c\_gen[B] \cup (in[B] - c\_kill[B]) \tag{4}$$

$$in[B] = \bigcap_{P \text{ is a predecessor of } B} out[P] \text{ for } B \text{ not initial} \tag{5}$$

$$in[B_1] = \emptyset \text{ where } B_1 \text{ is the initial block} \tag{6}$$

Note that we don't perform the step 3 in Figure 5 at this time. After performing the first two steps of the copy propagation algorithm in Figure 5, we keep every traversed nodes in the same data flow path into a list $L$. While finding out all possible nodes, we import these nodes in $L$ into the other equations (equation (1), and equation (3)) to find a data propagation path with the best profits. Finally, we propagate data according to the best data flow path. Note that we can choose not to take the data flow path if no path makes a profit. The algorithm in Figure 6 shows the whole processes of both the weight evaluation and the data flow selection.

The first step of enhanced data flow algorithm does the initial work to find out the concerned nodes of a propagation path from $node_n$ to $node_m$. The nodes form an acyclic data flow tree. Step 2 evaluates the initial weight of each edge $(i, j)$. By step 2, we can calculate the initial weight of this $n - m$ path. The initial weight can be estimated by $Gain(n, m)$ since they tell the same cost but from different views. In step 3, we perform both the equation (1) and the equation (3) to check if there are some short cuts to go. Note that the *gains* represent both the communication cost and the available copy assignments we can save by going through the short cut, and the *costs* show the extra inter/intra cluster costs on the short cut. We iterate several times over this tree graph, using $k$ as an index. On the $k$th iteration, we get the best profit solution to the propagation path finding problem, where the paths only use vertices numbered $n$ to $k$. Note that if this results in a better profit path, we remember it. Due to the comparison with initial weight, the outcome path must be no more than the weight of no-propagation method and naive propagation method. After iterations, all possible short cuts have been examined, and we output the proper propagation path by step 4. The algorithm produces a matrix $p$, which, for each pair of nodes $u$ and $v$, contains an intermediate node on the least cost path from $u$ to $v$. So the best profit path from $u$ to $v$ is the best profit path from $u$ to $p[u,v]$, followed by the best profit path from $p[u,v]$ to $v$. Step 3 of the algorithm is done with a flavor of the shortest path problem, but only now that we model the problem for copy propagation and register communications.

---

### Algorithm 1: Copy Propagation Algorithm

---

**Input**:  A flow graph G, with ud-chains.
c_in[B] represents the solution to Equation
(4), (5), (6). And du-chains.
**Output**: A revised flow graph.
**Method**: For each copy s: **x:=y** do the following.


1. Determine those uses of **x** that are reached by this
   definition of **x**, namely, s: **x:=y**.
2. Determine whether for every use of **x** found in (1),
   s is in c_in[B], where B is the block of this particular use, and moreover, no definitions of **x** or y
   occur prior to this use of **x** within B.
3. If s meets the conditions of (2), then remove s and
   replace all uses of **x** found in (1) by **y**.

**Fig. 5.** Copy Propagation Algorithm

## 4.2  Advanced Estimation Algorithm

The goal of the *Enhanced Data-Flow Analysis Algorithm* is to collect the information of the weights and gains of propagation at each point in a program. If
multiple nodes have the same ancestors, they should share the weights and gains
from their ancestors. The Figure 7 shows a new evaluating method to solve this
sharing problem on a propagation tree.

In the first step, we deal with the issue for shared edges for determining which
path is doing copy propagation and which path does not. In that case, the intermediate assignment will not be eliminated by dead code eliminations. This can
still be done, but we need to reflect this in our cost model for GAINS calculated
in equation (3). Three small steps are performed. In step 1.a, we first find the set
of all propagation paths. Note that we only need to find out those paths are not
sub-path of other paths, as dealing with the long path (non-proper sub-path) in
copy propagation will cover all cases. Next in Step 1.b, we try to mark the intermediate stops in all propagation paths according to output of Path routine in
Figure 6 for each path. Next in Step 1.c, we re-adjust the cost model for GAINS if
there are intermediate nodes which will not be eliminated eventually in dead code
elimination phase due to the share edge decides to keep the intermediate stops.

In step 2, we also deal with shared edges, but for fine-tuning the cost model. As
if there are shared edges, the gains of copy propagations should be counted only
once (or the benefit needs to be distributed among shared paths). A reference
counting scheme can be used to see the amount of sharing. This is done in Step
2.a. This information can then be used to re-adjust the cost model for GAINS
in equation (3).

---

**Algorithm 2: Enhanced Data Flow Analysis**

---

**Input**: Inputs in Copy Propagation Algorithm.
(Figure 5).
**Output**: A proper propagation path.

1. Perform the first and the second steps in Copy
   Propagation Algorithm in Figure 5 to traverse all
   possible propagation nodes on $n - m$ path .
2. **for** $i = n$ to $m$ **do**
       **for** $j = n$ to $m$ **do**
         /* Evaluate the initial weight, $w[i,j]$.    */
         /* This weight includes the communication*/
         /* costs and all the copy assignments    */
         /* along path before propagation.    */
         Estimate the initial weight $w[i,j]$;
       **end**
     **end**
3. **for** k $= n$ to $m$ **do**
       **for** i $= n$ to $m$ **do**
         Compute $Gain(i,k)$ and $Cost(i,k)$.
         **for** j $= n$ to $m$ **do**
         Compute $Gain(k,j)$ and $Cost(k,j)$.
         $profit = Gain(i,k) - Cost(i,k) +$
                      $Gain(k,j) - Cost(k,j)$;
         **if** $(w[i,j] - profit) < w[i,j]$ **do**
           $w[i,j] = w[i,j] - profit$;
           $p[i,j] = k$;
         **end**
         **end**
       **end**
     **end**
4. /* Output a proper propagation path from */
   /* u to v */
   Path $(u, v, p)$ {
       $k = p[u,v]$;
       **if** $(k == Null)$ **return**;
       Path$(u, k)$;
       output the node $k$;
       Path$(k, v)$;
   }

**Fig. 6.** The Enhanced Data Flow Analysis Algorithm

---

**Algorithm 3:**   Available Copy Assignment Estimation Algorithm

**Input:** A propagation tree
**Output:** Proper weights of all propagation paths

**Step 1.a:**
Find the set of all the propagation paths (all the
non-proper propagation paths), $PP$.
**Step 1.b:**
For each path $p \in PP$ do {
   Mark each element in the output of Path routine in Figure 6
   for $p$ as intermediate stop.
}
**Step 1.c:**
For each path $p \in PP$ do {
   Compare the elements of intermediate stops in $p$ with the
   elements from the output of Path routine in Figure 6 for $p$.
   If there are additional elements in the path of $p$ marked
   as intermediate stops, revise cost for the GAINS of $p$.
}
**Step 2.a:**
For each path $p \in PP$ do {
   Use reference counting to count the reference count
   for each node in $p$.
}
**Step 2.b:**
For each path $p \in PP$ do {
   Revise GAINS for $p$ by using the reference counting
   information acquired in the previous step.
}

---

**Fig. 7.** Available Copy Assignment Estimation Algorithm

## 5   Infrastructure Designs and Experiments

We now first describe our compiler testbed for our proposed copy propagations
over cluster-based architecture and distributed register files. Our compiler platform is based on ORC and we retarget the compiler infrastructure for PAC
architecture. ORC is an open-source compiler infrastructure released by Intel. It
is originally designed for IA-64. ORC is made up of different phases. The ORC
compilation starts with processing by the front-ends, generating an intermediate
representation (IR) of the source program, and feeding it in the back-end. The
IR , called WHIRL, is a part of the Pro64 compiler released by SGI [11]. PAC architecture introduces additional issues with register allocation under comparison

between different platforms. In our compiler infrastructure, we first implemented a partitioning scheme to partition the register file among clusters. This is known Ping-pong Aware Local Favorable (PALF) register allocation [12] [16] to obtain a preferable register allocation scheme that well partitions register usage into the irregular register file architectures in PAC DSP processor. The algorithm involves the proper consideration of various characteristics in accessing different register files, and attempts to minimize the penalty caused by the interference of register allocation and instruction scheduling, with retaining desirable parallelism over ping-pong register constraints and inter-cluster overheads. After the phase of register allocation and instruction selections, we then move into the phase of EBO (basic block optimizations). EBO was a phase originally in ORC for the basic block optimizations and carrying out optimization such as copy propagations, constant folding, dead code eleminations. Our enhanced copy propgation algorithm is implemented in this phase.

We use the PAC DSP architecture described in section 2 as the target architecture for our experiments. The proposed enhanced data flow analysis framework is incorporated into the compiler tool with PAC ORC [5], and evaluated by the ISS simulator designed by ITRI DSP team. We also implement the METIS graph partitioning library [6] for the register allocation scheme. The benchmarks used in our experiment are from the floating-point version of DSP-stone benchmark suite [7]. Notice that benchmarks are indexed with numbers to identify the specified basic block we used in this experiment. We focused on the major basic blocks as copy propagation was implemented in peephole optimizations for basic block optimizations.

Three versions are compared in our research work. The base version is one without copy propagation mechanism. The original version is one from a work that only performs the naive copy propagation algorithm in Figure 5. The Enhanced Data-Flow Analysis scheme proposed in our work is to perform all phases in Figure 6. Both the original version and the Enhanced Data-Flow Analysis scheme are incorporated with dead code elimination.

Figure 8 shows that our scheme can achieve an average of 15.0% reduction comparing to the base method. Note that from our experiment, the original copy propagation version (Figure 5) suffers a performance loss in benchmarks *real_update_BB_2*, *n_real_update_BB_3*, and *convolution_BB_2*. That's because the naive copy propagation produces lots of inter communication codes and register pressure in *real_update_BB_2* and *n_real_update_BB_3*. The test program *convolution_BB_2* suffers redundant inter communication codes. Although the naive propagation version can reduce some of the unnecessary copy assignments, it is still out-performed by our proposed scheme. The test programs *mat1x3_BB_3*, *dot_prod-uct_BB_3*, *fir2dim_BB_5*, and *matrix1_BB_5* show that our methods can keep the good nature of the naive propagation version. And the other benchmarks prove that our proposed methods can also reduce the performance anomaly over by distributed register files.

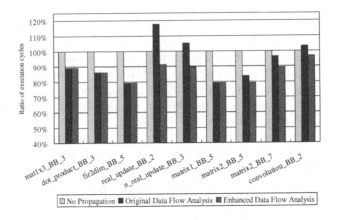

**Fig. 8.** Ratio of execution cycles in basic block codes

# 6   Related Work

High-performance and low-power VLIW DSP processors are of interests lately
for embedded systems to handle multimedia applications. To achieve this goal,
clustered architecture is one well-known strategy. Examples are given in this
work [8] [9] [10]. The presence of distributed register file architecture presents a
challenge for compiler code generations. Earlier work focused on the partitioning
of register file to combine with instruction scheduler [12] [13] [16]. While the
partitioning scheme for distributed register file is important, there are more
challenging problems ahead as evidenced in this work that we need to handle
copy propagations over such architectures. [17] provides techniques to support
copy propagation during register allocation which is known as node coalescing in
the interference graph. Our work presents an approximation to deal with these
issues in post register phase that we give cost models to guide the process for
copy propagations on embedded VLIW DSP processors with distributed register
files and multi-bank register structures.

Performance anomaly was earlier also found in the problem of array operation
synthesis. The work for Fortran 90 and HPF programs [14] [15] was done in the
context of array operations and source languages for distributed memory parallel
machines. With the distributed memory hierarchies moving from memory layers
into register levels, the performance anomaly was also observed in the register
layers. Previous work was done in loop levels and source levels, while this work
needs to carefully model register communication and architecture constraints in
the instruction levels.

# 7   Conclusion

In this paper, we presented an enhanced framework for copy propagations over
VLIW architectures with distributed register files. This presented a case study

to address the issues for how to address compiler optimizations for conventional optimizations schemes over distributed register file architectures. Experimental results show that our scheme can maintain the benefits of copy propagation optimizations while prevent performance anomaly. Future work will include the integration of cost models to cover more cases of compiler optimization schemes such as common available expression eliminations.

# References

1. David Chang and Max Baron: Taiwan's Roadmap to Leadership in Design. Microprocessor Report, In-Stat/MDR, December 2004. http://www.mdronline.com/mpr/archive/mpr_2004.html.
2. C. M. Overstreet, R. Cherinka, M. Tohki, and R. Sparks. Support of software maintenance using data flow analysis. Technical Report TR-94-07, Old Dominion University, Computer Science Department, June 1994.
3. C. M. Overstreet, R. Cherinka, and R. Sparks. Using bidirectional data flow analysis to support software reuse. Technical Report TR-94-09, Old Dominion University, Computer Science Department, June 1994.
4. Alfred V. Aho, Ravi Sethi, and Jeffrey D. Ullman. Compilers: Principles, Techniques and Tools. Addison-Wesley, November 1985.
5. Cheng-Wei Chen, Yung-Chia Lin, Chung-Ling Tang, Jenq-Kuen Lee. ORC2DSP: Compiler Infrastructure Supports for VLIW DSP Processors. *IEEE VLSI TSA*, April 27-29, 2005.
6. George Karypis and Vipin Kumar. A fast and highly quality multilevel scheme for partitioning irregular graphs. *SIAM J. Scientific Computing*, 20(1): 359-392, 1999.
7. V. Zivojnovic, J. Martinez, C. Schlager, and H. Meyr. DSPstone: A DSP-oriented benchmarking methodology. In *Proceedings of the International Conference on Signal Processing and Technology*, pp.715-720, October 1994.
8. T.J. Lin, C.C. Chang. C.C. Lee, and C.W. Jen. An Efficient VLIW DSP Architecture for Baseband Processing. In *Proceedings of the 21th International Conference on Computer Design*, 2003.
9. Tay-Jyi Lin, Chie-Min Chao, Chia-Hsien Liu, Pi-Chen Hsiao, Shin-Kai Chen, Li-Chun Lin, Chih-Wei Liu, Chein-Wei Jen. Computer architecture: A unified processor architecture for RISC & VLIW DSP. In *Proceedings of the 15th ACM Great Lakes symposium on VLSI*, April 2005.
10. S. Rixner, W. J. Dally, B. Khailany, P. Mattson, U. J. Kapasi, and J. D. Owens. Register organization for media processing. *International Symposium on High Performance Computer Architecture*, pp.375-386, 2000,
11. SGI - Developer Central Open Source - Pro64 http://oss.sgi.com/projects/Pro64/.
12. Yung-Chia Lin, Yi-Ping You, Jenq-Kuen Lee. Register Allocation for VLIW DSP Processors with Irregular Register Files. *International Workshop on Languages and Compilers for Parallel Computing*, January 2006.
13. R. Leupers. Instruction scheduling for clustered VLIW DSPs. In *Proceedings of International Conference on Parallel Architecture and Compilation Techniques*, pp.291-300, October 2000.
14. Gwan-Hwan Hwang, Jenq-Kuen Lee and Roy Dz-Ching Ju. A Function-Composition Approach to Synthesize Fortran 90 Array Operations. *Journal of Parallel and Distributed Computing*, 54, 1-47, 1998.

15. Gwan-Hwan Hwang, Jenq-Kuen Lee, Array Operation Synthesis to Optimize HPF Programs on Distributed Memory Machines. *Journal of Parallel and Distributed Computing*, 61, 467-500, 2001.
16. Yung-Chia Lin, Chung-Lin Tang, Chung-Ju Wu, Jenq-Kuen Lee. Compiler Supports and Optimizations for PAC VLIW DSP Processors. *Languages and Compilers for Parallel Computing*, 2005.
17. Preston Briggs, Keith D. Cooper, and Linda Torczon. Rematerialization. *Conference on Programming Language Design and Implementation*, 1992.
18. Yi-Ping You, Ching-Ren Lee, Jenq-Kuen Lee. Compilers for Leakage Power Reductions. *ACM Transactions on Design Automation of Electronic Systems*, Volume 11, Issue 1, pp.147-166, January 2006.
19. Yi-Ping You, Chung-Wen Huang, Jenq-Kuen Lee. A Sink-N-Hoist Framework for Leakage Power Reduction. *ACM EMSOFT*, September 2005.
20. Peng-Sheng Chen, Yuan-Shin Hwang, Roy Dz-Ching Ju, Jenq-Kuen Lee. Interprocedural Probabilistic Pointer Analysis. *IEEE Transactions on Parallel and Distributed Systems*, Volume 15, Issue 10, pp.893-907, October 2004.

# Optimal Bitwise Register Allocation Using Integer Linear Programming

Rajkishore Barik[1], Christian Grothoff[2], Rahul Gupta[1],
Vinayaka Pandit[1], and Raghavendra Udupa[1]

[1] IBM India Research Lab, Delhi
[2] University of Denver, Colorado

**Abstract.** This paper addresses the problem of optimal global register allocation. The register allocation problem is expressed as an integer linear programming problem and solved optimally. The model is more flexible than previous graph-coloring based methods and thus allows for register allocations with significantly fewer moves and spills. The formulation can also model complex architectural features, such as bit-wise access to registers. With bit-wise access to registers, multiple subword temporaries can be stored in a single register and accessed efficiently, resulting in a register allocation problem that cannot be addressed effectively with simple graph coloring. The paper describes techniques that can help reduce the problem size of the ILP formulation, making the algorithm feasible in practice. Preliminary empirical results from an implementation prototype are reported.

## 1  Introduction

This paper presents a family of new register allocation algorithms that are suitable for off-line computation of high-quality register allocations. The algorithm is targeted for embedded systems which need to run medium-sized applications with limited resources. In particular, we assume that the number of registers available is relatively small and that hardware optimizations such as out-of-order execution, caching and prefetching are not available to an extent that would nullify the cost of spilling. In this context, the compile-time cost for a critical method is almost irrelevant – even if the compilation takes extremely long, the resulting gain in either reduced hardware cost or possibly more important reduced energy consumption due to improved code performance is all that matters.

The traditional approach towards decent-quality register allocation is to color the interference graph [6]. If the number of colors exceeds the number of registers, temporaries are selected for spilling until the graph becomes colorable. The approach presented in this paper makes a radical departure from the graph coloring model, completely eliminating the boolean decision of spilling or not spilling a temporary. The basic idea is to allow temporaries to switch registers at any time and to use constraints to force temporaries that are used at a given instruction into appropriate registers only at the time of use. Moving a variable between registers or between registers and the stack is associated with a cost in the goal function of the integer linear program (ILP). The search space for the ILP solver is reduced using observations about the points in time at which it may make sense for a temporary to be spilled in an optimal allocation.

G. Almási, C. Caşcaval, and P. Wu (Eds.): LCPC 2006, LNCS 4382, pp. 267–282, 2007.

In order to show the expressive power of the approach, this work describes a way to perform optimal register allocation for architectures that allow bit-wise access to registers as proposed in [11]. Various applications, in particular from the embedded domain, make extensive use of sub-word sized values. Examples include network stack implementations and signal- and image-processing as well as hardware drivers. For these applications, bit-wise register allocation can reduce register pressure. Under the assumption that the cost of adding instructions that support sub-word access is smaller than the cost of adding additional registers (or increasing the processor speed to offset the spill-cost), bit-wise register allocation can help reduce total system cost.

The proposed approach uses Integer Linear Programming (ILP) [13]. Using minor variations to the integer linear program the model is able to encompass features from a large body of previous work on register allocation, including bit-wise allocation, co-alescing, spilling, use of registers for both spilling and ordinary temporaries, and a limited form of rematerialization [3].

The remainder of the paper is organized as follows. After an overview of related work in Section 2 the ILP formulation for the bit-wise register allocation is introduced in Section 3. Section 4 presents the implementation, performance data for various benchmarks and concludes the paper with a discussion of the benefits and limitations of this approach.

## 2   Related Work

Previous work has focused on register allocation at local, global, intraprocedural, and interprocedural levels. Intraprocedural register allocation is known to be a NP-hard problem and several heuristics have been proposed to solve the problem [4,5,6].

ILP has been used previously for register allocation and instruction scheduling. The optimal register allocator presented in [9] uses 0-1 linear programming to compute an optimal register allocation. Like this work, the ILP formulation there allows for a variable to moved between registers and memory. The primary difference is that in [9] models the register allocation problem as a sequence of binary decision problems: to allocate or not to allocate a register for a given variable at a given time. The objective function then accumulates the associated costs for each of the possible decisions. The decision model cannot cope with bitwise allocations, mostly because for a bitwise allocator the decision which temporaries should share a register is no longer binary. In [7] the ILP from [9] is transformed in order to improve the solution time while retaining optimality. This is achieved by reduction techniques that exploit the control-flow graph structure and live-ranges of the variables. The presented techniques implicitly assume that every register can only hold one variable and are thus not directly applicable to the model presented in this paper. The transformations resulted in a speed-up of a factor of 150 for solving the resulting ILP over the naïve model.

In [2], the authors solve the register allocation problem for CISC machines by dividing it into two subproblems - optimal spilling and register coalescing. The optimal spilling problem is solved optimally using ILP, while a variant of Park and Moon's heuristic [14] is used for solving the register coalescing problem (sub-optimally). The authors exploit the CISC instruction set to optimize the cost of loads and stores. They take into account that number of available registers may vary from program point to program point, but do not consider variable bit-width requirements of temporaries. In [12] an approach to speculative subword register allocation based on optimistic register allocation is proposed. The idea behind this paper is that there are more opportunities for subword allocation at runtime than what can be statically determined to be safe. The authors propose to use profiling data to speculatively pack variables that are most of the time sufficiently small into a register and to have the processor dynamically detect and flag the case where the size constraints are not met. This requires support by the processor which needs to keep an additional bit per register. If the flag is raised for a given register, the processor executes the appropriate stack accesses instead.

## 3   ILP Formulations

The key idea for the algorithm is to avoid assigning a temporary (both program defined variables and compiler generated temporaries) a fixed location and instead to formulate certain constraints on the location in the form of an integer linear problem (ILP) [13]. The goal function of the ILP captures the cost of the resulting register allocation. The ILP is then solved using off-the-shelf ILP solver technology.

The input to the ILP-solver is a set of constraints that describe the register allocation problem. The basic constraints are that each temporary must be assigned to exactly one register, and that each register must have enough space to hold all temporaries assigned to it. Dead temporaries do not use any space. Throughout the paper, the stack is modeled as a special register $\sigma$ that has no space constraints. All other registers can only store $b$ bits of information.

### 3.1   Basic Formulation

The basic formulation only considers allocating one register per temporary for the lifetime of that temporary. Moving a temporary between registers or between registers and the stack is not allowed in this model. The reader can choose to ignore the bit-wise nature of the register allocation and view the problem in a simplified manner where dead temporaries have a bit-width of zero and all live temporaries are word-sized. This would also be the natural simplification to the algorithm for architectures without bit-wise access to registers.

The input to the problem is sets of temporaries $i \in V$ and registers $r \in R$, spill costs $S_i$ for each temporary $i \in V$ and the size $w_{i,n}$ for temporary $i \in V$ at all nodes $n \in N$ in the control flow graph. The special register $\sigma \in R$ is used to represent the stack, which is not constrained in size and is used for spilling. All other registers $r \in R - \{\sigma\}$ are limited to $b$ bits ($b$ is typically 32). The result of the computation is an allocation $x_{i,r} \in \{0,1\}$, with $i \in V$ and $r \in R$, that assigns every temporary a unique register (or the stack $\sigma$). The problem can then be stated in a way suitable for integer-linear programming (ILP):

$$\min \sum_{i \in V} S_i \cdot x_{i,\sigma} \quad (1) \qquad \bigwedge_{i \in V} \sum_{r \in R} x_{i,r} = 1 \quad (3)$$

$$\text{such that} \quad \bigwedge_{\substack{r \in R - \{\sigma\} \\ n \in N}} \sum_{i \in V} x_{i,r} \cdot w_{i,n} \le b \quad (2) \qquad \bigwedge_{\substack{i \in V \\ r \in R}} x_{i,r} \in \{0,1\} \quad (4)$$

Equation (1) models the cost of the solution by summing up the cost of loading temporaries $i \in V$ that have been spilled ($x_{i,\sigma} = 1$) from the stack. Equation (2) states that at all times and for all registers except the stack, the total size of all temporaries stored in any register must not exceed the register size $b$. Equations (3) and (4) state that every temporary must be assigned exactly one location.

## 3.2   Control-Flow Graph Formulation

Let $(N, E)$ be the control-flow graph with nodes $n \in N$ and directed edges $(a, b) \in E \subseteq N \times N$. Note that the control-flow graph does not use basic blocks; instead, each individual statement corresponds to two nodes in the graph, one for the register allocation before the instruction and another one for the register allocation after the instruction.

The goal is to be more flexible in terms of *when* temporaries are spilled. The goal is to allow allocations where a temporary is spilled part of the time or where it is moved from one register to another (for example, in order to reclaim fragmented space in the registers in bitwise allocation). This problem can be formulated using linear constraints by introducing additional temporaries $c_{i,r,n} \in \{0, 1\}$ that capture at which nodes $n \in N$ register $r \in R$ has been allocated to a new temporary $i \in V$. Let $x_{i,r,n} \in \{0, 1\}$ be the decision function that places temporary $i \in V$ into register $r \in R$ at node $n \in N$.

Let $S_{i,n}$ be the spill cost of temporary $i \in V$ at node $n \in N$. The value of $S_{i,n}$ is zero if $i$ is neither defined in the instruction before $n$ nor used in the instruction after $n$ (whichever case applies). $S_{i,n}$ gives the cost of loading $i$ from the stack if $i$ is used at the instruction after node $n$. If $i$ is defined at the instruction before $t$, then $S_{i,n}$ is the cost of spilling $i$ to the stack. The cost estimate $S$ also includes a factor that estimates the execution count for spill operations at node $n$.

Let $\mu_{r,n} \in \mathbb{R}$ be the cost of moving a value to or from register $r \in R$ at node $n \in N$. Using $\mu_{r,n}$, the cost of a move at node $n$ between register $a$ and $b$ is assumed to be given by $\mu_{a,n} + \mu_{b,n}$. For example, given only one family of registers, the value for $\mu_{r,n}$ for $r \in R - \{\sigma\}$ is half the cost of a register-to-register move. In this case, if $\zeta_n$ is the cost of moving a value between the stack and a register at node $n$, then $\mu_{\sigma,n} = \zeta_n - \mu_{r,n}$. Unlike $S$, the value of $\mu$ is independent of the access pattern of the program. For $\mu_{r,n}$ the node $n \in N$ only plays a role in that it can again be used to factor in the fact that a move within a loop is more expensive than a move outside of loops.

Let $w_{i,n}$ be the number of bits that temporary $i \in V$ requires at node $n \in N$. The resulting integer linear program is shown in Figure 1.

The new goal function (5) adds the cost for moving a temporary $i$ from or to register $r$ at node $n$ in (indicated by $c_{i,r,n} = 1$) at cost $\mu_{r,n}$. The new formulation allows each variable to be spilled part-time while residing in registers at other times. Thus the spill cost is now differenciated into a per-node, per-variable access cost $S_{i,n}$ which is incurred if $x_{i,\sigma,n} = 1$, that is $i$ is spilled onto the stack $\sigma$ at node $n$.

Equation (6) directly corresponds to equation (2); the only change is that now also $x$ depends on $n \in N$. The new constraints (8) and (9) ensure that $c_{i,r,n}$ must be 1 each time that $x_{i,r,n} \neq x_{i,r,p}$ for some predecessor $p$ of $n \in N$. Equation (10) states that for any node $n$ a variable $i$ must either be assigned to register $r$ or not; a partial assignment is not allowed. While implied, equation (11) makes it obvious that $c_{i,r,n}$ is a boolean variable and that in particular values greater than 1 are not possible.

$$\min \sum_{\substack{i \in V \\ n \in N}} S_{i,n} \cdot x_{i,\sigma,n} + \sum_{\substack{i \in V \\ r \in R, n \in N}} \mu_{r,n} \cdot c_{i,r,n} \tag{5}$$

$$\text{such that} \bigwedge_{\substack{r \in R - \{\sigma\} \\ n \in N}} \sum_{i \in V} x_{i,r,n} \cdot w_{i,n} \leq b \tag{6}$$

$$\bigwedge_{\substack{i \in V \\ n \in N}} \sum_{r \in R} x_{i,r,n} \geq 1 \tag{7}$$

$$\bigwedge_{\substack{i \in V, r \in R \\ (p,n) \in E}} (x_{i,r,n} - x_{i,r,p}) + c_{i,r,n} \geq 0 \tag{8}$$

$$\bigwedge_{\substack{i \in V, r \in R \\ (p,n) \in E}} (x_{i,r,p} - x_{i,r,n}) + c_{i,r,n} \geq 0 \tag{9}$$

$$\bigwedge_{\substack{i \in V, r \in R \\ n \in N}} x_{i,r,n} \in \{0,1\} \tag{10}$$

$$\bigwedge_{\substack{i \in V, r \in R \\ n \in N}} c_{i,r,n} \in \{0,1\} \tag{11}$$

**Fig. 1.** ILP formulation for bitwise register allocation with a graph-based control flow model

### 3.3  Zero-Cost Moves

Dead temporaries can be moved between registers at no cost. The model so far considers all moves to be of equal cost, regardless of the liveness of the temporary. A good way to allow for zero-cost moves is to split all temporaries with multiple disjoint live-times into multiple temporaries, one for each live-time. While this increases the size of the set $V$, the simplification presented in the next section avoids significant growth of the problem due to this extension.

### 3.4  Optimizations to the ILP

The ILP stated so far can be optimized in order to achieve faster solution times. The basic idea is to reduce the search space for the ILP solver by adding constraints that fix the value of problem variables without changing the value of the goal function for the optimal solution.

Let $pred(n) := \{p | (p,n) \in E\}$ be the set of immediate predecessors of node $n \in N$. Let $L_n \subseteq V$ be the set of temporaries that are not accessed at nodes $n$ and $pred(n)$ and that are either dead or have maximum size at node $n \in N$. Considering that $S_{i,n}$ specifies the spill-cost for temporary $i$ at node $n \in N$, the exact definition of $L_n$ is

$$L_n := \left\{ i \in V \,\middle|\, w_{i,n} \in \{0,b\} \wedge \bigwedge_{d \in pred(n) \cup \{n\}} S_{i,d} = 0 \right\}.$$

Let $M \subseteq N$ be the set of nodes where the move cost is equivalent compared to all previous and next nodes (and thus performing the move earlier or later does not change the cost of the move). The intuitive meaning of $M$ is the set of nodes where the control-flow is linear. Formally

$$M := \left\{ n \in N \;\middle|\; \bigwedge_{p \in pred(n)} \bigwedge_{\substack{s \in succ(n) \\ r \in R}} \mu_{r,p} = \mu_{r,n} = \mu_{r,s} \right\}. \tag{12}$$

**Lemma 1.** *The optimality of the solution computed by the ILP solver is preserved if the constraint*

$$\bigwedge_{\substack{r \in R \\ n \in M}} \bigwedge_{\substack{i \in L_n \\ p \in pred(n)}} x_{i,r,n} = x_{i,r,p} \tag{13}$$

*is added. The constraint further implies that*

$$\bigwedge_{\substack{r \in R \\ t \in M}} \bigwedge_{i \in L_n} c_{i,r,n} = 0. \tag{14}$$

**Proof:** Suppose for some $r \in R$, $n \in M$, $i \in L_t$ an optimal solution to the ILP exists with $x_{i,r,n} \neq x_{i,r,pred(p)}$. If $x_{i,r,n} = 1$, then $i$ was moved at node $n$ out of register $r \in R$. If $w_{i,n} = 0$, performing the move earlier at time $p$ makes no difference at all (since the temporary is dead and only assigned a register pro-forma). Suppose $w_{i,n} = b$. In that case, $i$ must be moving from the stack into a register or vice versa, since moving $i$ from one register $r \in R - \{\sigma\}$ to another register $r' \in R - \{r, \sigma\}$ must be a useless move in an architecture with orthogonal registers and can thus not occur in an optimal solution.[1] Assume that $i$ is moved from $\sigma$ to register $r \in R - \{\sigma\}$. Then this move can be deferred until time $succ(n)$ (change to the previous optimal solution requires setting $x_{i,r,n} = 0$ and $x_{i,\sigma,pred(n)} = 1$). This is always possible, since deferring the move only reduces register pressure ($\sigma$ has no space constraint). Similarly, if the move is from register $r \in R - \{\sigma\}$ to $\sigma$, the move can be performed earlier at $pred(n)$ without changing the cost and again strictly reducing register pressure. The situation for $x_{i,r,n} = 0$ is analogous. $\qquad \square$

*Symmetry.* Another improvement in performance can sometimes be achieved by eliminating symmetry from the ILP formulation. Symmetry occurs in the ILP since all registers (in the same register family) are equal. Thus for $n$ registers, there exist $n!$ completely equivalent solutions. If symmetry is not addressed, the ILP solver may end up enumerating all of these. Symmetry can be reduced by adding constraints that eliminate redundant solutions.

Note that the register order can only be chosen arbitrarily for one specific node since in an optimal solution the selected permutation may limit the register order at other places. Since only live variables will impose constraints on neighboring nodes, the impact of selecting a register order can be increased by adding a constraint at a node where the number of variables in registers is high.

**Lemma 2.** *Let $n_S \in N$ be a node where the number of live variables is maximized. Let $W \subseteq V$ be the set of variables at node $n_S$ for which $w_{i,n_S} = b$.[2] Let $Q \subseteq R$ be a subset of*

---

[1] Note that this would not be true for $w_{i,n} \in (0,b)$, since such a move might defragment the available space in the registers in that case.

[2] $W$ could be defined to include all variables that at node $n_S$ cannot be co-located with others in the same register. However, this definition makes the proof simpler and more to the point.

*equivalent registers (that is, $S_{i,n} = S_{j,n}$ and $\mu_{i,n} = \mu_{r,n}$ for all $i, j \in Q$ and $n \in N$). For example, given a suitable architecture $Q := R - \{\sigma\}$. Let $<_Q$ be a total ordering of the registers and $<_W$ be a total ordering of the variables in $W$.*
  *Then, adding the constraint*

$$\bigwedge_{\substack{r_1,r_2 \in Q, i_1, i_2 \in W \\ r_1 <_Q r_2, i_1 <_W i_2}} x_{i_1,r_1,n_S} + x_{i_2,r_2,n_S} < 2 \tag{15}$$

*does not change the value of the optimal solution for the ILP.*

**Proof:** Let $x \in \{0,1\}^{V,R,N}$ be an optimal solution for the ILP without constraint (15). It needs to be shown that there exists a solution $x' \in \{0,1\}^{V,R,N}$ that satisfies (15) with the same cost. Equation (15) can be reformulated into a logical expression:

$$\bigwedge_{\substack{r_1,r_2 \in Q, i_1, i_2 \in W \\ r_1 <_Q r_2, i_1 <_W i_2}} x_{i_1,r_1,n_S} + x_{i_2,r_2,n_S} < 2$$

$$\Leftrightarrow \bigwedge_{\substack{r_1,r_2 \in Q, i_1, i_2 \in W \\ r_1 <_Q r_2, i_1 <_W i_2}} (x_{i_1,r_1,n_S} = 1) \Rightarrow (x_{i_2,r_2,n_S} = 0)$$

$$\Leftrightarrow \bigwedge_{\substack{r_1 \in Q \\ i_1 \in W}} \left( (x_{i_1,r_1,n_S} = 1) \Rightarrow \bigwedge_{\substack{r_2 \in Q, i_2 \in W \\ r_1 <_Q r_2, i_1 <_W i_2}} x_{i_2,r_2,n_S} = 0 \right)$$

For variable $i \in W$ let $r_i \in R$ be this register ($x_{i,r_i,n_S} = 1$) for the optimal solution $x$. Let $\tau^0 : R \to R$ be the identity permutation. For any permutation $\tau^k$ define $x^k_{v,r,n} := x_{v,\tau^k(r),n}$. While $x^k$ violates (15) define $x^{k+1}$ iteratively as follows:
  *Let $r^k \in Q$ be the smallest (with respect to $<_Q$) register for $r_1$ such that the above equation is not satisfied for $r_1 := -r^k$ and suitable choices for the other terms. Let $i^k \in W$ be the unique variable for which $x_{i^k,r^k,n_S} = 1$. Let $r_2 \in Q$ be the largest register $r^k <_Q r_2$ for which there exists an $j \in W$ with $x^k_{j,r_2,n_S} = 1$ and $i_k <_W j$. Define $\tau^{k+1} := \tau^k \circ \tau_{r^k,r_2}$.*
  Note that the permutation will eliminate the violation of the constraint since $r_2 >_Q r$ among all registers $r \in Q$ for which there exists an $i \in W$ with $x^k_{i,r,n_S} = 1$ and $i_k <_W i$. Note that precondition $w_{i,n_S} = b$ is important here since it implies that at most one variable from the set $W$ can be assigned to any given register ($\sum_{i \in W} x_{i,r,n_S} \leq 1$ for all $r \in R$). This ensures that there does not exist a $j \neq i$ for which $x^k_{j,r_{i_2},n_S} = 1$ also holds (which would result in (15) making the problem infeasible).
  The inductive definition of $x^k$ terminates with a solution $x' = x^{k_{max}}$ (with $k_{max} < |W|$) since in step $k+1$ the equation $j_{k+1} > W j_k$ holds and thus enforces progress. The result $x'$ is a feasible solution (using $c'_{v,r,n} = c_{v,\tau(r),n}$ gives the values for $c$) of equivalent cost (since $\tau(r) = r$ for $r \in R - Q$ implies that cost equivalence follows trivially from register equivalence for $r \in Q$) that satisfies (15). $\qquad\square$

## 3.5    Avoiding to Block Registers for Spilling

Whenever a spilled temporary is used by an instruction, some architectures require that it must be loaded into a register before execution of that instruction. Similarly, if an instruction produces a temporary that is not allocated a register at that point, the result may need to be temporarily stored in a register before it can be spilled onto the stack. A common technique addressing such requirements is to reserve a few registers for accessing spilled temporaries. These registers are then excluded from the ordinary register allocation process. The formulation presented so far assumes that a sufficient number of such registers exist outside of the set of available registers $R$ that is made available to the ILP solver.

Let $a_{i,n} \in \{0,1\}$ be a condition temporary that indicates that at node $n$ temporary $i$ is accessed (used or defined). Since $S_{i,n}$ gives the cost for accessing a spilled variable, this means $a_{i,n} := \text{sgn}(S_{i,n})$. Let $b_{r,n} \in \{0,1\}$ indicate that register $r$ is used for at least one assigned temporary at node $n$. The term "assigned temporary" is used to differentiate these temporaries from "spilled temporaries" in the classical sense. The following constraints are then sufficient to reserve registers for spilling (extending the ILP model from Section 3.2):

$$\bigwedge_{n \in N} \sum_{i \in V} a_{i,n} \cdot x_{i,\sigma,n} + \sum_{r \in R - \{\sigma\}} b_{r,n} \leq |R - \{\sigma\}| \tag{16}$$

$$\bigwedge_{\substack{i \in V, r \in R \\ n \in N}} b_{r,n} \cdot w_{i,n} \geq x_{i,r,n} \cdot w_{i,n} \tag{17}$$

$$\bigwedge_{\substack{r \in R \\ n \in N}} b_{r,n} \in \{0,1\} \tag{18}$$

In (17) the value of $b_{r,n}$ is forced to be one if a live temporary $i$ exists ($w_{i,n} \neq 0$) that is assigned to register $r$ at node $n$ ($x_{i,r,n} = 1$). As a result, $\sum_{i \in V} a_{i,n} \cdot x_{i,\sigma,n}$ is the number of registers that must be reserved for spilled temporaries at node $n$ and $\sum_{r \in R - \{\sigma\}} b_{r,n}$ is the number of registers assigned to registers at that instruction. Equation (16) describes that the number of allocated registers for both the spilled and register-allocated temporaries must not exceed the total number of registers.

Note that this formulation does *not* take bit-wise access to registers into account. While the ILP solution does allow assignment of temporaries to all registers at times, the formulation does not allow for the possibility of allocating just some bits of registers for the spilled temporaries. The problem with a formulation supporting this kind of allocation is that one would still have to ensure that the spilled temporaries are not scattered over multiple registers. This precludes a simple formulation over the sum of all bits assigned to temporaries.

## 3.6    Coalescing

Coalescing is an important step in register allocation that assigns the same register to temporaries that are connected by a move in order to reduce the number of move instructions. The problem with coalescing for previous register allocators is that forcing two temporaries to be in the same register can result in additional spilling. In [8] an algorithm is presented that attempts to minimize the number of moves without introducing any additional spills.

Since the ILP formulations presented in this paper (with the exception of the basic formulation in section 3.1) allow spilling temporaries on a per-instruction basis, they do not have the problem of additional spills due to too aggressive coalescing. Where in [5] the merging of move-connected temporaries would force these temporaries to be either spilled or kept in a register throughout their lifetime, the ILP formulation allows for partial spilling. Hence it is possible to merge all temporaries that are connected by moves upfront. The ILP solver will insert the necessary minimal number of moves and spills as required.

Also note that coalescing reduces the total number of variables and thus reduces the problem size of the ILP. From that perspective, coalescing should also be considered an optimization that improves the run-time of the register allocation algorithm.

### 3.7 Rematerialization

Rematerialization [3] is an important technique based on the realization that is sometimes cheaper to recompute a temporary than to load it from memory or to hold it in a register (and possibly spilling other temporaries). The simplest case for this is where the temporary is a constant value. Extending the presented formulation to the case where values need to be recomputed is not easily possible since this may change the lifetimes of the other temporaries that are used in the expression. On the other hand, rematerialization of constants can be handled easily by the ILP formulation.

Note that it would not be optimal to just replace all uses of a constant with a fresh temporary. Inserting an instruction to load a constant value can be more expensive than keeping the constant in a register if a register is available for free. The cost of loading an immediate value can be modeled precisely in the goal function. This can be achieved by modifying the goal function to allow for temporary-specific spill costs. Let $\mu_{i,r,n}$ be the cost of spilling temporary $i \in V$ at node $n \in N$ to or from register $r \in R$. For temporaries of constant value, the spill-cost to the stack would be zero. The spill-cost for loading a constant-value temporary from the stack would be the cost of a load-immediate instruction. The resulting goal function that incorporates the differentiated spill-cost due to constant rematerialization is then:

$$\min \sum_{\substack{i \in V \\ n \in N}} S_{i,n} \cdot x_{i,\sigma,n} + \sum_{\substack{i \in V \\ r \in R, n \in N}} \mu_{i,r,n} \cdot c_{i,r,n} \tag{19}$$

## 4   Results

The current implementation uses gcc [1] to generate the ILP problems. gcc was modified to support register allocation for hypothetical architectures with 4 to 8 orthogonal registers. The integer linear problems generated by gcc are then solved using ILOG's AMPL/CPLEX linear optimizer. Code generation based on the ILP results has not yet been implemented. Note that a target platform with bit-wise access does not yet exist to the best of our knowledge. However, platforms allowing subword-register allocation exist and while it is trivial to adjust the ILP model for these architectures the necessary modifications to gcc would be extensive. The various cost-parameters in the ILP formulation were set using gcc's built-in cost estimation functions.

The resulting performance metric is the cost estimate given by the goal function in the ILP formulation (5). While this does not allow us to deduce the overall speed-up that could be obtained from the proposed algorithm, this cost estimate should be a good general metric for comparing register allocators. In order to compare the new register allocation algorithm, the output of various other register allocation algorithms available for gcc was judged using the same metric.

For the evaluation, three previously published register allocators were compared with the various ILP-based allocators presented in this paper. The previously published register allocators are traditional graph coloring [5], linear-scan register allocation [15] and Tallam and Gupta's bitwidth aware global register allocation [17]. In order to allow a fair comparison with the graph coloring and linear scan allocators we give numbers for the ILP models for both bitwise and ordinary (wordwise) register allocation. Also, the bitwidth estimation algorithm used is the same for all allocators supporting bitwise allocation.

### 4.1   Bitwidth-Estimation

The bitwidth information for various temporaries at different program points are determined using the approach suggested by [17]. The bitwidth of a temporary $i$ at program point $n$ is represented in a pair $(ld, tr)$, where $ld$ represents the leading zero bits of $i$ at $n$ (leading dead bits) and $tr$ represents the trailing zero bits of $i$ at $n$ (trailing dead bits). In order to determine $(ld, tr)$ pairs for all temporaries at all program points, first a forward data flow analysis is performed to chain the definition of temporaries to their uses. Then a backward data flow analysis is performed to refine the $(ld, tr)$ pairs by chaining the use of temporaries to their respective definitions. The $(ld, tr)$ pair for all temporaries are computed simultaneously as they are interdependent on each other.

### 4.2   Benchmarks

The performance of the approach is evaluated using benchmarks from the Bitwise [16] and Mediabench [10] suites. These benchmarks are appropriate since they correspond to real-world applications where sub-word access to temporaries is common. Furthermore, using some of the same benchmarks as [17] enables comparison with prior work on bitwise register allocation.

### 4.3   Impact of the Optimizations

Applying Lemma 1 to the ILP formulation reduces the searchspace for the ILP solver. Depending on the benchmark the resulting constraints can eliminate up to 90% of the free variables. Note that the reduction of problem variables does not only reduce the space requirements but also significantly reduces the search space for the ILP solver. For example, mpegcorr with 8 registers takes 422s without the constraints allowed by Lemma 1, but only 46s with those constraints.

Surprisingly, using the constraints from Lemma 2 increases the cost for this benchmark, if applied together with Lemma 2 the solution time is between roughly 50 and 300s depending on the choice of $n_S$. While the additional constraints from Lemma 2 also reduce the search space, this reduction can somehow not offset the cost of evaluating the additional constraint for the specific ILP solver and any of the benchmarks that have been tested for this during our study.

Another possible optimization is to use any of the other register allocation algorithms to compute a feasible register allocation and to feed this as an input into the ILP solver. Such a feasible starting solution can help the solver in its branch and bound search to prune the search space. In our benchmarks, we use the best solution computed by either graph coloring, linear scan or Tallam's bitwise allocator as the starting solution. The resulting performance improvements vary depending on the benchmark. Typically smaller benchmarks see no improvement or even performance degradation, whereas larger benchmarks see (often minor) performance improvements. For example, the mpegcorr benchmark runs in 46s with a starting solution, but takes 418s without it. We speculate that the smaller search space for small benchmarks gives fewer opportunities for pruning and the given initial solution is further away in the search space from the optimal solution than the default infeasible starting point that would be used without a starting solution. Future work may result in some deeper understanding of the circumstances under which the various combinations of these optimizations (namely Lemma 1, Lemma 2 and giving a starting solution) are most effective.

The performance results reported for the benchmarks henceforth use a feasible starting solution in combination with the constraints from Lemma 1.

## 4.4  Performance

Figure 2 and Figure 5 shows the cost as estimated by the goal function (5) for the various register allocation algorithms for all benchmarks.

The time it took to solve the different ILP problems were obtained by running ILOG's cplex v9.1 on an Intel Xeon 3 Ghz with 4 GB memory running Linux 2.6.10. While the time may seem excessively long for some benchmarks, note that this is using a stock ILP solver that has not been specialized to the problem at hand. Furthermore, the run-times should still be feasible when compiling small programs or performance critical functions for embedded systems where high performance and low per-unit cost are paramount.

Note that various benchmarks show that adding more registers does not always have to increase the cost of the ILP – typically at some point computing an optimal solution becomes much easier because there are few or no points of register pressure left. In general, the runtime of the solver is rather unpredictable. For example, the adpcm benchmark with word-wise register allocation runs takes more than $10^5$s for 4 registers, runs rather quickly in 331s for 6 registers. Astonishingly, if the number of registers is increased to 8 the solver takes again significantly longer with 4162s.

Figure 8 gives some data comparing the size of the benchmarks and the respective runtime of the ILP. The size of the benchmark is determined by the number of local variables ($|V|$), the number of nodes ($|N|$) and edges ($|E|$) in the control flow graph.

| Benchmark | Reg. | adpcm | convolve | median | mpegcorr | NewLife | MotionTest | Histogram |
|---|---|---|---|---|---|---|---|---|
| Graph Coloring [5] | 4 | 1225415 | 0 | 91280 | 92400 | 2236190 | 4690 | 7515 |
| Linear [15] | 4 | 1450425 | 0 | 131217 | 127913 | 1752698 | 7060 | 106605 |
| Tallam [17] | 4 | 800330 | 0 | 91280 | 92400 | 2136180 | 4690 | 5160 |
| ILP GCF | 4 | 490124 | 0 | 44710 | 73850 | 599642 | 1919 | 3773 |
| ILP GCFB | 4 | 330071 | 0 | 44710 | 73850 | 599642 | 1916 | 2837 |
| Graph Coloring [5] | 6 | 750315 | 0 | 34575 | 34835 | 531305 | 260 | 1990 |
| Linear [15] | 6 | 1025311 | 0 | 82283 | 67444 | 743840 | 4560 | 4310 |
| Tallam [17] | 6 | 325230 | 0 | 34575 | 34835 | 531305 | 260 | 1195 |
| ILP GCF | 6 | 270084 | 0 | 17795 | 28550 | 251428 | 105 | 794 |
| ILP GCFB | 6 | 120045 | 0 | 17795 | 28550 | 251428 | 105 | 6 |
| Graph Coloring [5] | 8 | 275215 | 0 | 17870 | 8055 | 27915 | 0 | 0 |
| Linear [15] | 8 | 575214 | 0 | 72248 | 38415 | 218790 | 0 | 0 |
| Tallam [17] | 8 | 130 | 0 | 17870 | 8055 | 27915 | 0 | 0 |
| ILP GCF | 8 | 120054 | 0 | 6452 | 1062 | 11404 | 0 | 0 |
| ILP GCFB | 8 | 42 | 0 | 6452 | 1062 | 11404 | 0 | 0 |

**Fig. 2.** ILP GCF is the ILP model with the graph-based control flow model and without bitwise allocation. ILP GCFB is the graph-based control flow model with bitwise allocation. Memory load/store cost metric is 5.

| Benchmark | adpcm | convolve | median | mpegcorr | NewLife | MotionTest | Histogram |
|---|---|---|---|---|---|---|---|
| 4 registers | 53257s | 0s | 73s | 10s | 57s | 2s | 6s |
| 6 registers | $\geq 10^5$s | 0s | 44s | 35s | 163s | 3s | 11s |
| 8 registers | 454s | 0s | 80s | 46s | 312s | 1s | 6s |

**Fig. 3.** Solver time for the bitwise graph-based ILP formulation, ILP GCFB. Entries prefixed with > indicate that the ILP was timed out before completing.

| Benchmark | adpcm | convolve | median | mpegcorr | NewLife | MotionTest | Histogram |
|---|---|---|---|---|---|---|---|
| 4 registers | $\geq 10^5$s | 0s | 23s | 10s | 42s | 2s | 5s |
| 6 registers | 331s | 0s | 39s | 27s | 168s | 3s | 11s |
| 8 registers | 4162s | 0s | 80s | 43s | 286s | 1s | 6s |

**Fig. 4.** Solver time for the graph-based ILP formulation, ILP GCF

### 4.5 Discussion

At the surface the large and unpredictable ILP solution times seem to be the big problem with the presented approach. However, in practice, the optimal solution is computed rather quickly, especially given a good initial feasible starting solution. The solver spends most of its time proving that this solution is optimal. Naturally such a proof does not yield any speedups later, so it is perfectly reasonable to turn the presented algorithm into a heuristic by simply aborting the ILP solver if the computation takes too long without improving the solution. This will allow the user to select an appropriate trade-off between register allocation quality and compile-time.

| Benchmark | Reg. | bilint | edge-detect | levdurb | g721 | adpcm-coder |
|---|---|---|---|---|---|---|
| Graph Coloring [5] | 4 | 1225490 | 3331565 | 912080 | 90565 | 1419575 |
| Linear [15] | 4 | 687730 | 2134138 | 1424956 | 148124 | 1736976 |
| Tallam [17] | 4 | 975390 | 3331565 | 912080 | 87705 | 1028675 |
| ILP GCF | 4 | 260104 | 1333229 | 582787 | 29943 | 581829 |
| ILP GCFB | 4 | ≤80072 | ≤1333181 | 582787 | 29943 | 412035 |
| Graph Coloring [5] | 6 | 325130 | 2604260 | 427840 | 32040 | 955580 |
| Linear [15] | 6 | 487665 | 1535156 | 851177 | 98388 | 1409078 |
| Tallam [17] | 6 | 287615 | 2604260 | 427840 | 32040 | 539670 |
| ILP GCF | 6 | 142557 | ≤962851 | 260489 | 13608 | 401715 |
| ILP GCFB | 6 | ≤92537 | ≤952981 | 260489 | 13608 | 222531 |
| Graph Coloring [5] | 8 | 150060 | 2076610 | 193580 | 0 | 639035 |
| Linear [15] | 8 | 350125 | 1129861 | 489472 | 11945 | 1032645 |
| Tallam [17] | 8 | 150060 | 2076610 | 193580 | 0 | 234130 |
| ILP GCF | 8 | 72529 | ≤1346346 | 41844 | 0 | 278352 |
| ILP GCFB | 8 | ≤35014 | ≤1346346 | 41844 | 0 | 100776 |

**Fig. 5.** Solution cost for various larger benchmarks using the graph-based control flow model. Entries prefixed with ≤ indicate that the ILP solver was aborted prior to proving optimality. Memory load/store cost metric is fixed to 5.

| Benchmark | bilint | edge-detct | levdurb | g721 | adpcm-coder |
|---|---|---|---|---|---|
| 4 registers | $> 10^6$s | $> 10^5$s | 24s | 57s | 5545s |
| 6 registers | $> 10^5$s | $> 10^5$s | 102s | 321s | 845s |
| 8 registers | $> 10^5$s | $> 10^5$s | 138s | 41s | 648s |

**Fig. 6.** Solver time for the graph-based bitwise ILP formulation, ILP GCFB. Entries prefixed with > indicate that the ILP was timed out before completing.

| Benchmark | bilint | edge-detct | levdurb | g721 | adpcm-coder |
|---|---|---|---|---|---|
| 4 registers | 5s | 1342s | 26s | 443s | 3855s |
| 6 registers | 16s | $> 10^5$s | 60s | 311s | 935s |
| 8 registers | 18s | $> 10^5$s | 77s | 15s | 1588s |

**Fig. 7.** Solver time for the graph-based ILP formulation, ILP GCF

In addition to heuristics that abort the ILP solver earlier, solution times can be improved dramatically using straight-forward reductions of the ILP problem size. One possibility is to map multiple nodes from the original control-flow graph to one node in the ILP formulation. Also, on many processors bit-wise register allocation may not be useful or effective anyway. As the 32-bit timings have shown, using a more coarse allocation granularity can dramatically improve solution times. Changing the ILP formulation to other granularities such as nibbles or bytes is trivial. All of these changes can improve ILP solution times at the expense of reduced quality of the produced solutions. Future work will have to evaluate which graph reduction strategies will give the most effective trade-offs.

| Benchmark | $\|V\|$ | $\|E\|$ | $\|N\|$ | time (GCFB) |
|-----------|------|------|------|-------------|
| adpcm | 29 | 228 | 218 | 53257s |
| median | 34 | 190 | 184 | 73s |
| NewLife | 61 | 312 | 302 | 57s |
| levdurb | 37 | 206 | 199 | 24s |
| mpegcorr | 31 | 185 | 178 | 10s |

**Fig. 8.** This Table shows the relationship between benchmark size and the time it takes to solve the ILP for some selected benchmarks. The number of registers is fixed to 4.

## 5   Conclusion

This paper introduced a new ILP-based algorithm for bit-wise register allocation. The presented formulation expands the expressiveness of the model of existing ILP-based register allocation algorithms and hence allows for better solutions. The algorithm integrates previous techniques including coalescing, spilling, constant rematerialization and register families and allows for temporaries to be temporarily spilled. The formulation supports using the same register for access to spilled temporaries or direct temporary assignment at different times. Experimental results show that the resulting ILP problems can be solved by modern of-the-shelf ILP software, resulting in register allocations that substantially improve on allocations computed by state-of-the-art techniques.

### Acknowledgments

We thank Calin Cascaval, Satish Chandra, Nandivada V. Krishna and Jens Palsberg for their comments on earlier drafts of this paper.

### References

1. http://gcc.gnu.org/, 2004.
2. Andrew W. Appel and Lal George. Optimal spilling for cisc machines with few registers. In *Proceedings of the ACM SIGPLAN 2001 conference on Programming language design and implementation*, pages 243–253, 2001.
3. Preston Briggs, Keith D. Cooper, and Linda Torczon. Rematerialization. In *Proceedings of the Conference on Programming Language Design and Implementation (PLDI)*, volume 27, pages 311–321, New York, NY, 1992. ACM Press.
4. Preston Briggs, Keith D. Cooper, and Linda Torczon. Improvements to graph coloring register allocation. *ACM Transactions on Programming Languages and Systems*, 16(3):428–455, May 1994.
5. Gregory J. Chaitin. Register allocation and spilling via graph coloring. In *Proceedings of the ACM SIGPLAN '82 Symposium on Compiler Construction*, pages 98–105, Jun.
6. Gregory J. Chaitin, Marc A. Auslander, Ashok K. Chandra, John Cocke, Martin E. Hopkins, and Peter W. Markstein. Register allocation via coloring. *Computer Languages*, 6:47–57, 1981.
7. Changqing Fu and Kent Wilken. A faster optimal register allocator. In *MICRO 35: Proceedings of the 35th annual ACM/IEEE international symposium on Microarchitecture*, pages 245–256, Los Alamitos, CA, USA, 2002. IEEE Computer Society Press.
8. Lal George and Andrew W. Appel. Iterated register coalescing. *ACM Transactions on Programming Languages and Systems*, 18(3):300–324, May 1996.
9. David W. Goodwin and Kent D. Wilken. Optimal and Near-Optimal Global Register Allocation Using 0-1 Integer Programming, 1996.

10. Chunho Lee, Miodrag Potkonjak, and William H. Mangione-Smith. Mediabench: A tool for evaluating and synthesizing multimedia and communicatons systems. In *International Symposium on Microarchitecture*, 1997.
11. Bengu Li and Rajiv Gupta. Bit section instruction set extension of arm for embedded applications. In *Proceedings of the international conference on Compilers, architecture, and synthesis for embedded systems*, pages 69–78. ACM Press, 2002.
12. Bengu Li, Youtao Zhang, and Rajiv Gupta. Speculative subword register allocation in embedded processors. In *Proceedings of the LCPC 2004 Workshop*, 2004.
13. John L. Nazareth. *Computer Solution of Linear Programs*. Oxford University Press, 1987.
14. Jinpyo Park and Soo-Mook Moon. Optimistic register coalescing. In Jean-Luc Gaudiot, editor, *International Conference on Parallel Architectures and Compilation Techniques*, pages 196–204, Paris, October 1998. IFIP,ACM,IEEE, North-Holland.
15. Massimiliano Poletto and Vivek Sarkar. Linear scan register allocation. *ACM Transactions on Programming Languages and Systems*, 21(5):895–913, 1999.
16. Mark Stephenson, Johnathan Babb, and Saman Amarasinghe. Bitwidth analysis with application to silicon compilation.
17. Sriraman Tallam and Rajiv Gupta. Bitwidth aware global register allocation. *ACM SIGPLAN Notices*, 38(1):85–96, January 2003.

## A   ILP Progress over Time

The presented algorithm can easily be converted into a heuristic by aborting the ILP solver before optimality is established. In this context, it is interesting to know how fast the ILP solver finds good solutions. The following graphs show the improvement of

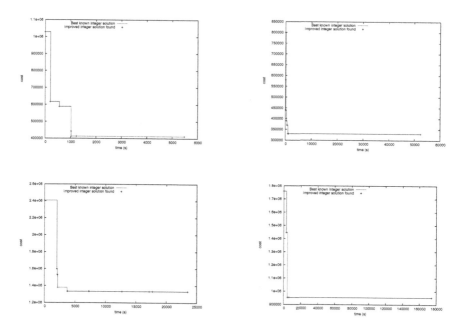

**Fig. 9.** For many benchmarks, near-optimal solutions are found quickly. Graphs for bitwise solutions for adpcm-coder (4 reg.), adpcm (4 reg.) and edge-detect (4 and 6 reg.).

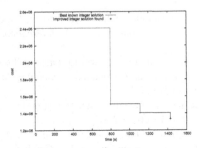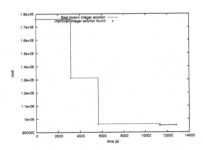

**Fig. 10.** For some benchmarks, it takes a while for better solutions to be found. Graphs for word-wise solutions for edge-detect q(4 and 6 registers).

the best known integer solution over time for some representative benchmarks (starting with the starting solution and ending with the optimal solution).

# Register Allocation: What Does the NP-Completeness Proof of Chaitin et al. Really Prove? Or Revisiting Register Allocation: Why and How

Florent Bouchez[1], Alain Darte[1], Christophe Guillon[2], and Fabrice Rastello[1]

[1] LIP, UMR CNRS-ENS Lyon-UCB Lyon-INRIA 5668, France
[2] Compiler Group, ST/HPC/STS Grenoble, France

**Abstract.** Register allocation is one of the most studied problems in compilation. It is considered NP-complete since Chaitin et al., in 1981, modeled the problem of assigning temporary variables to $k$ machine registers as the problem of coloring, with $k$ colors, the interference graph associated to the variables. The fact that this graph can be arbitrary proves the NP-completeness of this formulation. However, this original proof does not really show where the complexity of register allocation comes from. Recently, the re-discovery that interference graphs of SSA programs can be colored in polynomial time raised the question: Can we use SSA to do register allocation in polynomial time, without contradicting Chaitin et al's NP-completeness result? To address this question and, more generally, the complexity of register allocation, we revisit Chaitin et al's proof to identify the interactions between spilling (load/store insertion), coalescing/splitting (removal/insertion of register moves), critical edges (property of the control flow), and coloring (assignment to registers). In particular, we show that, in general, it is *easy* to decide if temporary variables can be assigned to $k$ registers or if some spilling is necessary. In other words, the real complexity does not come from the coloring itself (as a misinterpretation Chaitin et al's proof may suggest) but comes from critical edges and from the optimizations of spilling and coalescing.

## 1 Introduction

The goal of register allocation is to map the variables of a program into physical memory locations (main memory or machine registers). Accessing a register is usually faster than accessing memory, thus one tries to use registers as much as possible. When this is not possible, some variables must be transferred ("spilled") to and from memory. This has a cost, the cost of load/store operations that should be avoided as much as possible.

Classical approaches are based on fast graph coloring algorithms (sometimes combined with techniques dedicated to basic blocks). A widely-used algorithm is iterated register coalescing proposed by Appel and George [17], a modified version of previous developments by Chaitin et al. [9,8], and Briggs et al. [4]. In these heuristics, *spilling*, *coalescing* (removing register-to-register moves), and *coloring* (assigning variables to registers) are done in the same framework. Priorities among these transformations are done implicitly with cost functions. *Splitting* (adding register-to-register moves) can also be integrated in this framework. Such techniques are well-established and used in optimizing compilers. However, there are several reasons to revisit these

G. Almási, C. Caşcaval, and P. Wu (Eds.): LCPC 2006, LNCS 4382, pp. 283–298, 2007.

approaches. First, some algorithms not considered in the past, because they were too time-consuming, can be good candidates today: processors used for compilation are now much faster and, for critical applications, industrial compilers are also ready to accept longer compilation times. Second, the increasing cost on most architectures of a memory access compared to a register access suggests to focus on heuristics that give more importance to spilling cost minimization, possibly at the price of additional register-to-register moves. Finally, there are many pitfalls and folk theorems concerning the complexity of the register allocation problem that are worth clarifying.

This last point is particularly interesting to note. In 1981, Chaitin et al. [9] modeled the problem of allocating variables of a program to $k$ registers as the problem of coloring, with $k$ colors, the corresponding interference graph in which two vertices/variables interfere if they are simultaneously live. As any graph is the interference graph of some program and because graph $k$-colorability is NP-complete [15, Problem GT4], heuristics have been used for spilling, coalescing, splitting, coloring, etc. The argument "register allocation *is* graph coloring, therefore it is NP-complete" is one of the first statements of many papers on register allocation. It is true that most problems related to register allocation are NP-complete but this simplifying statement can make us forget what Chaitin et al's proof actually shows. In particular, it is commonly believed that, in the absence of instruction rescheduling, it is NP-complete to decide if the program variables can be allocated to $k$ registers with no spilling, even if live-range splitting is allowed. This is *not* what Chaitin et al. proved. We show that this problem is not NP-complete, except for a few particular cases that depend on the target architecture. This may be a folk theorem too but, to our knowledge, it has never been clearly stated. Actually, going from register allocation to graph coloring is just a way of modeling the problem, not an equivalence. In particular, this model does not take into account the fact that a variable can be moved from a register to another (live-range splitting), of course at some cost, but only the cost of a move instruction, which is often better than a spill.

Until very recently, only a few authors addressed the complexity of register allocation in more details. Maybe the most interesting complexity results are those of Liberatore et al. [22,14], who analyze the reasons why *optimal* spilling is hard for basic blocks. In this case, the coloring phase is of course easy because, after some variable renaming, the interference graph is an interval graph, but deciding *which* variables to spill and *where* is in general difficult. We completed this study for various spill cost models, and not just for basic blocks [2], and for several variants of register coalescing [3].

Today, most compilers go through an intermediate code representation, the (strict) SSA form (static single assignment) [12], which makes many code optimizations simpler. In such a code, each variable is defined textually only once and is alive only along the dominance tree associated to the control-flow graph. Some so-called $\phi$ functions are used to transfer values along the control flow not covered by the dominance tree. The consequence is that, with an adequate interpretation of $\phi$ functions, the interference graph of an SSA code is not arbitrary: it is chordal [18], thus easy to color. Furthermore, it can be colored with $k$ colors iff (if and only if) Maxlive $\leq k$ where Maxlive is the maximal number of variables simultaneously live. What does this property imply? One can try to decompose register allocation into two phases. The first phase decides which values are spilled and where, to get a code with Maxlive $\leq k$. This phase is called *allocation* in [22] as it decides the variables allocated in memory and the variables allocated in registers. The second phase, called *register assignment* in [22], maps variables to registers, possibly removing move instructions by *coalescing*, or introducing move instructions by *splitting*. These moves are also called *shuffle code* in [23]. When loads and stores are more expensive than moves, such an approach is worth exploring. It was experimented by Appel and George [1] and also advocated in [20,2,19].

The fact that interference graphs of strict SSA programs are chordal is not a new result if one makes the connection between graph theory and SSA form. Indeed, an interference graph is chordal iff it is the interference graph of a family of subtrees (here the live-ranges of variables) of a tree (here the dominance tree), see [18, Theorem 4.8]. Furthermore, maximal cliques correspond to program points. We re-discovered this property when trying to better understand the interplay of register allocation and coalescing for out-of-SSA conversion [13]. Independently, Brisk et al. [6], Pereira and Palsberg [25], and Hack et al. [19] made the same observation. A direct proof of the chordality property for strict SSA programs can be given, see for example [2,19].

Many papers [12,5,21,28,7,27] address the problem of how to go out of SSA, in particular how to replace efficiently $\phi$ functions by move instructions. The issues addressed in these papers are how to handle renaming constraints, due to specific requirements of the architecture, how to deal with the so-called critical edges of the control-flow graph, and how to reduce the number of moves. However, in these papers, register allocation is performed *after* out-of-SSA conversion: in other words, the number of registers is not a constraint when going out of SSA and, conversely, the SSA form is not exploited to perform register allocation. In [19] on the other hand, the SSA form is used to do register allocation. Spilling and coloring (i.e., register assignment) are done in SSA and some permutations of colors are placed on new blocks, predecessors of the $\phi$ points, to emulate the semantics of $\phi$ functions. Such permutations can always be performed with register-to-register moves and possibly register swaps or XOR functions. However, minimizing the number of such permutations is NP-complete [19].

All these new results related to SSA form, combined with the idea of spilling before coloring so that Maxlive $\leq k$, has led Pereira and Palsberg [26] to wonder where the NP-completeness of Chaitin et al's proof (apparently) disappeared: "Can we do polynomial-time register allocation by first transforming the program to SSA form, then doing linear-time register allocation for the SSA form, and finally doing SSA elimination while maintaining the mapping from temporaries to registers?" (all this when Maxlive $\leq k$ of course, otherwise some spilling needs to be done). They show that, if register swaps are not available, the answer is no unless P=NP. The NP-completeness proof of Pereira and Palsberg is interesting, but we feel it does not completely explain why register allocation is difficult. Basically, it shows that if we decide *a priori* what the splitting points are, i.e., where register-to-register moves can be placed (in their case, the splitting points are the $\phi$ points), then it is NP-complete to choose the right colors (they do not allow register swaps as in [19]). However, there is no reason to restrict to splitting points given by SSA. Actually, we show that, when we can choose the splitting points, when we are free to add program blocks to remove critical edges (the standard *edge splitting* technique), then it is easy, except for a few particular cases, to decide if and how we can assign variables to registers without spilling.

More generally, the goal of this paper is to revisit Chaitin et al's proof to clarify the interactions between spilling, splitting, coalescing, critical edges, and coloring. Our study analyzes the complexity of the problem "are $k$ registers enough to allocate variables without spill?" but, unlike Chaitin et al., we take into account live-range splitting. In Section 2, we analyze more carefully Chaitin et al's proof to show that the NP-completeness of the problem comes from critical edges. We then address the cases where critical edges can be split. In Section 3, we show how to extend Chaitin et al's proof to address the same problem as Pereira and Palsberg in [26]: if live-range splitting points are fixed at entry/exit of basic blocks and if register swaps are not available, the problem is NP-complete. In Section 4, we discuss the register swap constraint and show that, for most architecture configurations, if we can split variables wherever we want, the problem is polynomial. Section 5 summarizes our results and discusses how they can be used to improve previous approaches and to develop new allocation schemes.

## 2  Direct Consequences of Chaitin et al's NP-Completeness Proof

Let us examine Chaitin et al's NP-completeness proof. The proof is by reduction from graph $k$-coloring [15, Problem GT4]: Given an undirected graph $G = (V, E)$ and an integer $k$, can we color the graph with $k$ colors, i.e., can we define, for each vertex $v \in V$, a color $c(v)$ in $\{1, \ldots, k\}$ such that $c(v) \neq c(u)$ for each edge $(u, v) \in E$? The problem is well-known to be NP-complete if $G$ is arbitrary, even for a fixed $k \geq 3$.

For the reduction, Chaitin et al. build a program with $|V| + 1$ variables, one for each vertex $u \in V$ and an additional variable $x$, as follows. For each $(u, v)$ in $E$, a block $B_{u,v}$ defines $u$, $v$, and $x$. For each $u \in V$, a block $B_u$ reads $u$ and $x$, and returns a new value. Each block $B_{u,v}$ is a direct predecessor in the control-flow graph of $B_u$ and $B_v$. An entry block switches to all blocks $B_{u,v}$. Fig. 1 illustrates this construction when $G$ is a cycle of length 4, the example used in [26]. The program is given on the right; its interference graph (upper-left corner) is the graph $G$ (lower-left corner) plus a vertex for the variable $x$, connected to any other vertex. Thus $x$ must use an extra color. Therefore $G$ is $k$-colorable iff each variable can be assigned to a unique register for a total of at most $k + 1$ registers. This is what Chaitin et al. proved: for such programs, deciding if one can assign the variables, *this way*, to $k \geq 4$ registers is thus NP-complete.

Chaitin et al's proof, at least in its original interpretation, does not address the possibility of splitting [10] the live-range of a variable (set of program points where the variable is live [1]). In other words, each vertex of the interference graph represents the complete live-range as an atomic object and it is assumed that this live-range must always reside in the same register. Furthermore, the fact that the register allocation problem is modeled through the interference graph loses information on the program itself and the exact location of interferences. This is a well-known fact, which has led to many different register allocation heuristics but with no corresponding complexity study even though their situations are not covered by the previous NP-completeness proof.

---

[1] Actually, for Chaitin et al., two variables interfere only if one is live at the definition of the other. The two definitions coincide for *strict* programs, i.e., programs where any static control-flow path from the program start to a given use of a variable goes through a definition of this variable. This is the case for all the programs we manipulate in our NP-completeness proofs.

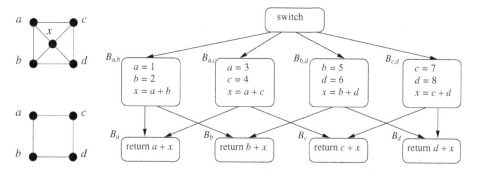

**Fig. 1.** Program built from a cycle of length 4 (bottom left) and its interference graph (top left)

This raises the question: What if we allow to split live-ranges? Consider Fig. 1 again and one of the variables, for example $a$. In block $B_a$, variable $a$ is needed for the instruction "return $a + x$", and this value can come from blocks $B_{a,b}$ and $B_{a,c}$. If we split the live-range of $a$ in block $B_a$ before it is used, some register must still contain the value of $a$ both at the exit of blocks $B_{a,b}$ and $B_{a,c}$. The same is true for all other variables. In other words, if we consider the possible copies live at exit of blocks of type $B_{u,v}$ and at entry of blocks of type $B_v$, we get the same interference graph $G$ for the copies and each copy must remain in the same register. Therefore, the problem remains NP-complete even if we allow live-range splitting. Splitting live-ranges does not help here because the control-flow edges from $B_{u,v}$ to $B_u$ are *critical* edges, i.e., they go from a block with more than one successor to a block with more than one predecessor. In Chaitin et al's model, each vertex is atomic and must be assigned a unique color. Live-range splitting redefines these objects. In general, defining precisely *what* is colored is indeed important as the subtle title of Cytron and Ferrante's paper "What's in a name?" pointed out [11]. However, here, because of critical edges, whatever the splitting, there remains atomic objects hard to color, defined by the copies live on the edges.

To conclude, we can interpret Chaitin et al's original proof as follows. It is NP-complete to decide if the program variables can be assigned to $k$ registers, even if live-range splitting is allowed, but only when the program has critical edges that cannot be split, i.e., when we cannot change the control flow graph structure and add new blocks.

## 3 Split Points on Entry & Exit of Blocks and Tree-Like Programs

In [26], Pereira and Palsberg pointed out that the construction of Chaitin et al. (as done in Fig. 1) is not enough to prove anything about register allocation through SSA. Indeed, any program built this way can be allocated with only 3 registers by adding extra blocks, where out-of-SSA code is traditionally inserted, and performing some register-to-register moves in these blocks. We can place the variable definitions of each block of type $B_{u,v}$ in 3 registers (independently of other blocks), e.g., $r_1$ for $u$, $r_2$ for $v$, and $r_3$ for $x$, and decide that variables $u$ and $x$ in each block of type $B_u$ are always expected in registers $r_1$ and $r_3$. Then, we can "repair" the coloring at each join point, when needed, thanks to an adequate re-mapping of registers (here a move from $r_2$ to $r_1$) in a new block along the edge from $B_{u,v}$ to $B_u$. We will use a similar block structure later, see Fig. 2.

More generally, when there are no critical edges, one can indeed go through SSA (or any live-ranges representation as subtrees of a tree), i.e., consider that different variable definitions belong to different live-ranges, and to color them with $k$ colors, if possible. This can be done in linear time, in a greedy fashion, because the corresponding interference graph is chordal. At this stage, it is easy to decide if $k$ registers are enough. This is possible iff Maxlive, the maximal number of values live at any program point, is less than $k$. Indeed, Maxlive is obviously a lower bound for the minimal number of registers needed, as all variables live at a given point interfere (at least for strict programs). Furthermore, this lower bound can be achieved by coloring because of a double property of such live-ranges: a) Maxlive is equal to the maximal size of a clique in the interference graph (in general, it is only a lower bound); b) the maximal size of a clique and the chromatic number of the graph are equal (the graph is chordal). Moreover, if $k$ registers are not enough, additional splitting will not help as this leaves Maxlive unchanged.

If $k$ colors are enough, it is still possible that the colors selected under SSA do not match at join points where live-ranges were split. Some "shuffle" [23], i.e., registers permutation, is needed along the edge where colors do not match. Because the edge is not critical, the shuffle will not propagate along other control flow paths. If some register is available at this point, any remapping can be performed as a sequence of register-to-register moves, possibly using the free register as temporary storage. Otherwise, an additional register is needed unless one can perform register swaps, either with a special instruction or with arithmetic operations such as XOR (but maybe only for integer registers). This view of coloring through permutations insertion is the base of any approach that optimizes spilling first [20,1,2,19]. Some spilling and splitting are done, optimally or not, to reduce Maxlive to at most $k$. In [1], this approach is even used in the most extreme form: live-ranges are split at each program point in order to solve spilling optimally, and there is a potential permutation between any two program points. Then, live-ranges are merged back, as much as possible, thanks to coalescing.

Thus, it seems that if we go through SSA (for example but not only), deciding if $k$ registers are enough becomes easy. The only possible remaining difficult case is if register swaps are not available. Indeed, in this case, no permutation except the identity can be performed at a point with $k$ live variables. This is the question addressed by Pereira and Palsberg in [26]: Can we easily choose an adequate coloring of the SSA representation so that no permutation is needed? The answer is no, the problem is NP-complete. Pereira and Palsberg use a reduction from the $k$-colorability problem for circular-arc graphs, which is NP-complete if $k$ is a problem input [16]. Basically, the idea is to start from a circular-arc graph, to cut all arcs at some point to get an interval graph, to view this interval graph as the interference graph of a basic block, to add a back edge to form a loop, and to make sure that $k$ variables are live on the back edge. Then, coloring the basic block so that no permutation is needed on the back edge is equivalent to coloring the original circular-arc graph. This is the same technique used in [16] to reduce the coloring of circular-arc graphs from a permutation problem. This proof shows that if we restrict to the split points defined by SSA, it is difficult to choose the right coloring of the SSA representation and thus decide if $k$ registers are enough. It is NP-complete even

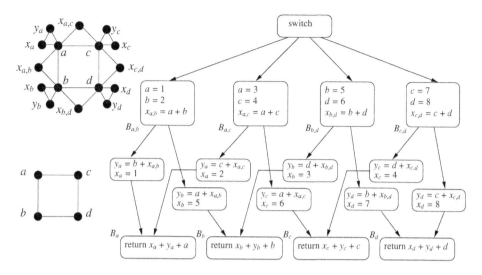

**Fig. 2.** Program built from a cycle of length 4 (bottom left) and its interference graph (top left)

for a simple loop and a single split point. However, if $k$ is fixed, this specific problem is polynomial as is the $k$-coloring problem of circular-arc graphs, by propagating possible permutations. We now show that, with a simple variation of Chaitin et al's proof, we can get a similar NP-completeness result, even for a fixed $k$, but for an arbitrary program.

Given an arbitrary graph $G = (V, E)$, we build a program with the same control-flow structure as for Chaitin et al's construction, but we split critical edges as shown in Fig. 2. The program has three variables $u$, $x_u$, $y_u$ for each vertex $u \in V$ and a variable $x_{u,v}$ for each edge $(u, v) \in E$. For each $(u, v) \in E$, a block $B_{u,v}$ defines $u$, $v$, and $x_{u,v}$. For each $u \in V$, a block $B_u$ reads $u$, $y_u$, and $x_u$, and returns a new value. For each block $B_{u,v}$, there is a path to the blocks $B_u$ and $B_v$. Along the path from $B_{u,v}$ to $B_u$, a block reads $v$ and $x_{u,v}$ to define $y_u$, and then defines $x_u$. An entry block switches to all blocks $B_{u,v}$. The interference graph is 3-colorable iff $G$ itself is 3-colorable. Its restriction to variables $u$ (those that correspond to vertices of $G$) is exactly $G$. Fig. 2 illustrates this construction, again when $G$ is a cycle of length 4. The interference graph is in the upper-left corner.

Assume that permutations can be placed only along the edges, or equivalently on entry or exit of the intermediate blocks, between blocks of type $B_{u,v}$ and type $B_u$. We claim that the program can be assigned to 3 registers iff $G$ is 3-colorable. Indeed, for each $u$ and $v$, exactly 3 variables are live on exit of $B_{u,v}$ and on entry of $B_u$ and $B_v$. Thus, if only 3 registers are used, no permutation, except the identity, can be done. Thus the live-range of any variable $u \in V$ *cannot be split*, i.e., each variable must be assigned to a unique color. Using the same color for the corresponding vertex in $G$ gives a 3-coloring of $G$. Conversely, if $G$ is 3-colorable, assign to each variable $u$ the same color as the vertex $u$. It remains to color the variables $x_{u,v}$, $x_u$, and $y_u$. This is easy: in block $B_{u,v}$, only two colors are used so far, the colors for $u$ and $v$, so $x_{u,v}$ can be assigned the remaining color. Finally assign $x_u$ and $y_u$ to two colors different than the color of $u$ (see Fig. 2 again to visualize the cliques of size 3). This gives a valid register assignment.

To conclude, this slight variation of Chaitin et al's proof shows that if we cannot split inside basic blocks but are allowed to split only on entries and exits of blocks (as in traditional out-of-SSA translation), it is NP-complete to decide if $k$ registers are enough. This is true even for a fixed $k \geq 3$ and even for a program with no critical edge.

# 4    If Split Points Can Be Anywhere

Does the study of Section 3 completely answer the question? Not quite. Indeed, who said that split points need to be on entry and exit of blocks? Why can't we shuffle registers at any program point, for example in the middle of a block if this allows us to perform a permutation? Consider Fig. 2 again. The register pressure is 3 on any control-flow edge, this was the key for the proof of Section 3. But it is not 3 everywhere; between the definitions of each $y_u$ and each $x_u$, it drops to 2. Here, some register-to-register moves can be inserted to permute 2 colors and, thanks to this, 3 registers are always enough for such a program. One can color independently the top (including the variables $y_u$) and the bottom (including the variables $x_v$), then place permutations between the definitions of $y_u$ and $x_u$. More precisely, for each block $B_{u,v}$ independently, color the definitions of $u$, $v$, and $x_{u,v}$ with 3 different colors, arbitrarily. For each block $B_u$, do the same for $u$, $x_u$, and $y_u$ (i.e., define 3 registers where $u$, $x_u$, and $y_u$ are supposed to be on block entry). In the block between $B_{u,v}$ and $B_u$, keep $u$ in the same register as for $B_{u,v}$, give to $x_u$ the same color it has in $B_u$ and store $y_u$ in a register not used by $u$ in $B_{u,v}$. So far, all variables are correctly colored except that some moves may be needed for the values $u$ and $y_u$, after the definition of $y_u$, and before their uses in $B_u$, if colors do not match. But, between the definitions of $y_u$ and $x_u$, only 2 registers contain a live value: one contains $u$ defined in $B_{u,v}$ and one contains $y_u$. These 2 values can thus be moved to the registers where they are supposed to be in $B_u$, with at most 3 moves in case of a swap, using the available register in which $x_u$ is going to be placed just after this shuffle.

## 4.1    Simultaneous Definitions

So, is it really NP-complete to decide if $k$ registers are enough when splitting can be done anywhere and swaps are not available? The problem with the previous construction is that there is no way, with simple statements, to avoid a program point with a low register pressure while keeping the reduction with graph 3-coloring. This is illustrated in Fig. 3: on the left, the previous situation with a register pressure drop to 2, in the middle, a situation with a constant register pressure equal to 3, but that does not keep the equivalence with graph 3-coloring. However, if instructions can define more than one value, it is easy to modify the proof. To define $x_u$ and $y_u$, use a statement $(x_u, y_u) = f(v, x_{u,v})$ that consumes $v$ and $x_{u,v}$ and produces $y_u$ and $x_u$ *simultaneously*, as depicted on the right of Fig. 3. Now, the register pressure is 3 everywhere in the program and thus $G$ is 3-colorable iff the program can be mapped to 3 registers (and, in this case, with no live-range splitting). Thus, it is NP-complete to decide if $k$ registers are enough *if two variables can be created simultaneously by a machine instruction* but swaps are not available, even if there is no critical edge and if we can split wherever we want. Such an instruction should consume at least 2 values, otherwise, the register pressure is

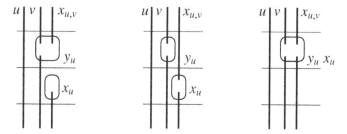

**Fig. 3.** Three cases: register pressure drops to 2 (on the left), is constant to 3 (middle and right)

lower just before and a permutation can be placed. Notice the similarity with circular-arc graphs: as mentioned in [16], coloring circular-arc graphs remains NP-complete even if at most 2 circular arcs start at any point (but not if only one can start).

Besides, if such machine instructions exist, it is likely that a register swap is also provided in the architecture (we discuss such architectural subtleties at the end of this section). In this case, we are back to the easy case where any permutation can be done and $k$ registers are enough iff Maxlive $\leq k$. Thus, it remains to consider only one case: what if *at most one* variable can be created at a given time as it is in traditional sequential assembly-level code representation and register swaps are not available?

### 4.2    At Most One Definition at a Time

If blocks can be introduced to split critical edges, if live-range splitting can be done anywhere and if instructions can define at most one variable, we claim it is polynomial to decide if $k$ registers are enough, in the case of a strict program. We proceed as follows.

The *register pressure* at a point is the number of variables live at this point; Maxlive is the maximal register pressure in the program. If Maxlive $> k$, it is not possible to assign the variables of a strict program to $k$ registers without spilling, as two simultaneously live variables interfere.[2] If Maxlive $< k$, it is always possible to assign variables to $k$ registers by splitting live-ranges and performing adequate permutations. The same occurs for a point with register pressure $< k$, as explained in Section 3: a color mismatch can always be repaired by an adequate permutation, thanks to an available register. Thus, for a strict program, the only problem may come from the sequences of program points where the register pressure remains equal to $k$. But, unlike Section 4.1 where the degree of freedom (at least 2) to choose colors leads to NP-completeness, here, the fact that at most *one* variable can be defined at a time simplifies the problem. It does not mean that $k$ registers are always enough, but it is easy to decide if this is the case. To explain this situation precisely, we need to define more formally what we mean by *color propagation*.

Liveness analysis defines, for each instruction $s$, *live_in(s)* and *live_out(s)*, the set of variables live just before and just after $s$. We color these sets locally, propagating the colors from instruction to instruction, i.e., coloring variables in neighbor sets with the same color, following the control-flow, possibly backwards or forwards, i.e., considering the

---

[2] Notice that it is not true for a *non-strict* program. We leave this case open.

control-flow as undirected. More formally, coloring a statement $s$ means defining two injective maps $col\_in(s)$ (resp. $col\_out(s)$) from $live\_in(s)$ (resp. $live\_out(s)$) to $[1..k]$. When we propagate colors from a statement $s_1$ to a statement $s_2$, forwards, we define $col\_in(s_2)$ so that $col\_in(s_2)(x) = col\_out(s_1)(x)$ for all $x \in live\_in(s_2) \cap live\_out(s_1)$ and we pick different colors for the other variables, arbitrarily. Then, we do the same to define $col\_out(s_2)$ from $col\_in(s_2)$. When we propagate backwards, the situation is symmetric; we define $col\_out(s_2)$ from $col\_in(s_1)$, then $col\_in(s_2)$ from $col\_out(s_2)$. Below, when we explain the effect of propagation, we assume the propagation is forwards; otherwise one just needs to exchange the suffixes "in" and "out".

We first restrict to the subgraph of the control-flow graph defined by the program points where the register pressure is equal to $k$, i.e., we only propagate between two instructions $s_1$ and $s_2$ such that both $live\_out(s_1)$ and $live\_in(s_2)$ have $k$ elements. We claim that, in each connected component of this graph, if $k$ registers are enough, there is a unique solution, up to a permutation of colors, except possibly for the sets $live\_out(s_2)$ where the propagation stops. Indeed, for each connected component, start from an arbitrary program point and an arbitrary coloring of the $k$ variables live at this point. Propagate this coloring, as defined above, backwards and forwards along the control flow until all points are reached. In this process, there is no ambiguity to choose a color. First, there is no choice for defining $col\_in(s_2)$ from $col\_out(s_1)$ as $live\_out(s_1) = live\_in(s_2)$: indeed they both have $k$ elements and, since there is no critical edge, either $live\_out(s_1) \subseteq live\_in(s_2)$ or the converse. Second, if $live\_out(s_2)$ has $k$ elements, then either $live\_out(s_2) = live\_in(s_2)$ or, as $s_2$ defines at most one variable, there is a unique variable in $live\_out(s_2) \setminus live\_in(s_2)$ and a unique variable in $live\_in(s_2) \setminus live\_out(s_2)$: they must have the same color. Thus, there is no choice for defining $col\_out(s_2)$ from $col\_in(s_2)$ either. Therefore, for each connected component, going backwards and forwards defines, if it exists, a *unique* solution up to the initial permutation of colors. In other words, if there is a solution, we can define it, for each connected component, by propagation. Moreover, if, during this traversal, we reach a program point already assigned and if the colors do not match, this *proves* that $k$ registers are not enough.

Finally, if the color propagation on each connected component is possible, then $k$ registers are enough for the whole program. Indeed, we can color the rest (with register pressure $< k$) in a greedy (but not unique) fashion. When we reach a point already assigned we can repair a possible color mismatch: we place an adequate permutation of colors between $s_1$ and $s_2$, in the same basic block as $s_1$ if $s_2$ is the only successor (resp. predecessor for backwards propagation) of $s_1$ or in the same basic block as $s_2$ if $s_1$ is the only predecessor (resp. successor) of $s_2$. This is always possible because there is no critical edge and there are at most $(k-1)$ live variables at this point. To summarize, to decide if $k$ registers suffice when Maxlive $\leq k$ (and color when possible), we first propagate colors, following the control flow, along program points where the register pressure is exactly $k$. If we reach a program point already colored and the colors do not match, more spilling needs to be done. Otherwise, we start a second propagation phase, along all remaining program points. If we reach a program point already colored and the colors do not match, we solve the problem with a permutation of at most $(k-1)$ registers, using an extra available register. We point out that we can also do the propagation in a unique phase, as long as we propagate in priority along points where the register pressure is exactly $k$. A work list can be used for this purpose.

### 4.3    Subtleties of the Architectures

To conclude this section, let us illustrate the impact of architectural subtleties with respect to the complexity cases just analyzed, when edge splitting is allowed. We consider the ST200 core family from STMicroelectronics, which was the target of this study.

As for many processors, some variables need to be assigned to specific registers: they are *precolored*. Such precoloring constraints do not change the complexity of deciding if some spilling is necessary. Indeed, when swaps are available, Maxlive $\leq k$ is still the condition to be able to color with $k$ registers as we can insert adequate permutations, possibly using swaps, when colors do not match the precolored constraints. Reducing these mismatches is a coalescing problem, as in a regular Chaitin-like approach. Now, consider the second polynomial case, i.e., when no register swap is available and instructions define at most one variable. Even with precolored constraints, a similar greedy approach can be used to decide, in polynomial time, if $k$ registers are enough. It just propagates colors from precolored variables, along program points with exactly $k$ live variables, i.e., with no freedom, so it is easy to check if colors match. A similar situation occurs when trying to exploit auto-increments $r_x$++, i.e., $r_x = r_x + 1$. An instruction $x$++ apparently prevents the coloring under SSA as $x$ is redefined, unless first rewritten as $y = x + 1$. A coalescer may then succeed in coloring $y$ and $x$ the same way. To enforce this coloring, one can also simply ignore this redefinition of $x$ and consider that the live-range of $x$ goes through the instruction, as a larger SSA-like live-range.

The possible NP-complete cases are due to the fact that register swaps are not available and that some machine instructions can define more than one variable. In the ST200 core family, two types of instruction can create more than one variable: the function calls that can have up to 8 results and the 64 bits load operations that load a 64 bits value into two 32 bits registers. For a function call, the constraint Maxlive $\leq k$ needs to be refined. Spilling must be done so that the number of live variables at the call, excluding parameters and results, is less than the number of callee-save registers. In the ST200, the set of registers used for the results is a *strict* subset of the set of caller-save registers. Thus, just after the call and before the possible reloads of caller-saved registers, at least one caller-save register is available to permute colors if needed. The situation is similar before the call, reasoning with parameters. Therefore, function calls do not make the problem NP-complete, even if they can have more than one result. Also, if no caller-save register was available, as results of function calls are in general precolored, this situation could also be solved as previously explained. What about 64 bits loads, such as $r_x, r_y = \text{load}(r_z)$? Such a load instruction has only one argument on the ST200. So, if the number of live variables is $k$ after defining $r_x$ and $r_y$, it is $< k$ just before, so a permutation can be done if needed. We can ensure that $r_x$ and $r_y$ are consecutive thanks to a permutation just before the load to make two successive registers available. Thus, again, despite the fact that such an instruction has two results, it does not make the problem NP-complete because it has only one variable argument.

Finally, even if no swap operation is available in the instruction set, a swap can be simulated thanks to the parallelism available in the ST200 core family. In the compiler infrastructure, one needs to work with a pseudo-operation swap $R_x, R_y = \text{swap}(R_i, R_j)$, which will then be replaced by two parallel operations scheduled in the same cycle: $R_x = \text{move}(R_i)$ and $R_y = \text{move}(Rj)$. Also, for integer registers, another possibility to swap without an additional register is to use the instruction XOR. In conclusion, when edge splitting is allowed, even if one needs to pay attention to architectural subtleties, the NP-complete cases where deciding if some spilling is necessary seem to be quite artificial. In practice, swaps can usually be done and one just has to check Maxlive $\leq k$. If not, one can rely on a greedy coloring, propagating only along program points where the register pressure is $k$. Instructions with more than one result could make this greedy coloring non deterministic (and the problem NP-complete) but, fortunately, at least for the ST200, these instructions have a neighbor point (just before or just after) with $< k$ live variables. Thus, it is in general easy to decide if some spilling is necessary or if, at the price of additional register-to-register moves, the code can be assigned to $k$ registers.

## 5  Conclusion

In this paper, we tried to clarify where the complexity of register allocation comes from. Our goal was to recall what Chaitin et al's original proof really proves and to extend this result. The main question addressed by Chaitin et al. is of the following type: Can we decide if $k$ registers are enough for a given program or if some spilling is necessary?

### 5.1  Summary of Results

The original proof of Chaitin et al. [9] proves that this problem is NP-complete when live-range splitting is not allowed, i.e., if each variable can be assigned to only one register. We showed that the same construction proves more: the problem remains NP-complete when live-range splitting is allowed but not (critical) edge splitting.

Recently, Pereira and Palsberg [26] proved that, if the program is a simple loop, the problem is NP-complete if live-range splitting is allowed but only on a block on the back edge and register swaps are not available. This is a particular form of register allocation through SSA. The problem is NP-complete if $k$ is a problem input. We showed that Chaitin et al's proof can be extended to show a bit more. When register swaps are not available, the problem is NP-complete for a fixed $k \geq 3$ (but for a general control-flow graph), even if the program has no critical edge and if live-range splitting can be done on any control-flow edge, i.e., on entry and exit of blocks, but not inside basic blocks.

These results do not address the general case where live-range splitting can be done anywhere, including *inside* basic blocks. We showed that the problem remains NP-complete only if some instructions can define two variables at the same time but register swaps are not available. Such a situation might not be so common in practice. For a strict program, we can answer the remaining cases in polynomial time. If Maxlive $= k$ and register swaps are available, or if Maxlive $< k$, then $k$ registers are enough. If register swaps are not available and at most one variable can be defined at a given program point, then a simple greedy approach can be used to decide if $k$ registers are enough.

This study shows that the NP-completeness of register allocation is *not* due to the coloring phase, as may suggest a misinterpretation of the reduction of Chaitin et al. from graph $k$-coloring. If live-range splitting is taken into account, deciding if $k$ registers are enough or if some spilling is necessary is not as hard as one might think. The NP-completeness of register allocation is due to three factors: the presence of critical edges or not, the optimization of spilling costs (if $k$ registers are not enough) and of coalescing costs, i.e., which live-ranges should be fused while keeping the graph $k$-colorable.

## 5.2   Research Directions

What does such a study imply for the developments of register allocation strategies? Most approaches decide to spill because their coloring technique fails to color the live-ranges of the program. But, for coloring, a heuristic is used and this may generate some useless spills. Our study shows that, instead of using an *approximation heuristic* to decide when to spill, we can use an *exact algorithm* to spill only when necessary. Such a test is fundamental to develop register allocation schemes where the spilling phase is decoupled from the coloring/coalescing phase, i.e., when one considers better to avoid spilling at the price of register-to-register moves. However, we point out that this "test", which is, roughly speaking, to make sure that Maxlive $\leq k$, does not indicate which variables should be spilled and where the store/load operations should be placed to get an optimal code in terms of spill cost (if not execution time). Optimal spilling is a much more complex problem, even for basic blocks [22,14], for which several heuristics, as well as an exact integer linear programming approach [1], have been proposed.

Existing register allocators give satisfying results, when measured *on average* for a large set of benchmarks. However, for some applications, when the register pressure is high, we noticed some possible improvements in terms of spill cost. In Chaitin's first approach, when all variables interfere with at least $k$ other variables, one of them is selected to be spilled and the process iterates. We measured, with a benchmark suite from STMicroelectronics, that such a strategy produces many *useless* spills, i.e., a variable such that, after spilling all chosen variables except this one, Maxlive is still less than $k$. A similar fact was noticed by Briggs et al. [4] who decided to delay the spill decision to the coloring phase. If a potential spill does not get a color during the coloring phase, it is marked as an *actual spill*, else it is useless. This strategy significantly reduces the number of useless spills compared to Chaitin's initial approach. Other improvements include biased coloring, which in general reduces the number of actual spills, or conservative/iterated register coalescing [17], as coalescing can reduce the number of neighbors of a vertex in the interference graph.

We applied a very simple strategy in our preliminary experiments: in the set of variables selected for spilling, we choose the most expensive useless spill and remove it from the set. We repeat this process until no useless spill remains. This simple additional check is enough to reduce the spill cost of Chaitin's initial approach to the same order of magnitude as a biased iterated register coalescing. Also, even for a biased iterated register coalescing, this strategy still detects some useless spills and can improve the spill cost. With this more precise view of necessary spills, one can also avoid the successive spilling phases needed for a RISC machine: for a RISC machine, a spilled live-range leaves small live-ranges to perform the reloads, and a Chaitin-like approach needs to iterate. With an exact criterion for spilling needs, we can take into account the new live-ranges to measure Maxlive and decide if more spilling is necessary at once.

Once spilling is done, variables still have to be assigned to registers. The test "Is some spilling necessary?" does not really give a coloring. For example, if swaps are available, the test is simply Maxlive $\leq k$. One still needs to ensure that coloring with Maxlive registers is possible. A possibility is to split all critical edges and to color in polynomial time with Maxlive colors, possibly inserting color permutations. The extreme way to do so is to color independently each program point, whose corresponding interference graph is a clique of at most Maxlive variables, and to insert a permutation between any two points. This amounts to split live-ranges everywhere, as done in [1]. Such a strategy leads to a valid $k$-coloring but of course with an unacceptable number of moves. This can be improved thanks to coalescing, although it is in general NP-complete [3]. As there are many moves to remove, possibly with tricky structures, a conservative approach does not work well, and an optimistic coalescing seems preferable [24,1]. Another way is to color independently each basic block, with Maxlive colors, after renaming each variable so that it is defined only once. This will save all moves inside the blocks. Then permutations between blocks can be improved by coalescing. One can try to extend the basic blocks to larger regions, while keeping them easy to color. This is the approach of fusion-based register allocation [23], except that the spilling decision test is Chaitin's test, thus a heuristic that can generate useless spills. One can also go through SSA, color in polynomial time, and place adequate permutations. This will save all moves along the dominance tree, but this may not be the best way because this can create split points with many moves. A better way seems a) to design a cost model for permutation placement and edge splitting, b) to choose low-frequency potential split points to place permutations, and c) to color the graph with a coalescing-coloring algorithm, splitting points – and thus live-ranges – on the fly when necessary. In the worse case, the splitting will lead to a tree (but not necessarily the dominance tree) for which one can be sure that coloring with Maxlive registers is possible. The cost of moves can be further reduced by coalescing and permutation motion.

Designing and implementing such a coloring mechanism has still to be done in details. How to spill remains also a fundamental issue. Finally, it is also possible that a too tight spilling, with many points with $k$ live variables, severely limits the coalescing mechanism. In this case, it is maybe better to spill a bit more so as to balance the spill cost and the move cost. Such tradeoffs need to be evaluated with experiments before concluding. The same is true for edge splitting versus spilling, but possibly with less importance, as splitting an edge does not always imply introducing a jump.

## Acknowledgments

The authors would like to thank Philip Brisk, Keith Cooper, Benoît Dupont de Dinechin, Jeanne Ferrante, Daniel Grund, Sebastian Hack, Jens Palsberg, and Fernando Pereira, for interesting discussions on SSA form and register allocation.

## References

1. A. W. Appel and L. George. Optimal spilling for CISC machines with few registers. In *Proceedings of PLDI'01*, pages 243–253, Snowbird, Utah, USA, June 2001. ACM Press.
2. F. Bouchez, A. Darte, C. Guillon, and F. Rastello. Register allocation and spill complexity under SSA. Technical Report RR2005-33, LIP, ENS-Lyon, France, Aug. 2005.

3. F. Bouchez, A. Darte, C. Guillon, and F. Rastello. On the complexity of register coalescing. Technical Report RR2006-15, LIP, ENS-Lyon, France, Apr. 2006.
4. P. Briggs, K. Cooper, and L. Torczon. Improvements to graph coloring register allocation. *ACM Transactions on Programming Languages and Systems*, 16(3):428–455, May 1994.
5. P. Briggs, K. D. Cooper, T. J. Harvey, and L. T. Simpson. Practical improvements to the construction and destruction of static single assignment form. *Software: Practice and Experience*, 28(8):859–881, 1998.
6. P. Brisk, F. Dabiri, J. Macbeth, and M. Sarrafzadeh. Polynomial time graph coloring register allocation. In *14th International Workshop on Logic and Synthesis*, June 2005.
7. Z. Budimlić, K. Cooper, T. Harvey, K. Kennedy, T. Oberg, and S. Reeves. Fast copy coalescing and live range identification. In *Proc. of PLDI'02*, pages 25–32, 2002. ACM Press.
8. G. J. Chaitin. Register allocation & spilling via graph coloring. In *Proceedings of Compiler Construction (CC'82)*, volume 17(6) of *SIGPLAN Notices*, pages 98–105, 1982.
9. G. J. Chaitin, M. A. Auslander, A. K. Chandra, J. Cocke, M. E. Hopkins, and P. W. Markstein. Register allocation via coloring. *Computer Languages*, 6:47–57, Jan. 1981.
10. K. D. Cooper and L. T. Simpson. Live range splitting in a graph coloring register allocator. In *Proceedings of Compiler Construction (CC'98)*, volume 1383 of *LNCS*, pages 174–187. Springer Verlag, 1998.
11. R. Cytron and J. Ferrante. What's in a name? Or the value of renaming for parallelism detection and storage allocation. In *Proceedings of the 1987 International Conference on Parallel Processing*, pages 19–27. IEEE Computer Society Press, Aug. 1987.
12. R. Cytron, J. Ferrante, B. Rosen, M. Wegman, and K. Zadeck. Efficiently computing static single assignment form and the control dependence graph. *ACM Transactions on Programming Languages and Systems*, 13(4):451–490, 1991.
13. A. Darte and F. Rastello. Personal communication with Benoît Dupont de Dinechin, Jeanne Ferrante, and Christophe Guillon, 2002.
14. M. Farach-Colton and V. Liberatore. On local register allocation. *Journal of Algorithms*, 37(1):37–65, 2000.
15. M. R. Garey and D. S. Johnson. *Computers and Intractability: A Guide to the Theory of NP-Completeness*. W. H. Freeman and Company, 1979.
16. M. R. Garey, D. S. Johnson, G. L. Miller, and C. H. Papadimitriou. The complexity of coloring circular arcs and chords. *SIAM J. of Algebr. Discrete Methods*, 1(2):216–227, 1980.
17. L. George and A. W. Appel. Iterated register coalescing. *ACM Transactions on Programming Languages and Systems*, 18(3):300–324, May 1996.
18. M. C. Golumbic. *Algorithmic Graph Theory and Perfect Graphs*. Academic Press, New York, 1980.
19. S. Hack, D. Grund, and G. Goos. Register allocation for programs in SSA-form. In *Proceedings of Compiler Construction (CC'06)*, volume 3923 of *LNCS*. Springer Verlag, 2006.
20. K. Knobe and K. Zadeck. Register allocation using control trees. Technical Report No. CS-92-13, Brown University, 1992.
21. A. Leung and L. George. Static single assignment form for machine code. In *Proceedings of PLDI'99*, pages 204–214. ACM Press, 1999.
22. V. Liberatore, M. Farach-Colton, and U. Kremer. Evaluation of algorithms for local register allocation. In *Proceedings of Compiler Construction (CC'99)*, volume 1575 of *LNCS*, pages 137–152, Amsterdam, 1999. Springer Verlag.
23. G.-Y. Lueh, T. Gross, and A.-R. Adl-Tabatabai. Fusion-based register allocation. *ACM Transactions on Programming Languages and Systems*, 22(3):431–470, 2000.
24. J. Park and S.-M. Moon. Optimistic register coalescing. In *Proceedings of PACT'98*, pages 196–204. IEEE Press, 1998.
25. F. M. Q. Pereira and J. Palsberg. Register allocation via coloring of chordal graphs. In *Proceedings of APLAS'05*, pages 315–329, Tsukuba, Japan, Nov. 2005.

26. F. M. Q. Pereira and J. Palsberg. Register allocation after classical SSA elimination is NP-complete. In *Proceedings of FOSSACS'06*, Vienna, Austria, Mar. 2006.

27. F. Rastello, F. de Ferrière, and C. Guillon. Optimizing translation out of SSA using renaming constraints. In *Proceedings of CGO'04*, pages 265–278. IEEE Computer Society, 2004.

28. V. C. Sreedhar, R. D. Ju, D. M. Gillies, and V. Santhanam. Translating out of static single assignment form. In A. Cortesi and G. Filé, editors, *Proceedings of the 6th International Symposium on Static Analysis*, volume 1694 of *LNCS*, pages 194–210. Springer Verlag, 1999.

# Custom Memory Allocation for Free[*]

Alin Jula and Lawrence Rauchwerger

Texas A&M University , College Station, Texas
alinj@cs.tamu.edu, rwerger@cs.tamu.edu

**Abstract.** We present a novel and efficient container-centric memory allocator, named *Defero*, which allows a container to guide the allocation of its elements. The guidance is supported by the semantic-rich context of containers in which a new element is inserted. Defero allocates based on two attributes: size and location. Our policy of allocating a new object *close* to a related object often results in significantly increased memory reference locality. Defero has been integrated to work seamlessly with the C++ Standard Template Library (STL) containers. The communication between containers and the memory allocator is very simple and insures portability. STL container modification is the only needed code change to achieve custom memory allocation. We present experimental results that show the performance improvements that can be obtained by using Defero as a custom allocator for STL applications. We have applied our memory allocator to the molecular dynamics and compiler applications and obtained significant performance improvements over using the standard GNU STL allocator. With our approach custom memory allocation has been achieved without any modification of the actual applications, i.e., without additional programming efforts.

## 1 Introduction

Memory allocation is performed from various information-rich contexts, such as containers, libraries, and domain specific applications. Yet, traditional allocation schemes do not use the semantic information present in these rich contexts, but rather allocate memory based only on the *size* of the request. For example, to solve the spatial data locality for dynamically allocated memory, we need to analyze the memory based on its *location*, not its size. Data locality cannot be solved based on size only. Thus, we need better memory allocation to improve data locality.

This paper studies how memory allocation automatically benefits from the knowledge present in the STL containers, and how this knowledge gets communicated from the containers to the memory allocator, in order to increase containers' data locality.

Data locality has been given a great deal of attention. Compiler techniques offer a plethora of optimizations, such as tiling, register allocation, and field reorganization, which increase data locality for regular data structures [27,7,6]. However, compiler analysis is less effective for dynamic data structures. The intrinsic dynamic property of these structures inhibits the analysis. This is because the information necessary to

* This research supported in part by NSF Grants EIA-0103742, ACR-0081510, ACR-0113971, CCR-0113974, EIA-9810937, ACI-0326350, and by the DOE Office of Science.

G. Almási, C. Caşcaval, and P. Wu (Eds.): LCPC 2006, LNCS 4382, pp. 299–313, 2007.

perform the optimization is not available at compile time, but it becomes available only at run time as the program executes.

We present a novel and efficient container-centric memory allocator, named *Defero*[1], which allows a container to guide the allocation of its elements. The guidance is supported by the semantic-rich context in which a new element is inserted, by suggesting where to allocate each element. The communication between containers and the memory allocator allows Defero to automatically increase data locality for containers.

We integrated Defero to work automatically with the C++ Standard Template Library (STL) containers [12]. The integration yielded improvements in data locality for applications that use STL. Applications benefit from the performance improvement provided by Defero while maintaining their portability, without having to design a custom memory allocator. Thus, applications can get the best of both worlds: the improved performance of custom memory allocation and the hassle-free portability of general memory allocation.

This paper makes the following contributions:

- *A container-centric memory allocation with a simple interface* which guides the allocation process. It allows users or compilers to easily specify various memory allocation policies at the container instantiation level.
- *Allocation based on multiple attributes.* Defero allocates based on 'size' and 'location' . The policy of allocating a new object *close*(in memory space) to a related object (hinted by the user or compiler) results in improved memory reference locality. This approach also minimizes the external fragmentation.
- *An adjustable memory scheme, K-Bit*, which allows data locality to be controlled with a simple number. We also present a novel allocation predicate, named Path, which increases data locality for balanced trees.

We present experimental results from various areas, such as molecular dynamics, network simulation, and compilers, as well as micro-kernels.

The remainder of the paper is organized as follows. Defero's design and implementation, along with examples are presented in Section 2. Several allocation policies are discussed in Section 3, while Section 4 reasons upon the criteria used to select a certain allocation scheme. Defero's automatic interaction with containers, as well as its integration in libraries is described in Section 5. Experimental results are described in Section 6, and Section 7 discusses related work. Conclusions are presented in Section 8.

## 2   Defero Memory Allocator

Memory allocation schemes fall into two main categories. On one end of the spectrum, a large number of memory allocation schemes use a *general* memory allocation policy for all applications. These policies are memory allocation centric, in which the focus is on memory allocation alone. They are rigid and do not adapt to the application's needs, and therefore are not optimal. On the other end of the spectrum, *custom* allocation schemes are tailored to specific applications. These schemes are application-centric, in

---

[1] In Latin, *defero* means *"to hand over, carry down, communicate, offer, refer"*.

which the focus is on that specific application's memory allocation alone. They have a tremendous impact on performance, but they are not portable.

Defero is different. It is *container-centric*, which means that containers guide the memory allocation. Containers collect their specific semantic information and pass it to Defero. Based on this information, Defero guides the allocation and deallocation routines. Therefore, Defero communicates with applications through their containers.

The result of container-centric memory allocation is a custom memory allocation policy nested into each container. It has the performance advantage of custom memory allocation, without its portability disadvantage. Defero can be integrated in STL, and thus the portability is shifted from the application, to STL. Applications need not change a single line of code to take advantage of the customized allocation scheme provided by STL containers. Defero, thus, provides custom memory allocation for free. Section 5 provides more details on Defero integration into applications.

### 2.1  Design

**Memory Partition.** We now present how Defero partitions the memory and how it manages its free chunks. Defero regards all its free memory chunks as an algebraic space of memory addresses. Defero properly partitions this address space into *equivalence classes*, based on an *equivalence relation*. An example of such an equivalence relation is "congruent to modulo 5" between integers.

This generic space partitioning based on an equivalence relation provides flexibility in the way Defero manages its free memory chunks. Because of its flexibility, previous allocation policies can also be implemented with our design. Consider the segregated lists approach, first described by Weinstock in [24]. It manages small object classes, for example up to 128 byte-objects, rounded up to a multiple of 8. All objects of a certain size are kept together in a linked list. The segregated lists partition can be expressed as an equivalence relation in Defero: let x and y be memory addresses, then $x \equiv y$ if $(size(x) \geq 128 \wedge size(y) \geq 128)$ or $(\lfloor \frac{size(x)}{8} \rfloor = \lfloor \frac{size(y)}{8} \rfloor)$ otherwise.

New partitions can also be created using this generic space partition. In this paper we analyze a new equivalence relation, named *K-Bit*, which improves data locality. K-Bit is defined as: if x and y are memory addresses, they are equivalent iff the first K higher-order bits are the same. K-Bit partition keeps the memory organized in groups of addresses where the first K bits are identical. The K-Bit partition results in $2^K$ groups, each with a maximum size of $2^{32-K}$. This is an invariant throughout the whole program execution. At any point in the program execution, regardless of the deallocation pattern or distribution, the memory is organized into classes of available contiguous chunks. This property is not true for traditional allocators, since out-of-order deallocations violate this invariant. K-Bit ensures that even the most complicated allocation patterns will not affect Defero's memory organization.

The K parameter is adjustable. Assuming a 32-bit system and a virtual page size of $2^K$ bytes, the equivalence classes coincide with the system's virtual pages. With the appropriate K, memory can also be partitioned in cache lines.

Defero orders these equivalence classes based on an *order predicate*, which allows equivalence classes to be compared against each other. An example is the trivial order predicate $'less' = '\leq'$, which orders the K-Bit equivalence classes based on the first K bits. Equivalence and order predicates are traits associated with memory management. The user can select the equivalence and order predicates or use the defaults provided by Defero. The equivalence classes are ordered, thus searchable, by virtue of having an order predicate.

**Allocation Predicate.** We can now focus on searching the memory partition. The idea behind flexible space partitioning is to facilitate the allocation/deallocation process. An *allocation predicate* stores a target equivalence class, with the intention of allocating a memory chunk from that specific equivalence class. The allocation predicate has two critical pieces of information: (i) a target class, the equivalence class from which the memory chunk is allocated, and (ii) a search algorithm, which describes how to find that specific equivalence class. The allocation's searching algorithm is implemented as a ternary predicate:(i) 0 for found; 'I found it, stop searching', (ii)-1 for moving left ; 'I need a smaller one' and (iii) 1 for moving right ; 'I need a bigger one'. This binary search guides the searching process among the ordered equivalence classes.

Defero's generic interface allows users to select their own memory partition and allocation predicate. This flexibility allows different containers to have different allocation policies within the same application.

## 2.2   Implementation

While other equivalence relations can be easily integrated in Defero, the focus of this article is on K-Bit equivalence relation. We analyze K-bit partitioning and K's impact on memory allocation. We define *K-class* as the equivalence class which contains all the memory address that have the same K first bits. In the remainder of the paper we will use the term K-class as an equivalence class instance, without loss of generality.

Now that we have the generic framework, we can proceed to concrete instantiations. Defero organizes its memory in a 2-dimensional space. The first dimension is based on 'size' and is partitioned using the segregated-lists approach. The second dimension is the 'address' , and is partitioned using K-Bit. Consequently Defero sees the memory as a 2-dimensional space, with 'size' and 'address' as orthogonal dimensions.

The first dimension, 'size', is organized in segregated classes. The benefit of segregated size classes is that they generally work well on a large class of applications. We followed the SGI STL allocator guidelines for the size dimension [17]. All free chunks of a certain size are partitioned and ordered according to the K-Bit partition. This design benefits from the empirically proven segregated lists approach, while it also allows for a custom partition of the memory space. Fig. 1(a) shows Defero's implementation where each size class has its own K-Bit partition.

The second dimension, 'address', is organized by the K-Bit partition. Defero organizes the K-classes of K-Bit partition into an ordered red-black balanced tree, based on the order predicate. A node in the tree represents a K-class, and all of the elements in the same K-class are stored in a linked list. Fig. 1(b) depicts the K-Bit's organization.

The allocation process selects a free chunk of memory from a 2-dimensional memory space. The allocation takes into consideration both dimensions. The first dimension selects size, and the second dimension selects locality. Allocation based on 'size' is performed using the traditional segregated-lists allocation, where the size of the memory request determines the appropriate entry into the hash table. It then selects a K-class

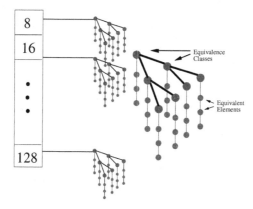

**Fig. 1.** (a) K-Bit organization (b) Defero's internal structure

within this tree, based on the allocation predicate. A memory chunk from the selected K-class is returned as the allocated memory.

To improve locality, the allocation searches for the 'closest' available address to a *hint* address. This hint address is automatically provided by the container semantics. For example, an element to be inserted at the back of a list, can be allocated near the tail, which is the hint address. This information is not known at compile time, and only the container has that information at run-time. If the K-class of the hint address is found, then an equivalent address from that class is returned. There is no guarantee which one, only that the returned address is equivalent with the hint address. Otherwise, the 'closest' K-class is considered, according to the order predicate, and an element from this class is returned.

Upon deallocation, the memory address is returned to its designated K-class. If its K-class exists in the tree, then the address is inserted in the K-class linked list, otherwise, a new tree node is inserted in the tree.

The allocation complexity depends on two variables: the allocation predicate and the number of K-classes in the tree. The deallocation complexity depends only on the number of K-classes in the tree. Both allocation and deallocation complexities are $O(K)$.

**Examples.** *Defero*'s interface is similar to the STL allocator interface. The STL allocator accepts the size of the memory request as input parameter, along with an optional hint address [12]. Defero generalizes the hint address to an allocation predicate. In Section 3 we show how the allocation predicate can hold a hint address or address distribution information. The deallocation interface remains unchanged. Fig. 2 shows an example of how Defero is used. Lines 1-2 show allocation with different predicates, while lines 3-4 show different container instances using different allocation predicates.

It is worth noting that the selection and modification of an allocation policy, can be done with only few lines of code. Users can easily experiment with different policies. Different architectures and containers can benefit from specific memory partitions and allocation predicates. Defero's generic interface allows for an easy selection of these salient attributes.

```
        // Allocate 4 bytes with First predicate
1. int * y= defero :: allocate (4, First (0));
        // Allocate z near x, or the closest
2. int * z= defero :: allocate (4, Best(x));
        // List with Defero(K–Bit, First)
3. list <int, defero <int, Kbit<12>, less <int > >, First > my_smart_list_1;
        // List with Defero(K–Bit, Best)
4. list <int, defero <int, Kbit<12>, less <int > >, Best > my_smart_list_2;
```

**Fig. 2.** Example of Defero using Equivalence, Order and Allocation Predicates

## 3  Allocation Predicates

In this section we describe two existing allocation predicates and introduce a novel one, named *Path*. We describe each individual one and then discuss the advantages and disadvantages when combining them with K-Bit partition.

**First** allocation predicate selects the K-class situated at the root of the tree. If the root class has elements, it returns the first element in the list, otherwise, it returns the root. First guarantees consecutive allocations from the same K-class, regardless of the allocation pattern. Thus, First favors programs which exhibit *temporal locality*. The allocation complexity is O(1) amortized, and deallocation complexity is O($K$).

**Best** allocation predicate takes a hint address and returns the closest available address to this hint address. It is a binary search performed on a tree, with the key as hint address. If the hint address's K-class is found in the tree, an equivalent address is returned, else an element from the closest K-class is returned. Best can be described as a best match fit with regard to address location.

Best exploits *spatial locality*, by attempting to allocate objects close to each other. Best favors irregular allocation patterns by explicitly ensuring spatial locality. The closeness metric is dictated by K. The allocation/deallocation complexity is O($K$).

**Path** is a novel allocation predicate designed to improve locality for sorted tree containers. Balanced trees perform rebalancing operations that modify the structure of the tree and hurt the spatial locality. An example is the red-black trees with its *rotate left* and *rotate right* rebalancing operations. The Path allocation predicate attempts to solve the spatial locality problem introduced by the rebalancing operations. When an element is inserted in a tree, a top-down search is performed. The search path is recorded as a series of bits: 0 for visiting the left sub-tree and 1 for visiting the right sub-tree. Path then allocates elements with similar paths together, since it is very likely they will end up in the same part of the tree. The complexity of Path is O(K).

The idea behind Path is that low values should be allocated together and high values should be allocated together, regardless of the order in which they were inserted in the tree. Values that create similar paths are allocated together, since they are likely to be to be close in the tree. The tree passes the path to the allocator, and the allocator follows this path in its own top down tree search. Path maps values to addresses. Elements that have approximately the same value are allocated together, thus likely to be accessed together. Intuitively, it makes sense to allocate together the elements which are logically grouped by the application. The allocation process follows a given path into the K-Bit

**Table 1.** Strengths and weaknesses of allocation predicates with K-Bit

| K-Bit with ⇒ | First | Best | Path |
|---|---|---|---|
| Advantage | + Temporal Locality<br>+ Fast | + Spatial Locality<br>+ Container aware<br>+ Worst case allocation pattern | + Logical Locality<br>+ Container aware |
| Disadvantage | - Not container aware | - Slower | - Slower |

searching tree. This allows for directing the allocation requests toward a certain part of the tree. In Table 1 we summarize the strengths and weaknesses for each allocation predicate when used with K-Bit.

# 4   Selecting K

In this section we characterize and discuss the dynamic property of containers and how it helps in selecting an optimal K. We start by asking how dynamic is a container? The answer depends on how the application operates the container. Assuming we know the operations applied on the container by the application, we now quantify the dynamic property of containers. First, we classify the types of operations on a container into two categories: (i) *modifying* (M) operations, such as insertion or deletion and (ii) *non-modifying*(NM) operations, such as traversals or element access[2]. M operations stress the memory allocator, while NM operations stress the locality of the container.

Next, we define the **dynamism** of a container as a measurable metric which represents the percentage of modifying operations in the total operations:

$$D = \frac{M}{NM + M} * 100, withD \in (0, 100), M \geq 1, NM \geq 1 \tag{1}$$[3]

Intuitively, the dynamism describes the rate of change in a data structure. The more often it changes, the higher the dynamism. The dynamism of the container is highly correlated with memory behavior. The higher the dynamism, the more important the speed of the memory allocation becomes, while data locality diminishes in its importance. The lower the dynamism, the more important locality is, while memory allocation's speed becomes less dominant.

K is an adjustable parameter. It varies between 0 and the size of the pointer, 32 or 64 depending of the system. On one end, when K is the size of the pointer, each memory chunk is its own K-class. In this case the equivalence relation is the classic equal predicate '='. On the other end, when K is 0, all memory chunks are equivalent, and there is only one K-class in the tree, the whole memory. Therefore, K dictates the ratio between trees' and lists' sizes and the number of K- classes it creates.

To reduce the allocation overhead, one might consider either reducing K to obtain fewer K-classes, or choosing an allocation predicate that selects faster, like First. To

---

[2] Modifying can be regarded as Write operations and Non-Modifying as Read operations.

[3] Each container has at least 1 M operation, the creation of that container. Every container has at least 1 NM operation. If it didn't have one, it meant that that container was never accessed by the program and thus would be dead code.

increase data locality, one might consider either increasing K for a better refinement of the space or choosing an allocation predicate that selects better, like Best.

Therefore, high values of K speed up NM operations, but slow down M operations. Low values of K reverse the trend. Selecting K is dictated by the application needs. A highly dynamic container requires a low K, and vice-versa. Low K though does not help locality, and a high K does not allocate fast. For each application there is a "sweet spot" for which these two antagonistic characteristics are balanced.

## 5   Integration of Defero with STL

The advantage of integrating Defero with STL is knowing the information rich context from where memory is allocated. The container allocates its elements and is the perfect candidate to provide allocation guidelines to its elements' allocation. Defero allows the communication of this semantic context to the allocation policy.

We integrated Defero into the C++ STL. The library provides various generic data containers, such as lists, sets, and trees. STL container's modular design made Defero's integration easy. For list-like containers, traversals imply a linear order of their elements. Elements in these containers find themselves in a partial order. Because of this intrinsic invariant property, the best place to allocate a new element to improve locality, is in the proximity of its neighbors. This neighbor(s) context is passed to the allocation predicate, which is then passed to the allocation routine.

For tree-like containers, insertion is based on the new element's value, a run-time variable. This insertion context is more complex than the list's. One can think of several allocation predicates that increase locality: allocation close to the parent, allocation close to the sibling, allocation based on the value distribution, etc.

Each container can benefit from selecting its own allocation predicate by providing the best allocator for the application. Applications use theses STL containers, without the knowledge of their allocators. Consequently, Defero keeps the application portable and thus provides custom memory allocation for free.

## 6   Experimental Results

We tested Defero using several dynamic applications from various areas, such as compiler infrastructure, molecular dynamic, network simulation, as well as in-house microkernels. These applications use STL containers. Defero integration effort was minimal. The integration required the inclusion of the modified STL in the include path of the compilation command. We did not modify the applications.

We conducted the experimental results on a Intel(R) Xeon(TM) 3.00 GHz, 1GB memory, using GNU C++ compiler $g$++ version 3.3.6, with -O3 level of optimization.

We compared Defero against Doug Lea's allocator (DL), the GNU STL allocator [17]. The DL allocator uses a size-segregated approach, and boundary tags. This allocator is considered the best overall memory allocator [14,15]. Berger et al. [2] show that it competes with custom memory allocators, and sometimes even outperforms them. The GNU STL allocator is a segregated list allocator, with first fit policy and no coalescing. This allocator was based on a SGI implementation. We set the GNU STL allocator as our base allocator because of its portability and ubiquity. It is worth noting that the difference between the GNU STL allocator and Defero is exactly the K-Bit partition. Consequently, any improvement over the GNU STL allocator is solely attributed to K-Bit partition with allocation predicates.

Defero, DL and GNU STL allocators used exactly the same amount of memory for all applications analyzed in this paper. The minimum memory request was 12 bytes, which was rounded up by the GNU STL allocator to 16 bytes, while Defero requires a memory chunk threshold of at least 16 bytes, the same threshold as the one required by DL.

### 6.1   Micro-kernels

**Lists.** For this experiment we created a list of one million random integers. The memory was warmed up by allocating two millions integers and then we randomly erased one million, in order to simulate a real scenario where the application randomly allocates and deallocates objects. We then created a list of elements alternating *push_back* and *push_front* methods. We then invoked two STL algorithms: list's own *sort* and *for_each* with incrementing the elements as the called function. All measurements are relative to the native GNU STL allocator.

Fig. 3 (a) shows the list creation. Defero improves data locality which eventually reduces the execution time. Fig. 3 (b) shows the list deletion. Best performs almost 2 times faster than First and 3.5 times faster that DL allocator. Fig. 3 (c) shows the STL foreach algorithm. A higher precision of the partition implies an improved the locality. Best reduces the execution time by almost 90% and it is 9 times faster than the DL allocator. Fig. 3 (d) shows the execution time of the list's sorting algorithm.

The experimental results corroborate our hypothesis: high locality precisions favor traversal operations, such as for_each, sort, at the expense of modifying operations, such

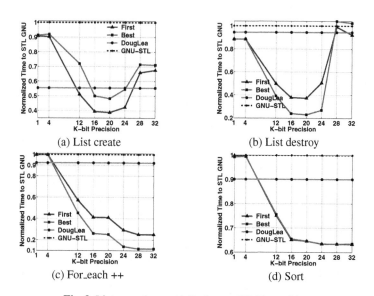

(a) List create          (b) List destroy

(c) For_each ++          (d) Sort

**Fig. 3.** List operations with Defero and K-bit partition

as insert and clear. The sweet spot is determined by the ratio of these two operations. For traversals, the Best allocation predicate performs two times better than First, but First is faster for modifying operations.

**Trees.** In this experiment the memory was warmed up in a similar fashion as in the list experiment. An STL tree with nine million integers was allocated and then three million elements were randomly erased. We then created an STL red-black tree of three million random integers. Then each key was randomly selected and searched in the tree. We then applied a for_each algorithm, after which the tree was destroyed.

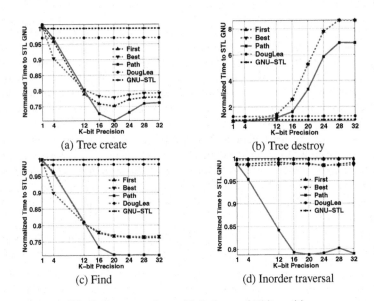

(a) Tree create

(b) Tree destroy

(c) Find

(d) Inorder traversal

**Fig. 4.** Tree operations with Defero and Kbit partition

Fig. 4 (a) and (b) show the tree creation operation. Defero with Path improves the execution time by 30% over GNU STL allocator and 25% over the DL allocator. Fig. 4 (b) shows the tree deletion which observed a slow-down. The inorder traversal is not substantially sped up to compensate for the extra memory management involved in deallocation. Fig. 4 (c) shows three million top-down traversals performed by *find* operation. Defero with Path improves the execution time by 28% over the GNU STL and 25% over the DL allocator. Fig. 4 (d) shows the for_each algorithm. While Defero with Best and First did almost the same as DL and the GNU STL allocators, Defero with Path improved the execution time by 20% over all of them.

These experiments show that specialized allocation predicates benefit different containers. For example Path works best for trees, while First and Best work best for lists.

While we do not expect real applications to exhibit such improvements, these algorithms and operations are the basic blocks of each application. Understanding the impact of memory allocation on these basic yet fundamental, algorithms, is important for a better understanding of real applications.

## 6.2 Applications

In order to evaluate our technique in a realistic setting we have applied it to two real and very dynamic programs, a molecular dynamics code and a compiler. In Table 2 we list the benchmarks and their pertinent characteristics, such as inputs used, the size (number of lines of code), their execution time, total memory allocated, maximum memory used, number of allocation and deallocation performed, and the average size of the memory allocation requests.

**Table 2.** Benchmarks General Characteristics

| Application | Input | Code size (lines) | Exec. Time (sec) | Total (MB) | Max Mem (MB) | Alloc/Dealloc (Mil) | Avg. Size (bytes) |
|---|---|---|---|---|---|---|---|
| MD | 7000 particles | 1800 | 88.32 | 167.34 | 14.68 | 13.9 / 12.7 | 12 |
| Polaris | Spec89, Perfect | 600,000 | 300 | 128.921 | 18.977 | 3.9 / 3.7 | 32.73 |

**Table 3.** Benchmarks Containers Characterization

| Applications | Containers | #Containers | Total Op. (Mil) | # NM (Mil) | # M (Mil) | Dynamism |
|---|---|---|---|---|---|---|
| MD | list,tree | 6,912 | 551.46 | 524.75 | 13.93 / 12.78 | 2.58 |
| Polaris | list | - | 27.47 | 18.75 | 3.93 / 3.78 | 17.15 |

In Table 3 we show the characteristics of the data containers used by these benchmarks, such as their numbers, type, total number of operations they perfrom. "Interesting" properties such as the number of non-modifying operations and modifying operations, along with the average dynamism of the containers are also displayed here.

**Molecular Dynamics.** The code we have used for our experiment was written by Danny Rintoul from Sandia National Laboratories. The application fully utilizes STL containers, such as lists and trees and STL algorithms such as for_each, sort. It is a classical molecular dynamics code that computes the molecule interactions at every time step.

Fig. 5(a) shows the normalized execution time of the whole application. While the DL allocator reduces the execution time by 22%, Defero comes in very close. Defero

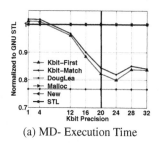
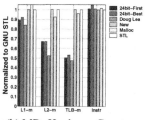

(a) MD- Execution Time    (b) MD- Hardware Counters

**Fig. 5.** Molecular Dynamics

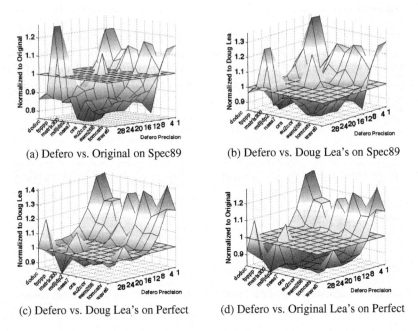

(a) Defero vs. Original on Spec89    (b) Defero vs. Doug Lea's on Spec89

(c) Defero vs. Doug Lea's on Perfect    (d) Defero vs. Original Lea's on Perfect

**Fig. 6.** Execution time of Polaris with Defero vs. Original and DL allocator

with First improves by 20%, and Defero with Best by 18%. Fig. 5(b) shows a comparison of five hardware counters : L1, L2, TLB misses and Issued Instructions. These hardware counters were collected for the following memory partitions and allocation policies: 24-bit with First, 24-bit with Best, DL, native 'new' and native 'malloc'. The vertical line in figure 5(a) represents K=20, the system's native virtual page partition.

Molecular dynamics is a discrete event simulation. In between time steps, the application releases its memory to the system, only to allocate it again in the next step. This behavior benefits the DL allocator, which reduces external fragmentation by coalescing.

**Polaris** is a Fortran restructuring compiler [22]. At its core, the most used container is a list similar to an STL list which stores various semantic entities, such as statements, expressions, constants, etc. We used Defero as the underlying memory allocator for these lists. The algorithms that we used in Polaris are compiler passes that perform program transformations, such as forward substitution, removing multiple subprogram entries, fixing type mismatches, etc.

We ran Polaris with inputs from Perfect and Spec 89 benchmarks. For each input we varied the K from 0 to 32. Fig. 6(a) and 6(b) show the performance of Polaris using Defero with First relative to the original memory allocation. First outperformed Best with Polaris. In the figures, anything below the plane is faster and anything above is slower. There is up to 22% improvement relative to the original implementation. Fig. 6(c) and 6(d) show a relative improvement of up to 12% over the DL allocator.

It is worth noting the consistency in improving execution time across all inputs of the two benchmarks. Almost all inputs exhibit the same pattern with respect to K's variance. For the Spec 89 input, the average improvements are 15% over the original and 10% over the DL allocator. For the Perfect input the average improvements are 10% over the original and 5% over the DL allocator.

In summary, Defero improves data locality, especially large applications with complex allocation patterns. Defero increases data the temporal or spatial locality through the use of the specified allocation predicates. The Best allocation predicate improves spatial locality, while First improves the temporal one. Different containers can benefit from different allocation predicates. For example, the Path allocation predicate encapsulates the semantic structure of the tree and helps improving tree locality. Path is specific to balanced trees while lists may benefit more from First or Best policies.

# 7   Related Work

There has been a significant amount of work related to memory allocation and its customization. This section will present only the research that is strictly related to *Defero*.

Lattner and Adve [13] developed a compiler technique to identify logical data structures in the program. Once a data structure has been identified, its elements are allocated in a designated memory pool. Defero works at the library level, thus it already has the rich information environment, without compiler support. Chilimbi et al. in [5] investigated the idea of cache-conscious data structures. They present two tools for improving cache locality for dynamic data structures, namely *ccmorph* and *ccmalloc*. Chilimbi's tools are not available[4], so we could not empirically compare them against Defero. Nonetheless, Defero works automatically with containers, while Chilimbi's tools are semi-automated and require programmer intervention and hardware knowledge about the system. Ccmorph works only with static trees that do not change once created, while Defero does not impose this restriction. On the contrary, Defero offers several policies that benefit different dynamic behaviors.

HeapLayers [3] is an infrastructure for building memory allocators. Unfortunately we could not use HeapLayers since Defero's design requires a generic template allocation scheme, a generic template memory partition, and a new allocation interface. Huang et al. [11] used the Jikes RVM adaptive compiler to sample the methods used by the program at run-time, and when they become "hot", they get compiled. This approach increases data locality by profiling at garbage time, while Defero improves locality through semantics at allocation time.

Grunwald et al. [10] profile the performance of five memory allocation schemes (first-fit, gnu g++, BSD, gnu local, quick-fit) and conclude that efforts to reduce memory utilization, such as coalescing adjacent free blocks, will increase both the execution time and reduce program reference locality. Barret and Zorn [1] show that 90% of all bytes allocated are short-lived. Short-lived and long-lived objects are placed in separate arenas, implicitly increasing locality. Shuf et al. [18] show that prolific type objects can benefit from allocating them together, since they tend to be related and short-lived.

Seidl and Zorn [16] present an algorithm for predicting heap object reference and lifetime behavior at the allocation time. Calder et al. [4] present a profile driven compiler technique for data placement (stack, global, heap and constants) in order to reduce data cache misses. Grunwald and Zorn [9] present a custom memory allocator based on

---

[4] Personal communication with the author.

profiling. Users profile an application, and based of the object sizes the application uses, customalloc creates segregated lists with the frequently used class sizes.

Doug Lea's allocator, DL, uses boundary tags in its implementation and a size-segregation organization [14,15]. Boundary tags allow for quick coalescing, which improves data locality. Defero does coalescing at allocation, explicitly through the allocation predicate, while DL does coalescing at deallocation using boundary tags.

Gay and Aiken [8] study region based memory management. A pseudo region-based allocation is supported by Defero implicitly as a K-class region with the locality advantage. There are other memory allocation schemes worth mentioning which attempt to improve performance by speed [23] or by padding [21].

# 8   Conclusions

We presented Defero, a container-centric memory allocator, which allows high level semantic information present in the allocation context to be communicated to the memory allocator. Defero is automatically integrated in STL, thus applications need not change a single line of code. The approach provides custom memory allocation for free, i.e., without programmer intervention.

Defero's generic interface allows users to select their own partition and allocation policy, thus making Defero highly tunable. We analyzed a novel and adjustable K-Bit memory scheme. K-Bit performs best when it is virtual page aware and partitions its space into pages. We explored several allocation policies on several applications. We show that containers benefit from specialized allocation predicates. We propose a novel allocation predicate named Path, which produces better locality for balanced trees. It outperforms First and Best allocation predicates, and even Doug Lea's allocator. For list containers, First and Best produce the best locality improvement.

# References

1. Barret, D., Zorn, B.: . Using Lifetime Predictors to Improve Memory Allocation Performance. ACM SIGPLAN PLDI, Albuquerque, NM, 1993.
2. Berger, E., Zorn, B., McKinley, K.: Reconsidering Custom Memory Allocation. ACM OOPSLA, Seattle, WA, 2002.
3. Berger, E., Zorn, B., McKinley, K.: Composing High-Performance Memory Allocators. ACM SIGPLAN PLDI, Snowbird, UT, 2001.
4. Calder, B., Krintz, C., John, S., Austin, T.: Cache-Conscious Data Placement. ACM ASPLOS, San Jose, CA, 1998.
5. Chilimbi, T., Davidson, B., Larus, J.: Cache-conscious structure definition. ACM SIGPLAN PLDI, Atlanta, GA, 1999.
6. Chilimbi, T., Hill, M., Larus, J.: Cache-conscious structure layout. ACM SIGPLAN PLDI, Atlanta, GA, 1999.
7. Ding, C., Kennedy, K.: Improving cache performance in dynamic applications through data and computation reorganization at run time. ACM SIGPLAN PLDI, Atlanta, GA, 1999.
8. Gay, D., Aiken, A.: Memory Management with Explicit Regions. ACM SIGPLAN PLDI, Montreal, Canada, 1998.
9. Grunwald, D., Zorn, B.: CustoMalloc: Efficient Synthesized Memory Allocators. Technical Report CU-CS-602-92, Dept. of Computer Science, Univ. of Colorado, Boulder, CO 1992.

10. Grunwald, D., Zorn, B., Henderson, R.: Improving the Cache Locality of Memory Allocation. ACM SIGPLAN PLDI, Albuquerque, NM 1993.
11. Huang, X., Blackburn, S., McKinley, K., Moss, J., Wang, Z., Cheng, P.: The garbage collection advantage: improving program locality. ACM OOPSLA, Vancouver, BC, Canada 2004.
12. International Standard ISO/IEC 14882. 1998. Programming Languages C++. 1st edn.
13. Lattner, C., Adve, V. Automatic Pool Allocation: improving performance by controlling Data Structure Layout in the Heap. ACM SIGPLAN PLDI, Chicago, IL 2005.
14. Lea, D.: Some storage management techniques for container classes. The C++ Report *http://g.oswego.edu/pub/ papers/C++Report89.txt* 1990
15. Lea, D.: A memory allocator. Unix/Mail, Hanser Verlag *http://gee.cs.oswego.edu/dl/html/malloc.html* 1996.
16. Seidl, M., Zorn, B.: Segregating Heap Objects by Reference Behavior and Lifetime. ACM SIGPLAN PLDI, San Jose, CA, 1998.
17. SGI: SGI STL Allocator Design. *http://www.sgi.com/tech/stl/alloc.html*
18. Shuf, Y., Gupta, M., Franke, H., Appel, A., Singh, J.: Creating and Preserving Locality of Java Applications at Allocation and Garbage Collection Times. ACM OOPSLA, Seattle, WA, 2002.
19. Standish, T.: Data Structures Techniques. Addison-Wesley Press 1980.
20. Tofte, M., Talpin, J.: Region-Based Memory Management. Symposium on Principles of Programming Languages, Portland, OR 1994.
21. Truong, D., Bodin, F., Seznec, A.: Improving cache behavior of dynamically allocated data structures. Int. C. on Parallel Architectures and Compilation Techniques, Paris, 1998.
22. W. Blume, *et. al.* Advanced Program Restructuring for High-Performance Computers with Polaris. *IEEE Computer*, 2912:78–82, 1996.
23. Vo, K.: Vmalloc: A General and Efficient Memory Allocator. Software Practice Experience, 263, 1996, 357-374.
24. Weinstock, C.: Dynamic Storage Allocation Techniques. Doctoral dissertation, Carnegie-Mellon University, Pittsburgh, April 1976
25. Wilson, P., Johnstone, M., Neely, M., Boles, D.: Dynamic storage allocation: A survey and critical review. Int. Workshop on Memory Management, Kinross, UK, 1995.
26. Wolf, M., Lam, M.: A Data Locality Optimizing Algorithm. ACM SIGPLAN PLDI, Toronto, Canada, 1991.
27. Wolfe, M.: Iteration Space Tiling for Memory Hierarchies. SIAM Conf. on Parallel Processing for Scientific Computing, Los Angeles, CA, 1987.

# Optimizing the Use of Static Buffers for DMA on a CELL Chip

Tong Chen, Zehra Sura, Kathryn O'Brien, and John K. O'Brien

IBM T.J. Watson Research Center, Yorktown Heights, NY 10598
{chentong,zsura,kmob,caomhin}@us.ibm.com

**Abstract.** The CELL architecture has one Power Processor Element (PPE) core, and eight Synergistic Processor Element (SPE) cores that have a distinct instruction set architecture of their own. The PPE core accesses memory via a traditional caching mechanism, but each SPE core can only access memory via a small 256K software-controlled local store. The PPE cache and SPE local stores are connected to each other and main memory via a high bandwidth bus. Software is responsible for all data transfers to and from the SPE local stores. To hide the high latency of DMA transfers, data may be prefetched into SPE local stores using loop blocking transformations and static buffers. We find that the performance of an application can vary depending on the size of the buffers used, and whether a single-, double-, or triple-buffer scheme is used. Constrained by the limited space available for data buffers in the SPE local store, we want to choose the optimal buffering scheme for a given space budget. Also, we want to be able to determine the optimal buffer size for a given scheme, such that using a larger buffer size results in negligible performance improvement. We develop a model to automatically infer these parameters for static buffering, taking into account the DMA latency and transfer rates, and the amount of computation in the application loop being targeted. We test the accuracy of our prediction model using a research prototype compiler developed on top of the IBM XL compiler infrastructure.

## 1 Introduction

The design of computing systems is trending towards the use of multiple processing units working collaboratively to execute a given application, with communication interfaces that enable high bandwidth data transfers between the processor and memory elements of the system. The CELL architecture[4] is one example of such a system, primarily designed to accelerate the execution of media and streaming applications. It includes two kinds of processing cores on the same chip: a general-purpose Power Processor Element (PPE) core that supports the Power instruction set architecture, and eight Synergistic Processor Element (SPE) cores that are based on a new SIMD processor design[3].

G. Almási, C. Cașcaval, and P. Wu (Eds.): LCPC 2006, LNCS 4382, pp. 314–329, 2007.

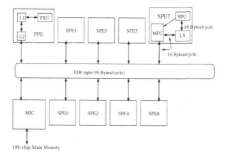

**Fig. 1.** The CELL Architecture

## 1.1  CELL Architecture

Figure 1 shows the elements of the CELL architecture and the on-chip data paths that are relevant to the discussion in this paper. The PPE includes the Power Execution Unit (PXU) that accesses main memory via its L1 and L2 caches. Each SPE includes a Synergistic Processor Unit (SPU), a Local Store (LS), and a Memory Flow Controller (MFC). Load/store instructions executed on an SPU can only load from and store to locations in the LS of that SPE. If an SPU needs to access main memory or the LS of another SPE, it must execute code that will issue a DMA command to its MFC explicitly instructing the MFC to transfer data to or from its LS. All the SPE local stores, the PPE's L2 cache, and the Memory Interface Controller (MIC) that provides access to the off-chip main memory, are inter-connected via a high bandwidth (16 Bytes/cycle on each link) Element Interconnect Bus (EIB). It is possible for a DMA transaction on the EIB that involves the LS of one SPE to be initiated by another SPU or by the PXU. However, the code transformations discussed in this paper only involve DMA transactions between main memory and an SPE LS that have been initiated by the corresponding SPU.

The hardware architecture maintains coherence between copies of data in the main memory, data in the PPE caches, and data being transferred on the EIB. However, the hardware does not keep track of copies of data residing in an LS, and software is responsible for coherence of this data. Each LS is a small 256KB memory that is completely managed in software. It contains both the code and data used in SPU execution. The latency of DMA operations between an LS and main memory is quite high, approximately in the order of 100-200 SPU cycles[11]. However, for consecutive DMA operations, it is possible to overlap the latency for the second operation with the DMA transfer of the first, as the MFC can process and queue multiple DMA requests before they are issued to the EIB.

## 1.2  DMA Buffering

The example code in Figure 2(a) shows a loop that iterates N times, and in each iteration it loads the $i^{th}$ element of array A, multiplies this value by a scalar

```
/* A and B are in main memory */
/* S is a scalar residing in LS */

for (i=0; i<N; i++) {
    B[i] = A[i] * S;
}
```
**(a) Example Code**

```
/* S, tA, and tB reside in LS */

for (i=0; i<N; i++) {
    DMA get A[i] to tA;
    tB = tA * S;
    DMA put tB to B[i];
}
```
**(b) Naive Buffering**

```
for (ii=0; ii<N; ii+=bf) {
    n = min(ii+bf, N);
    DMA get A[ii:n] to tA;
    for (i=ii; i<n; i++) {
        tB[i] = tA[i] * S;
    }
    DMA put tB to B[ii:n];
}
```
**(c) Single Buffering**

```
/* Uses non-blocking DMA */

t=0; /* Decides buffer 1 or buffer 2 */
n = min(bf, N);
DMA get A[0:n] to tA[t], tag=t;
t = (t+1) % 2;

for (ii=0; ii<N; ii+=bf) {
    n = min(ii+bf, N);
    m = min(ii+2*bf, N);
    DMA get A[ii+bf:m] to tA[t], tag=t;
    t = (t+1) % 2;
    DMA wait, tag=t;

    for (i=ii; i<n; i++) {
        tB[t][i] = tA[t][i] * S;
    }

    DMA put tB[t] to B[ii:n], tag=t;
}
DMA wait, tag=t;
```
**(d) Double Buffering**

**Fig. 2.** Example to Illustrate DMA Buffering

S, and stores the result in the $i^{th}$ element of array B. If this code is targeted to execute on an SPE, the elements of A and B must be located in the LS for the SPU to be able to operate on them. However, A and B maybe allocated in main memory, perhaps because they are also being accessed by other cores, or because they are too large to fit in the limited LS space. In this case, the code is modified to include DMA operations to *get* elements of A into a temporary buffer tA in the LS, and *put* elements of B from a temporary buffer tB in the LS to main memory, as illustrated in Figure 2(b). Since the latency of DMA transfers is high, it is more efficient to transfer multiple array elements in a single DMA operation, effectively pre-fetching data for computation. Figure 2(c) shows how the example code is transformed to do this by blocking the loop using a blocking factor of *bf*, buffers tA and tB of size equivalent to *bf* array elements instead of a single array element, and one DMA get and one DMA put operation per iteration of the outer blocked loop.

The problem with the code in Figure 2(c) is that it allows no overlap between DMA transfer time and SPU computation time. Each instance of the inner blocked loop must wait for the preceding DMA get operation to complete before the inner loop can execute. This restriction can be overcome using a double-buffer scheme, as illustrated in Figure 2(d). Instead of using one *bf*-element buffer for each array data stream, the code uses two such buffers for each data stream. Before the SPU starts computing with the data fetched in one buffer, it initiates a DMA transfer using the other buffer to get data that will be used in the next iteration of the outer blocked loop. This transformation requires that there be no loop-carried flow dependencies among the iterations within one instance of the inner blocked loop. The DMA operations used are non-blocking versions, and they are tagged with an integer identifying the LS buffer being used in the DMA transfer. The SPU can continue execution of the inner blocked loop while a DMA transfer is in progress. To wait for specific DMA operation(s) to complete, the code calls a DMA wait function with the tag corresponding to a previously issued DMA operation passed as a parameter.

The double-buffer scheme can be extended to use $k$ buffers for each data stream to increase the amount of DMA that is overlapped with the computation in one instance of the inner blocked loop.

## 1.3   Problem Description

Execution time of a loop blocked for DMA buffering varies with the amount of DMA overlapped with computation. For a $k$-buffer scheme, the amount of DMA overlap increases both with the value of $k$, and with the size of the buffers used. In the SPE, all the buffers occupy space in the LS, which is only 256KB in size. This limited LS space is a prime resource, since it is being used for both code and data, and the available space limits the applicability of optimizations that increase code size or require more space to buffer data. Due to the LS size constraint, a restricted amount of space is available for DMA buffering.

The problem we address in this paper is that given a budget for the amount of space to be used for DMA buffering, determine the buffering scheme that will result in the best execution time performance. Since the total buffer size is fixed, performance of a $k$-buffer scheme needs to be compared with the performance of a $(k+1)$-buffer scheme that uses individual buffers of a size smaller than the buffers used in the $k$-buffer scheme. Once the optimal buffering scheme is known, it may be the case that all possible DMA overlap is attained using a buffer size smaller than the maximum buffer size allowed by the total buffer space budget. Note that there is a limit to how much performance can be improved using DMA overlap before the application becomes computation-bound. Thus, we want to determine both the optimal buffering scheme and the smallest buffer size that maximize performance, when constrained by the total buffer space available.

We find that the performance of DMA buffering depends on several factors, including the set-up time for each DMA operation, the DMA transfer time, the amount of computation in the loop, the number of buffers being used, and the size of each individual buffer. We develop a model to relate each of these factors to the execution time, and use this model to predict the relative merit of using different buffering schemes and different buffer sizes. Also, we obtain performance numbers for a small set of applications running on a CELL chip using single-, double-, and triple-buffer, and various buffer sizes. We correlate the experimental data with our model. Our experiments are restricted to consider only the innermost loop in a loop nest, where this loop operates on a number of array data streams, has a large iteration count, has no loop-carried dependences, and has no conditional branches within the loop body.

In Section 2, we develop the model used to predict performance for a given buffering scheme. In Section 3, we describe how the model can be used to determine the optimal buffering scheme and buffer size in a compiler transformation for static buffering. In Section 4, we describe the experiments we performed to validate our model against actual performance data. We discuss related work in Section 5, and conclude in Section 6.

# 2   Modeling Buffering Schemes

## 2.1   Assumptions

We assume that a loop is a candidate for DMA buffering optimization if it satisfies the following conditions:

- The loop operates on array data streams. The buffering optimizations considered are not interesting for scalar data, or data accessed through unpredictable indirect references.
- There are no loop-carried dependences between accesses to elements of the array data streams. This enables the loop to be transformed for any $k$-buffer scheme since the DMA get and put operations can be freely moved out of the inner blocked loop.
- There is no conditional branch statement within the loop body. This is important to be able to accurately gauge the amount of computation in the loop body, which is one of the factors that determines relative performance of different buffering schemes.
- Elements in the array data streams that are accessed in consecutive loop iterations are contiguous in memory, or not spaced too far apart. This is to ensure that when buffers are used to DMA contiguous memory locations in a single operation, the majority of the data being transferred is in fact useful.
- DMA buffers are assigned such that each buffer is only used for a single array data stream, and no buffer is used in both DMA get and put operations. This is a conservative assumption to ensure that a DMA operation on one buffer does not have to wait for a DMA operation on another buffer to complete.
- The loop iteration count is large enough that any prologue or epilogue generated when the loop is blocked has a negligible impact on performance.
- The array data streams are aligned on 128-byte boundaries, and this alignment is known at compile-time. If this is not the case, then code has to be generated to explicitly check alignment at runtime, and to issue DMA operations such that misaligned data is correctly handled. This changes the DMA set-up time, which is one of the factors used to determine the relative performance of different buffering schemes.

## 2.2   Latency of DMA Operations

We approximate the latency of one DMA operation with the formula $S + D * b$, where $S$ is the set-up time for one DMA operation, $D$ is the transfer time for one byte, and $b$ is the number of bytes transferred by this DMA operation.

When two non-blocking DMA operations for $b_1$ and $b_2$ bytes are issued in sequence, the set-up of the second DMA operation can be overlapped with the

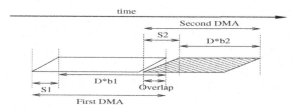

**Fig. 3.** Latency of DMA Operations

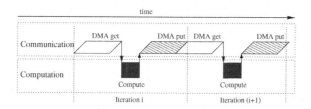

**Fig. 4.** Execution Sequence for Single-Buffer

data transfer of the first, as illustrated in Figure 3. When the set-up of the second DMA operation ($S_2$) is less than or equal to the set-up of the first DMA operation ($S_1$), it can be completely overlapped. In this case, the combined latency of the two DMA operations will be $S_1 + D * (b_1 + b_2)$. For different values of $S_1$ and $S_2$, the amount of overlap of set-up time with transfer time will be different.

In the CELL architecture, the value of $S$ is different for DMA get and put operations[11]. The DMA get operation has a higher value of $S$ because it includes the main memory access time to retrieve data, whereas a DMA put can complete before data is actually written to its main memory location.

In general, a sequence of $n$ DMA transfers will have latency $S+D*(b_1+...+b_n)$, where $S$ is a function of $S_1, ..., S_n$.

### 2.3 Latency for Single-Buffer

Figure 4 illustrates the execution sequence for the code in Figure 2(c). Ignoring the prologue and epilogue, and clubbing together consecutive DMA operations, each iteration of the outer blocked loop comprises of a DMA put corresponding to the previous iteration, a DMA get to fetch data for the current iteration, and the computation of one instance of the entire inner blocked loop. Note that non-blocking DMA operations can be used, with a DMA wait inserted just before the inner blocked loop. Thus, the latency of one iteration of the outer blocked loop is the latency of both the DMA transfers plus the computation latency of the inner blocked loop. Let $N$ be the iteration count of the original loop, and assume the loop has been blocked using a blocking factor of $bf$. Let $D_1$ be the DMA transfer time for one byte, $b$ be the number of bytes transferred in all DMA operations corresponding to one iteration of the outer blocked loop, and $S$ be the

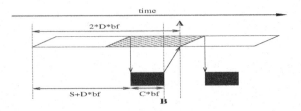

**Fig. 5.** Execution Sequence for DMA-bound Double-Buffer

composite set-up time for the sequence of non-blocking DMA operations corresponding to one iteration of the outer blocked loop. Also, let $C$ be the computation time for one iteration of the inner blocked loop. The value for C is expressed as $(C_{inner} + C_{outer}/bf)$, where $C_{inner}$ is the compute time for each iteration of the inner blocked loop, and $C_{outer}$ is the overhead for issuing DMA requests in an iteration of the outer blocked loop. This overhead primarily includes the function call and runtime checking overhead in compiler-generated code for DMA transfer requests, and it gets amortized over $bf$ iterations of the inner blocked loop. In practice, we expect $C_{outer}$ to be small, and $bf$ to be large, so that $C$ can be approximated by $C_{inner}$. The total latency of the entire loop is given by: $((S + D_1 * b * bf) + C * bf) * (N/bf) = (S/bf + D_1 * b + C) * N$ For simplicity, let $D = D_1 * b$ be the DMA transfer time for all data accessed in one iteration of the inner blocked loop. Thus, latency for single-buffer is $(S/bf + D + C) * N$.

## 2.4 Latency for Double-Buffer

In the following discussion, the terms $N$, $bf$, $C$, $S$, and $D$ have the same meaning as in the single-buffer case discussed earlier. For clarity, the following examples refer to DMA for one pair of buffers. However, the discussion also applies to examples using a set of double buffers, with $S$ corresponding to the set-up delay for a composite sequence of non-blocking DMA operations issued for each set.

**Case 1: DMA-Bound.** Figure 5 illustrates the case when double-buffer is used and the application is DMA-bound. In this case, there is no delay between any two successive DMA operations. The sequence of DMA operations and computations alternate between using the first buffer and the second buffer. The first and second DMA operations are issued successively before any computation begins. The third DMA operation is issued only after the first computation of the inner blocked loop finishes. If there is to be no delay between the second and third DMA operations, then the time to complete the first computation (point B in the figure) must be less than or equal to the time to complete the first two DMA operations (point A in the figure). This translates to the condition:

$$(S + D * bf + C * bf) \leq (2 * D * bf), \quad \text{or} \quad D \geq (C + S/bf)$$

When this condition holds, the execution pattern repeats throughout the loop and the application is DMA-bound. The latency for the entire loop is

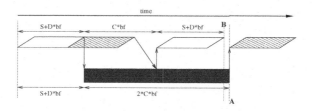

**Fig. 6.** Execution Sequence for Computation-bound Double-Buffer

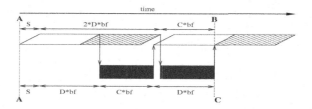

**Fig. 7.** Execution Sequence for Double-Buffer When $C \leq D < (C + S/bf)$

approximated by the time taken by all the consecutive DMA operations, i.e. $S + D * N$. When $N$ is large, this can be simplified to $D * N$.

**Case 2: Computation-Bound.** Figure 6 illustrates the case when double-buffer is used and the application is computation-bound. In this case, there is no delay waiting for DMA to complete between any two successive computations of the inner blocked loop. The sequence of DMA operations and computations alternate between using the first buffer and the second buffer. The first and second DMA operations are issued successively before any computation begins. The third DMA operation is issued only after the first computation of the inner blocked loop finishes. If there is to be no delay between the second and third computations, then the time to complete the third DMA operation (point B in the figure) must be less than or equal to the time to complete the first two computations (point A in the figure). This translates to the condition:

$$(S + D * bf + C * bf + S + D * bf) \leq (S + D * bf + 2 * C * bf), \text{ or } D \leq (C - S/bf)$$

When this condition holds, the execution pattern repeats throughout the loop, and the application is computation-bound. The latency for the entire loop is approximated by the time taken by all the consecutive computations, i.e. $C * N$, when $N$ is large.

**Case 3: Incomplete Overlap.** A loop that is neither DMA-bound nor computation-bound has incomplete overlap of DMA operations with computation. We analyze this case by splitting it into two sub-cases: when $C \leq D < (C + S/bf)$, and when $(C - S/bf) < D < C$. The total latency of the loop in both cases is the same: $(S/bf + D + C) * N/2$.

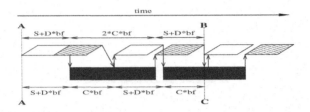

**Fig. 8.** Execution Sequence for Double-Buffer When $(C - S/bf) < D < C$

**Case A: When** $C \leq D < (C + S/bf)$: Figure 7 illustrates this case. Here, the set-up of the third DMA operation is not fully overlapped with the second DMA transfer. Also, there is a delay between the first and second computation, waiting for the second DMA transfer to complete. The second computation finishes at point B in the figure, and it can only start after the second DMA transfer has completed. From the beginning (point A in the figure), the latency for the second computation to finish is $S + 2 * D * bf + C * bf$. From a DMA point of view, the earliest that the fourth DMA operation can start is after the third DMA transfer reaches point C. The third DMA transfer can start only after the first computation finishes. The latency from point A in this case is $S + D * bf + C * bf + D * bf$. The two latencies from A to B and A to C are the same, which means that the fourth DMA starts at the same point that the second computation finishes, and the execution repeats the pattern illustrated in the figure. The delay between the second and third DMA operations is $S + D * bf + C * bf - 2 * D * bf = S + (C - D) * bf$. The total latency of the loop is the latency of all DMA transfers plus the extra delays due to incomplete overlap that occur after every two DMA operations. This latency is given by:

$$N * D + (S + (C - D) * bf) * N/bf/2 = (S/bf + D + C) * N/2.$$

**Case B: When** $(C - S/bf) < D < C$: Figure 8 illustrates this case. Here, the set-up of the third DMA operation is not overlapped with the second DMA transfer. Also, there is no delay between the first and second computation, but there is a delay between the second and third computation, waiting for the third DMA transfer to complete. The data for the fourth computation will be ready at point B in the figure, made available only after the first DMA transfer, the first two computations, and the fourth DMA transfer have completed. From the beginning (point A in the figure), the latency for the fourth DMA transfer to complete is $S + D * bf + 2 * C * bf + S + D * bf$. From a computation point of view, the third computation will finish at point C in the figure, and it can start only after the third DMA transfer completes. The third DMA can start only after the first computation finishes. The latency from point A in this case is $S + D * bf + C * bf + S + D * bf + C * bf$. The two latencies from A to B and A to C are the same, which means that the fourth DMA completes at the same point that the third computation finishes, and the execution repeats the pattern illustrated in the figure. The delay between the second and third computations is $S + D * bf - C * bf = S + (D - C) * bf$. The total latency of the loop is the latency of all computations plus the extra delays due to incomplete overlap that occur after every two computations. This latency is given by:

$$N * C + (S + (D - C) * bf) * N/bf/2 = (S/bf + D + C) * N/2.$$

### 2.5   Latency for $k$-Buffer

**Case 1: DMA-Bound.** Analogous to the case of double-buffer, we can derive the condition for a $k$-buffered loop to be DMA-bound, i.e. if the first computation finishes and starts up the $(k+1)$th DMA operation in time less than or equal to the time it takes to transfer data for $k$ DMA operations. This condition evaluates to $D \geq (C + S/bf)/(k-1)$. The initial pattern repeats throughout the loop when $D > C$. Thus, the loop is DMA-bound when $D \geq max(C, (C + S/bf)/(k - 1))$. The latency of the entire loop is approximated by $D * N$.

**Case 2: Computation-Bound.** Analogous to the case of double-buffer, we can derive the condition for a $k$-buffered loop to be computation-bound, i.e. if the DMA transfer corresponding to the $(k + 1)$th computation finishes in time less than or equal to the time it takes to complete the first $k$ computations occuring consecutively one after another, without any intervening delays due to DMA waits. This condition evaluates to $D \leq (k - 1) * C - S/bf$. The initial pattern repeats throughout the loop execution when $D < C$. Thus, the loop is computation-bound when $D \leq min(C, (k - 1) * C - S/bf)$. The latency of the entire loop is approximated by $C * N$.

**Case 3: Incomplete Overlap.** Analogous to the case of double-buffer, the latency of a $k$-buffered loop that is neither DMA-bound nor computation-bound is $(S/bf + C + D) * N/k$. We do not discuss details of this case here.

## 3   Compiler Analysis

In this section, we describe how the latency formulae derived in Section 2 can be applied to determine the optimal buffering scheme and buffer size for a loop with limited amount of memory available for buffer space. We expect that the algorithm described here will be used in a compiler that automatically transforms code for DMA buffering. In the following discussion, we restrict the choice of buffering schemes to single-, double-, or triple-buffer.

Assume that the amount of memory available for buffering is specified in terms of the largest block factor (say B) that can be used when transforming the loop for a single-buffer scheme[1]. Then the maximum block factor for double-buffer is B/2, and for triple-buffer is B/3.

The performance of a loop will be optimal if it is computation-bound or DMA-bound. Therefore, a DMA-bound double-buffered loop (latency $D * N$) or

---

[1] Therefore, in the case of single-buffer, the actual size of an individual buffer will be B times the size of an array element.

```
Algorithm: bool Choose_Double_Buffer (C, D, S, B) {

    float C: the computation per iteration;
    float D: the DMA transfer time per iteration;
    float S: the set-up latency for DMA;
    int B: buffer space constraint in terms of the maximum
          block factor used in a single-buffering scheme;

    if (D > C) {
        if (S/(D-C) <= B/2)
            return TRUE;
    } else if (D < C) {
        if (S/(C-D) <= B/2)
            return TRUE;
    }

    return FALSE;
}
```

**Fig. 9.** Algorithm to Choose Between Double- and Triple-Buffer Schemes

a computation-bound double-buffered loop (latency $C * N$) should be better than a single-buffered loop (latency $(S/B + D + C) * N$). When the double-buffered loop has incomplete overlap, its latency will be $(S/B/2 + D + C) * N/2$. In this case, the difference between the latencies of double-buffer and single-buffer is $(D + C) * N/2 > 0$. So double-buffer should always outperform single-buffer.

The algorithm in Figure 9 shows how to choose between double-buffer and triple-buffer. When the same performance can be achieved by different buffering schemes, the scheme with less number of buffers is preferred. When $D > C$, the double-buffer scheme becomes DMA-bound when $D \geq C + S/B/2$, which is the same as $S/(D - C) \leq B/2$. In this case, we choose the double-buffer scheme since it is DMA-bound and optimal. Similarly, when $D < C$, the double-buffer scheme becomes computation-bound for $D \leq C - S/B/2$, which is the same as $S/(C-D) \leq B/2$, and we choose the double-buffer scheme. In all other cases, we choose the triple-buffer scheme since it can provide a greater amount of overlap.

Once the loop becomes DMA-bound or computation-bound, performance will not improve with increasing buffer sizes. In such cases, memory resources can be saved by choosing the smallest buffer size that is optimal. The memory space saved can then be used by other components contending for it, e.g. more local memory can be assigned to the outer blocked loops to increase data re-use, or the size of code buffers can be increased to reduce the frequency of swapping code partitions to and from the SPE LS. Based on the conditions derived in Section 2 for the execution to be DMA-bound or computation-bound, the block factor for double-buffer need not be larger than $S/abs(D - C)$. The block factor for DMA-bound triple-buffer need not be larger than $S/(2 * D - C)$, and for computation-bound triple-buffer need not be larger than $S/(2 * C - D)$.

## 4   Experiments

To verify how precise our analysis models are, we performed experiments on a CELL blade. The clock rate for the PPU and SPU in the blade is 3.2GHz. All our experiments were run using a single SPE. We use the IBM XL CELL

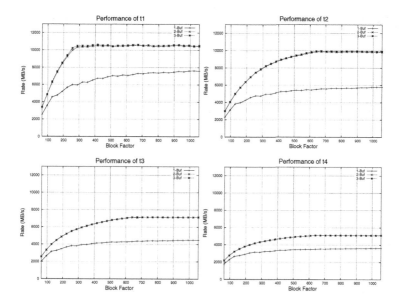

**Fig. 10.** Performance of Applications with Varying Buffer Schemes and Buffer Sizes

single-source compiler [2] to automatically apply single-, double-, and triple-buffer schemes to a set of test applications. This compiler uses OpenMP directives to decide what parts of the code will execute on the SPE(s), and it automatically handles DMA transfers for all data in an SPE LS.

We adapted a simple streaming benchmark to obtain a set of test kernels with varying amount of computation in the loop. Currently, we report results for 4 test cases: t1, t2, t3, and t4. The amount of computation in the kernel loop increases from t1 to t4. Each test case has only one OpenMP parallel loop that has a very large iteration count (15 million), and is invoked multiple times. The four test cases use the same data types, and have the same data access pattern: two reads and one write. Performance is measured in terms of throughput (MB/s).

To apply our formula, we have to determine the values of D, S, and C. For D and S, we ran code that only performs a large number of DMA operations, and inferred the values of D and S using linear regression analysis on the performance results of this code. To determine C for each test case, we used a profiling tool called Paraver [5] to instrument code and measure the amount of computation time for each iteration of the outer blocked loop. This was done for each test case using a single-buffer scheme and a large block factor to amortize the overhead. The constant values that were determined are S=130ns, $D_1$=0.0877ns per byte, $C_{outer}$=300ns (for all test cases), $C_{inner}$=0.51ns(t1), 1.73ns(t2), 2.83ns(t3), and 3.93ns(t4). All of these benchmarks need to transfer 24 bytes of data per iteration of the inner blocked loop, so the D per iteration is 2.112ns.

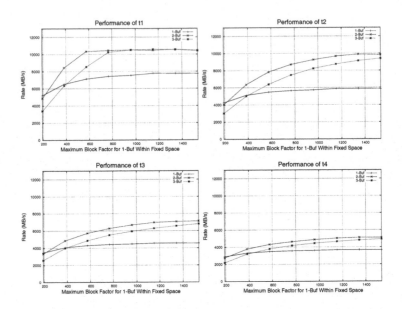

**Fig. 11.** Comparison of Buffering Schemes Using a Fixed Space Constraint

The performance of single-buffer (1b), double-buffer (2b), and triple-buffer (3b) for the 4 test cases is shown in Figure 10. The x-axis is the block factor, and the y-axis is the performance. Here, different buffer schemes are compared when they use the same block factor. We notice that 2b and 3b have a similar performance curve, while the performance of 1b is much lower. We also observe that the performance of 2b and 3b becomes flat when the block factor becomes large enough. t1 and t2 reach almost the same peak performance. Since their values of $C_{inner}$ are smaller than the value of D per iteration, they should become DMA-bound. On other hand, the values of $C_{inner}$ in t3 and t4 are larger than the value of D, and they become computation-bound. Their peak performance is determined by the amount of computation, $C_{inner}$. The overall performance trend conforms to our model. In Figure 11, we compare the performance of different buffering schemes with a fixed amount of space available for buffering. The x-axis is the block factor of the 1b scheme. Within the same available space, the corresponding block factor for 2b should be half, and one-third for 3b. For large block factors, the performance trend conforms to our analysis. However, for small block factors, in all 4 test cases, 1b outperforms 2b and 3b. This is contradictory to the analysis presented earlier. In the analysis in Section 2, we assumed C could be approximated by $C_{inner}$. However, when the block factor is small and the overhead of issuing a DMA request is high, the $C_{outer}/bf$ component of C dominates. In this case, the difference between the latencies of the whole loop for 1b and 2b evaluates to $(D + C_{inner}) * N/2 - C_{outer} * N/B$ (as opposed to $(D+C) * N/2$, derived in Section 3), which may or may not be positive. With fixed space, 1b can use a larger block factor than 2b

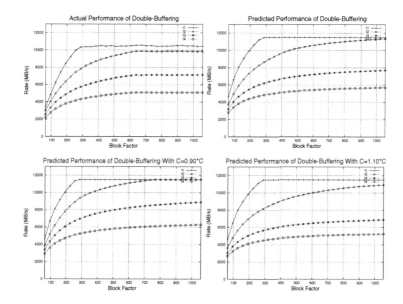

**Fig. 12.** Actual and Predicted Performance for Double-Buffer

and 3b, thus issuing fewer DMA requests and paying the $C_{outer}$ overhead fewer times. This results in higher performance for 1b, as observed. We performed experiments to manually code the 1b, 2b, and 3b versions of our test cases, and determined that the $C_{outer}$ overhead can be made small enough such that the $C_{outer}/bf$ component of C is always negligible. It is possible to do this in the compiler, but we do not have this implemented yet.

In Section 3, we discuss how to choose the block factor so as to avoid wasting memory resources. Figure 12 shows the actual and the predicted performance of double-buffer when using different block sizes. Overall, the prediction is quite precise in terms of the shape of the performance curve. The relative performance of each test case is correctly predicted. However, the absolute performance of all test cases is over-estimated by about 15%. The values of S and D need to be determined just once, and precise values for these constants can be obtained empirically on a given machine. However, the value of C is application-specific, and may need to be estimated by the compiler. The in-order, statically scheduled SPU architecture enables a high degree of accuracy in compiler estimation. However, compiler optimizations that occur after the DMA buffering transformation can significantly affect the code generated. Therefore, it may be necessary to use an extra compiler pass to feedback the estimated value of C to the DMA buffering optimization. To investigate the sensitivity of our prediction to the value of C, we also plot in Figure 12 the performance predicted using a value of C that is 10% less and 10% more than the value determined by profiling. We observe that the variation in predicted performance is 6% on average, and 15% maximum.

## 5   Related Work

In [11], the performance of DMA on a CELL chip is studied, and the latencies of DMA operations for different workload characteristics are determined. The use of loop stripmining and unrolling to optimize network communications is studied in [7]. This work focuses on determining the minimum size for stripmining to avoid performance degradation. In [12], the dependencies and communication time between tasks in a parallel execution are modeled with the aim of identifying possible computation-communication overlap. In our work, we optimize both performance and local memory usage.

In [1], remote accesses in UPC programs are optimized in the compiler by coalescing small accesses into one large access, and by using one-way communication supported in the underlying network layer. The work in [8] also discusses optimization of remote accesses in UPC programs, using runtime synchronization and scheduling. In [10], a stream programming model is used to inform the compiler of the high-level program structure. The compiler then uses this information to optimize scheduling and buffering for execution on the Imagine stream processor. A compiler-based loop optimization targeted to improve the communication-computation overlap is described in [9]. The technique of communication pipelining for distributed memory systems is discussed in [6][13].

## 6   Conclusion

We have developed a model to predict the performance of different buffering schemes and the optimal buffer size for DMA buffering in the CELL SPE local stores. We compare the predicted and actual performance for a set of kernels with varying amounts of computation in the loop, and observe a high degree of correlation between the two. In this work, we have considered the use of a single SPE, but we plan to extend our model to multiple SPEs in future work.

## References

1. W. Chen, C. Iancu, and K. Yelick. Communication optimizations for fine-grained UPC applications. *Parallel Architecture and Compilation Techniques*, 2005.
2. A.E. Eichenberger et al. Optimizing compiler for the CELL processor. *Parallel Architecture and Compilation Techniques*, September 2005.
3. B. Flachs et al. A streaming processing unit for a CELL processor. *IEEE International Solid-State Circuits Conference (ISSCC)*, February 2005.
4. D. Pham et al. The design and implementation of a first-generation CELL processor. *IEEE International Solid-State Circuits Conference*, February 2005.
5. European Center for Parallelism of Barcelona (CEPBA). Paraver: Parallel program visualization and analysis tool reference manual. November 2000. URL: http://www.cepba.upc.es/paraver.
6. S. Hiranandani, K. Kennedy, and C-W. Tseng. Evaluation of compiler optimizations for Fortran D on MIMD distributed memory machines. *International Conference on Supercomputing*, 1992.

7. C. Iancu, P. Husbands, and W. Chen. Message strip mining heuristics for high speed networks. *6th International Meeting of VECPAR*, 2004.
8. C. Iancu, P. Husbands, and P. Hargrove. HUNTing the overlap. *Parallel Architecture and Compilation Techniques*, September 2005.
9. K. Ishizaki, H. Komatsu, and T. Nakatani. A loop transformation algorithm for communication overlapping. *International Journal of Parallel Programming*, 2000.
10. U.J. Kapasi, P. Mattson, W.J. Dally, J.D. Owens, and B. Towles. Stream scheduling. *Proceedings of the 3rd Workshop on Media and Streaming Processors*, 2001.
11. M. Kistler, M. Perrone, and F. Petrini. CELL multiprocessor communication network: Built for speed. *IEEE Micro*, 26(3), May/June 2006.
12. J.S. Leu, D.P. Agrawal, and J. Mauney. Modeling of parallel software for efficient computation communication overlap. *Proceedings of the 1987 Fall Joint Computer Conference on Exploring Technology: Today and Tomorrow*, 1987.
13. D.J. Palermo, E. Su, J.A. Chandy, and P. Banerjee. Communication optimizations used in the PARADIGM compiler for distributed memory multicomputers. *International Conference on Parallel Processing*, August 1994.

# Runtime Address Space Computation
# for SDSM Systems

Jairo Balart, Marc Gonzàlez, Xavier Martorell, Eduard Ayguadé, and Jesús Labarta

Barcelona Supercomputing Center (BSC),
Computer Architecture Department, Technical University of Catalunya (UPC),
Cr. Jordi Girona 1-3, Mòdul D6, 08034 – Barcelona, Spain
{jbalart,marc,xavim,eduard,jesus}@ac.upc.edu

**Abstract.** This paper explores the benefits and limitations of using a inspector/executor approach for Software Distributed Shared Memory (SDSM) systems. The role of the inspector is to obtain a description of the address space accessed during the execution of parallel loops. The information collected by the inspector will enable the runtime to optimize the movement of shared data that will happen during the executor phase. This paper addresses the main issues that have been considered to embed an inspector/executor model in a SDSM system: amount of data collected by the inspector, the accurateness of this data when the loop has data and/or control dependences, and the computational overhead introduced. The paper also includes a description of the SDSM system where the inspector/executor model has been embedded. The proposal is evaluated with four applications from the NAS benchmark suite. The evaluation shows that the accuracy of the inspection and the small overheads introduced by the approach allow its use in a SDSM system.

## 1 Introduction

Software Distributed Shared Memory (SDSM) systems has been one of the approaches proposed to provide a shared address space and overcome the programming difficulties of programming models based on message passing. Co-Array Fortran [19], Unified Parallel C (UPC) [3] or OpenMP [1] can simplify the programming of SDSM systems if the appropriate support is provided by the compiler and/or runtime system. In such systems both components are significantly stressed, and become responsible for the memory consistency and the data sharing, being these issues the most critical aspects in any SDSM system.

The inherent data movement overheads added to the overheads of this compiler/runtime support need to be minimized in order to take benefit of the potential performance of the parallel execution. On one hand, each memory access has to be monitored in order to check if it corresponds to a shared data. This memory monitoring can be performed in different ways. For instance, UPC implementations are based on the injection of runtime calls to intercept any memory access to shared data. In most SDSM implementations of OpenMP [6][8][10], the memory monitoring is done through the handling of the page fault exceptions. On the other hand, data and control communication are considered important sources of overhead. The impact of data communication overheads can be reduced by overlapping communication and

G. Almási, C. Caşcaval, and P. Wu (Eds.): LCPC 2006, LNCS 4382, pp. 330–344, 2007.

computation. Control communication is associated to the memory consistency protocol, and no matter the basis of the SDSM system implementation, it is always one of the main concerns for developers, and therefore the target of several optimization techniques [4][5][6][10].

The usual approach in most SDSM implementations is to perform both data and control communication on-demand during the parallel execution of the computation. At each page fault or memory access interception, the runtime is invoked in order to serve memory access requests and interchange the necessary control messages. Computation and communication alternate according the application requirements. The chances of the runtime system to foresee near-future data and control communication requirements are clearly limited by the amount of information available. The inspector/executor approach might play an interesting role by inspecting the set of memory addresses generated before the execution takes place and building an accurate description of them. From this information, the runtime can derive the strictly necessary data and control communication requirements and reduce the overhead associated to the memory consistency implementation. This information can be reused as long as the data access pattern has no significant changes.

This paper explores the possibility of using an inspector/executor approach in SDSM systems. The main objective is to show that applications can afford the overheads associated with building the data structures that record shared-memory memory access and computing the data distribution from the information collected in these data structures. The structure of this paper is as follows: section 2 outlines related work on the use of runtime approaches to optimize the performance of SDSM systems. Section 3 describes the main issues to consider while embedding the inspector/executor model within a SDSM system. Section 4 describes our prototype implementation that is evaluated in section 5. Finally, section 6 concludes the paper and outlines future work.

## 2 Related Work

This section comments some recent contributions related with data and control communication optimization in SDSM systems.

UPC implementations [2][3] perform address space monitoring through a deep coordination of the compiler and the runtime system. The compiler is in charge of detecting any suspicious memory access that might refer to shared data. Runtime calls are injected to intercept those memory accesses, and invoke the appropriate communication actions. Coalescing communication is an important source of optimization. Parallel loops are the target of the compiler, looking for statements where the set of memory references can be grouped and then served with a single communication action [4]. Beside that, the runtime tries to schedule the iterations in order to overlap the computation and the communication.

In SDSM-based OpenMP implementations [6][8][10], the address space monitoring is implemented through the pagination system. The page fault signal is intercepted to embed the communication protocol responsible for the memory consistency and data sharing. Each time a page fault takes place, the runtime system checks if the accessed page corresponds to shared data, and if necessary, takes the appropriate actions to maintain the memory consistency. Avoiding false sharing is one of the main concerns. The compiler can force particular memory alignments by inserting memory padding, which has been shown to be a reliable solution [5]. Some runtime techniques have been also proposed to modify the default assignment of work to threads in parallel loops. The runtime needs to be provided with the necessary services and structures to relate page faults (data movement) to the iterations where they occur [6]. With this information the runtime can redistribute the set of iterations in order to avoid false sharing, to minimize as much as possible the number of page movements, and to pre-send data and control messages in order to overlap computation and communication.

Regarding the data distribution, there have been some proposals that place the problem at the programming language level. For example, the ZPL [16] programming model includes several constructs and operators to specify data movements. Based on the *gather/scatter* operations, the language allows the programmer to control these operations through the content of variables, which are used as array indexes to specify the array elements to be selected within a *gather/scatter* operation.

The Co-Array Fortran [19] proposal follows the main guidelines of the traditional message-passing paradigm, but introduces considerable improvements on the data communication. Communication actions are hidden by a special treatment of the array-reference operator. This operator is overloaded and allows the specification of data distribution and remote memory accesses. Data distribution is accomplished by declaring a distributed object with extra array dimensions. The programmer controls the distribution by the shape the extra dimensions provide the object with. All memory accesses to shared and distributed data need to be expanded with particular values in the extra dimensions. The runtime derives the data location according to the defined distribution.

The introduction of the *inspector/executor* model for DSM environments was already proposed for HPF [18][19]. Our main contributions with respect those previous works are the parallel inspection process and the ability of recording the data produced by the inspector for reusing it along the different instances of the parallel code.

## 3   The Inspector/Executor Model in SDSM Systems

The aim of this section is to point out the main issues that have been considered to embed the *inspector/executor* model within a SDSM system. One of the main constraints of the *inspector/executor* model is its implicit computational overhead. Although the overhead of determining how shared data is accessed during the parallel execution may seem to be huge, we will show that for SDSM systems can be affordable. This is based on the following observations:

- It is generally accepted that in SDSM systems, unnecessary communication has much more incidence in performance than the overheads related to the execution of the runtime code. This could be summarized with something like *"better execute than communicate"*. The *inspector/executor* model follows this line.

- Most of the accesses performed in parallel codes allow the injection of a highly optimized inspector. For instance, loops represent the most common source of parallelism, and their execution usually defines a data distribution that is maintained along the whole application execution. Usually, shared data is organized as vectors or matrices, and the access pattern to those structures can be accurately described at compile time [7]. With reasonable compiler technology, it is possible to avoid the inspection of all the memory accesses at runtime, and still get an exact description of what data is referenced.
- Parallel loops are usually executed several times, giving the chance of reusing the information provided by the inspection mechanism. Therefore the execution of the inspector phase can be avoided if the data access patterns remain constant along the several instances of a parallelized loop. We are going to see that this is the most common case.
- It is possible to perform the execution of the inspector code in parallel. This is giving the runtime much space to perform the inspection without interfering with unacceptable overheads.
- One of the main limitations of the *inspector/executor* approach is the existence of control and data dependences that take part in the computation of memory addresses. This is the case when control flow statements and/or pointers appear within the body of a parallel loop. Typically, parallel loops affected with such dependences can not be treated with an optimized inspector. In the worst case, when dealing with parallel loops highly loaded with data and/or control dependences, the inspector will provide with an as much as possible accurate description of the address space used in each parallel flow. Beyond the inspector limits, the native SDSM mechanisms implementing the data sharing and memory consistency will apply. Depending on how accurate the description is, the more chances for optimizing the communications will appear, and hence, speeding up the parallel code execution.
- Finally, another important issue that needs to be considered with more detail is the amount of data that the inspector can produce, which may cause unacceptable overheads within the data distribution. This relation exists since the algorithm responsible for the data distribution totally depends on the data produced by the inspector.

All the issues comented before have conditioned the implementation of the *inspector/executor* approach that is going to be described in the next section.

## 4 Implementation

This section describes a specific SDSM system implementation where the *inspector/executor* model has been embedded. The implementation has been guided towards a main objective: evaluate the effectiveness of the *inspector/executor* model for SDSM systems as a source for optimization. Consequently, it has been reasonable to force the implementation to stress to the limit the inspector role, leading to a system that totally relies on the information provided by the inspection mechanisms. Therefore, the inspection process must provide the information from where to derive all the communications. For the purposes of this paper, it must be noted that all the code transformations and the generation of the inspector code have been done by hand. However, the compilation technology required by them is reasonable and should be available in any compiler.

In our implementation, computation and communication are decoupled. This forces the implementation to guarantee that shared data is available to the parallel flows prior to the execution of the parallel code. With that, we want to show that the inspector can provide with very accurate descriptions of the working sets used in each parallel flow. An immediate consequence of such approach is that three different phases can be differentiated along the parallel execution: inspection phase, communication phase and execution phase. No matter the phase, the current implementation works under a master/slave scheme, and the memory consistency protocol implements relaxed consistency.

During the inspection phase, the loop parameters (iteration space and scheduling) are broadcasted to all the slaves. Each slave computes the chunk of iterations that have been assigned to it, and the code inspection is executed. The result of the inspection consists of a list of pages that are read and/or written by each execution flow, and each slave sends this information to the master process. At this point, the communication phase starts, and the master computes the necessary page movements and which pages are written by two or more processes (conflicting pages). This computation gets as input the data produced by the inspector, and according to that, page queries are sent. Page distribution takes place, and then all processes start the parallel loop execution (execution phase). After execution, conflicting pages are treated with *diff* operations. The resulting differences are sent to the master thread. Although computation and communication could be overlapped, our current prototype implementation does not include this feature.

The current prototype is limited to loop-level parallelism. Parallel loops are specified using the OpenMP PARALLEL DO construct. Only STATIC schedules are supported with PRIVATE and SHARED data scoping clauses. REDUCTION operations have been implemented through variable expansion of the variable holding the reduction operation.

The following points describe the main aspects of the prototype implementation, according to the main issues that have been enumerated in the previous section. The code inspection process is the most critical part in the implementation so that we will try to reduce the computational overhead of the inspection process and to face the amount of data the inspection process is going to produce.

## 4.1 Basic Inspector Implementation

A simple but costly implementation can be easily achieved by intercepting any memory access in the parallel loop. For each statement in the loop body, memory accesses can be replaced by a runtime call that will record the address in internal runtime structures. It is obvious that only shared data must be monitored, so it is needed that the compiler can identify which objects are private and which are shared. This classification can be easily done by the compiler through the data scoping clauses in OpenMP. This strategy represents the simplest inspector implementation and the worst case in terms of overhead. Taking this basic approach as a baseline, several optimizations can be applied. Consider the parallel code shown in Figure 1.

```
#pragma omp parallel for
for (i=0; i<DIMX; i++) {
  for (j=0;j<DIMY;j++) {
    a[i][j] = a[i][j]*a[i][j];
    compute_row(a[i]);
  }
}
```

**Fig. 1.** Simple parallel loop

### 4.2 Amount of Data Produced by the Inspector

A critical aspect to consider is the granularity level at which the inspector structures work. Trying to record each of the memory addresses can generate an amount of data impossible to deal with. So, it is better to work with a coarser memory unit. We propose to make the inspection at page level, being a page a continuous portion of the memory address space, similarly as in the pagination system. Even if the inspected code follows a fully predictable access pattern, the inspection mechanisms work at page level. Notice that nothing is forcing the implementation to define a uniform size for all the variables the application deals with. It might be interesting to work with smaller or bigger pages depending on the memory portion a page refers to. It is well known that particular data alignment can cause false sharing, stressing the SDSM implementation with a considerable source of control communication. Scalar variables involved in reduction operations or structured data structures (vectors, matrices) are well studied examples [5].

### 4.3 Parallelizing the Inspector Code

The inspector loop can be executed in parallel, scheduling the iterations with the same scheduled that wil be used for the loop execution. Computing the inspection of a chunk of iterations can be done applying the basic strategy described in section 4.1, but just over a subset of the whole iteration space.

Figure 2 shows the code skeleton, responsible for the inspection process. This code is executed by each parallel flow. The runtime call to *dsm_begin_for_sampling* allocates a Loop Descriptor. This subroutine forces all the threads to wait for a control message containing the loop parameters coming from the master process. The last parameter of the runtime call informs the runtime about if the information produced by the inspection can be reused in case the loop is executed several times (see section 4.6). For this example, nothing forbids to do so. The *while* statement makes the executing thread to be continuously asking for iterations to the runtime system until all the loop iterations have been executed. In the current implementation, only STATIC scheduling is supported, thus the call to *dsm_next_iters_sampling* runtime service updates the variables start and end only once, defining the chunk of iterations to execute.

```
int a[DIMX][DIMY];
int low,upper,step;
int start,end;
int i,j;
dsm_begin_for_sampling(&low,&upper,&step,1);
while (dsm_next_iters_sampling (&start,&end))
{
  for (i=start;i<=end;i+=1)
    for (j=;j<=DIMY;j+=1)
    {
      stmt_sample(&a[i][j],1,& a[i][j]);
      insp_compute_row(a[i]);
    }
}
dsm_end_for_sampling ();
```

**Fig. 2.** Inspection code for parallelized loop

## 4.4   Predictable Access Patterns

Even if the code inspection is done in parallel, it is necessary to look for more chances for optimization. Statements with invariant memory addresses can be omitted in the inspection process for all iterations, and treated just once. Predictable memory addresses, such as linear accesses to vectors or multidimensional matrices, can be managed with a single runtime service, summarizing the memory portion accessed by each execution flow. Figure 3 shows an optimized version of the inspecting code. Notice that interprocedural analysis phase is required to detect that the call to *compute_row* subroutine is invariant across the *j-loop* iterations. For similar cases where the inspection process can be optimized, the data produced by the inspector is organized at page level, as it has previously mentioned in section 4.2.

```
int a[DIMX][DIMY];
int low,upper,step;
int start,end;
int i,j;
dsm_begin_for_sampling(low,upper,step,1);
while (next_iters_sampling (&start,&end))
{
  for (i=start;i<=end;i+=1)
  {
sample_region(&a[i][0],DIMY,1,&a[i][0],DIMY);
    insp_compute_row(a[i]);
  }
}
```

**Fig. 3.** Optimized inspecting loop code

## 4.5   Pointers and Control Dependences

Pointers and control dependences represent a considerable limitation to the *inspector/executor* model. Current implementation does not include any specific support for dealing with pointers. The case of index vectors is treated with the most conservative approach, which forces the inspector to assume that the variable accessed through an index vector will be totally referenced. In terms of communication, this is going to be translated to a broadcast operation of the variable. In case pointers appear to be invariant along the parallel loop execution, the inspector still can be executed with no limitation. Under any other circumstance, the inspection is inhibited.

Control dependences also limit the inspection process. When a control flow statement breaks the sequential execution, the inspector cannot always know which branch will be executed. If private data determines the branch, the *inspector* can include all the necessary operations to evaluate the control dependence. If not, a conservative approach is taken and the *inspector* inspects all the possible branches.

Although the current support to overcome the limitations related with pointers and control dependences is very small, this is not going to have a significant impact on the inspector functionality. It is quite common that parallel loops show a particular ratio between the amount of data and operations related to memory addresses computation and the total loop computation. Usually, parallel loops present a small percentage of data and operations related to memory addresses computations. Under such situation, the inspector code can still be applied, and the most conservative solutions that have been described are not going to suppose a significant loose of accurateness or an unacceptable increment of overhead.

### 4.6  Reuse of the Inspector Data

It is clear that having the possibility of reusing the *inspector* data becomes an important source of optimization. Detecting if this data can be reused along the different instances of a parallelized loop is not a simple task and the necessary compiler and runtime support to automate such issue is not available in the prototype. So, the current implementation is based on information provided by the programmer to specify if the inspector data can be reused. We have analyzed each parallelized loop and determined for each one, if data reuse was possible to be applied. In the evaluation section, the number of loops with reused inspector is discussed, as well as the impact of the reuse in performance.

## 5  Evaluation

The aim of this section is to describe and measure the limits on the *inspector/executor* model in SDSM systems. Hence, not the whole SDSM implementation is evaluated, just the effects of the inspection and data distribution mechanisms. Speedup and execution time numbers are the initial metrics for the evaluation process, but then broken down in different parts: communication associated to application itself, communication required by the runtime, computation time of the application code and computation time inside the runtime. The effects of the inspection process are mostly noticeable within two implementation mechanisms: the inspection execution and the algorithm responsible for deriving the data communication. Therefore, these two aspects are specifically measured. No comparison of the current prototype with other systems has been included. The main reason for that, is that the evaluation is centered around the effects of the inspection process and the accurateness of the data produced. In that direction, for all the tested applications, two versions of the inspector code have been considered: a non optimized and an optimized version. For each case, the optimizations are described.

The evaluation has been done using four applications from the NAS parallel benchmark suite: EP, IS, FT and CG, all of them in their C version [9][10]. The experiments have been performed in the *Marenostrum* [15] platform available at the Barcelona Supercomputing Center (BSC). The machine is composed by 2406 dual nodes based on PowerPC970FX, 2.2 GHz and Myrinet with a total amount of 9.6 TB of memory. A subset of 8 nodes was used for the evaluation.

## 5.1  EP

The *Embarrassingly Parallel* benchmark computes pairs of Gaussian random deviates, according to a specific scheme. The benchmark works mainly with private data and performs a reduction operation over two global variables. The whole computation is organized as a single loop executed just once. This benchmark allows for measuring the impact of the inspection process, conditioned by three issues. First, no reuse can be applied, as the computation takes place only once. Second, the inspection process has to deal with a considerable amount of private computation, needed to point out what private data has to be accessed in the reduction operations. Two versions of the inspection process can be studied, one including the private computations, the other not. Finally, negligible data communication is about to happen, since shared data is only composed by two objects, the global variables where the output of the reduction operations are stored.

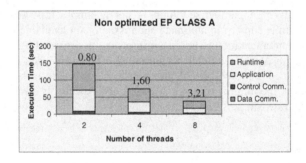

**Fig. 4.** Non optimized EP CLASS A

Figure 4 shows the performance obtained in the execution of the EP (class A) benchmark, with 2, 4 and 8 threads and non optimized inspection. The numbers on top of the columns correspond to the speedup obtained in each experiment. The *Y* axis shows the execution time, which is broken down (top to bottom) in Runtime and Application code execution, and Data and Control communication. The serial time is 119,39 seconds and corresponds to the unmodified benchmark executed sequentially. The Runtime and Application code take near 93% of the execution time. The cost of the inspection process is included in the Runtime measurements and represents about 51% of total execution time. This behavior is maintained with 2, 4 and 8 threads, and suggests there is much space for optimization. The inspection process is too heavy and represents about having to execute twice the benchmark computation. The reason of such overhead is that all computations related to private data are inspected. Notwithstanding, some speedup is observed (3.21 with 8 threads).

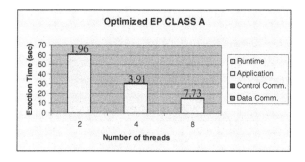

**Fig. 5.** Optimized EP CLASS A

Figure 5 shows the performance for the optimized inspection process. In this case, private computations have been taken out from the inspection code. This process could be easily done by means of the PRIVATE clause in the parallelism specification. Clearly, the benchmark performance is now improved, obtaining speedups of 1.96, 3.91, and 7.73. The Runtime execution time ranges from 0.17% (2 threads) to 1.16% (8 threads). The inspection process and the computation of the data distribution represent about 1.72% and 1.22% over the total execution time.

These results show that with a simple compiler optimization (avoiding the inspection of private data), the process can be implemented without noticeable overhead. In addition, the accuracy of the data produced by the *inspector* is enough to totally determine the data distribution in this simple benchmark.

## 5.2  IS

The Integer Sort benchmark works with a shared vector, uniformly distributed among all parallel processes. The computation is organized in a single parallel loop, executed several times. After each loop instance, a reduction operation is performed. That forces the parallel flows to flush some data back to the master process. The output of the inspection process can be reused along the benchmark execution, so it is only computed once. Two versions of the inspection process can be implemented: a non optimized inspection, which goes along the iteration space and records all memory accesses; and, an optimized version, where the inspection is done through a single runtime call, summarizing the access pattern to the shared vector.

Figure 6 shows the performance for the IS (class B) execution, with 2, 4 and 8 threads, and non optimized inspection. The serial time is 46.0 seconds. For the non optimized version each memory reference to a shared variable is intercepted. The execution of the application code scales with the number of threads, but not the execution of the runtime system. Data communication also increases with the number of threads. This is caused by an *all-to-one* communication pattern related to the reduction operation, previously mentioned. Notice that Control communication represents a very small percentage (0.01%, 0.02% and 0.03 with 2, 4, and 8 threads) of all the communication. This is caused because the *inspector* provides the runtime system with all the necessary information regarding the memory consistency (conflicting pages, written by more than one thread).

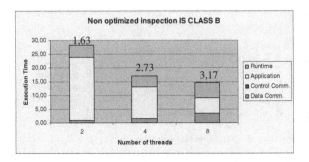

**Fig. 6.** Non optimized IS CLASS B

For the optimized version, predictable access patterns are assumed to be detected by the compiler. Linear memory accesses to shared vectors have been inspected through a single runtime call describing the access to the vector. The results in Figure 7 show the reduction of the execution time spent in the runtime system.

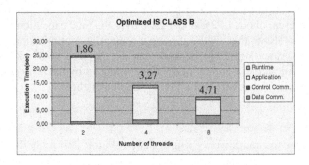

**Fig. 7.** Optimized IS CLASS B

## 5.3  FT

The *Fourier Transformation* benchmark computes a Fourier transformation over a three dimensional matrix. The computation is organized in four subroutines: *evolve, cffts1, cffts2* and *cffts3*. All execute one after the other and update the content of the main structure, the three dimensional matrix. This is repeated several times, depending on the input benchmark. Each subroutine implements the computation with three nested loops, one per dimension on the working set. While *evolve, cffts1* and *cffts2* distribute the data cross the same dimension, the computation in *cffts3* completely changes the data distribution. This causes this benchmark to be highly loaded with *Data* communication overhead. The output of the inspection process in each subroutine can be reused except for *evolve, cffts1* and *cffts3*, so for these subroutines, the code inspection is performed each time they are executed. Again, two versions of the inspection process have been tested.

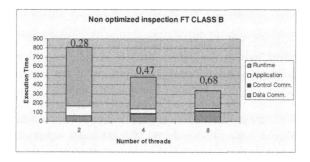

**Fig. 8.** Non optimized FT CLASS B

Figure 8 shows the performance of the non optimized version. The serial time is 232.33 seconds. Clearly, the unacceptable overhead produced by the inspection is preventing any chance for speeding up the execution. Although *Data* communication represents 7.64%, 17.09% and 33.72% of overhead, the weight for the inspection process (76.32%, 63.79% and 45.41%) is the main factor that degrades the performance. The inspection overhead comes out because of the structure of the inspected code: the nest of three loops. Running over the whole iteration space sinks any possibility of taking profit of the information gathered during the inspection process.

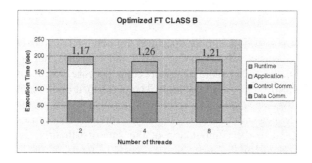

**Fig. 9.** Optimized FT CLASS B

Figure 9 shows the results for the optimized case. Although this version obtains very poor speedup, just 1.17, 1.26 and 1.22 for 2, 4 and 8 threads, now the time spent under the runtime execution is about 11.79, 18.33 and 21.82. If those percentages are broken down, we see that the inspection process is about 1.08%, 0.6% and 0.3% of the overall execution time. Therefore, the influence of the inspection process is not the point. Those overheads are related to *diff* operations needed for the memory consistency protocol. Anyway, Data communication becomes critical as it represents 32.26%, 49.22% and 63.20% of total execution time.

Notice that the data movement is totally determined by the application. The overhead contributions coming from the inspection process and the data distribution algorithm are negligible in front of Data communication times.

## 5.4  CG

The CG NAS parallel benchmark computes an approximation to the smallest eigenvalue of a large, sparse, symmetric, positive definite matrix using a conjugate gradient method. As in previous codes, two versions of the application have been evaluated. In the non-optimized version (in which each memory access to shared data is intercepted), the overheads related to the inspection process and the computation of the data distribution can be afforded by the application when running up to 4 threads (speedups of 1.87 and 2.89). With 8 threads the grain size assigned to each process becomes too small to be worth for parallel execution, compared to the amount of data that needs to be communicated. Figure 10 shows the results for this version.

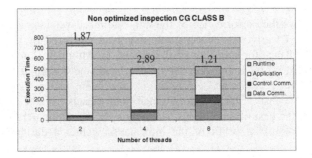

**Fig. 10.** Non optimized CG CLASS B

For the optimized version, similar speedups are obtained. The overheads related to the inspection are reduced when running with 2 and 4 threads, but not with 8 threads. This is not translated to an increase of speedup because the accuracy in the data produced by the inspector is not very high. The performed optimizations are based on broadcast operations of shared data referenced through index vectors. The inspector assumes the whole data structure is used by all the threads. This causes an increment of the overhead related to the computation of the data distribution, as this mechanism depends on the output of the inspection process, in terms of the number of pages involved in the data distribution. Figure 11 shows the results for the optimized version.

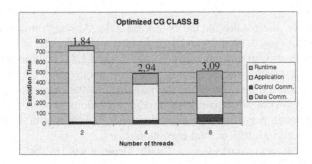

**Fig. 11.** Optimized CG CLASS B

# 6  Conclusions

This paper shows benefits and limitations of the *inspector/executor* model within a SDSM system. The role of the *inspector* is to provide an accurate (as mush as possible) description of the references to shared data in each processor during the parallel execution. It has been proved that delivering this information to the runtime system creates many chances for optimizing the communication. The limits of the model are defined by the overheads, implicit to the basis model, but can be overcome by several optimization techniques, smoothing the impact of the inspection process on the overall execution time.

Our experiments with four benchmarks of the NAS parallel benchmark suite have demonstrated that it is possible to generate very accurate inspectors. It is possible to build on top of the *inspector/executor* model a SDMS implementation, and execute the parallel code performing the strictly necessary communication.

## Acknowledgements

This work has been supported by the Ministry of Education of Spain under contract CICYT-TIN2004-07739-C02-01, and the Barcelona Supercomputing Center.

## References

[1]  OpenMP Application Program Interface, Version 2.5, May 2005, www.openmp.org.

[2]  T. El-Ghazawi and F. Cantonet. "UPC Performance and Potential: a NPB experimental Study". Proceedings of the 2002 ACM/IEEE International Conference on Supercomputing (ICS). 2002.

[3]  T. El-Ghazawi, W. Carlson and J. Drapper. "UPC Language Specifications V1.1.1". Oct 2003.

[4]  W. Yu Chen, C. Iancu and K. Yelick. "Communication Optimizations for Fine-grained UPC Applications", Proceedings of the 14th International Conference on Parallel Architectures and Compilation Techniques, (PACT2005)

[5]  H. Lu, A. L. Cox, S. D. R. Rajamony and W. Zwaenepoel. "Compiler and Software Distributed Shared Memory Support for Irregular Applications". Proceedings of the Sixth ACM SIGPLAN Symposium on Principles and Practice of Parallel Programming (PPoPP), 1997.

[6]  J.J Costa, T. Cortés, X. Martorell, E. Ayguadé and J. Labarta. "Running OpenMP applications efficiently on an everything-shared SDSM". Proceedings of the 18th International Parallel and Distributed Processing Symposium (IPDPS). Santa Fe, New Mexico, USA. 2004.

[7]  Basumallik, R. Eigemann. "Towards Automatic Translation of OpenMP to MPI". Proceedings of the 19th Annual International Conference on Supercomputing (ICS). Cambridge, Massachusetts, USA. 2005.

[8]  Y. Charlie Hu, Honghui Lu, Alan L. Cox, and Willy Zwaenepoel. "OpenMP for Networks of SMPs". Journal of Parallel and Distributed Computing, vol. 60 (12), pp. 1512-1530, December 2000.

[9]  M. Sato, S. Satoh, K. Kusano and Y. Tanaka. "Design of OpenMP Compiler for SMP Cluster". Proceedings of the 1st European Workshop on OpenMP (EWOMP). 1999.

[10]  M. Sato, H. Harada and Y. Ishikawa. "OpenMP Compiler for a Software Distributed Shared Memory System SCASH". Proceedings of the 1$^{st}$ Workshop on OpenMP Applications and Tools (WOMPAT). 2000.

[11]  NanosMercurium Compiler Infrastructure, www.cepba.upc.es/mercurium.

[12]  S. D. Sharma, R. Ponnusamy B. Moon, Y. Hwang, R. Dasand J. Saltz. "Runtime and compile-time support for adaptive irregular problems". Proceedings of Supercomputing'94, 1994.

[13]  H. Jin M. Frumkin, and J. Yan. "The OpenMP Implementation of the NAS Parallel Benchmarks and its Performance". Technical Report NAS-99-011, NASA Ames Research Center, October 1999.

[14]  C. Koelbel and P. Mehrotra. "Compiling Global Name-Space Parallel Loops for Distributed Execution". IEEE Transactions on Parallel and Distributed Systems, vol. 2(4), pp. 440–451, October 1991.

[15]  Barcelona Supercomputing Center, www.bsc.es.

[16]  S. J. Deitz, B. L. Chamberlain, S-Eun Choi, and L. Snyder. "The Design and Implementation of a Parallel Array Operator for the Arbitrary Remapping of Data",.Proceedings of the ACM SIGPLAN symposium on principles and practice of parallel programming (PPoPP 2003)

[17]  C. Koelbel and P. Mehrotra. "Supporting shared data structures on distributed memory architectures". Proceedings of the 2nd ACM SIGPLAN Symposium on Principles and Practice of Parallel Programming (PPOPP). 1990.

[18]  R.V. Hanxleden, K. Kennedy, C. Koelbel, R. Das, and J. Saltz. "Compiler analysis for irregular problems in Fortran-D". Proceedings of the 5$^{th}$ Workshop on Languages and Compilers for Parallel Computing (LCPC), 1992.

[19]  Y. Dotsenko, C. Coarfa, J. Mellor-Crummey. "A Multiplatform CoArray Fortran Compiler". Proceedings of the 13$^{th}$ International Conference on Parallel Architecture and Compilation Techniques (PACT), 2004.

# A Static Heap Analysis for Shape and Connectivity: Unified Memory Analysis: The Base Framework

Mark Marron, Deepak Kapur, Darko Stefanovic, and Manuel Hermenegildo

University of New Mexico
Albuquerque, NM 87131, USA,
{marron, kapur, darko, herme}@cs.unm.edu

**Abstract.** Modeling the evolution of the state of program memory during program execution is critical to many parallelization techniques. Current memory analysis techniques either provide very accurate information but run prohibitively slowly or produce very conservative results. An approach based on abstract interpretation is presented for analyzing programs at compile time, which can accurately determine many important program properties such as aliasing, logical data structures and shape. These properties are known to be critical for transforming a single threaded program into a version that can be run on multiple execution units in parallel. The analysis is shown to be of polynomial complexity in the size of the memory heap. Experimental results for benchmarks in the Jolden suite are given. These results show that in practice the analysis method is efficient and is capable of accurately determining shape information in programs that create and manipulate complex data structures.

## 1 Introduction

Research on automatic thread level parallelization techniques makes extensive use of the *shape* [4,16] of data structures in memory. As an example, in [6] Ghiya used a notion of shape to enable the extraction of *foreach* thread-level parallelism from common heap-based data structures. The notion of shape and sharing can also be used to enable the parallelization of recursive algorithms [15,8]. In many programs the availability of accurate shape information and the application of these two transforms enables the extraction of a substantial portion of the available parallelism. Unfortunately, the applicability of these parallelization techniques has been limited by the difficulty of performing shape analysis with the required level of accuracy. The advent of commonly available multi-processor systems, the slowing of improvements in single threaded processor performance and the increasing use of object oriented languages (which make extensive use of heap allocated memory and rich pointer structures) have renewed interest in shape driven parallelization techniques.

This paper uses an abstract interpretation framework for performing static analysis of programs and introduces a graph based abstract heap model that can represent all the information on aliasing, shape and logical data structures [10] that are required to perform thread level parallelization transformations. Along with accurately representing the required information on shape, aliasing and logically related regions, the framework enables accurate simulation of the evolution of these properties through many

G. Almási, C. Caşcaval, and P. Wu (Eds.): LCPC 2006, LNCS 4382, pp. 345–363, 2007.

important program idioms, e.g. sorting, copying, destructive reversal, and element insertion/deletion. A theoretical analysis of the runtime and our experience running the method on the Jolden benchmarks indicates that the technique is accurate, efficient and scalable.

A key factor in achieving these results is the use of a novel technique for undoing the *summarization* of information (the analysis must use a bounded representation to summarize unbounded recursive structures). For efficiency, it is important to make the summary representations as compact as possible. However, this summarization may lead to the loss information which is needed to accurately simulate the effect of program statements on the heap model. Seminal work on heap analysis [16] introduced the notion of refinement but the proposed technique results in an exponential runtime (due to the desire to model the program with maximal precision). This paper presents a technique for refinement that sacrifices some accuracy in less common cases to ensure that the worst case exponential time is avoided and that the method is fast in practice.

## 1.1 Related Work

There are two research activities closely related to the work presented in this paper. One is the research on shape analysis by Ghiya [4] and the second is the TVLA (3-valued Logic Analysis) framework introduced by Reps, Sagiv and Wilhelm [16].

Ghiya's method is efficient and is able to model simple structures in programs that do not use destructive updates. In this work shapes are defined on the entire portion of the heap that is reachable from a variable. This implies that any extraneous sharing of the heap (due to the use of the *singleton* design pattern or sharing of data that is unrelated to the computation that is being parallelized) will result in very conservative results. Further, the analysis is unable to strongly update heap based storage. Thus, the analysis is unable to accurately handle situations where a section of the heap, through destructive updates, temporarily takes on a more general shape and then returns to the original shape (e.g. Tree → DAG → Tree).

The TVLA framework is very powerful and highly expressive in the sense that it can be used to represent the shape and aliasing properties needed for extracting thread-level parallelism. In addition to being expressive enough to model the relevant program properties, the TVLA framework is able to model the evolution of these properties through destructive updates [17,12] and is able to model shape on a more localized basis. In the TVLA framework destructive updates are handled by allowing the summary representations of recursive data structures to be refined into a number of distinct objects which can be strongly updated. Since there may be ambiguity about how to refine the summarization TVLA enumerates all the possibilities. This results in a potentially exponential runtime and in practice leads to large analysis times. There has been work on reducing the cost of running TVLA or restricted variations of the method [20,7] but they do not eliminate the exponential worst case time and have had mixed results in reducing the execution time on various benchmarks.

To compare the proposed method with existing shape analysis techniques we look at some simple examples with lists and with benchmarks from the Jolden suite. The list benchmarks demonstrate that the proposed method handles simple heap based structures accurately and that in practice it is over an order of magnitude faster than existing analysis techniques of similar precision. The Jolden tests indicate that the proposed analysis method can determine the correct shape for the majority of heap based data structures even in programs that build and manipulate relatively complex data structures while maintaining an acceptable analysis time.

# 2  Concrete Domain

Our analysis works on the strongly-statically typed, single-inheritance, thread-free, exception-free, object-oriented imperative core of languages like Java or C#. Using this simplified language enables us to focus on the central issues of the analysis and allows the analysis to be extended to a large class of source languages.

## 2.1  Concrete Language and Semantics

Our source language MIL (Mid-Level Intermediate Language) is a structured intermediate representation. The language has function and method invocations, a conditional construct (if ... else if ... else) and a looping construct with break statements (do ... while and break). The state modification operations and expressions (load, store and assign along with the standard collection of logical, arithmetic and comparison operators) are in a standard three-address form [11,18].

MIL supports objects and arrays. We use $\sigma$ to denote the set of all user-defined object types. Each object type, $\upsilon \in \sigma$, has a set of fields $F_\upsilon$ associated with it. The set of all field offsets that are defined in a program is $F = \bigcup \{F_\upsilon | \upsilon \in \sigma\}$. MIL has the primitive types $\rho = \{\texttt{int}, \texttt{float}, \texttt{char}, \texttt{bool}\}$. Arrays can contain either primitive types, $\rho$, or objects, $\sigma$. The set of all legal array types for a program is $\sigma_A = \{\upsilon[\,] | \upsilon \in \rho \vee \upsilon \in \sigma\}$. The set of all types in the program is $\tau = \rho \cup \sigma \cup \sigma_A$. We assume that the types of all variables are explicitly declared. Since this paper is focused on the operation of the abstract heap model and the local data flow analysis, we omit any description of how function and method calls are handled.

## 2.2  Concrete Heap Definition

The concrete heap is modeled as a multi-graph with labeled edges where objects and arrays are the vertices and the pointers are labeled directed edges in the graph. We use the term *cell* to indicate either an object or an array on the heap and *offset* to indicate the field or array index that a pointer is stored at in a cell. Thus, the set of edge labels (offsets) is, $L = F \cup \mathbb{N}$. Edges are modeled as a relation on the cells and the labels. Given a set of cells $C$ and the set of labels $L$ the edge relation $E \subseteq C \times L \times C$. Variables are modeled as a partial map from variable names to cells. Given a set of variables, $V$, the variable map is a function, $V_m : V \mapsto C$. The set of all concrete heaps (which we define as being the heap graph plus the program variable map) is, $H_s = \mathscr{P}(C) \times \mathscr{P}(E) \times \{V_m\}$ and the concrete domain $H = \mathscr{P}(H_s)$.

## 2.3  Heap Properties of Interest

*Points-to and Paths.* Given cells $a$, $b$ and offset $o$, $(a, o) \rightarrow_p b$ denotes a pointer $p$ that has the label $o$ (is stored at offset $o$) $a$ and points to $b$. We use $a \rightarrow_p b$ to indicate that $\exists$

offset $o$ s.t. $(a,o) \to_p b$. Two cells can be connected by a *path* $\psi$. We use $(a,o) \leadsto_\psi b$ to indicate the sequence of pointers $\langle p_1 \dots p_n \rangle$ s.t. $p_1$ has the label $o$, starts at cell $a$, $p_n$ points to $b$ and $\forall p_i, p_{i+1}$ in the path $p_i$ ends at the same cell, $c_i$, that $p_{i+1}$ begins at ($\exists o'$ s.t. $p_{i+1}$ is stored at $o'$ in $c_i$). Define $a \leadsto_\psi b$ to denote that $\exists o$ s.t. $(a,o) \leadsto_\psi b$. We abuse the notation $\phi \subseteq P$ to denote that all the pointers in the path $\phi$ are contained in the set of pointers $P$.

*Regions of the Heap.* A *region* of memory $\mathfrak{R}$ is a subset of the cells in memory, all the pointers that connect these cells and all the cross region pointers that start or end at a cell in this region. Given $C \subseteq \{c \mid c \text{ is a cell in memory}\}$, let $P = \{\text{pointer } p \mid \exists a, b \in C, a \to_p b\}$. Let $P_c = \{\text{pointer } p \mid \exists a \in C, x \notin C, a \to_p x \oplus x \to_p a\}$ Then a region is the tuple $(C, P, P_c)$.

*Connectivity.* Connectivity within a region describes how cells in the region are connected. For a region $\mathfrak{R} = (C, P, P_c)$ and cells $a, b \in C$, cells $a$ and $b$ are connected if they are in the same weakly-connected component of the graph $(C, P)$; cells $a$ and $b$ are disjoint if they are in different weakly-connected components of the graph $(C, P)$. Figure 2 shows examples of connected and disjoint concrete heaps. In Figure 2(a) the cells $c, d$ are disjoint in the region $Z$, while in Figure 2(b) and Figure 2(c) the cells $c, d$ are connected in the region $Z$.

*Structure Traversals.* An important property for program transformations is the layout of data structures in memory [4,5]. The idea is to track the layout of the heap as it appears to a program traversing a data structure. Ghiya considered the shape of the section of the heap that could be accessed starting from each variable.

Our heap analysis identifies logically related sections of the heap (regions). To improve the accuracy of the shape information we define data structure layouts on these logically related regions instead of the entire section of the heap reachable from a given variable. Given a region $\mathfrak{R} = (C, P, P_c)$, we can define several layout predicates on the graph $(C, P)$ to indicate what kinds of traversal patterns a program can use to navigate through the data structures in the region. A region admits a traversal type if there is a subregion that satisfies the corresponding layout predicate. Note that these traversals are not mutually exclusive and that *Tree* traversal $\Rightarrow$ *List* traversal $\Rightarrow$ *Singleton* traversal. In the following definitions, let $a, b$ be cells and $\phi, \psi$ be paths.

- Cycle Traversal iff $\exists$ graph $(C', P'), C' \subseteq C, P' \subseteq P$ s.t. $\exists a \in C', \phi \subseteq P'$ s.t. $a \leadsto_\phi a$.
- MultiPath Traversal iff $\exists$ graph $(C', P'), C' \subseteq C, P' \subseteq P$ s.t. $\exists a, b \in C', \phi, \psi \subseteq P'$ s.t. $(a \neq b) \wedge (\phi \neq \psi) \wedge (a \leadsto_\phi b) \wedge (a \leadsto_\psi b) \wedge (C', P')$ does not admit a Cycle Layout.
- Tree Traversal iff $\exists$ graph $(C', P'), C' \subseteq C, P' \subseteq P$ s.t. $(\exists a \in C', a$ has 2 or more successors in $C') \wedge (C', P')$ does not admit a Cycle or Multipath Layout.
- List Traversal iff $\exists$ graph $(C', P'), C' \subseteq C, P' \subseteq P$ s.t. $(\forall a \in C', a$ has one or zero successors in $C') \wedge (\exists b \in C', b$ has one successor in $C') \wedge (C', P')$ does not admit a Cycle or Multipath Layout.
- Singleton Traversal holds for all regions.

Figure 1 shows several concrete heaps; the cells are the circles labeled with letters and the edges represent pointers. Since we are interested in the most general way a program could traverse a region of the concrete heap we must assume that a program variable could begin its traversal of the region at any of the cells in the region. Thus, the figures omit the program variables. Figure 1(a) shows a concrete heap with three cells $(a,b,c)$. Since there are no edges connecting these cells the only way a program can traverse them is by individually referencing each cell. Figure 1(b) shows a concrete heap that admits a *List* traversal (both $b \rightarrow a$ and $c \rightarrow a$). It also admits a *Singleton* traversal since a program can always treat the cells as if they were disconnected. Figure 1(c) shows a concrete heap that admits a *Tree* traversal $(b,a,d)$ as well as *List* and *Singleton* traversals. Finally, Figure 1(d) adds an edge, $c \rightarrow b$ that changes the region to admit a *MultiPath* traversal $(c,b,a)$.

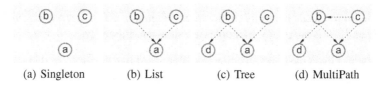

(a) Singleton          (b) List          (c) Tree          (d) MultiPath

**Fig. 1.** Concrete Heaps, Admissible Traversals and Layout Types for the Regions

## 3   Abstract Domain

The abstract domain is based on an abstract heap graph model [2,19,9]. Each node represents a set of concrete cells and each edge represents a set of pointers. The model provides a natural framework for representing connectivity, aliasing, and region identification information. This section introduces a number of instrumentation domains that when added to the nodes and edges in the abstract heap graph allow aliasing and connectivity to be tracked more accurately and enable the modeling of shape.

*Numeric Quantities.* The only requirement we place on the numeric abstraction is that it differentiates the case where the value is exactly one and the case where the value is in the range $[0,\infty]$. This gives the binary domain $1 < \#$ (unknown), where $1$ represents the interval $[1, 1]$ and $\#$ represents the interval $[0, \infty]$. Given this domain, $a \sqcup a' = 1$ if $a = a' = 1$ and $\#$ otherwise. In the later algorithms we also need an interpretation, $\bar{+}$, for $+$. This is given by, $a \bar{+} a' = \#$.

*Types.* Each node represents a set of cells and each cell is either an object (has type $\upsilon \in \sigma$) or an array ($\upsilon \in \sigma_A$). Since MIL has dynamic method invocation as well as type casting it is important to model the types of cells that a given node might represent. The domain for representing the types of each node is $\mathscr{P}(\sigma \cup \sigma_A)$. As usual the join operation $\sqcup$ is $\cup$ and the $\leq$ relation is $\subseteq$.

*Offsets.* Each edge in the model represents a set of pointers and each pointer has an offset (label) associated with it. Since there are only a finite number of fields in a given program the model can be completely sensitive with respect to field offsets (by construction two pointers with different offsets are never represented by the same edge). However, there may not be a bound on the size of arrays. So, we treat arrays as having a single offset, ?, that contains a summary of all the elements that may be in the array. Thus, the offsets that are used in the field sensitive parts of the analysis is the set $F \cup \{?\}$.

*Abstract Layout.* Each node, $n$, in the graph represents a region, $\mathfrak{R}$ on the heap. To track the traversals that may be admissible in the region $\mathfrak{R}$ that $n$ represents we use a set of layout types *Layouts* $= \{Singleton, List, Tree, MultiPath, Cycle\}$.

- if $n$ has a *Singleton* Layout, then $\mathfrak{R}$ only admits *Singleton* traversals.
- if $n$ has a *List* Layout, then $\mathfrak{R}$ only admits *Singleton* or *List* traversals.
- if $n$ has a *Tree* Layout, then $\mathfrak{R}$ only admits *Singleton*, *List* or *Tree* traversals.
- if $n$ has a *MultiPath* Layout, then $\mathfrak{R}$ only admits *Singleton*, *List*, *Tree* or *MultiPath* traversals.
- if $n$ has an *Cycle* Layout, then any traversal pattern may be admissible in $\mathfrak{R}$.

This definition leads naturally to the order: *Singleton* < *List* < *Tree* < *MultiPath* < *Cycle*. Then $l \sqcup l'$ is $max(l, l')$. Examples are shown in Figure 1.

*Connectivity.* Given the concretization operator $\gamma$ and two edges $e_1, e_2$ that start or end at the node $n$, the predicates that define connectivity in the abstract domain are:

- $e_1, e_2$ connected with respect to $n$ if: $\exists p_1 \in \gamma(e_1) \land \exists p_2 \in \gamma(e_2) \land \exists a, b \in \gamma(n)$ s.t. ($p_1$ starts or ends at $a$) $\land$ ($p_2$ starts or ends at $b$) $\land$ ($a$, $b$ connected).
- $e_1, e_2$ disjoint with respect to $n$ if: $\forall p_1 \in \gamma(e_1) \land \forall p_2 \in \gamma(e_2) \land \forall a, b \in \gamma(n)$ ($p_1$ starts or ends at $a$) $\land$ ($p_2$ starts or ends at $b$) $\Rightarrow a, b$ are disjoint.

Edges $e_1$, $e_2$ are *outConnected* if: $\exists n$ s.t. ($e_1, e_2$ are out edges from $n$) $\land$ ($e_1$, $e_2$ are connected in $n$).

Edges $e_1$, $e_2$ are *inConnected* if: $\exists n$ s.t. ($e_1, e_2$ are in edges to $n$) $\land$ ($e_1$, $e_2$ are connected in $n$).

Figure 2 shows overlays of the abstract and concrete heaps. The concrete cells and pointers are shown as dotted circles and lines while the abstract nodes and edges are represented with solid boxes and lines. Edge $E$ is an abstraction of pointer $p$, edge $F$ is an abstraction of pointer $q$. Node $Z$ abstracts cells $c, d, e$. Nodes $X, Y$ abstract cells $a, b$ respectively. In Figure 2(a) we can see that the targets of $p$, $q$ (cells $c$, $d$) are disjoint. By the definition of the connectivity abstraction, edges $E$ and $F$ are also disjoint with respect to $Z$. In Figure 2(b) there is an additional pointer which connects cells $d, c$. This means that $c$, $d$ are connected and in the abstraction, $E$, $F$ are connected with respect to $Z$ and thus $E$, $F$ are also *inConnected*. Finally, Figure 2(c) shows the case where cells $c, d$ are connected indirectly (but according to the definition they are still connected). Thus $E$, $F$ are also *inConnected*.

*Interference.* Each graph edge represents a set of inter-region pointers. When combining nodes, it is important to know if all the pointers that the edge represents point into disjoint subregions or if there may exist a cell that two or more pointers may be able to reach and thus they *interfere*. An edge $e$ represents interfering pointers if there exist pointers $p, q \in \gamma(e)$ such that the cells that $p, q$ point to are connected. We use a two-element lattice, $np < ip$, $np$ for edges with all non-interfering pointers and $ip$ for edges with potentially interfering pointers. This abstraction is a complement to the connectivity relation. The connectivity relation tracks reachability information between the start or end cells of pointers represented by different edges while interference tracks reachability information between the end cells of pointers represented by the same edge.

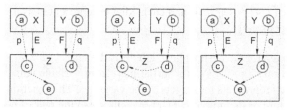

(a) Disjoint in Z    (b) Connected in Z   (c) Connected in Z

**Fig. 2.** Concrete and Abstract Connectivity

In Figure 3, Edge $E$ is an abstraction of pointers $p$ and $q$, node $Z$ abstracts cells $c, d, e$, and $X$ abstracts cells $a$ and $b$. In Figure 3(a) the targets of $p$, $q$ (cells $c$, $d$) are disjoint. Thus, the pointers do not interfere and the edge, $E$, that abstracts them should be *np*. In Figure 3(b) there is an additional pointer which connects cells $d$, $c$. This means that $c$ and $d$ are connected and edge $E$ should be *ip*. In Figure 3(c) the cells $c, d$ are connected indirectly. Thus, the edge $E$ is again *ip*.

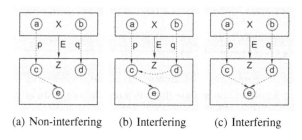

(a) Non-interfering    (b) Interfering    (c) Interfering

**Fig. 3.** Concrete Connectivity and Abstract Interference

*Nodes.* The types of the concrete cells that a node represent are stored in a set called *types*. To track the total number of cells that may be in the region represented by this node we use the *size* property. The internal layout of a node is represented by the *layout* component. Finally, we introduce a binary relation $connR \subseteq E \times E$ to track the connectivity of the edges that are incident to this node. If $(e_1, e_2) \in connR$ then $e_1, e_2$ are connected with respect to this node otherwise $e_1, e_2$ are disjoint with respect to this node. The abstract domain for the nodes, $N = \mathscr{P}(\sigma \cup \sigma_A) \times Layouts \times \{1, \#\}, \times \mathscr{P}(E \times E)$ and each node in the graph is represented as a record of the form [types layout size]. For clarity we omit a representation of the *connR* relation, as the inclusion of this information complicates the figures substantially. In the cases where the connectivity relation is of interest we will mention it in the description of the figure.

*Edges.* As in the case of the nodes, we combine several component abstractions to create the edge abstraction. The *offset* component indicates the offsets (labels) of the pointers that are abstracted by the edge. The number of pointers that this edge may represent is tracked with the *maxCut* property. The *interfere* property tracks the possibility that the edge represents pointers that interfere. The domain of the edges is,

$E = (F \cup \{?\}) \times \{1, \#\} \times \{np, ip\}$, and each edge is represented as a record $\{$offset maxCut interfere$\}$.

*Graph.* The domain for the abstract heap graphs is the set $G \subseteq \mathscr{P}(N) \times \mathscr{P}(E) \times \{V_n\} \times \{M_e\}$. The function $V_n : V \mapsto N$ is a partial map from variable names to nodes in the heap graph, which represents the targets of the variables. The function $M_e : E \to N \times N$ defines the structure of the graph by mapping edges $e$ to the pair of nodes $(n_s, n_e)$ such that $e$ begins at $n_s$ and ends at $n_e$. We use the notation $M_e(e) = (*, n)$ or $M_e(e) = (n, *)$ in the case were we do not care about the identity of the start/end node of the edge.

We restrict the abstract domain by defining a normal form for heap graphs. This normal form simplifies the structure of the abstract domain and it has several properties that improve the accuracy of the analysis.

First, we define what it means for two nodes to to be *recursive* (for this work we assume single level recursion but the definitions can be generalized [3]). This definition is used to make the abstract heap domain finite for a given program. If we limit the maximum size of the graph structure then, since the domains for the nodes and the edges are finite, the number of graphs is finite. This is done by forcing recursive structures to have bounded representations. Define two nodes $n, n' \in N$ to be *recursive* if:

- $\exists e \in E$ s.t. $M_e(e) = (n, n')$.
- $n.types \cap n'.types \neq \emptyset$.
- $\nexists$ variable $v$ s.t. $V_n(v) = n \vee V_n(v) = n'$.

Another useful concept is that of ambiguous edges. We would like to be able to assume that given an offset and a node there is a unique outgoing edge that is incident to this node with that offset. Define a node $n$ as having an ambiguous offset if: $\exists e, e' \in E$ s.t. $e \neq e' \wedge M_e(e) = (n, *) \wedge M_e(e') = (n, *) \wedge e.offset = e'.offset$.

A graph $g = (N, E, V_n, M_e)$ is in normal form if:

- It has no unreachable nodes: $\forall n \in N, \exists$ variable $v$ s.t. $V_n(v) = n \vee (V_n(v) = n' \wedge \exists$ path $\phi$ s.t. $n' \leadsto_\phi n)$.
- It has no recursive nodes: $\nexists n_1, n_2 \in N$ s.t. $n_1, n_2$ are recursive.
- It has no ambiguous edges: $\nexists n \in N$ s.t. $n$ has an ambiguous offset.
- No refinement rules can be applied, See Section 5.

## 4   Example: Building a List

We use two examples to demonstrate our analysis, Figure 4. The first is a loop that constructs a linked list. The second example copies a linked list (and is the subject of Section 7). We assume that the datatypes ListNode and DataNode have been defined. In an actual program the data elements in the list might be other data structures (lists, trees, arrays, etc) or composite user defined objects. However, the exact nature of the data components of the list does not fundamentally alter the behavior of the algorithm on our examples. Thus, for simplicity we use DataNode as a dummy type to represent whatever data is of interest. ListNode has a next field which points to the next node in the list and a data field which points to a DataNode.

| Build a List | Copy a List (in reverse, for simplicity) |
|---|---|

```
ListNode p, q                    ListNode q, x, t
p = null                         x = p
for(int i = 0; i < M; ++i)       q = null
    q = new ListNode()           while(x != null)
    q.data = new DataNode             t = q
    q.next = p                        q = new ListNode()
    p = q                             q.next = t
                                      q.data = x.data
                                      x = x.next
```

**Fig. 4.** List Example Code

Figure 5(a) shows the state of the abstract heap after allocating the `ListNode` (abbreviated LN). The variable q points to a node of type `ListNode` and since we just allocated the object that this node represents we know that the node represents exactly one cell and has a *Singleton* layout (abbreviated S). Figure 5(b) shows the state of the heap after allocating and assigning the data object, a cell of type `DataNode` (DN). The data node is also a node of size one with a *Singleton* layout. The connecting edge is stored at the `data` offset and since it was just created it must represent a single pointer and be *np*. Figure 5(c) shows the heap at the end of the first loop iteration: p points to the newly created list entry and q is nullified since it is dead.

Figure 5(d) shows the abstract heap at the end of the second loop iteration. New nodes represent the `ListNode` and `DataNode` cells allocated in this iteration. The newly allocated list entry has been put at the head of the list and the old list (shown dotted) is linked in with an edge stored at the `next` offset. If we were to continue, the heap abstraction would grow in an unbounded manner. To prevent this, we normalize the abstract heap. This is described in detail in Section 6 but for this example the important point is that we merge the two `ListNode` nodes into a single summary node that represents the combined information from these two nodes and the edge between them. By looking at the edge connecting the two nodes and the internal layouts we can determine that the internal layout of the summary node is *List* (abbreviated L) since we have two *Singleton* regions connected by an edge of size one. Since each region is of size one the summary region must be of size larger than one, represented by # in our abstract domain. Finally, we update the internal connectivity information for the summary node. In particular, the two edges are *outConnected*. The state of the heap after this merge is shown in Figure 5(e).

After combining the list nodes we have ambiguous targets (two out edges from the same node with the same label, `data`) This ambiguity is removed by merging the potential targets into a single summary node and by combining the edges that refer to these targets into a single summary edge. Merging these nodes is similar to the merge of the list nodes except that the two incoming edges are *disjoint*. After merging the nodes we merge the two edges. Since the summary edge represents two pointers its *maxCut* is #. To determine the value of the *interfere* property we check if either edge is *ip* or if the targets of the edges are *inConnected*. Because the edges pointed to disjoint nodes they are not *inConnected* and therefore cannot *interfere*. Thus, the interference property of the summary edge is *np*. The result is shown in Figure 5(f), which is also the fixed point for the analysis of the loop.

## 5   Refinement

During the data flow analysis portions of the abstract heap graph are summarized into single nodes to improve efficiency and to eliminate unbounded recursive data structures. This summarization can cause a substantial loss of accuracy if it is too aggressive. We define a method that (for the most common cases encountered) allows us to undo the summarization by transforming a summary node into a number of nodes (and edges) so that relationships between variables and regions of the heap can be more accurately modeled.

There are three layout types that we refine. The first is a node that represents several disjoint regions of the concrete heap. In this case we expand each sub-region into a separate node in the abstract graph. The second is a list node with a single incoming edge. In this case we make explicit the unique memory location that the variable must refer to in the list structure. The third is a tree with a single incoming edge. This case is analogous to the list so we do not discuss it separately.

*Disjoint Region Separation.* It is possible for a single summary node to represent several entirely disjoint regions. If this is the case then there is a partition of incoming edges (from variables or pointers) based on the *inConnected* relationship. Using this partition we transform the node into a number of new nodes, each new node representing a single element from partition of edges in the original node. An important special case is when a node has a *Singleton layout* and there is a single incoming edge of *maxCut* 1. If a node has these properties we can safely assume that the node represents a single cell, which enables strong updates in later analysis steps.

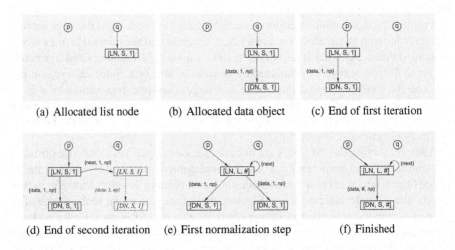

    (a) Allocated list node    (b) Allocated data object    (c) End of first iteration

    (d) End of second iteration    (e) First normalization step    (f) Finished

**Fig. 5.** Building a linked list

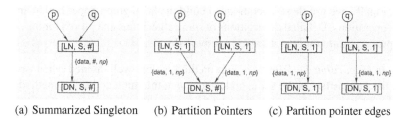

(a) Summarized Singleton    (b) Partition Pointers    (c) Partition pointer edges

**Fig. 6.** Refinement of a region with disjoint sub-regions

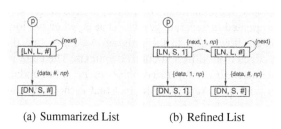

(a) Summarized List              (b) Refined List

**Fig. 7.** Refinement of a node with a list layout

Consider the case in Figure 6(a) where the variables p and q point to the same node, and assume that the edges from p and q are not *inConnected*. Partitioning results in Figure 6(b) where the summary node has been partitioned based on the *inConnected* relation from the variables. Since the edge that was split contained all non-interfering pointers the two edges incident to the node representing the *DataNode* cells cannot be *inConnected*. This now allows us to apply refinement again—the results are shown in Figure 6(c).

*Refinement on Lists.* Refinement on lists is more complex than refinement of disjoint regions. Since disjoint region refinement is applied before list or tree refinement we know that all the incoming edges to the given list node may be connected. Further, if there are multiple incoming edges we cannot determine an ordering for them in the list, so we only consider lists with a single incoming edge with a *maxCut* of 1.

Figure 7(a) shows a list with one incoming variable. Figure 7(b) shows the most general way in which a list can be referred to by a single program variable; there is a single cell that the variable points to and a section of the list after this cell. We can safely ignore the section of the list before the cell that the variable refers to since it is unreachable and therefore cannot affect the program in any way. Since the data edge contains all non-interfering pointers we apply the disjoint region separation rule to the data components of the list.

# 6    Dataflow Operators

This section describes the principal algorithms used in the analysis. We first address merging nodes and edges. Then we define the normalization routines for nodes and

356     M. Marron et al.

graphs. Finally, we use these operations to build the heap graph upper bound and comparison operations. Detailed descriptions of some algorithms and proofs for the required safety properties are omitted; see [13] for more details.

*Edge Join (Algorithm 1).* The edge join method is only well defined when two edges start at the same offset in the same node and end at the same node. The method checks the end connectivity information to determine how the component abstraction should be combined. If the edges are *inConnected* then the pointers that these edges represent may interfere and we set the summary edge as *ip*, otherwise we take the join of the *interfere* types of the edges. For the rest of the components that are used to represent an edge, we can simply combine them component-wise with respect to the possibility that these edges originated in separate graphs. That is, when we join two heap graphs that are from separate flow paths in the program we know that there can be no interaction between edges from different control contexts. The edge join algorithm uses the function *updateInternalConnInfoEdgeJoin*$(n_s, n_e, e_a, e_b)$ to update the internal connectivity info in $n_s$ and $n_e$ to represent the fact that $e_a$ now represents pointers from $e_a$ and $e_b$.

---

**Algorithm 1.** Join Edges ($\sqcup_e$)

---

**input** : $g$ the heap graph, $e_a, e_b$ edges, $n_s, n_e$ the nodes, $e_a, e_b$ start and end at
**if** $(e_a, e_b$ *from the same context*) **then** $e_a$.maxCut $\leftarrow e_a$.maxCut $\widetilde{+}$ $e_b$.maxCut;
**else** $e_a$.maxCut $\leftarrow e_a$.maxCut $\sqcup$ $e_b$.maxCut;
**if** $e_a, e_b$ *are inConnected* **then** $e_a$.interfere $\leftarrow ip$;
**else** $e_a$.interfere $\leftarrow e_a$.interfere $\sqcup_{\text{interfere}}$ $e_b$.interfere;
updateInternalConnInfoEdgeJoin$(n_s, n_e, e_a, e_b)$;
deleteEdge$(g, e_b)$;

---

*Node Join and Combine.* When summarizing two nodes, $n_a$ and $n_b$, there are three possibilities. The first is neither node can reach the other. In this case we *join* them. If there are only edges in one direction between nodes, from $n_a$ to $n_b$ or $n_b$ to $n_a$, then we *combine* them. If there are edges from $n_a$ to $n_b$ and from $n_b$ to $n_a$, then we replace $n_a, n_b$ with a single node $n_c$ that is a safe approximation of $n_a, n_b$.

Figures 5(e) and 5(f) show that the node join is a purely component-wise operation. The combine operation on a pair of nodes that have a connecting edge is more complicated, as it can be seen in Figures 5(d) and 5(e), where the two nodes with type ListNode are combined into a single summary node. In particular we need to account for the fact that the edge(s) connecting nodes $n_a$ and $n_b$ will affect the layout and the internal connectivity in the new summary node.

The algorithm *combineLayout*$(l_a, l_b, ebt)$, is based on a case analysis of the internal layout that results from the possible combinations of layouts for $n_a, n_b$ along with the total number of pointers represented by *ebt* and the potential that any pointers in the edges represented by *ebt* interfere. We enumerate the possible combinations of the *ebt* edges and the layout types. Then for each case we use the semantics of the edge and layout properties to determine the most general layout type that may result from this particular case.

---

**Algorithm 2.** Combine Nodes ($\widetilde{+}_{node}$)

---

**input** : graph $g$, $n_a, n_b$ nodes, $ebt$ set of edges from $n_a$ to $n_b$
$n_a$.type $\leftarrow n_a$.type $\cup n_b$.type;
$n_a$.size $\leftarrow n_a$.size $\widetilde{+} n_b$.size;
$n_a$.layout $\leftarrow$ combineLayout($n_a$.layout, $n_b$.layout, $ebt$);
$n_a$.connR $\leftarrow$ combineConnR($n_a$.connR, $n_b$.connR, $ebt$);
remap all edges incident to $n_b$ to be incident to $n_a$;
deleteNode($g$, $n_b$);

---

**Algorithm 3.** combineLayout

---

**input** : $l_a, l_b$ layout types, $ebt$ set of edges from $n_a$ to $n_b$
**output**: the layout of the combined node
$mayInterfere \leftarrow \bigvee \{e \in ebt | e.\text{interfere} = ip\}$;
$totalCut \leftarrow \sum \{e \in ebt | e.\text{maxCut}\}$;
$notSingletons \leftarrow s_a \neq \text{Singleton} \wedge s_b \neq \text{Singleton}$;
$isDAGgraph \leftarrow totalCut > 1 \wedge notSingletons$;
$l_r \leftarrow l_a \sqcup_{layout} l_b$;
**case** ($mayInterfere \vee isDAGgraph$) **return** $l_r \sqcup_{layout} MultiPath$;
**case** ($l_a = List$) **return** $l_r \sqcup_{layout} Tree$;
**case** ($l_a = l_b = Singleton$) **return** $l_r \sqcup_{layout} List$;
**otherwise return** $l_r$;

---

The *combineConnR* function updates the internal connectivity information in $n_a$ to reflect that it now represents the combined regions for $n_a$ and $n_b$. This involves computing the binary connectivity relation for all the edges that are incident to the new summary node based on the connectivity information in the argument nodes $n_a, n_b$, and the edges that connect the argument nodes, *ebt*.

*Normalization/Join Operators.* To normalize a node we check if there are two edges that start at this node and have the same offset. If they exist and they end at different nodes, we merge the target nodes and then join the edges. If they already end at the same node, we just join the edges.

To normalize a heap graph we normalize all the nodes, then apply the refinement rules to all the nodes that they can be applied to and finally we compress all the recursive nodes in the graph. This process is repeated until the heap graph is no longer changing.

To compute the upper approximation for two heaps, we first normalize both heaps and mark which graph each edge and node belonged to originally. Then we take variables with the same name and union their targets. Once this is done the resulting graph is normalized.

*Heap Graph Equivalence.* Defining equivalence on the heap graphs is simple if we require that they are in normal form. This implies that each abstract storage location has a unique edge and we can compare the graphs for structural equality and equality of the data in the nodes and edges.

---

**Algorithm 4.** Normalize Node

---

**input** : node $n$, graph $g$, $n \in g$
**output**: None
**while** $\exists$ *offset $o$ with more than 1 edge* **do**
    $e_1, e_2 \leftarrow$ two edges with offset $o$;
    $n_1 \leftarrow$ endpoint of $e_1$;
    $n_2 \leftarrow$ endpoint of $e_2$;
    **if** $n_1 \neq n_2$ **then**
        **if** $\exists$ *edges from $n_1$ to $n_2$ and $n_2$ to $n_1$* **then**
            replace $n_1, n_2$ with the $\top$ from the lattice of nodes;
        **else if** $\exists$ *edges from $n_1$ to $n_2$* **then**
            combine($g, n_1, n_2$);
        **else if** $\exists$ *edges from $n_2$ to $n_1$* **then**
            combine($g, n_2, n_1$);
        **else**
            join($g, n_1, n_2$);

    $\sqcup_e(e_1, e_2, g)$;

---

**Algorithm 5.** Normalize Graph

---

**input** : graph $g$
**output**: None
Remove all unreachable nodes from $g$;
**while** $g$ *is changing* **do**
    **while** $\exists$ *node $n$ s.t. $n$ can be normalized* **do**
        normalize($n, g$);

    **while** $\exists$ *node $n$ s.t. $n$ can be refined* **do**
        apply the applicable refinement rule to $n$;

    **while** $\exists$ *nodes $n, n'$ that are recursive* **do**
        combineNodes($g, n, n'$);

---

**Algorithm 6.** Heap Graph Upper Bound, $\sqcup$

---

**input** : graph $g_a, g_b$
**output**: None
$g_{an} \leftarrow$ normalize($g_a$);
set all nodes/edges in $g_{an}$ as context $a$;
$g_{bn} \leftarrow$ normalize($g_b$);
set all nodes/edges in $g_{bn}$ as context $b$;
$g_{res} \leftarrow g_{an} \cup g_{bn}$;
normalizeGraph($g_{res}$);

# 7   Example: Copying a List

During the copy operation (Figure 4) there are several attributes that we want to preserve: the source list should be unaffected, the copy should be a list, and, if the source
list contained all independent data elements so should the copy. For simplicity assume
that we know that the source list is already pointed to by p. Figure 8(a) shows the list at
the start of the copy. Figure 8(b) shows the results at the end of the first loop iteration.
The head of the list has been copied; t is nullified and x has been indexed down the
list. Note that in indexing down the list we refined the list on the next edge so that the
node that x refers to is made explicit (the node is a singleton of size 1). We show the
newly materialized list and data node using dotted lines.

Figure 8(c) shows the heap during the second iteration of the loop after creating the
new list node and assigning it to point to the next data node in the source list. At the end
of the loop 8(d) we have again indexed the variable x. We now have recursive nodes
(for simplicity assume that we know that keeping p, q refined does not matter—if we
keep them refined the result is the same, it just takes an extra loop iteration and results
in a larger graph). Thus, we compress them during normalization. The resulting graph
shown in Figure 8(e). This is the fixed point of the loop and if we interpret the exit
condition we see that the result of the copy loop is the heap graph in Figure 8(f).

# 8   Performance

*Theoretical Performance.* In order to analyze a program, the model presented in this
paper can plugged into any dataflow analysis framework. The total cost of analyzing the
program is affected by the cost of the model operations and the runtime of the dataflow
framework that is chosen. In this paper we do not assume a specific framework so our
runtime analysis only looks at the cost of the model operations.

We assume that the number of nodes in the abstract heap graph is $n$, that each node
has at most $k$ edges and there are $t$ user defined types. The most expensive part of
running the heap model is the graph normalization step, so we only present the analysis
for this and the node combine operation, which is the dominant cost of the normalization
algorithm.

The execution of *Combine Nodes* (Algorithm 2), requires combining the type sets,
$O(t)$, remapping the incident edges, $O(k)$, calling *combineLayout* (which computes the
shape of the combined nodes), $O(k)$ and calling the *computeConnR* method (which
computes the transitive closure of the two connectivity relations), $O(k^3)$. Thus, The
total time is $O(t + k + k + k^3)$. If we assume that $t$ is a small constant, the time to
normalize a node is $O(k^3)$.

The graph normalization step requires:

- Removing all the unreachable sections of the heap graph, $O(nk)$.
- Normalizing each node, visit each edge of each node and potentially combine
  edges, $O((nk)k^3)$.
- Refining all possible nodes, visit each node and potentially refine it, $O(nk)$.
- Removing all recursive nodes, visit each node and potentially combine two nodes,
  $O((nk)k^3)$.

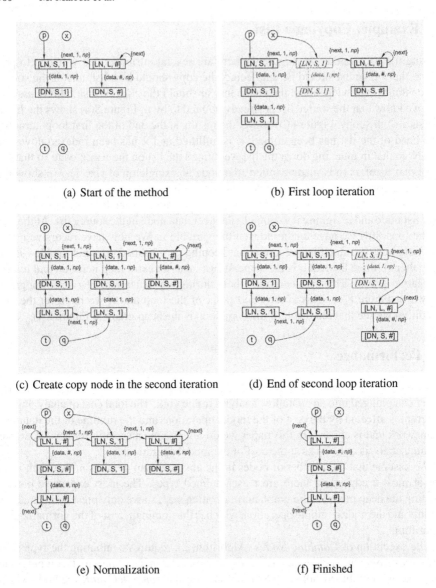

(a) Start of the method

(b) First loop iteration

(c) Create copy node in the second iteration

(d) End of second loop iteration

(e) Normalization

(f) Finished

**Fig. 8.** Copying a linked list (in reverse order)

These operations need to be done until none can be applied. Since the refine operation can only be applied to a node twice and the combine operation replaces two nodes by a single node (which cannot be refined), the algorithm cannot continue for more than $O(n)$ iterations. Thus the total time for the normalization routine is $O(n) * O((nk)k^3) = O(n^2k^4)$.

*Benchmarks.* In this section we compare the runtime cost of the UMA (Unified Memory Analysis) method with TVLA (tvla-2-alpha) and a simple flow-sensitive equality-based points-to method (which is not capable of shape analysis but provides a performance baseline). Then, we examine the accuracy and utility of the information that the UMA analysis method provides. All measurements were made on a Pentium M 1.5 GHz laptop with 1 GB of RAM.

We use two sets of benchmarks. The first is a number of simple list manipulation methods that are useful for validating that the information computed by this analysis is accurate. These benchmarks include list insertion, deletion, find and copy operations. The goal is to ensure that the listness and data independence properties are preserved through all of these operations. The first entry in Figure 9 shows the runtime for TVLA, the points-to and the UMA analysis. In all of the simple list tests, our analysis is able to determine that the result of each list operation is a region with the *List* shape.

List Analysis Times

| Benchmark | Copy | Find | Insert | Delete | Reverse |
|-----------|------|------|--------|--------|---------|
| TVLA | NA | 0.91s | 1.52s | 8.00s | 3.01s |
| Points-to | 0.05s | 0.03s | 0.04s | 0.06s | 0.03s |
| UMA | 0.25s | 0.10s | 0.15s | 0.19s | 0.13s |

Jolden Analysis Times and Shape Results

| Benchmark | bisort | em3d | health | mst | power | treeadd | tsp |
|-----------|--------|------|--------|-----|-------|---------|-----|
| Points-to | 2.10s | 1.48s | 12.20s | 0.54s | 0.42s | 0.16s | 0.70s |
| UMA | 12.30s | 6.90s | 40.90s | 5.70s | 4.20s | 1.80s | 5.08s |
| Accurate | Partial | Yes | Partial | Yes | Yes | Yes | Yes |

**Fig. 9.** Benchmark Results

The second set of benchmarks is from the Jolden suite [1] (we have not finished implementing the virtual method dispatch analysis, so bh, perimeter and voronoi are omitted from the table). This set of benchmarks is designed to test how well the analysis method scales to non-trivial code sizes and as a first test for the ability of the heap analysis method to provide useful shape information for parallelization transforms. Current work on interprocedural versions of TVLA indicate that even simple programs take upwards of 30s to analyze [14] and no results for programs as complex as the Jolden suite have been published so we omit the TVLA analysis from the table. The second entry in Figure 9 shows the time to run the analysis on each of the benchmarks and indicates if the analysis was able to correctly determine the shape information required to perform basic thread level *foreach* and *recursive tree* parallelization. In the table we have two categories for the accuracy of the shape analysis. *Yes* is used when the shape analysis was able to provide the correct shape information for all of the relevant heap structures in the program. *Partial* indicates that the analysis was able to determine the correct shape for some of the heap data structures but that some important properties were missed.

There were no cases where the analysis failed to produce a non-trivial amount of useful information on data structure shapes. In the cases where the UMA algorithm is unable to provide completely accurate information for parallelization the causes can be traced back to the simple modeling of arrays (health) or the crude technique we are currently using for interprocedural analysis in recursive functions (bisort and health).

## 9   Conclusion and Future Work

This paper presented a graph-based heap model that can be used with a standard data flow framework to analyze the evolution of the heap during program execution. The model is shown to be capable of representing heap properties (aliasing, shape and logical data structure identification) that are needed to extract thread level parallelism from single threaded programs. The paper then outlined the model operations required to perform the program analysis. A key component of the operations was the use of a refinement operator that enables the accurate simulation of important program operations (copying, reversing, destructive updates, etc.). Unlike Ghiya's work where extremely conservative approximations must be made in the presence of destructive updates, the proposed model is able to retain enough information to provide meaningful shape information even when destructive updates are being performed. Theoretical analysis shows that all the program operations on the model are $O(k^4)$ and the upper bound/equality operations are $O(n^2k^4)$ where $n$ is the number of nodes in the heap graph and $k$ is the number of edges incident to a node. This polynomial runtime is due to our conservative refinement operator (which only refines unambiguous cases) which is in contrast to the TVLA refinement operator (which resolves ambiguity by enumerating all possible cases).

The method has been implemented and run on several benchmarks. The first set of benchmarks is designed to test the ability of the analysis method to model fundamental list operations. The method analyzed this set quickly while discovering all the relevant list properties. Next, we analyzed several codes from the Jolden benchmark suite. Analysis times on these benchmarks scaled acceptably given that a simplistic and fully context-sensitive interprocedural analysis method was used. The method correctly identified the shapes (*Singleton, List, Tree, MultiPath, Cycle*) for almost all of the data structures in the programs.

These results are a critical step toward the goal of transforming modern single threaded programs that make extensive use of pointer rich, heap based structures into multithreaded parallel programs. Our future work is focused on improving the accuracy, performance and scope of this analysis technique. We identified recursive procedures that rely on destructive updates as a major issue in accurately modeling shape and handling these cases is the next step in our research. The method is local in the sense that all abstract program operations only refer to and modify small portions of the heap, we plan to utilize this to enable memoization and localization of procedure calls, both of which are crucial to improving scalability. Since modern programming languages make extensive use of built in collection libraries (hashtables, trees with parent pointers, iterators, etc.) we are working on how to model these important data structures and generic programming concepts.

## Acknowledgements

This material is based upon work supported by the National Science Foundation (grants 0085792, 0238027, and 0540600). Any opinions, findings, and conclusions or recommendations expressed in this material are those of the author and do not necessarily reflect the views of the sponsors.

The first author would like to thank Jack, John, Mario and Stefan for their input and comments on the work presented in this paper.

# References

1. B. Cahoon and K. S. McKinley. Data flow analysis for software prefetching linked data structures in Java. In *PACT*, 2001.
2. D. R. Chase, M. N. Wegman, and F. K. Zadeck. Analysis of pointers and structures. In *PLDI*, 1990.
3. A. Deutsch. Interprocedural may-alias analysis for pointers: Beyond *k*-limiting. In *PLDI*, 1994.
4. R. Ghiya and L. J. Hendren. Is it a tree, a dag, or a cyclic graph? A shape analysis for heap-directed pointers in C. In *POPL*, 1996.
5. R. Ghiya and L. J. Hendren. Putting pointer analysis to work. In *POPL*, 1998.
6. R. Ghiya, L. J. Hendren, and Y. Zhu. Detecting parallelism in C programs with recursive darta structures. In *CC*, 1998.
7. B. Hackett and R. Rugina. Region-based shape analysis with tracked locations. In *POPL*, 2005.
8. L. J. Hendren and A. Nicolau. Parallelizing programs with recursive data structures. *IEEE TPDS*, 1(1), 1990.
9. N. D. Jones and S. S. Muchnick. Flow analysis and optimization of lisp-like structures. In *POPL*, 1979.
10. C. Lattner and V. Adve. Data Structure Analysis: An Efficient Context-Sensitive Heap Analysis. Tech. Report UIUCDCS-R-2003-2340, Computer Science Dept., Univ. of Illinois at Urbana-Champaign, Apr 2003.
11. C. Lattner and V. Adve. LLVM: A Compilation Framework for Lifelong Program Analysis & Transformation. In *CGO*, 2004.
12. T. Lev-Ami and S. Sagiv. TVLA: A system for implementing static analyses. In *SAS*, 2000.
13. M. Marron, D. Kapur, D. Stefanovic, and M. Hermenegildo. Unified memory analysis. Tech. Rep. TR-CS-2006-06, University of New Mexico, Apr. 2006. Available at *"http://www.cs.unm.edu/~treport/tr/06-04/uma.pdf"*.
14. N. Rinetzky, M. Sagiv, and E. Yahav. Interprocedural shape analysis for cutpoint-free programs. In *SAS*, 2005.
15. R. Rugina and M. C. Rinard. Automatic parallelization of divide and conquer algorithms. In *PPOPP*, 1999.
16. S. Sagiv, T. W. Reps, and R. Wilhelm. Solving shape-analysis problems in languages with destructive updating. In *POPL*, 1996.
17. S. Sagiv, T. W. Reps, and R. Wilhelm. Parametric shape analysis via 3-valued logic. In *POPL*, 1999.
18. R. Vallée-Rai, L. Hendren, V. Sundaresan, P. Lam, E. Gagnon, and P. Co. Soot - a Java optimization framework. In *CASCON*, 1999.
19. R. P. Wilson and M. S. Lam. Efficient context-sensitive pointer analysis for C programs. In *PLDI*, 1995.
20. E. Yahav and G. Ramalingam. Verifying safety properties using separation and heterogeneous abstractions. In *PLDI*, 2004.

# Author Index

# Lecture Notes in Computer Science

For information about Vols. 1–4382

please contact your bookseller or Springer